D1418437

ASCAP

COPYRIGHT LAW SYMPOSIUM

Number Twenty-Seven

COPYRIGHT LAW SYMPOSIUM

Number Twenty-Seven

NATHAN BURKAN
MEMORIAL COMPETITION

SPONSORED BY THE

American Society of Composers
Authors and Publishers

COLUMBIA UNIVERSITY PRESS
NEW YORK
1982

Columbia University Press
New York   Guildford, Surrey

Library of Congress Catalog Card Number: 40–8341

International Standard Book Number 0–231–05296–0

ISSN Number 0069–9950

Printed in the United States of America

Contents

Foreword

THE YEAR 1977 was a special time in the history of copyright. It fell between the enactment of the 1976 Copyright Act on October 19, 1976, and the Act's effective date of January 1, 1978. The intervening transition period provided an opportunity for students of copyright to ponder the new Act and prepare for its effects. The Nathan Burkan Memorial Competition supplied a forum for this study, and encouraged the best young legal minds in the area of copyright to share their ideas. Volume 27 of the ASCAP Copyright Law Symposium represents the cream of that year's exemplary crop of articles, and contain the six essays we have judged to be the best contributions to the literature of copyright.

Henry David Fetter of the Harvard Law School received First Prize for his treatment of a subject that is certain to be hotly disputed in the years to come: the effect of the 1976 Act's preemption provision on state misappropriation laws. Mr. Fetter presents a thorough and insightful analysis of the new statutory provisions. He considers issues left unanswered by the statute—issues that require an accommodation of state and federal law. The task of achieving such accommodation, he concludes, will fall to the judiciary, as have so many other delicate problems.

Second Prize was awarded to Mary S. Lawrence of the University of Oregon School of Law for her study of fair use.

There has been much discussion of the interplay of the judicially created fair use doctrine and first amendment safeguards. Mr. Lawrence contends that the two are harmonious, and that codification of fair use in the 1976 Act reflects the doctrine's constitutional underpinnings.

Craig Hayes, a student at the University of North Carolina School of Law, won Third Prize. He addresses an issue that has been vigorously debated for fifty years: performance rights in sound recordings. Mr. Hayes argues that performers should be accorded equal legal status with other authors of creative works, and advocates a performance royalty that will compensate performers for the commercial exploitation of their recorded performances.

Fourth Prize went to Robert T. Mowrey of the Southern Methodist University School of Law for his lively exploration of the "rise and fall of record piracy." Thanks to the protection against unauthorized duplication provided by the Sound Recording Act of 1971, and the new Act's establishment of copyrightability for sound recordings, record piracy, he thinks, is one problem whose solution seems close at hand.

Two papers were deemed equally deserving of national Fifth Prize honors, and we declared a tie between Gregg Oppenheimer of the Boalt Hall School of Law, University of California at Berkeley, and Ellyn Sue Roth of the George Washington University National Law Center.

Mr. Oppenheimer grapples with the elusive concept of originality in art reproductions, criticizing the traditional "distinguishable variation" test for infringement as too vague. He proposes a standard based upon a "reasonable inspection of the reproduction by a would-be copyist": A reproduction bearing a copyright notice would trigger a close examination by the would-be copyist for variations from the original work. The copyist would be expected to eliminate such variations from his own copy.

Ms. Roth examines the notice provisions of the copyright

law. She concludes that the technical notice requirements for copyright protection are more burdensome to the creator than they are helpful to the user. Although the 1976 Act simplifies many of the requirements, it still represents a compromise between the interests of creators and users. Ms. Roth suggests mandatory registration as a means of furnishing users with copyright information; she would remove entirely the provisions requiring copyright notice.

These six well-written and analytical articles on subjects which have continuing vitality reaffirm the value of the Nathan Burkan Competition as a vehicle for the dissemination of scholarship and creative thinking in the field of copyright.

HON. CHARLES D. FERRIS
Former Chairman,
Federal Communications Commission

HON. ROBERT W. KASTENMEIER
Member of Congress

HON. BARBARA A. RINGER
Former Register of Copyrights

Preface

The Nathan Burkan Memorial Competition continues to attract outstanding, young legal talent in the field of Copyright Law. The Competition continues to enjoy enthusiastic support from law school deans and faculty. Volume 27 presents six outstanding papers judged to be the finest contributions to the study of copyright law from among eighty-four papers submitted by fifty-six law schools throughout the country.

Each year of the Competition, a panel of distinguished judges generously gives its time and guidance to selecting the national winners. The year 1977 fell between the enactment of the 1976 Copyright Act and the Act's effective date. This transitional period encouraged students to speculate intelligently and creatively on the future of Copyright Law. The Nathan Burkan Memorial Competition provided a means of acknowledging the important research and writing these students accomplished. The Competition was extremely fortunate to have three judges whose vast experience and knowledge was invaluable to the selection process.

Charles Ferris graduated from Boston College Law School. He served as Chairman of the Federal Communications Commission from 1977 until 1981. Previously, he served as a trial attorney in the Civil Division of the United States Department of Justice and in various capacities for the United

States Senate from 1963 to 1977, first as Associate General Counsel to the Democratic Policy Committee and then as General Counsel to the Policy Committee, Chief Counselor to the Majority Leader and Chief Counsel for the Senate Majority.

Robert Kastenmeier received his LL.B. from the University of Wisconsin. He has served as a member of the House of Representatives from Wisconsin since January, 1959. As a member of the Judiciary Committee and Chairman of the Subcommittee on Courts, Civil Liberties and the Administration of Justice, he was the sponsor of the copyright revision bill which he piloted through the House of Representatives, and which became the 1976 Copyright Act.

Barbara Ringer graduated from Columbia University Law School and served as Register of Copyrights from 1973 until 1980. Her expertise in the practice of Copyright Law is demonstrated by almost three decades of involvement in the field, from the time she joined the Copyright Office as an examiner in 1949. She has served as Director of the Copyright Division of UNESCO, as a Trustee of the Copyright Society of USA, and as Vice-President of the Inter-American Copyright Society. She has received the President's Award for Distinguished Federal Civilian Service.

I can think of no panel of judges more qualified in the field of copyright than these three distinguished public servants. The Competition is honored by their participation.

HERMAN FINKELSTEIN

Rules Governing the Competition

1. *Participating Law Schools:* All accredited law schools are invited to participate in the Competition.
2. *Eligible Students:* Third-year students. In the discretion of the dean, second-year students also may be eligible.
3. *Subject Matter:* Any phase of *copyright law.*
4. *Determination of Awards:* The prizes will be awarded to the students who shall, in the sole judgment of the dean—or such other person or committee as he may delegate—prepare the two best papers. The dean may in his discretion withhold the awards entirely, if in his opinion no worthy paper is submitted, or may award only the first or second prize.
5. *Prizes: A first prize of $500* and a *second prize of $200,* to be paid through the dean, upon his written certification.
6. *Formal Requirements, Right of Publication, etc.:*
   (a) Manuscript must be typewritten: double-spaced on 8½″ × 11″ paper, 1″ margin all around; indent and single space all quotations exceeding four lines.
   (b) Manuscript must not exceed 50 pages.
   (c) Citations must be in approved law review form.
   (d) Submit *two* copies of manuscript.
   (e) Cover for manuscript: any standard form stiff cover with label on outside showing title of paper, your name, and permanent *home address.*
   (f) Two copies of winning papers will be forwarded by the dean to the Society, which may authorize publication.
   (g) Papers may appear in law review, provided their entry in the Nathan Burkan Memorial Competition is duly noted.
7. As papers are presumed to represent individual study, collaboration with others in their preparation is not permitted.
8. *Closing Date:* August 15th—or any earlier date the dean may spec-

ify. Winning papers must be certified to the Society not later than August 31st.

9. *National Awards:* The best papers certified to the Society will be selected for National Awards of *$3,000, $2,000, $1,500, $1,000* and *$500*, respectively. The award papers selected by the judges will be printed in the form of a "Copyright Law Symposium."

Questions concerning the Competition may be addressed to the Director of the Competition, Herman Finkelstein, One Lincoln Plaza, New York, N.Y. 10023.

Barbara Ringer

Charles D. Ferris

Robert W. Kastenmeier

ASCAP

COPYRIGHT LAW SYMPOSIUM

Number Twenty-Seven

NATIONAL FIRST PRIZE

Articles

Copyright Revision and the Preemption of State "Misappropriation" Law: A study in Judicial and Congressional Interaction

HENRY DAVID FETTER*

HARVARD LAW SCHOOL

I. THE PROBLEM AND ITS SETTING

On October 19, 1976, President Ford signed the bill of the general revision of the United States copyright law (the "Revision").[1] Section 301 [2] of the law, entitled "Preemption with Respect to Other Laws," replaces the dual system of federal and state copyright protection which has existed since 1790 with a unitary system of federal protection for all copyrightable works. Section 301 spells out in detail what in state law has and has not been preempted by the Revision. This article examines the status of state law relief for "mis-

* Mr. Fetter is an associate in the Beverly Hills, California, law firm of Kaplan, Livingston, Goodwin, Berkowitz & Selvin. He wishes to thank his third-year written work supervisor, Prof. Raya S. Dreben, for her guidance and encouragement and for making available the Justice Department Letter which appears in Appendix IV and is discussed in some detail in the text. Mr. Fetter is also grateful to his classmates, Barry Klayman and James Lopes, for lending him important and useful material which greatly facilitated his work.

[1] General Revision of the United States Copyright Law, Pub.L. No. 94–553, 90 Stat. 2541 (codified as 17 U.S.C.).

[2] The text of Section 301 is set out in Appendix I.

appropriation," as expounded in *International News Service v. Associated Press,*[3] within the general preemptive design of the statute. It begins with a brief survey of the doctrinal and institutional setting in which the current post-Revision problem of "misappropriation" preemption arises.

In 1918 the United States Supreme Court, in *International News Service v. Associated Press,* recognized the tort law doctrine of "misappropriation." Mr. Justice Pitney, writing for the Court, concluded that "the news has an exchange value to one who can misappropriate it" and held the Associated Press ("AP") entitled to relief against INS's copying (or paraphrasing) and competitive use of the AP's *noncopyrighted* news reports.[4] The injunction issued entirely apart from the remedial machinery of federal copyright law. An expansive "unfair competition" analysis, focusing on the profit accruing to INS as a result of AP's expenditures and efforts (and wholly divorced from traditional conceptions of false representation), was the basis for decision.[5]

Concurring in *INS,* Justice Holmes pronounced as a general principle that

[3] 248 U.S. 215 (1918).

[4] *Id.* at 239–240. "The International News Service (INS), its correspondents barred from the European battle fields for breaches of censorship regulations, had been supplying war news to its West Coast subscriber newspapers by copying the 'news' as reported by the Associated Press in the East, and transmitting verbatim or paraphrased news reports westward, where the news was still fresh and competitive with the reports in the AP member papers." *See,* B. KAPLAN, AN UNHURRIED VIEW OF COPYRIGHT 86 (1967).

[5] "[D]efendant [INS], by its very act, admits that it is taking material that has been acquired by complainant [AP] as the result of organization and the expenditure of labor, skill, and money, and which is salable by complainant for money, and that defendant in appropriating it and selling it as its own is endeavoring to reap where it has not sown, and by disposing of it to newspapers that are competitors of complainant's members is appropriating to itself the harvest of those who have sown. Stripped of all disguises, the process amounts to an unauthorized interference with the normal operation of complainant's legitimate business precisely at the point where the profit is to be reaped, in order to divert a material portion of the profit from those who have earned it to those who have not; with special advantage to defendant in the competition because of the fact that it is not burdened with any part of the expense of gathering the news." 248 U.S. at 239–240.

> When an uncopyrighted combination of words is published there is no general right to forbid other people repeating them—in other words, there is no property in the combination or in the thoughts or facts that the words express. Property, a creation of law, does not arise from value. . . . Property depends upon exclusion by law from interference. . . .[6]

Without having recourse (or at least apparent recourse) to the property protection offered by the federal copyright act, AP successfully obtained protection under an alternative common law theory: a judicially crafted remedy substituted for an unavailable statutory one. To adopt Holmes's analysis, property rights supplementary to those recognized by the copyright statute were created. That which was open to copying under the copyright statute was to be protected under the common law of tort.

After the decision of *Erie R.R. v. Tompkins*,[7] this tension between statute and common law was recast into a more pointed, though for a time, latent, confrontation between federal and state law. The holding in *Erie*, of course, did potentially undermine the continuing authority of *INS* as a decision of "federal general common law" uprooted by that case. Whatever this fallout effect of *Erie* on the subsequent precedential force of *INS*, the misappropriation doctrine found a secure place in *state* tort jurisprudence. (This was especially true in the law of New York—by happenstance or not—then home base to the lion's share of the intellectual property industries.)[8] Once "misappropriation" relief provides under state law protection not available under *federal* law, clear preemption issues are apparent. Preemption problems come before the courts in the course of the judicial exercise of the obligation to decide cases and controversies.[9]

[6] *Id.* at 246.

[7] 304 U.S. 64 (1938).

[8] *See, e.g.*, Metropolitan Opera Ass'n., Inc. v. Wagner-Nichols Recording Corp., 199 Misc. 786, 101 N.Y.S. 2d 483 (Sup. Ct. 1950).

[9] *See generally*, Note, *Pre-Emption as a Preferential Ground: A New Canon*

Decision of cases, in turn, requires judicial adherence to the constitutional command that federal law be supreme with respect to state law. The judicial function is both premise and condition of the court's preemptive role.[10]

The 1909 Copyright Act made no general provision for the adjustment of federal and state law respecting intellectual property, save for the traditional preservation of state common law authority over "unpublished" works in section 2. This failure of explicit statement is, of course, the general pattern; it is the rare federal statute which explicitly confronts the question of the preemption or "saving" of state law operating within the ambit of federally affected subject matter.[11]

The Revision Bill is such a statute. Section 301 of the 1976 Act is an express preemption provision intended by Congress

> to preempt and abolish any rights under the common law or statutes of a State that are equivalent to copyright and that extend to works within the scope of the Federal copyright law. The declaration of this principle in section 301 is intended to be stated in the clearest and most unequivocal language possible, so as to foreclose any possible misinterpretations of its unqualified intention that Congress shall act preemptively, and to avoid the development of any vague borderline areas between State and Federal protection.[12]

Has "misappropriation" then been withdrawn from the

---

of Construction, 12 STAN. L. REV. 208 (1959); Note, *The Preemption Doctrine*, 75 COLUM. L. REV. 623 (1975); *Nuclear "Moratorium" Legislation in the States and the Supremacy Clause: A Case of Express Preemption*, 76 COLUM. L. REV. 392 (1976); Hirsch, *Toward a New View of Federal Preemption*, 1972 U. ILL. L.F. 515.

[10] The analysis in Note, *The Preemption Doctrine: Shifting Perspectives on Federalism and the Burger Court*, 75 COLUM. L. REV. 623 (1975), tends to advocate a role for the courts in adjusting federal-state relations that appears to overstep the limits of the judicial function in these cases.

[11] *See* the material cited in note 9, *supra*.

[12] S. REP. No. 473, 94th Cong., 1st Sess. 114 (1975), [hereinafter S. REP.]. The explanatory language of this Senate Report was repeated verbatim in H.R. REP. No. 1476, 94th Cong., 2d Sess. 130 (1976) [hereinafter H.R. REP.], reprinted in 1976 U.S. CODE CONG. & AD. NEWS 5659, 5746.

"vague borderline" between federal and state law, its status definitely settled by Congress? The legislative history suggests that this question remains open.

Section 301(b)(3) of the Senate Revision Bill (S.22) [13] and the bill as reported favorably by the House Judiciary Committee in 1976 [14] specifically referred to state law "rights against misappropriation" as rights expressly *not* preempted by the federal statute; and the illustration provided in the accompanying report on the Revision Bill was the *INS* case itself.[15]

The continuing legitimacy of *INS*-type relief within the preemptive scheme of the Revision Bill was, however, pointedly put into question by an amendment suggested by the Justice Department [16] and introduced in final debate in the House of Representatives in September 1976,[17] to strike out the specific "saving" reference to "rights against misappropriation" contained in the Senate Bill. In the debate, the potential post-Revision availability of state law "misappropriation" relief under the general, as enacted, "saving" language of section 301(b)(3) was evaluated in confusing and sharply contradictory terms. Whether any cutback of existing law was intended was left unclear by the colloquy in the House preceding its passage.[18] The accepted amendment was agreed to by the House-Senate conference and enacted as law.[19] Therein lies the specific problem of statutory inter-

[13] S.22, 94th Cong., 1st Sess. § 301 (1975). The text of the Senate Bill is set out in Appendix III.

[14] H.R. Rep. *supra* note 12.

[15] S. Rep., *supra* note 12, at 116.

[16] Letter from Michael M. Uhlmann (Assistant Attorney General, Legislative Affairs) to Congressman Robert Kastenmeier, Chairman of the Subcommittee on Courts, Civil Liberties, and the Administration of Justice (July 27, 1976). The relevant portions of the text of the letter are set out in Appendix IV.

[17] 122 Cong. Rec. H10910 (daily ed., September 22, 1976).

[18] *Id.* The House of Representatives' debate is discussed in the text at note 138, *infra.*

[19] House Conference Report 94–1733, *reprinted in* [1976] U.S. Code Cong. & Ad. News 5810, 5819–5820. The change was noted without comment.

pretation to which this paper eventually turns: working out the consequences of this express preemption provision absent clearcut exposition of legislative intent.

Such an exploration of the Revision preemption plan must be placed in the context provided by the previous developments that its own evolution and formulation reflect. The "misappropriation" preemption problem is not the novel, unprecedented product of the Revision but instead has been cognizable ever since *INS* was decided. Its resolution has heretofore been weighed, not in the Congress, but in the courts, subject to some of the vagaries of the amorphous doctrine at issue.

Preemption adjudication, however, came slowly to this area of law. That judicial resolution of any such claim was not demanded for so long a period of time may have been, in part, because the formulations of "misappropriation" claims allegedly implicated interests separate from those involved in copyright litigation. Starting with *INS*, judges analyzed misappropriation problems in terms of the wrongful taking of the fruits of the labors and investments of others. Copyright claims turned, on the other hand, on allegations and proofs of "copying."

This skewing of analyses may account, in part, for the delayed arrival of preemption adjudication to the area. To further complicate and confuse matters—and to postpone conclusive adjudication—the "misappropriation" doctrine expanded over time, and when preemption challenges were raised, they were addressed to fact situations quite dissimilar to that posed in *INS* itself. Three main lines of "misappropriation" cases appear to have emerged. First, *INS* and the opinion of New York Supreme Court Justice Greenberg in *Metropolitan Opera Ass'n v. Wagner-Nichols Recording Corp.* exemplified classic, straightforward judicial justifications of relief founded on characterization of the charged party's *conduct* as wrongful: that "the effort to profit from the labor, skill, expenditures, names and reputation of others which appears in this case constitutes unfair competition which will be enjoined" and that in such a case the issuance of an injunction "simply quarantines business conduct which is abhorrent to good conscience and the most elementary principles of law and equity." [20]

Second, however, are cases in which state protective power in the face of a failure of federal protection is grounded on the exclusion from the federal scheme of the *subject matter* in question; such cases have also fallen under the "misappropriation" rubric—with the consequences in *Goldstein v. California* [21] traced below. This line of analysis developed in the course of judicial response (a notable example being the Second Circuit's influential opinions in *Capitol Records v. Mercury Records*) [22] to preemptive problems not faced by the pioneering exponents of the "misappropriation" doctrine. Further confusion is provided by the *sub silentio* interweaving between these two classes of cases: the same issue—that of the availability of "misappropriation" relief for the unauthorized duplication of sound recordings—was considered in both *Metropolitan Opera Ass'n* and *Capitol Records,* and in entirely different analytical frameworks. A third type of "misappropriation" case is *Grove Press, Inc. v. Collectors Publication, Inc.,*[23] in which state relief was held not preempted, on reasoning which leaves the basis for decision obscurely balanced somewhere between the conduct and subject-matter foci.

These threads of judicial response to preemption issues as litigated under the 1909 Act and of the complications introduced into the judicial delineation of preemption by the existence of these varieties of "misappropriation" claims will

[20] 199 Misc. 786, 101 N.Y.S.2d 483 (Sup. Ct. 1950), *aff'd* 279 App. Div. 632, 107 N.Y.S.2d 795 (1st Dep't 1951).

[21] 412 U.S. 546 (1973).

[22] 221 F.2d 657 (2d Cir. 1955).

[23] 264 F. Supp. 603 (C.D. Cal. 1967).

continue to engage attention as the background to section 301 of the Revision is developed in closer detail. First, this article explores the climax of judicial preemption analysis in *Goldstein v. California* and that case's implications for decision under the 1909 Act. Second, the congressional history of section 301, with particular scrutiny of the interpenetration of judicial and legislative developments is described. Finally, the article assesses the continued legitimacy of *INS*-type "misappropriation" relief under the regime established by the Revision law, which entered into force after January 1, 1978.

II. GOLDSTEIN V. CALIFORNIA JUDICIAL PREEMPTION METHODOLOGY

In *Goldstein v. California*,[24] a "misappropriation" preemption case finally came before the Supreme Court. Within the "universe" of misappropriation cases two points distinguished the facts in the case. First, the state statute challenged as preempted by the federal copyright scheme asserted protective power over the specific subject matter category of sound recordings. California was not exercising corrective process to remedy a general, wrongful business practice—*sub nomine* unfair competition, or "misappropriation." The subject matter defined the actionable wrong. Second, the state policy was enforced through a criminal statute, not through a judicial decision. The statute, unlike an opinion announcing a common law right, defined specific, proscribed conduct, *without*, however, framing its analysis in traditional "misappropriation" terms. The validity of what the Court confidently labeled a state copyright statute was the preemption issue squarely presented by *Goldstein*.

[24] 412 U.S. 546 (1973).

For the first time, the Court essayed a full-dress discussion of the preemptive force of federal constitutional and statutory law regarding copyright. The Court elaborately reconstructed and formulated the balance struck by the Framers and, subsequently, legislators, between federal and state regulation of intellectual property, all of which was set within an analytical framework explicitly borrowed from the *general* mode of preemption adjudication.[25]

The implications of this methodological choice are explored below. What merits emphasis now is that it was not an inevitable approach to the specific preemption issues posed in *Goldstein*. The novelty of the Court's analysis may be gauged by comparison with a case which rested on very similar facts,[26] decided by the Second Circuit in 1955, *Capitol Records v. Mercury Records*.[27]

In *Capitol Records*, both the majority opinion of Judge Dimock and the dissent of Judge Learned Hand were crafted along analytical lines specific to intellectual property law. In fact, the area of agreement shared by the two opinions was quite extensive. Both concluded that recorded renditions were potentially copyrightable under the Constitution but had not been made copyrightable under federal statutory law. Both held that the Copyright Act [28] *by itself* exercised no preemptive force barring state protection respecting such noncopyrightable material. Finally, the two opinions agreed

[25] *Id.* at 555–557.

[26] Capitol Records v. Mercury Records Corporation, 221 F.2d 657 (2d Cir. 1955), presented facts quite comparable with *Goldstein*. The actionable wrong in *Capitol* could not easily be framed in the typical "misappropriation" language of the taking of another's skill, enterprise, or investment. The recordings of public domain compositions had not been originally produced by either party to the action. The defendant did not "misappropriate" time and labor that the plaintiffs had invested in the recording process. Both parties had pressed their records from matrices originally produced by a common third party source. The "misappropriation" issue in the case—decided by the majority under the law of New York—turned squarely on the simple sale of copies by the defendant: the wrong defined by statute in *Goldstein*.

[27] 221 F.2d 657 (2d Cir. 1955).

[28] 17 U.S.C. § 1 *et seq.* (1909).

that "publication" extinguished the possibility of state law relief against unauthorized copying: but here significant divergence is evident. The majority only impliedly accepted such a conception—which *could be* so derived as the history of the Revision Bill demonstrates below—as the traditional rule in American copyright law, the consequence of *Wheaton v. Peters.*[29] This is nowhere spelled out, yet without such an implied assumption, the labored exposition of the majority *on the issue* upon which the decision turned makes little sense. For Judge Hand, "publication" cut off state law because of the force of the constitutional copyright clause itself, with its prescription of limited times and implication of a uniform national rule.[30]

Beyond these points of agreement, majority and dissent divided on the specific issue of whether New York State law or federal law determined whether the plaintiffs' sales of the recordings had "dedicated" the recorded renditions to the public, that is, which law provided the applicable standard to test whether "publication" had occurred. Hand argued that the Constitution itself required a federal standard to apply; and tested by that standard, the records had been "published" and dedicated. Finding no preemptive mandate in the copyright statute, the majority, however, held state law dispositive to conclude that, under state law, sale did not constitute a "dedication" to public use, relying on Justice

[29] 33 U.S. (8 Pet.) 591 (1834).

[30] I cannot believe that the failure of Congress to include within the Act all that the Clause covers should give the states so wide a power. To do so would *pro tanto* defeat the overriding purpose of the Clause, which was to grant only for "limited Times" the untrammelled exploitation of an author's "Writings." Either he must be content with such circumscribed exploitation as does not constitute "publication," or he must eventually dedicate his "work" to the public. . . . I would hold that the clause has that much effect *ex proprio vigorè;* and that the states are not free to follow their own notions as to when an author's right shall be unlimited both in user and in duration. Such power of course they have as to "works" that are not "Writings"; but I submit that, once it is settled that a "work" is in that class, the Clause enforces upon the author the choice I have just mentioned; and if so, it must follow that it is a federal question whether he has published the 'work.'" 221 F.2d at 667.

Greenberg's holding in *Metropolitan Opera Ass'n v. Wagner-Nichols Records Corp.*[31] (an opinion, of course, in which none of the preemption-"publication" questions at issue in *Capitol Records* had been considered).

In *Goldstein v. California,* the issues as argued and decided were considerably recast from the approaches taken in *Capitol Records.* The shared assumptions, as well as the points of division, were brushed aside in *Goldstein. Capitol Records* had pointed a way to resolve the legality of state protection of sound recordings through an analysis closely geared to the particular problems of copyright law. In *Goldstein,* the issue of "publication"—the very focus of *Capitol*—was virtually dismissed. Impetus for *Goldstein's* broader inquiry was provided by the ambiguous legacy of *Sears, Roebuck & Co. v. Stiffel Co.,*[32] and *Compco Corp. v. Day-Brite Lighting, Inc.*[33] *Sears-Compco* were interpreted as having implications for copyright as well as patent law. Decided in 1964, *Sears-Compco* could be read—and were so read by *Goldstein*[34]—as dramatically departing from the view of both Dimock and Hand in *Capitol Records* that the Copyright Act itself held no preemptive consequences for material not brought within its coverage. The conclusion appeared to be that material that could not be federally copyrighted could not then find alternative protection under state law.

The sound recording preemption question therefore took on a different cast after *Sears-Compco.* The petitioners in *Goldstein* relied on the copyright statute to support their claim that the California criminal sanctions were preempted—an

[31] 199 Misc. 786, 101 N.Y.S. 2d 483 (Sup. Ct. 1950).
[32] 376 U.S. 225 (1964).
[33] 376 U.S. 234 (1964).
[34] At least this is true to the extent that Goldstein v. California did in fact "reaffirm today" those holdings, departing from them only to the extent required by the results of the factual inquiry conducted as to congressional intention regarding sound recording protection.

argument rejected all around in *Capitol Records;* and they also pressed arguments based, following the *Capitol Records* dissent, on the Constitution itself.

In *Sears,* the Court found that a national policy for uniformity was manifested in both patent and copyright laws. The Court concluded that "the patent system is one in which uniform federal standards are carefully used to promote invention while at the same time preserving free competition." State encroachment—direct or indirect—upon federal law was barred, of course, by the Supremacy clause. "An unpatentable article, like an article on which the patent has expired, is in the public domain and may be made and sold by whoever chooses to do so."[35]

Although *Sears* and its companion case, *Compco,* treated matter that had not qualified under the *patent laws,* their preemptive example had certain—if unclear—implications for copyright adjudication and the reconciliation of state unfair competition or "misappropriation" protection with the federal copyright law's failure to protect. Distinctions between copyright and patent could be drawn.[36] But the general teaching derived from *Sears-Compco* appeared to be that statutory enactments under the copyright clause should be seen as reaching to the full extent of the constitutional power, effectively barring state entry into the field.[37]

To frame the statutory preemption issue, the Court in *Goldstein* began with a reconstruction of the first principles embodied in the constitutional grant of federal copyright power. Next, it applied the general tenets of preemption analysis to evaluate the preemptive impact of the Copyright

[35] 376 U.S. at 231.

[36] As was noted in the aftermath of Goldstein v. California in Brown, *Publication and Preemption in Copyright Law: Elegiac Reflections on Goldstein v. California,* 22 U.C.L.A. L. Rev. 1022 (1975).

[37] For a range of views of the time, *see* Leeds, Handler, Derenberg, Brown and Bender, *Product Simulation: A Right or a Wrong?* 64 Colum. L. Rev. 1178 (1964).

Act's failure to protect sound recordings upon protection under state law for such a class of "writings." In a brief footnote to this line of analysis, the Court summarily denied that the concept of "publication" provided a demarcation point between state and federal power.[38]

Goldstein's rejection of the *Capitol Records* approach was implicit but fundamental. Analysis focused on the particular nuances of copyright law was transformed into an analysis framed in terms of general preemption principles. The relevance of these principles was not accorded any critical self-examination but was accepted *a priori.* Derived from the classic fount of preemption litigation—commerce power cases—they offered the Court a readily available framework for resolution of the *copyright* preemption issue facing it.

Throughout our legal history, preemption adjudication has been preeminently a matter of the adjustment of federal and state power to regulate commerce. Preemption cases have traced out the changing distributions of power in the federal system, with solicitude for the uniform, national sway of federal law alternating with greater toleration of state exercises of local regulatory and police power.[39]

Within the commerce context three general guides to preemption adjudication have emerged in recent decades.[40] First, the exercise of state police powers was not to be superseded unless such was "the clear and manifest purpose of Congress." Second, state regulatory and police power enactments had to be measured against, as a fundamental structural limit, the Constitution's affirmative grant of power to the Congress to regulate interstate commerce. The decision of *Cooley v. Board of Wardens*[41] had fashioned the *con-*

[38] 412 U.S. at 570 n. 28.

[39] Influential recent accounts of this history of preemption adjudication appear in Engdahl, *Preemptive Capability of Federal Power,* 45 U. Colo. L. Rev. 51 (1973); Hirsch, *supra* note 9; and *The Preemption Doctrine, supra* note 10.

[40] These principles have been distilled from the leading cases, especially Rice v. Santa Fe Elevator Corp., 331 U.S. 218 (1947).

stitutional standards for testing state commerce legislation: matters inherently national, requiring one uniform rule, were declared by force of the constitutional provision itself to be beyond the legislative capacities of a state. Third, state legislation which trenched upon activities already subject to some federal legislative enactment had to be examined by the courts to determine whether their enforcement would frustrate the federal policies represented by the federal statute in question. This task is imposed upon the courts by the Constitution's Supremacy Clause.

As federal legislation proliferated, preemption problems increased. If the appropriate test for preemption had once been *actual* conflict or *explicit* congressional intent to displace state law, such formally exacting standards could not long be maintained. Intent, of course, had never been the constitutional command; the assurance of supremacy of federal law always was. To see judicial analysis of preemption problems as narrowly focused on the explication of a platonic congressional intent misunderstands the judicial function in cases where state law is challenged as preempted by federal law. Congressional intent is not of itself the relevant constitutional standard. The command of the Supremacy Clause is. Intent provides an index of potential conflict by delineating what the operative scope of *supreme* federal law is to be, but it is only an index. The judicial role in preemption cases is, in this critical way, necessarily independent of specific tracings of congressional intention, nebulous as they so frequently are. This independent judicial role in determining whether state law has been preempted is most clearly exercised when Congress has in enacting legislation made no explicit provision for its impact on state law. However, even where an express preemption statute (such as section 301) is involved, the statutory language may not clearly

[41] 53 U.S. 298, 12 How. 299 (1851).

indicate its preemptive scope, and congressional intention may similarly fail to provide a court with definitive guidelines for judgment. The court is remitted therefore to its general techniques of adjudicating preemption claims to ensure that the supremacy of federal law is not frustrated. That such is the necessary judicial response to section 301 as it respects state "misappropriation" rights will be argued in the text accompanying notes 158–160, *infra.*[42] As federal regulation expanded, discrete standards for testing congressional intent to preempt tended to merge together.[43] A finding of "occupation of the field" could be rephrased as reflecting a judicial finding that the Congressional legislation in question had fixed the balance of rights or powers to prevail and that supplementary state legislation would upset that balance.[44] The case becomes one of actual conflict and clearly appropriate for a preemptive holding. This pattern of analysis was especially marked in the labor law cases.[45]

These premises and principles were primarily fashioned in commerce cases. Preemption analysis came very belatedly to other areas. Not until 1941 and the decision of *Hines v. Davidowitz*[46] did a preemption case involve legislation which did not regulate commerce. In *Hines*, state (Pennsyl-

[42] Note, *Pre-Emption as a Preferential Ground,* 12 Stan. L. Rev. 208 (1959).

[43] The criteria enumerated in the leading case of Rice v. Santa Fe Elevator Corp., 331 U.S. 218, 230 (1947), were the pervasiveness of the federal scheme, the dominant federal interest in the field affected, the evidence of the object to be obtained or obligations imposed, and whether state and federal results would be inconsistent. All these criteria of intent are rarely run through in any single case; for one notable example *see* Pennsylvania v. Nelson, 350 U.S. 497 (1956).

[44] For a survey of "occupation of the field" cases, *see* Note, *"Occupation of the Field" in Commerce Clause Cases, 1936–1946; Ten Years of Federalism,* 60 Harv. L. Rev. 262 (1946).

[45] *See, e.g.,* Hill v. Florida, 325 U.S. 538 (1945), *and* Garner v. Teamsters, Chauffeurs, and Helpers Local Union No. 776, 346 U.S. 485 (1953), for analysis basically rooted in the conception that labor law regulation, *once* undertaken by Congress, becomes a subject for which only national uniform action is permissible to avoid upsetting the federal scheme. Conflict is a function of subject matter description.

[46] 312 U.S. 52 (1941).

vania) registration requirements for aliens were challenged as barred by the Constitution's grant of naturalization power to Congress *and* by federal legislation regulating alien presence in the United States. The *Hines* case produced a frequently cited distillation [47] of the test for preemption, carried over, in turn, into commerce cases.

An emphasis on the *subject matter* at issue emerged from this development of preemption standards. Characterization of subject matter enters the preemption inquiry at two stages. First, irrespective of congressional intention of purpose, the Constitution itself poses a fundamental limit on state action affecting a certain range of subject matter—that "inherently national." [48] Second, congressional action upon subject matter that is not so "inherently national" may yet remove that subject matter from the range of permissible state action. Such a finding of subject matter as statutorily national is a basic pivot for the various tests of preemption. Such preemption tests as intent, conflict, and occupation of the field may be reduced in many cases to the determination that the affected subject matter requires national treatment. Characterization of the subject matter may determine preemption or preservation of state law.[49]

This approach to subject matter characterization was reflected in *Goldstein.* Paul Goldstein commented that the Court "comfortably rephrased" the preemption issue in *Goldstein* "to reflect an emphasis more congenial to an expansive view of state power." [50] Set within the chosen context of

[47] "Our primary function is to determine whether, under the circumstances of this particular case, [the state] law stands as an obstacle to the accomplishment and execution of the full purposes and objectives of Congress." 312 U.S. at 67. This was cited in Goldstein v. California, 412 U.S. 546, 561 (1973).

[48] For example, in the trial court in *Hines*, the state law had been struck down as barred by force of the "naturalization" clause of the Constitution, U.S. Const., art. I, § 8, cl. 4. Davidowitz v. Hines. 30 F. Supp. 470 (M.D. Pa. 1939).

[49] *See, e.g.*, Florida Lime and Avocado Growers, Inc. v. Paul, 373 U.S. 132 (1963).

[50] Goldstein, "*Inconsistent Premises*" *and the* "*Acceptable Middle Ground*"*: A Comment on Goldstein v. California*, 21 Bull. Copyright Soc'y 25, 28 (1974).

general preemption analysis, the Court's issue-framing was not surprising. *Goldstein* was decided within a framework taken over from the commerce cases; and we see the Court commencing in familiar fashion, by postulating the validity of state regulatory legislation,[51] the basic starting point of modern preemption adjudication.

The Court then spun out a commerce clause-type inquiry. The focus was on the subject matter, the sound recordings. The Court reasoned that no constitutional withdrawal of the states' "reserved" powers to grant copyrights existed. Explicitly drawing on *Cooley v. Board of Wardens*, the Court reaffirmed Congress's exclusive power to "legislate over matters which are *necessarily* national in import"; however, categories of intellectual property did not necessarily require such uniform, federal treatment.[52]

The copyright clause issue settled in favor of the reserved power of the states, the Court turned to the Supremacy clause, distinguishing the state laws struck down in *Sears-Compco*. California's statute prohibiting recording duplication, the Court held, did not conflict with federal law, despite the failure of the 1909 Act to protect sound recordings. Congress had not occupied the field to the exclusion of state law as to subject matter not within the federal scheme: no balance had been drawn.[53]

[51] 412 U.S. at 552–53.

[52] *Id.* at 554. "It is unlikely that all citizens in all parts of the country place the same importance on works relating to all subjects. Since the subject matter to which the copyright clause is addressed may thus be of purely local importance and not worthy of national attention or protection, we cannot discern such an unyielding national interest as to require an inference that state power to grant copyrights has been relinquished to *exclusive* federal control. *Id.* at 557–58.

[53] "The application of state law in [*Sears-Compco*] to prevent the copying of articles which did not meet the requirements for federal protection disturbed the careful balance which Congress had drawn and thereby necessarily gave way under the Supremacy Clause of the Constitution. No comparable conflict between state law and federal law arises in the case of recordings of musical performances. In regard to this category of 'Writings,' Congress has drawn no balance. . . ." *Id.* at 569–70.

The Court's handling of copyright subject matter again parallels treatment of commerce subject matters. No special inferences were drawn from the Copyright Act. Rather, the focus was on subject matters considered as discrete entities—not as part of any overall scheme of federal regulation of protection and competition. The Court's handling of the statutory issue rather disingenuously tracks the constitutional analysis, once no manifest congressional intent to withdraw protection is found. The field to be occupied appears to be made up of each separate category of "writings" and in the absence of manifest congressional intent, the constitutional finding that "writings" may be of local character will, of course, control resolution of this analytically distinct question.

At this point, a problem with the Court's assimilation of copyright preemption to commerce preemption becomes clear. In commerce cases, the *Constitution itself* provides an outer limit to state power.[54] This is a limit not found by the Court in the copyright area. No "writings" category is described as necessarily national; all are open to state action in the absence of congressional directive.[55] The Court's commerce analogy is incomplete—fatally incomplete from the standpoint of the federal interest in copyright regulation. The Court did not close the constitutional circle which re-

[54] *See* Cooley v. Board of Wardens, 53 U.S. 298, 12 How. 299 (1851).

[55] 412 U.S. at 560. This aspect of the reasoning in *Goldstein* was vigorously criticized in *The Preemption Doctrine, supra* note 9, at 641: "Considering the nature of the modern communications industry . . . the viability of local copyright regulation is doubtful. The promotion, distribution and marketing of sound recordings can hardly be deemed an 'intrastate' activity. If the 'necessarily national' character leg of the Court's test is to have any practical applicability, recordings should have come within it. The Court therefore seems to have extended protection to questionable state interests and in the process ignored potential federal interests in uniform regulation of a subject matter which does not admit of local treatment." This article was, in general, more favorably disposed to the Goldstein decision, viewed from the framework of preemption adjudication generally, than were the more specialized critiques of Brown, *supra* note 36, or Goldstein, *supra* note 50.

strains state exercises of commerce and police power. There is no constitutional barrier to state copyright legislation; only positive congressional action can cut off state lawmaking. And even the vast industry of music recording is left open to state copyright activity.

This imperfect symmetry between the copyright and commerce clauses was accepted without qualm by the Court. The *Goldstein* emphasis on subject matter dovetailed with an established body of preemption law which organized its lines of inquiry around the characterization of subject matter as national or local. The commerce clause analogy provided a ready-made approach to the sound recording problem posed by *Goldstein;* and its application in that case, however unsatisfactory in terms of copyright law tradition, could gain some plausibility as a simple and natural extension of general preemption principles. But if it was a simple extension, it also was a limited one. Once the focus of preemption analysis is no longer the protectibility of a particular, discrete category of subject matter, its analytic powers are exhausted.

III. AFTER GOLDSTEIN: PROBLEMS

The decision in *Goldstein v. California* recast the "misappropriation" preemption issue. A recent district court case illustrates the shifting dimensions of the problem, as it appeared after *Goldstein* and before the Revision.

In *Triangle Publications, Inc. v. Sports Eye, Inc.,*[56] plaintiff, publisher of *The Daily Racing Form,* brought suit for a preliminary injunction alleging that the defendant's publication had infringed plaintiff's copyright *and* had violated state unfair competition law.

Judge Lord began his statement of the case by explaining

[56] 415 F. Supp. 682 (E.D. Pa. 1976).

that plaintiff's newspaper (specifically its "Past Performances" section) "contains a wealth of information about horse races which are to be run at various tracks around the country" gathered at considerable expense.[57] Defendant's publication, *Fast Performances*, provided analytic charts of upcoming races with evaluations of horses' performances [58] based upon information appearing in *The Daily Racing Form* and compiled by referring to the *Form*.[59]

The court denied plaintiff's motion for relief.[60] There was no dispute that plaintiff had obtained a valid copyright of the *Form* and its "Past Performances" section.[61] But,

[57] *Id.*, at 683. As Judge Lord explained the plaintiff's business procedures: "The information published in plaintiff's paper is gathered at considerable expense and effort. Plaintiff has employees at all operating tracks in North and receives reports from them for each race. Plaintiff compiles and maintains these statistics using data processing equipment at its plant in New Jersey." *Id.* at 683–84.

[58] *Id.* at 684. Describing the content of *Fast Performances*, Judge Lord compared it to plaintiff's publication: "*Fast Performances* contains some thirty-two categories in four broad areas for each race covered. For each such race, *Fast Performances* names only those horses which fall into these categories. For example, one category is 'Beaten Within One Length of Winner Last Race.' . . . Other categories are comparative, such as 'Fastest Comparative Speed in Recent Races.' Thus, unlike *Past Performances* which give a plethora of facts about each and every horse entered in a given race, *Fast Performances* only mentions a given horse if it falls within one or more of its categories." Id.

[59] "[D]efendant obtains the information which it uses to prepare *Fast Performances* from plaintiff's publication. When the Form is first published, an employee of defendant purchases a copy and, using blank forms, prepares a draft copy of *Fast Performances*. The information is then telephoned to defendant in New York. . . . Defendant's employee was apparently able to prepare an issue of *Fast Performances* in less than an hour and, upon occasion, in fifteen or twenty minutes. At times he would be eating dinner or talking simultaneously with his preparation of the charts." Id. at 684.

[60] At this preliminary injunction stage the motion was, of course, subject to the general restrictions imposed on the issuance of such relief. The case will be read here for more than its procedural content with attention focused, for present purposes, on the issues raised without special regard for the plaintiff's particular unmet burdens here of making "a clear showing of probable success on the merits" and sufficient affirmative showing of irreparable injury. *See id.* at 684, for treatment of this aspect of the case.

[61] *Id.* at 684. Judge Lord relied here on Triangle Publications, Inc. v. New England Newspaper Publishing Co., 46 F. Supp. 198 (D. Mass. 1942) (Wyzanski, J.), the leading case holding that racing charts and past performance compilations were copyrightable. It was in that case that Judge Wyzanski offered the celebrated observation, "I could hardly be unmindful of the probability that

comparing the publications in question, the Court found that "both in visual and factual apprehension . . . the two papers differ substantially" and therefore the "substantial similarity" standard for infringement had not been met.[62] Judge Lord perceptively observed that plaintiff's complaint was grounded in the defendant's "use of the *Form,* without significant cost to prepare its own publication. . . ."[63] But "[i]n applying this test [of copying and substantial similarity] it must be remembered that while the form or mode of expressing an idea (or in this case data) may be copyrighted, the data or ideas may not be."[64] Precisely in these respects, however, allegations insufficient to support relief grounded on copyright infringement appear to present a classic case for "misappropriation" relief, congruent with the plaintiff's claim in *INS* itself.

The court recognized this linkage between the plaintiff's two allegations when it addressed the "unfair competition" plea for relief. Without any critical analysis[65] of the "fit" between plaintiff's claims and the law of unfair competition, the court simply commented that "[t]his cause of action was recognized and expounded upon by the Supreme Court in *International News Service v. Associated Press.*"[66] Relying

---

a majority of the present justices of the Supreme Court of the United States would follow the dissenting opinion of Mr. Justice Brandeis in the International News case. . . ." 46 F. Supp. at 204. *See* KAPLAN, *supra* note 4 at 61.

[62] 415 F. Supp. at 685.

[63] "Plaintiff's real complaint in this case, as it was in *Salkeld* [Universal Athletic Sales Co. v. Salkeld, 511 F.2d 904 (3d Cir.), *cert. denied sub. nom.* Universal Athletic Sales Co. v. Pinchock, 423 U.S. 863 (1975)], is defendant's use of the *Form,* without significant cost, to prepare its own publication—a publication which then competes in the marketplace with the plaintiff's paper. But, the answer is, as it was in *Salkeld,* that it is only the method or form for expressing the data that is copyrightable [citation omitted]. And on the present state of the record, plaintiff has not demonstrated a copyright infringement of its mode of disseminating the horseracing data it gathers." *Id.* at 685.

[64] *Id.* at 685.

[65] Triangle v. Sports Eye can be distinguished from the facts in *INS* to a point. *Sports Eye* was "using" *Triangle's* information to prepare its abstracts rather than simply directly "copying" or rewriting the "news" (the *INS* situation).

[66] 415 F. Supp. at 686.

on *Sears-Compco* and carefully limiting the plaintiff's use of *Goldstein,* Judge Lord qualified the continuing authority of *INS* [67] and concluded that no relief could be had on the state law claim, which was held to be preempted by federal law.

Triangle's analysis took as a starting point the view that "[t]he *Sears-Compco* decisions have been understood as holding that state regulation of unfair competition is pre-empted as to matters falling within the broad confines of the copyright clause of the United States Constitution. U.S. Const. Art. I, § 8." *Goldstein* "merely limited *Sears-Compco,* holding that the copyright and supremacy clauses by themselves, in the absence of Congressional expression, did not prohibit any state incursions on the area." Unlike *Goldstein,* which treated a field where Congress had not acted, "in the instant case Congress has taken action to afford copyright protection to the paper which plaintiff publishes. This is precisely the situation where the *Sears-Compco* preemption doctrine remains applicable." To grant plaintiff relief would precipitate a conflict, to quote *Goldstein,* between state protection and "that which Congress intended to be free from restraint." [68]

Without reference to the briefs and arguments to the court it is not, of course, possible to fully reconstruct the patterns of reasoning which provided the basis for the court's reading of the authoritative cases.[69] And much that can be extrap-

[67] "Since that time [when *INS* was decided], however, the Court has cut back substantially on the protection which a state may afford under the rubric of unfair competition." Id.

[68] *Id.* at 686.

[69] For example, the point of plaintiff's argument that grant of the injunction would not contravene federal policy and so should be authorized remains obscure in the opinion. Whether it is a *Goldstein* argument at all is questionable: it appears to owe more force to the subsequent opinion in Kewanee Oil Co. v. Bicron Corp., 416 U.S. 470 (1974). In *Kewanee,* state trade secret protection for patentable (but not actually patented) articles was held not preempted. Plaintiff's argument may have been that since it had obtained federal statutory copyright,

olated from the *Triangle* analysis was either left implicit or only developed in conclusory fashion. Taking up, first, *Triangle's* reading of the constitutional implications of *Sears* and, second, its treatment of *Goldstein's* limitation of this constitutional analysis will, however, open the way for a reconstruction of the potential preemption problems raised by *Goldstein.*

Triangle explicitly treated the *Sears-Compco* preemption rule as having a basis in the Constitution as well as the Copyright Act.[70] Resting the *Sears-Compco* doctrine on the force of the constitutional copyright clause is, however, problematic. Although the two cases may be read in tandem as announcing one common doctrine, it is curious that the quoted language from *Compco* comes from that opinion's explication of *Sears* and application of its holding over the *Compco* case facts. The holding in *Sears* itself directly relies on the Constitution only to establish the basis for the statutory exercise of patent power. In an imprecise analysis of the role of state unfair competition law within the federal patent system, Justice Black in *Sears* relied primarily on the policy of the patent *statute* as the bar to the challenged state laws.[71] However, the opinion did observe that the state law

---

state law relief would not have conflicted with a federal policy that authors rely on statutory copyright for copyrightable subject matter.

[70] *Triangle* quote from *Compco* as follows: "Today, we have held . . . that when an article is unprotected by a patent or copyright, state law may not forbid others to copy that article. To forbid copying would interfere with the federal policy, found in Art. I, § 8, cl 8, of the Constitution and in the implementing federal statutes, of allowing free access to copy whatever the federal patent and copyright laws leave in the public domain." 415 F. Supp. at 686, quoting 376 U.S. at 237.

[71] Although some reference was made to the "limited times" standard that controls the federal patent system by force of the constitutional enabling clause, the description offered of the federal patent system's relationship to state law concentrated on the *statutory* policies at stake: "The patent system is one in which uniform federal standards are carefully used to promote invention while at the same time preserving free competition. Obviously a State could not, *consistently with the Supremacy Clause of the Constitution,* extend the life of a patent beyond its expiration date or give a patent on an article which lacked the level of

of unfair competition might allow protection for articles unqualified "under *federal constitutional standards*" [emphasis added] and therefore should be held invalid.[72]

The shifting between constitutional and statutory references by Justice Black leaves unclear the source of the federal patent policy being applied to bar state protection of articles not qualifying under federal standards. Implicit in the *Sears* analysis is the apparent identification of the constitutional and statutory requirements of "invention,"[73] which state law may not ease. In this reading, *Sears* announces a statutory policy whose contours are informed by the constitutional definition of what is deserving of patent under federal law—and which *pro tanto* determines what may not be protected by the states.

Recasting the *Sears* constitutional argument in the copyright area has not squarely been done—although Judge Lord applied his constitutional perception of *Sears* to *Triangle's* facts despite the problems of transference.[74] If *Sears* is

---

invention required for federal patents. To do either would run counter *to the policy of Congress of granting patents only to true inventions*, and then only for a limited time. Just as a State cannot encroach upon the federal patent laws directly, it cannot, under some other law, such as that forbidding unfair competition, give protection of a kind that clashes with the *objectives of the federal patent laws*." [Emphasis added.] 376 U.S. at 230–31.

[72] As Justice Black explained: "To allow a State by use of its law of unfair competition to prevent the copying of an article which represents too slight an advance to be patented would be to permit the State to block off from the public something which federal law has said belongs to the public. The result would be that *while federal law* grants only 14 or 17 years' protection to genuine inventions [citation omitted], States could allow perpetual protection to articles too lacking in novelty to merit any patent at all *under federal constitutional standards*. This would be too great an encroachment on the federal patent system to be tolerated." [Emphasis supplied.] 376 U.S. at 231–32.

[73] The Constitutional Provision respecting copyright and patents (U.S. Const. art. I § 8, cl. 8) provides that "The Congress shall have Power . . . To promote the Progress of Science and useful Arts, by securing for limited Times to Authors and *Inventors* the exclusive Right to their respective Writings and *Discoveries*." [Emphasis added.]

[74] Ralph Brown, discussing the potential carryover of *Sears-Compco* into copyright adjudication, attempted to recast that holding into comparable literary property terms in a formulation that may have been overbroad: "[T]he objects in

read as enforcing a federal policy [75] derived from a constitutional definition (incorporated by the patent statute) of "discovery" or "invention," the constitutional limit on state power manifested by the Patent/Copyright Clause itself (apart from statutory preemption by virtue of the Supremacy Clause), the analogous copyright law issue would turn on the power of states to protect subject matter that are *not* Constitutional "writings" at all. This is the conclusion to which the *Sears* constitutional analysis pushes when brought to bear on copyright.[76] But Judge Lord did not follow this through.

The need to accommodate the decision in *Goldstein v. California* with *Sears-Compco* intervened at this point—with a consequent confusion of what the constitutional force of *Sears-Compco* could have been as decided. We return to *Triangle* to trace the impact of *Goldstein* on Judge Lord's analysis.

Goldstein, Judge Lord indicated, had undercut the constitutional basis of *Sears* [77]—and it deflected his reasoning away from the constitutional conclusion toward which his

---

Sears and *Compco* were unpatentable because they did not meet the qualitative standards of invention, not because lamps and lighting fixtures as such were not patentable machines or patentable designs. The copyright equivalent to the lamp in *Sears* would be works that are unoriginal or that are too abstract to be considered expressions." Brown, *supra* note 36, at 1037.

[75] The policy as described by Justice Black: "[T]he patent system is one in which uniform federal standards are carefully used to promote invention while at the same time preserving free competition."
376 U.S. at 230.

[76] Interestingly, when so pushed, the analysis ends up with a different formulation of the constitutional restrictions on state power from the one which it originally advanced. Judge Lord described *Sears-Compco* as "understood as holding that state regulation of unfair competition is pre-empted as to matters falling within the broad confines of the copyright clause of the United States Constitution," 415 F. Supp. at 686, but the *Sears* constitutional point is that state law is barred as to matters falling outside the constitutional standard. This simply indicates the difficulty of giving lucid explanation of the *Sears* result, understood as a constitutional decision.

[77] "*Goldstein* merely limited *Sears-Compco,* holding that the copyright and supremacy clauses *by themselves,* in the absence of congressional expression, did not prohibit any state incursions into the area."
415 F. Supp. at 686.

use of *Sears* appeared to be heading. Nevertheless, *Triangle* held that plaintiff's reliance on state law was barred and that *Sears-Compco,* even as "limited" by *Goldstein,* compelled preemption.[78] Judge Lord found support for this continued preemptive reading of *Sears-Compco* in a recent decision of a federal district court in New Hampshire, *Jacobs v. Robitaille.*[79]

Jacobs was an unsuccessful action by a publisher of a weekly classified advertisement booklet to enjoin a competitor who had issued his own booklet reprinting plaintiff's published material. Plaintiff alleged copyright infringement and unfair competition. The copied advertisements were copyrightable under the federal law.[80] Plaintiff had not, however, obtained statutory copyright before publication. The court held that such a publication dedicated the booklet to the public. *Goldstein* did not authorize state protection of copyrightable advertisements which were not, in fact, copyrighted. The court concluded that what had been thereby placed in the public domain could not be subsequently removed by state action.[81]

Judge Lord concluded that *Jacobs* presented "indistinguishable facts" with *Triangle.*[82] Concentrating on *Jacobs* for a moment, plaintiff's suit was aimed at enjoining the "copying" *per se* of the advertisements first published in his booklet. The result does not surprise when the allegations of wrong-doing are viewed from this perspective.

[78] Judge Lord concluded: "In the instant case Congress has taken action to afford copyright protection to the paper which plaintiff publishes. This is precisely the situation where the *Sears-Compco* pre-emption doctrine remains applicable. Otherwise 'a conflict would develop if a State attempted to protect that which Congress intended to be free from restraint or to free that which Congress had protected.' *Goldstein,* supra 412 U.S. at 559." 415 F. Supp. at 686–87.

[79] 406 F. Supp. 1145 (D.N.H., 1976).

[80] And necessarily, therefore, constitutional "writings."

[81] 406 F. Supp. at 1153.

[82] 415 F. Supp. at 687.

State law was invoked in *Jacobs* precisely to provide the protection against unauthorized copying that had been forfeited by failure to secure federal copyright. The copied advertisements were "writings" in both constitutional and statutory senses. Preemption could be held even within the "subject-matter"-focused framework that Goldstein had applied to limit the reach of *Sears-Compco. Goldstein* had concluded that "sound recordings of original artistic performances were constitutional, but not statutory, 'writings.' " Therefore, premised on the constitutional reservation of state power, subject matter that was not under the statute could be protected by state law. In holding that as to a "writing" copyrightable under the statute the state law protection, *sub nomine* unfair competition, claimed by the plaintiff was *barred, Jacobs* simply worked out the preemptive consequences of *Goldstein's* protective result.[83]

Judge Lord applied a similar understanding of *Goldstein's* acceptance of preemption with respect to "writings" that Congress had brought within the copyright statute. Plaintiff's newspaper was afforded copyright protection by Congress. State law could not—to fill in what the opinion left unarticulated—be relied upon in such a situation; federal law *exclusively* determined the range of protection available. And support for preemption of *additional* state relief was found in *Jacobs v. Robitaille*.[84]

Accepting Judge Lord's own characterization of plaintiff's allegations, the intermediate conclusion that *Jacobs* rested on "indistinguishable facts" is open to question; and the re-

[83] The reasoning in *Jacobs*, limiting *Goldstein*, was: "I do not believe that *Goldstein* can be read to allow the states, under the aegis of their common law, to exercise control over 'writings' which are copyrightable. . . . I find that the advertisements were copyrightable 'writings' and that the *Sears-Compco* decisions, even as refined by *Goldstein*, preempt a state action for unlawful competition." Jacobs v. Robitaille, 406 F. Supp. at 1153.

[84] 415 F. Supp. at 687.

sulting treatment of *Goldstein* may be queried as not adequately reflecting that decision's potential impact—or range of impacts—on misappropriation cases.[85]

The extent of *Goldstein's* reservation of state protective powers over subject matter not within the scope of the federal statute had not been settled by that decision. In its aftermath, emblematic of the destabilizing effect of *Goldstein* on traditional and rather settled conceptions of the federal system allocation of intellectual property power, speculative commentaries charted the consequences of Goldstein's subject-matter analysis.[86] In *Goldstein,* Ralph Brown observed,

> [w]e have the new recognition of a state copyright power that may extend to any kind of work that is not explicitly preempted. . . . It is also possible that another historic dividing-line in copyright is threatened, namely the separation between "ideas," which cannot be monopolized, and their "expression"—which is essentially the sphere of copyright.[87]

Such a reading of the possible reach of *Goldstein* places the *Triangle* plaintiff's "misappropriation" claim in a novel light—and suggests that *Triangle's* facts are not "indistinguishable" from those in *Jacobs.* For *Triangle's* "misappropriation" claim, as recast following *Goldstein,* can be seen as involving two distinct subject-matter categories: copyrightable (under statute) "literary expression" and the non-federally copyrightable "facts" compiled and reported. Since the "facts," considered as a category of subject matter *per se,* could *not be federally copyrighted, Goldstein* might be read to open the way for nonpreempted state law protection thereof.

This is the configuration of subject-matter claims that ex-

[85] The issue here is not the "correctness" or "justice" of the *Triangle* decision, but rather whether its reasoning adequately canvassed the implications of *Goldstein.*

[86] *See, e.g.,* Kaul, *And Now State Protection of Intellectual Property?*, 60 A.B.A.J. 198 (1974).

[87] Brown, *supra* note 36, at 1044–45.

ists in all classic *INS* "misappropriation" claims, but which was not present, for example, in *Jacobs v. Robitaille.* The misappropriation preemption issue posed in *Triangle* becomes, after *Goldstein,* a more difficult one. To see *Triangle* as involving two tiers of subject matter transforms analysis of classic misappropriation cases: the analysis emerges as the curious skewed evolution of the doctrine. Set within the factual situation of an *INS* "misappropriation" case, an open-ended reading of *Goldstein* poses the question whether federal law preempted state protection of the noncopyrightable subject matter involved: the *data* collected by the plaintiff in *Triangle,* the use of which, by the defendant, as Judge Lord had accurately noted, was crucial to plaintiff's complaint.

Judge Lord could have rejected plaintiff's "misappropriation" claim by pursuing the constitutional line developed in *Sears-Compco* and holding that such *data* was not a "writing" and, much like a non-"discovery" in patent law, was not within state protective purview by force of the Constitution. This conclusion could have been reached without upsetting the *Goldstein* holding. *Goldstein* had, of course, treated preemption problems concerning state protection of constitutional "writings." The Supreme Court in *Goldstein* had found no constitutional preclusion of state power to protect "writings" as an original proposition; and the simple failure of Congress to accord copyright to a class of "writings" [88] did not preempt—as a matter of statutory construction—state protective action.[89] As to the constitutional

[88] The classification of "sound recordings as renderings of original artistic performances" as constitutional "writings" presented no problem in *Goldstein,* 412 U.S. at 561–62.

[89] *Goldstein* distinguished *Sears-Compco:* "*Sears* and *Compco,* on which petitioners rely, do not support their position. . . . In regard to mechanical configurations, Congress had balanced the need to encourage innovation and originality of invention against the need to insure competition in the sale of identical or substantially identical products. The standards established for granting federal patent protection to machines thus indicated not only which articles in the par-

preclusion analysis apparently developed in *Sears-Compco*, *Goldstein*—in its focus on "writings"—might have been regarded as simply not relevant.

Judge Lord did not pursue such a line of analysis, however. His failure to do so—although subject to the problems below—makes puzzling the forthright reiteration of *Sears-Compco* as constitutional, as well as statutory, decisions, since their ascribed constitutional rationale was not at issue in *Goldstein*. The judgment of preemption, shorn of such a constitutional basis, lacks a clear foundation as a result.

Problems with pushing this constitutional argument as far as this are quite apparent. First, the extension of this constitutional definitional limit on state power from patent "discoveries" to copyright "writings" would have run headlong into considerable authority to the contrary, including that of Judge Hand, dissenting in *Capitol Records v. Mercury Records* itself. Concluding that the application of state law to protect publicly disseminated sound recordings (constitutional "Writings") was preempted, Hand also confidently asserted the reservation of state power over " 'works' that are not 'writings.' "[90] Second, the dimensions of the general class of constitutional "writings" exceeds the usage we might ordinarily apply to the concept.[91] Judicial enforcement of a

ticular category Congress wished to protect, but which configurations it wished to remain free. The application of state law in these cases to prevent the copying of articles which did not meet the requirements for federal protection disturbed the careful balance which Congress had drawn and thereby necessarily gave way under the Supremacy Clause of the Constitution. No comparable conflict between state law and federal law arises in the case of recordings of musical performances. In regard to this category of "Writings," Congress has drawn no balance; rather, it has left the area unattended, and no reason exists why the State should not be free to act." 412 U.S. at 563.

[90] "[T]he states are not free to follow their own notions as to when an author's right shall be unlimited both in user and in duration. Such power of course they have as to 'works' that are not 'Writings.' " Capitol Records, Inc. v. Mercury Records Corp., 221 F.2d 657, 667 (2d Cir. 1955) (Hand, J., dissenting).

[91] *Goldstein* expressed the standard view on this question of construction: "By Art. I, § 8, cl. 8 of the Constitution, the States granted to Congress the power to

perceived constitutional bar to state protection of non-"writings" would, as a result of the elasticity ascribed to the constitutional language, build an enduring tension between courts and Congress into the copyright system. The range of future congressional extension of statutory copyright, presumably limited to "writings," would be subject to the considerable volume of previous judicial classifications, requiring continual reexamination by the courts. At the same time, judicial readiness to avoid this barrier by holding various state-protected subject matters to be "writings" would lead the inquiry to the level of potential statutory preemption.

Preemption in *Triangle* did not take this difficult constitutional tack. Rather, state law was barred on the ground that the copyright offered as to the form for expressing the data by Congress—and accepted by the plaintiff—determined the limits of protection available. State law could

---

protect the 'Writings' of 'Authors.' These terms have not been construed in their narrow literal sense but, rather, with the reach necessary to reflect the broad scope of constitutional principles. While an 'author' may be viewed as an individual who writes an original composition, the term, in its constitutional sense, has been construed to mean an 'originator,' 'he to whom anything owes its origin.'" [Citation omitted.] 412 U.S. at 561. The 1909 and Revision statutes both observe such a "physical rendering," or "fixation," standard. But whether even it provides an outer limit to the scope of constitutional "writings" may be an issue. Without jumping ahead too much, this passage from the House Committee Report of 1967, commenting on the Revision's—as then proposed—exclusions from subject matter coverage, probed the permeable boundaries of the Constitutional grant: "Without implying that they would be wholly without protection [under the statute], or that they are *necessarily* [emphasis supplied] the 'writings' of an author in the constitutional sense, we cite the following as examples. These are areas of subject matter now on the fringes of literary property but not intended, solely, as such, to come within the scope of the bill: typography, unfixed performances or broadcast emissions; blank forms and calculating devices; titles, slogans and similar expressions; certain three-dimensional industrial designs; interior decoration; ideas, plans, methods, systems, mathematical principles; formats and synopses of television series and the like; color schemes; news and factual information considered apart from the compilation or expression. . . . any protection for them as separate copyrightable works is not here intended and will require action by a future Congress." H.R. Rep. No. 83, 90th Cong. 1st Sess. 98 (1967). For further discussion of H.R. Rep. No. 83 *see* text at note 144, *infra*.

not supplement the degree and kind of protection provided by federal law.[92] Unlike in *Goldstein,* Congress had acted; and state law cannot be applied within the ambit of federal law.

Goldstein's suggestive implications as to the possibility of state protection of "facts" or ideas—by extension, racing data or "news"—considered as a category of subject matter not included within the federal statute, and not preempted, are not treated at all.

A holding analogous to *Triangle* in *Goldstein* itself could have barred state protection on the ground that Congress had indeed afforded copyright protection in the *area* at issue, limited simply to the underlying musical composition recorded. It must be assumed that Judge Lord accepted *Goldstein's* holdings with respect to *its* facts. Nothing was said, however, in *Triangle* to distinguish and limit *Goldstein* on this point.[93] Any special problems suggested by the consideration of "facts" or information as a subject matter class were not raised or faced; the potential recasting of misappropriation complaints in such a subject matter framework went unmentioned.

This discussion of *Triangle* is open ended, even speculative, intended to throw into relief some of the complications introduced into preemption analysis by *Goldstein,* but not to

[92] 415 F. Supp. at 686.

[93] To be sure, *Goldstein* disclaimed the possibility of restraint "on the use of an idea or concept." However, this *caveat* was then specifically explained on the narrower grounds that "petitioners and other individuals remain free to record the same compositions in precisely the same manner and with the same personnel as appeared on the original recording." 412 U.S. at 571. This freedom is, of course, due to the particular provisions of the Copyright Law respecting compulsory licensing; it does not necessarily cut across the entire sphere of intellectual property. The implications we have derived from *Goldstein* were not definitively foreclosed, although sound policy reasons could surely be urged for a broad reading of this language in *Goldstein.* The points we focus on here are, again, simply the problems opened up by *Goldstein's* preemptive method and the difficulty in assimilating the particular interest balancings of copyright law within its generalized and abstracted approach.

settle them. The enactment of the Revision has, of course, placed the misappropriation preemption problem in a new context. Discussion of these issues must move on to consider them in this transposed key. The Revision's preemption provisions were expressly intended to clearly and definitely mark out the border between federal and state intellectual property law.[94] Whether definite answers will, even so, be forthcoming, is the next subject for analysis.

IV. AFTER REVISION: SOLUTIONS?

Section 301,[95] "one of the bedrock provisions of the bill,"[96] sets out the Revision's plan concerning "Preemption with Respect to other Laws." The provisions outlined briefly are:

1. Subsection (a) provides that all legal or equitable rights "equivalent" to the "exclusive rights within the general scope of copyright" specified in section 106(i) in works of authorship; (ii) fixed in a tangible medium of expression; (iii) within the subject matter of copyright specified by sections 102 and 103; (iv) whether published or unpublished, "are defined exclusively by this title."

2. Subsection (b) provides that the federal copyright statute *shall not preempt* state law rights or remedies with respect to (i) subject matter *not* within the subject matter of copyright specified by sections 102 and 103 (subsection [b][1]), or (ii) activities violating rights not within the scope of copyright as specified by section 106 (subsection [b][3]).[97]

[94] *See* S. Rep. at 114 and H.R. Rep. at 130, *supra* note 12.

[95] The text of section 301 is set out in Appendix I.

[96] H.R. Rep., *supra* note 12, at 129, *reprinted in* 1976 U.S. Code Cong. & Ad. News, *supra* note 12, at 5745.

[97] Section 301(b)(2) simply preserves state law rights or remedies with respect to those causes of action "arising from undertakings commenced before January 1, 1978," the effective date of the Copyright Act.

Section 301's preemption scheme takes this general form. Subsection (a) sets out the general rule of preemption of state law respecting intellectual property "fixed in a tangible medium of expression." Subsection (b) complements (a), qualifying federal preemption by explicitly preserving state law with respect to both subject matter and activities considered beyond the scope of the preemptive regime. The contours of what is preempted and what is "saved" in state law are, in turn, defined by reference to the sections of the Act which describe the subject matter of copyright and the rights within the scope of copyright. Determining the impact of section 301 therefore requires reference to sections 102 and 103 ("subject matter of copyright") and 106 ("Exclusive rights in copyrighted works").[98]

Whether "misappropriation" remains a permissible state law-based cause of action must be determined by testing it against the interacting preemptive-saving provisions of section 301. Ultimate pronouncement of preemption remains a judicial task; but enactment of section 301 provides an attempt by Congress to express an explicit design for the relationship between state and supreme federal law. Before working through the Revision, however, important background for evaluating its relative success or failure in providing a conclusive solution to the misappropriation preemption problem is presented. Several pages of history—even of legislative history—illuminate much, especially in an area of the law where logic has consistently been slighted in favor of accommodating special interests.

Section 301 has a lengthy history behind it.[99] The inclu-

[98] Set out in Appendix III.

[99] The legislative process which culminated in the enactment of the Revision Bill of 1976 began with efforts by the Copyright Office to assemble a body of information, analysis and interested comment which, taken together, would provide the revision task with a firm point of departure. Beginning in the mid-1950's, the Copyright Office commissioned expert studies on legal and business aspects of copyright law, assembled panels of practitioners (leavened with a few aca-

sion of a preemption provision in the Revision Bill had its conceptual origins in the desire to resolve the tensions generated by the interaction of the intransigent doctrine of "publication" with modern technological developments in the arts,[100] and not in the interaction between state law protectionism and the federal public domain, the flash point of "misappropriation" preemption problems. "Publication" had traditionally marked the dividing line between state and federal intellectual property jurisdiction. It provided the foundation for the dual system—of state common law and federal statute—of protection which had prevailed since 1790. The continuing coherence of this dual system had fallen victim to the attenuated significance of the traditional "publication" concept. The first preemption proposals of the Copyright Office were narrowly drawn and rather tightly directed at meeting the "publication" problem.[101]

---

demics) for discussion of particular problems, and eventually prepared a draft bill which was introduced in Congress in 1964. These efforts are traced in considerable detail in *Copyright Law Revision: Hearing on H.R. 2223 Before the Subcomm. on Courts, Civil Liberties and the Administration of Justice of the House Comm. on the Judiciary*, 94th Cong., 1st Sess., 99, 101 (1975) (Statement of Barbara Ringer) [hereinafter HEARINGS]. Consideration of federal preemption of state laws has been a part of the Revision effort, "a key provision of the statute," since it commenced in the latter 1950's. Provisions effectuating preemption have appeared in the successive Revision drafts beginning with the Preliminary Draft for Revised U.S. Copyright Law submitted by the Copyright Office in July 1964. "Preliminary Draft for Revised U.S. Copyright Law" appearing in U.S. Copyright Office, COPYRIGHT LAW REVISION, 88th Cong., 1st Sess., Report of the Register of Copyrights (Comm. Print. 1964) [hereinafter COPYRIGHT LAW REVISION].

[100] *See* COPYRIGHT LAW REVISION, 87th Cong., 1st Sess. 39 (Comm. Print 1961).

[101] In the Report of the Register of Copyrights on the General Revision of the U.S. Copyright Law [hereinafter the "1961 Report"] the Copyright Office distilled from previous studies and discussions a recommendation to recast the scheme, replacing "publication" with a less technical concept of "public dissemination." State law protection would be reserved only for copyrightable works that had not been "publicly disseminated." The scope of federal law would be extended, but the dual system would not be entirely superseded. 1961 REPORT, *supra* note 100, at 43. This proposed substitution of "publication" by "public dissemination" as the trigger for protection under federal law within a dual system was sharply criticized at the panel discussions convened by the Copyright Office in 1961–1962 to work over the proposals in the 1961 Report. *See* COPYRIGHT LAW

When the Copyright Office submitted a Preliminary Draft Revision Bill in 1963,[102] section 19(a), entitled "Pre-emption with Respect to Other Laws," set out—as the precursor of section 301(a) of the enacted Revision—the general rule of preemption, abolishing state copyright for works copyrightable under the statute. Whether published or unpublished, all rights in such a work in the nature of copyright would be governed by federal law exclusively. This general rule of preemption was restated in section 19(a) of the 1964 Revision Bill and subsequently in section 301(a) of the 1965 bill.[103] It retains a very similar formulation in the 1976 Act.

The complement to this primary focus on creating a unified system of federal copyright protection to resolve the "publication" problem was the lack of close analysis of the limits—set out in subsection (b) of successive drafts and bills—of the preemptive regime. Beginning with the Preliminary Draft prepared by the Copyright Office, the preemption section of the Revision was drafted to provide that "preemption is not intended to extend to subject matter or to causes of action outside the scope of the Federal Copyright Statute."[104] Section 19(b)(3) of the Draft set out

---

REVISION, Pt. 2 at 72–84 (1963). Copyright Office advocacy of the scheme was hamstrung by its forthright recognition of the advantages that would be gained by creating a single system of federal protection of copyrightable works. 1961 REPORT, *supra* note 100 at 41.

[102] Preliminary Draft, *supra* note 99.

[103] The text of section 19(a) of the Preliminary Draft appears in Appendix II. The comparative texts of the successive preemption provisions of these Bills are set out in Appendix III. The 1964 Revision Bill (introduced as H.R. 11947 and S. 3008 on July 20, 1964, in the 88th Cong., 2d Sess.) was described and discussed in COPYRIGHT LAW REVISION, Pt. 5 (1965); the 1965 Bill (introduced as H.R. 4347 and S. 1006 on February 4, 1965, in the 89th Cong. 1st Sess.) was discussed in COPYRIGHT LAW REVISION, Pt. 6, SUPPLEMENTARY REPORT OF THE REGISTER OF COPYRIGHTS (1965), reporting the relevant panel discussions [hereinafter SUPPLEMENTARY REPORT].

[104] The 1961 Report, *supra* note 100, of the Copyright Office had not discussed at all the accommodation of the Federal copyright system to state causes of action outside the statute's scope.

a specific listing of nonpreempted causes of action,[105] primarily involving deceptive business practices but pointedly omitting the modern extensions of "unfair competition law."[106] This exclusion of "unfair competition" from the listing of nonpreempted causes of action was repeated in both the 1964 and 1965 Revision Bills.[107] Prepared in the expansive aftermath of *Sears-Compco,* the 1965 Supplementary Report of the Register of Copyrights[108] (analyzing the 1965 Revision Bill) justified the omission of "unfair competition" from clause (3)'s illustrative[109] listing of rights under state law not equivalent to copyright:

[105] The text appears in Appendix II.

[106] A panel discussion on section 19(b) of the Draft concentrated on expanding this listing and on abandoning itemization in favor of the expression of a general principle. There was considerable comment urging incorporation of "acts of unfair competition" within section (b)(3) to reflect the fact that "[n]either fraud nor actual confusion is necessary under modern concepts of the law of unfair competition." Nowhere—in the public panel discussions at any rate—was explicit, extended consideration given to the place of the *INS* holding within the preemptive design. However, the remarks of Harry R. Olsson, Attorney for the American Broadcasting Company, at the panel convened to discuss the Preliminary Draft in August 1963, are suggestive in the context of subsequent developments. Olssen noted that "[f]or a long time there has been a tendency in some of the State courts to supply protection for matter to which the Federal Courts of the United States have decided no copyright protection should be given. . . . Frequently, the misappropriation theory is invoked." Olssen explained that "[t]here are very definitely 'idea' cases in which State courts have given property-type protection to ideas. . . . The State Courts to a very large extent, under the guise of unfair competition, have tended to supply copyright protection for things which the Federal courts have decided should not be protected over a very, very long period of time on policy grounds." One question elicited by these remarks—"Are you trying to overrule the *INS* case?"—was more the occasion for laughter than for continued analysis, unfortunately. COPYRIGHT LAW REVISION (Further Discussion and Comments on the Draft Revision Bill) 8–10 (1964).

[107] Texts of (b)(3) in both bills in Appendix III.

[108] SUPPLEMENTARY REPORT, *supra* note 103, at 81.

[109] Note that in each of the Revision Bills, unlike the Draft, the listings in b(3) of specific state law causes of action are stated only to illustrate the general principle that the Federal law does not preempt state law "with respect to activities violating rights that are not equivalent to any of the exclusive rights of copyright . . ." The SUPPLEMENTARY REPORT, discussing the 1965 Bill in detail, explained: "While the third clause of section 301(b) is not intended to represent an exhaustive listing, its purpose is to illustrate rights and remedies that are different in nature from copyright and that are preserved under State

The language of clause (3) has been worded very carefully in an effort to avoid saying too much or too little. In particular, we have resisted use of the ambiguous term "unfair competition," which in recent years has gone through some wide shifts in meaning. In some States it was greatly broadened to become, under the name "misappropriation," the virtual equivalent of copyright; and it has been cut back, by the Supreme Court's decision in *Sears, Roebuck, and Co. v. Stiffel Co.*, to the traditional concept of "passing off." There is no intention to pre-empt causes of action for unfair competition involving false labeling and fraudulent representation but, *to the extent that a right against "unfair competition" is merely copyright by another name, section 301 is intended to abolish it as a common law cause of action.*[110] [Emphasis supplied.]

This position was taken, however, without specific attention to "misappropriation," understood in the distinctive framework of *INS*. The framework of preemption was set by 1965. The system proposed in the 1965 Bill reflected preemption's origins in the "chaotic" situation produced by the role of "publication" in the traditional dual system.[111] What to do about "misappropriation" never received focused consideration. The 1965 Bill appeared to preempt its extensive application, but this result was based on an undifferentiated assimilation of the *INS* holding to the general law of "unfair competition," or to *Goldstein*-type facts.

An indication of the relatively marginal place held by the "misappropriation" preemption problem within the overall design of the unified federal system can be gleaned from testimony of the Register, Barbara Ringer, before the House Subcommittee on Courts, Civil Liberties and the Administration of Justice, in 1975.[112] The Supplementary Report (1965)

---

common law or statute. Some examples might include, depending upon the particular circumstances in the case: The unauthorized exploitation of a person's name or photograph for commercial advertising; The unauthorized use of the title of a work in such a way as to constitute passing off or fraud; The unauthorized disclosure and exploitation of a trade secret." *Id.* at 85.

110 *Id.* at 85.

111 *Id.* at 81.

112 HEARINGS, *supra* note 99, at 1910.

had described preemption as "[p]erhaps the most fundamental issue underlying the entire revision program."[113] Reviewing preemption's progress in the intervening decade, Ringer observed that

> at one time [preemption], was unquestionably the most controversial and debated issue in copyright revision. This has not, however, been true for at least 10 years and probably quite a bit longer than that. I believe that the concept of a single Federal system of copyright is now almost universally accepted. There was no opposition to this concept in your hearings in 1975.[114]

Ringer continued, laying a foundation for several recommended changes to the 1965 Bill's text:

> The Federal preemption provision in the bill has stayed pretty much the same since the early 1960's. What has happened is the result of a series of decisions by the courts, including the Supreme Court, which have had a sort of roller coaster effect with respect to Federal preemption, but which under the present law, as I think most people interpret it, requires *some technical changes in section 301.*[115] [Emphasis added.]

What Ringer termed "technical changes" entailed, in fact, a sweeping transformation of the place to be accorded—by explicit legislative command—"misappropriation" within the preemptive scheme. To term this a "technical change" suggests that as a general matter of law-making, the status of "misappropriation" had not been canvassed thoroughly.

Consideration of these "technical changes" made in section 301 in response to *Goldstein v. California* provides a further piece of the background against which the enacted preemption provisions should be evaluated. The impact of *Goldstein* on the Revision program was an accident of legislative history. In April 1967, the House of Representatives passed a Revision Bill which bodily incorporated the preemp-

[113] SUPPLEMENTARY REPORT, *supra* note 103, at 81.
[114] HEARINGS, *supra* note 99, at 1910.
[115] *Id.* at 1910.

tion section first included in the 1965 Bill. Preemption—and the specific form given it in the Revision legislation—had ceased to be a disruptive issue. Other problems, however, remained unresolved and the subject of profound disagreement. In 1967, the "legislative momentum began to slow more and more" and "it was increasingly apparent that cable television had become the make-or-break issue for copyright revision." Legislative progress stalled out, starting up only in the early 1970's (after a Supreme Court decision helped clear the contentious cable television air).[116]

Meanwhile, the *Goldstein* decision had been handed down in 1973. When the House Subcommittee on Courts, Civil Liberties and the Administration of Justice convened hearings on the Revision Bill in 1975, the Copyright Office submitted a Report[117] recommending the acceptance of changes made in the preemption section of the Senate Revision bill passed earlier that year. This section had not been modified since 1965. The 1975 Copyright Office Report concluded that:

> In view of the recent Supreme Court decisions in the *Goldstein* and *Kewanee* cases, referred to above, Congress should reconsider the wording of section 301 and subsection (b) in particular. The word "unpublished" in clause (1) of subsection (b) is probably inconsistent with the *Goldstein* decision, and additions to the specific references in clause (3) appear justified by this judicial trend.[118]

The Senate draft of section 301(b) provided:

> (b) Nothing in this title annuls or limits any rights or remedies under the common law or statutes of any State with respect to:
>
> (1) *subject* matter that does not come within the subject matter of copyright as specified by sections 102 and 103, including works of authorship not fixed in any tangible medium of expression; or
>
> (2) ****

[116] The legislative history is laid out in HEARINGS, *supra* note 99, 101 ff. (statement of Barbara Ringer).

[117] HEARINGS, *supra* note 99, 2051, 2079.

[118] *Id.* at 2081–2082. The reference is to Kewanee Oil Co. v. Bicron Corp., 416 U.S. 470 (1974). *See* note 69 *supra.*

(3) activities violating legal or equitable rights that are not equivalent to any of the exclusive rights within the general scope of copyright as specified by section 106, including *rights against misappropriation not equivalent to any of such exclusive rights,* breaches of contract, breaches of trust, trespass, conversion, invasion of privacy, defamation, and deceptive trade practices such as passing off and false representation.[119] [Emphasis supplied.]

The Senate Committee Report passed over the change made in clause (1) without comment but did discuss its "novel" inclusion of "misappropriation" among the illustrative nonequivalent causes of action in clause (3). For the first time in the legislative process, the *INS* problem was considered.

"Misappropriation" is not necessarily synonymous with copyright infringement, and thus a cause of action labeled as "misappropriation" is not preempted if it is in fact based neither on a right within the general scope of copyright as specified by section 106 nor on a right equivalent thereto. For example, state law should have the flexibility to afford a *remedy (under traditional principles of equity) against a consistent pattern of unauthorized appropriation by a competitor of the facts (i.e. not the literary expression) constituting "hot" news,* whether in the traditional mold of *International News Service v. Associated Press,* 248 U.S. 215 (1918), or in the newer form of data updates from scientific, business or financial data bases.[120] [Emphasis supplied.]

The direct impact that *Goldstein* had on preemption legislation is somewhat surprising. *Goldstein,* by rejecting preemptive inferences drawn from the Constitution, had, after all, based its holding squarely on the Congressional design manifested in the 1909 Act: Chief Justice Burger specifically left the distribution of protective power inferred from the statute open to future adjustment by Congress.[121] The lim-

[119] S. 22, *supra* note 13.

[120] S. REP., *supra* note 12, at 116.

[121] At any time Congress determines that a particular category of "writing" is worthy of national protection ". . . federal copyright protection may be authorized. Where the need for free and unrestricted distribution of a writing is thought to be required by the national interest the Copyright Clause and the Commerce Clause would allow Congress to eschew all protection." 412 U.S. at 559.

itation on state protection of subject matter contained in section 301(b)(1)—*unpublished*[122] subject matter outside the scope of the Federal act—was, even under *Goldstein*, clearly within Congress's power to enact. It is perhaps even more obscure why *Goldstein*—taken together with *Kewanee* —should have been read to create an apparently affirmative command to specifically include rights against "misappropriation" in clause (3) of section 301(b). These decisions, based on statutory construction and inference, did not extend of their own force beyond the particular statutory scheme— the 1909 Act—with which they worked.

Explanations may be suggested, however, for the decision of the Copyright Office and Congress to consciously tailor the Revision to these recent decisions under the 1909 Act— but only "suggested" since authoritative, official views about the necessary interrelationships between the 1909 statute, the Supreme Court holdings, and the Revision Bill were not spelled out.

First, most generally, the changes in section 301(b) can be seen as an effort to bring the Revision into line with the current understanding of the distribution of protective powers in the federal system. The Revision is intended as a codification of preemption doctrine, not as a total departure from the existing accommodation of state and federal law even when placed within a greatly extended preemptive framework.

Second, and this may be true especially with respect to clause (3), the changes made signaled recognition that "until recently, the wording as well as the underlying intent behind section 301 appeared to be consistent with the *judicial trend of limiting the rights of States to enforce rights similar to patent and copyright protection.*"[123] [Emphasis supplied.] And *Goldstein* and *Kewanee*, without explicitly overruling

[122] Publication is to be tested by a federally defined standard; *see* § 101 ("Definitions") in the 1965 Bill.
[123] HEARINGS, *supra* note 99, at 2080.

tolerated, limited by "traditional principles of equity," within the preemptive regime.[132] As to the preemption of those varieties of "misappropriation" which turned under federal law (exemplified by *Goldstein* itself with respect to the 1909 Act) the 1975 Senate Bill offered a similarly decisive answer: state power to protect was extended by clause (1), whether the subject matter concerned was "published" or "unpublished." The specific holding of *Goldstein* was here directly translated into the Revision Bill,[133] squarely reversing the projected result under the previous Revision text. As a consequence, the open-ended implications of *Goldstein* traced out in the analysis of *Triangle v. Sports Eye* remained live issues, to be considered again in the Revision context.

These were the changes induced in section 301 by the decision in *Goldstein.* Although not compelled to do so, Congress thereby tailored the legislation to conform to the pattern perceived by the Court in the very system that the Revision Bill was intended to replace.[134] Only at the very last minute, upon the initiative of the Justice Department (in a letter to Representative Kastenmeier, the Chairman of the Subcommittee which had considered the bill),[135] was the reference to "misappropriation" stricken (along with the other specific listings of nonequivalent state causes of action) from the text of sec-

[132] S. Rep., *supra* note 12, at 116.

[133] Again, Professor Brown's comments on the pre-*Goldstein* Revision bill are instructive as to the changes wrought: "If unpublished material not within section 102 is left to the states, published material in these categories is pre-empted. It is, for the present, left unprotected either by state law or the statute." Brown, *supra* note 36, at 1050.

[134] The history of the drafting of these changes in response to *Goldstein* is somewhat troubling. These modifications greatly extended the scope of state protection within the preemptive system. Apparently they were drafted by members of the copyright bar—whose general inclinations, to judge from the objective conditions of their employment and from the view expressed in the earlier panel discussions—are favorably disposed to protection at the expense of competition. *See* Hearings, *supra* note 99, at 1910 (Statement of Barbara Ringer) for a brief comment on the drafting of the changes.

[135] Letter, *supra* note 16. The letter appears as Appendix IV.

tion 301.[136] Congressional understanding of the effect of this proposed change was, however, confusing and unclear.[137]

Congressman Railsback accepted the amendment based on his understanding that "by striking the word 'misappropriation,' the gentleman in no way is attempting to change the existing state of the law, that is as it may exist in certain states that have recognized the right of recovery relating to misappropriation."

Congressman Seiberling, who introduced the amendment, accepted this formulation, whereupon Representative Kastenmeier added that the amendment was agreeable to him because "the amendment . . . is consistent with the position of the Justice Department."[138] The Justice Department view, as expressed in the letter, was decidedly against "any attempt to limit nondeceptive copying of uncopyrighted or unpatented subject matter by the general public. We believe that sound policy reasons underlie the weight of authority that opposes the *INS* 'misappropriation' doctrine."[139] If Railsback's expressed understanding is added to Kastenmeier's apparent endorsement of this Justice Department position, we can see that their expression of agreement is illusory, the amendment's preemptive force unresolved.

Upon this uncertain foundation, section 301 (as enacted) can be tested as a solution of the misappropriation preemption issue by examining the provisions of the statute in more detail.

Section 301's resolution of the misappropriation preemption issue cannot be worked out without reference to sections 102 and 103 (specifying the subject matter of copyright) and section 106 (specifying the rights within the scope of copyright). The preemptive scope of 301(a) as well as the non-

[136] The comparative texts are in Appendix III.

[137] As evidenced by the debate on the house floor reported in CONG. REC., *supra* note 17.

[138] *Id.* at H10910.

[139] Letter, *supra* note 16, at 5, set out in Appendix IV.

preemptive counterpoint provided by section 301(b) are determined by the contours of the federal system as drawn in these other sections of the Act.[140] The premise of the analysis offered is that *both* clauses (1) and (3) of section 301(b) must be examined to gauge whether, in fact, the Revision has preempted state law relief for "misappropriation," as specifically represented by the *INS* case.

Two points about the enacted text of section 301(b) may be quickly made. First, section 301(b)(1) provides a clear-cut answer to the preemption issues faced by the judiciary in cases such as *Goldstein v. California* and *Grove Press, Inc. v. Collectors Publications, Inc.*[141] Both cases could be analyzed as involving claims to state law protection for subject matter not copyrightable under federal law: sound recordings of performances in *Goldstein* and typography in *Grove Press.*[142] Section 301(b)(1) explicitly endorses state law protection for subject matter not within the coverage of the federal statute. It enacts into law the *Goldstein* approach: excepting from preemption state law actions against the copying of such subject matter *whether published or unpublished.*[143] Clause (1) both announces a generous, protective policy and—by offering a route for the exercise of state copyright authority—will result in an analytically more controlled application of the "misappropriation" doctrine. This clause effectively cuts the varieties of "misappropriation" back to the *INS* core, providing affirmative federal statutory legitimacy for claims that have previously sailed under that doctrine's confused colors.

Second, the Justice Department letter to Representative Kastenmeier did succeed in provoking the deletion of

[140] Texts in Appendix I.

[141] 264 F. Supp. 603 (C.D. Cal. 1967).

[142] It is not clear, however, that this was how the facts were analyzed in *Grove Press.* That case's issue-framing is discussed in text at note 23, *supra.*

[143] Sound recordings themselves are covered in section 301(c).

"rights against misappropriation not equivalent to any of such exclusive rights"[144] from the draft that was finally enacted and signed into law. No explicit federal statutory sanction of such state law rights appears in section 301(b) as enacted.

The Justice Department, expressing the concern that statutory sanction of state "misappropriation" rights "is almost certain to nullify preemption," concentrated its fire on the inclusion of "misappropriation" among the nonpreempted causes of action enumerated in clause (3).[145] Tracing the development of the "misappropriation" doctrine back to the "much-criticized" *INS* decision, the Department's letter argued,

> The misappropriation theory is vague and uncertain. The "misappropriation" provision of section 301 does not indicate what it is that is not to be appropriated. . . . Neither the *INS* case, other cases, nor proposed paragraph (3) adequately defines the conduct prohibited, or establishes any standard for distinguishing improper, as opposed to proper, copying.[146]

"Under the amorphous theory of misappropriation," state action could be undertaken precisely in the realm of avowedly exclusive federal jurisdiction: "This apparently would permit states to prohibit the reproduction of the literary expression itself. . . . Any copying of copyrightable subject matter

[144] The reference is to the "exclusive rights within the general scope of copyright as specified by section 106." *See* Appendix III.

[145] While emphasizing the special threat to preemption posed by clause (3)'s incorporation of "rights against misappropriation," the Justice Department advised striking all of the illustrative nonpreempted causes of actions from the clause: "While 'misappropriation' is almost certain to nullify preemption, any of the causes of action listed in paragraph (3) . . . may be construed to have the same effect. For example, a court could construe the copying of an uncopyrighted, published book to be an invasion of the author's right to privacy, i.e., the right to keep the control of the publication of his book privately to himself." Letter, *supra* note 16, at 6.

[146] *Id.* at 5–6.

that has not been federally protected could be prohibited. . . ."[147]

This analysis of the potential effect of clause (3) apparently derives from a paradigmatic conception of the thwarting of a federal preemption if "misappropriation" under state law is available; the reliance on state law where federal protection has been forfeited.[148] This is, however, not a direct response to the declared congressional intention behind the "saving" or "rights against misappropriation." The Senate Report supported the draft of clause (3) that was challenged by the Justice Department as preserving state flexibility to bar a "consistent pattern of unauthorized appropriation by a competitor of the facts . . . constituting 'hot news,' "[149] impliedly recognizing that a state bar to the copying of the "literary expression" would be merely a replication of an *exclusive federal right conferred by section 106.* Such protection against use of the facts (or "hot news") *itself* by a competitor is not an exclusive federal right under section 106. This particular application of the misappropriation doctrine—the original one as expressed in *INS*—is not discussed in the Justice Department letter. Its own status as a right not equivalent to the rights granted by federal copyright law is not evaluated. The letter is instead a caveat of the potential emanations of an "amorphous" doctrine.

The coherency of the Justice Department position with respect to preemption of core "misappropriation" is further undercut by the letter's exclusive attention to clause (3)'s enumeration of "rights against misappropriation." The letter implicitly recognizes the broad concession of state protection of noncopyrightable subject matter made by the preemp-

147 *Id.* at 6.

148 This was the type of state law claim rebuffed in Jacobs v. Robitaille, 406 F. Supp. 1145 (D.N.H. 1976), discussed in text at note 79, *supra.*

149 S. Rep., *supra* note 12, at 116.

tion provisions, by not questioning or limiting section 301(b)(1). The possible interplay between "misappropriation" and section 301(b)(1) (which enacts this subject matter reservation) is not considered.

To the extent that clause (1) adopts the *Goldstein* perspective—and rejects "publication" as a barrier to the exercise of state power—the clause raises anew the implications of *Goldstein* canvassed in the discussion of *Triangle v. Sports Eye.*[150] If "facts" or "hot news" is considered as a distinct subject matter category, then it is arguable that *INS*-misappropriation rights may find an enabling authority under clause (1), wholly apart from clause (3). The Senate Report on sections 102 and 103 does not treat the range of subject matter which exists beyond those sections' specifications of what is within the federal domain (and therefore preempted under section 301 (a)). The House Report of 1967 did (in the passage quoted earlier) [151] observe that there are "areas of existing subject matter that this bill does not propose to protect," and specifically included "news and factual information considered apart from its compilation or expression" in its listing.[152] The consequence of toleration of state protection over such subject matter was, in the context of the 1967 bill, limited by the reservation of state power to "unpublished" material only, with publication to be tested by a uniform federal standard.

The 1975 Senate Report does comment on the "nature of copyright" as illuminated by section 102(b).[153] The Report stated:

Copyright does not preclude others from using the *ideas or informa-*

[150] In text beginning at note 69, *supra.*
[151] Text of Report in note 91, *supra.*
[152] H.R. Rep., *supra* note 91.
[153] Section 102(b) provides: "In no case does copyright protection for an original work of authorship extend to any idea, procedure, process, system, method of operation, concept, principle, or discovery, regardless of the form in which it is described, explained, illustrated, or embodied in such work."

tion revealed by the author's work. It pertains to the literary, musical, graphic, or artistic form in which the author expressed intellectual concepts.

. . . .

. . . Section 102(b) in no way enlarges or contracts the scope of copyright protection under the present law. Its purpose is to restate, in the context of the new single Federal system of copyright, that the basic *dichotomy between expression and idea* remains unchanged.[154] [Emphasis supplied.]

The implications of this for the scope of state protection under section 301(b)(1) are not clear. It might be read as expressing a basic policy of federal copyright law which *the states* cannot abridge or infringe upon. That is, state protection for "hot news" under clause (1)'s enabling grant would trench on section 102's limitation of federal subject matter protection[155] to the literary expression embodied in the newspaper which reported the "news." Yet the force of this reading of 102(b) as expressing a limit which both operates *within* the federal statute and enforces a consequent condition on the grant of state power under 301(b)(1) is undercut by the simultaneous—until it was deleted—safeguarding of state misappropriation rights in section 301(b)(3). The Senate Report describes the federal copyright nonequivalence of "misappropriation" required for inclusion in clause (3) as turning on the *possible protection under state law of "hot news" or facts* not available under section 106 of the federal law. To coherently read section 102(b) together with the Senate version of 301(b)(3) (remembering they were both part of the same legislation) suggests that section 102(b) and the Senate Report's analysis simply restates well-understood standards pertinent only to qualification for federal copyright protection. On its face, section 301(b)(1) leaves the final reckoning of *Goldstein's* implications—as filtered through *Triangle*—inconclusively resolved.

[154] S. Rep., *supra* note 12, at 54.
[155] As a "literary work" described in section 102(a)(1).

After the amendment secured by the Justice Department, how well are the contours of federal preemption of state "misappropriation" doctrines defined? Section 301(b)(1) still awaits a more definite reading; its scope is uncertain. Section 301(b)(3) would "save" "misappropriation" rights provided the general nonequivalence standard is met—and the Senate Report did provide an explanation of how *INS*-type "misappropriation" might do so. "Misappropriation" is, however, something of an anomaly [156] as a clause (3) action, its nonequivalence defined in terms of the scope of protection provided, not in terms of activities condemned under state law for reasons which are extraneous to the law of intellectual property and to the *fact* of copyright (and which express general state policies of proper conduct). The *underlying conduct* implicated in a "misappropriation" claim and expounded as the classical basis for the action does not stand scrutiny as nonequivalent in this sense. To grant relief against a competitor's "*misappropriation*" of one's labor and investment by imitation, use or copying of material is to act on a restatement of the policies which underlie the grant of exclusive federal rights under section 106; yet the Senate Report's own analysis and justification of nonequivalence remains to be tested.

V. BEYOND THE REVISION

With the reconstruction and explication of the statute, a significant end-point of this inquiry is reached. Our conclusions, thus far, are limited, derived from an examination of the statutory language; they simply do not respond to deeper structural questions about the accommodation of state and federal law. A few thoughts are now offered regarding the "misappropriation" preemption issues whose resolution lies beyond the text of section 301.

[156] As compared with actions for breach of contract, defamation, etc.

The Justice Department letter had attacked "misappropriation" relief as a challenge to federal copyright preemption. A "misappropriation" (as raised in *INS* or *Triangle*) claim can arise in two copyright settings. First, the "literary expression" involved may have been copyrighted under federal law. If a "misappropriation" claim to bar the use of "hot news" by a competitor is pressed as to a work whose "literary expression" has been copyrighted, state law would be providing more protection than the federal statute; but it would not be invoked as a substitute for compliance with federal law.

Second, it could be used as a *substitute* for federal *copyright* protection. Where no federal copyright had been taken out for the "literary expression" published, the consequences of state relief are disturbing: the state protection would be more sweeping than the federal rights which had been forsaken. A state injunction to bar a competitor's publication of facts or "hot news" which had been "published" *without* securing federal copyright protection represents the paradigmatic threat to preemption set out by the Justice Department: the erosion by state law of the dimensions of the public domain as defined by federal law.[157] Simple compliance with the federal law is undermined. Here, state and federal law appear to collide; and state law should fall under the Supremacy Clause.

This would be the probable result under *Kewanee Oil Co. v. Bicron Corp.*,[158] the Supreme Court's exercise in the judicial preemptability of state law causes of action which, in part, effectuate policies that are separate from those represented by federal copyright and patent law (i.e., nonequivalent in the clause (3) sense). In *Kewanee*, the Court tested state trade secret law (concerned with the maintenance of standards of commercial ethics *as well as* the patent law objective of encouraging invention) and concluded that its

[157] *See* Letter, *supra* note 16.
[158] 416 U.S. 470 (1974). The case is briefly discussed in note 69, *supra*.

operation did not obstruct or frustrate the policy balances struck by the patent laws. State law did not, therefore, fall under the Supremacy Clause.[159]

With respect to section 301, however, express preemption has failed as a mechanism of clear statement: the legislative history appears thoroughly confusing.[160] The force of the *Kewanee* methodology *after* the Revision's legislative preemption scheme is, however, problematic. Under the statute, a finding of nonequivalence[161] substitutes for the *Kewanee* examination of impacts on federal policy: nonequivalence states the federal policy under the Revision. Yet, for the working out of a clear-cut solution to the *INS*-preemption issue, the statute provides only a rough charting of the relevant terrain.

The drafting of the Revision was intended explicitly to declare the law regarding the scope of state protection,[162] not simply to provide a basis for judicial reconstruction of that policy. However, the status of *INS*-"misappropriation" was not directly analyzed by the Justice Department letter. The vague conclusion of the colloquy between Representatives Seiberling and Railsback that "the existing state of the law" was not changed by striking the illustrative examples from section 301 (b)(3) ironically illustrates the Jus-

[159] "Although an express preemption provision does not automatically supersede all state laws, it does establish a more certain rule of preemption than that available under the doctrine of implied preemption. When there is no congressional declaration, the court is free to consider the degree of conflict and various presumptive factors of intent to occupy the field—all in an effort to determine whether Congress intended preemption. This inquiry is significantly narrowed by an express preemption provision. The court's role is limited to an evaluation of a statute's legislative history and of congressional purpose in order to determine whether a particular state law or regulation is of the type which Congress intended to supersede. The contrast between these types of inquiry is not a subtle distinction without a difference; an express preemption provision substantially limits the court's role in determining the allocation of governmental power in our federal system." *Nuclear Moratorium Legislation, supra* note 9, at 445.

[160] As discussed in text, particularly at notes 137–138, *supra*.

[161] The relevant standard of § 301(b)(3).

[162] S. Rep., *supra* note 12, at 114.

tice Department's concern about the uncertain ramifications of state "misappropriation" law, *INS* on its own facts—or on *Triangle's*—slips through this express preemption net, its disposition uncertain. Despite these appearances, we are not, though, really back at the beginning. In the beginning was *Goldstein;* and *Goldstein's* analysis cannot furnish a guide to decision of *this* "misappropriation" preemption question. In *Triangle,* Judge Lord clearly, if baldly, felt that it would be an infirm incongruity to allow state protection of the "facts" to supplement the federal grant of copyright for only the "literary expression" of the facts. Judge Lord insisted that federal law is the source and limit of such specifically intellectual property rights. The limits of *Goldstein's* style of analysis of the preemption problem, when applied to the distinctive issues and values of copyright law, are here revealed: discrete subject matter analysis, treated on a national-local scale, does not intelligently address, let alone resolve, the problem of explaining Judge Lord's appealing position.

The problem goes to the fundamental nature of copyright as a protective mechanism with a disseminating goal. This is the view taken by the constitutional copyright clause, a source for preemption analysis not seriously explored in *Goldstein.* The *INS*-"misappropriation" preemption issue may provide occasion for invocation of the constitutional command, which necessarily frames all congressional action. "To promote the progress of Science and useful Arts, by securing for limited Times to Authors and Inventors the exclusive Right to their respective Writings and Discoveries" represents the constitutional delineation of purpose and right.[163] Within this framework Congress has been charged with striking a balance to secure the constitutional result; and one could argue that the states cannot either supplement or sub-

[163] U.S. CONST., art. I, § 8, cl. 8.

stitute the measure of protection made available under this mandate by Congress. "Literary expression" is protected precisely as a device to encourage the wide distribution of "ideas" or "hot news" or "facts," which cannot in turn be protected. The purpose of the copyright scheme is precisely to place such "hot news" in the public domain.

Similar reasoning about constitutional and congressional balancing was rejected in *Goldstein*. The sharper conjuncture of the relationship of federal competitive and state protective determinations raised in the *INS* situation may yet invite a different result, but it has been *Goldstein's* legacy to couch the problem in the troublesome subject-matter formulation. Whether state "misappropriation" law is preempted remains for the judiciary to determine. Congress, by its Revision, has not done so.

APPENDIX I

THE ENACTED PREEMPTION PROVISIONS

§ 301. PREEMPTION WITH RESPECT TO OTHER LAWS

(a) On and after January 1, 1978, all legal or equitable rights that are equivalent to any of the exclusive rights within the general scope of copyright as specified by section 106 in works of authorship that are fixed in a tangible medium of expression and come within the subject matter of copyright as specified by sections 102 and 103, whether created before or after that date and whether published or unpublished, are governed exclusively by this title. Thereafter, no person is entitled to any such right or equivalent right in any such work under the common law or statutes of any State.

(b) Nothing in this title annuls or limits any rights or remedies under the common law or statutes of any State with respect to—

(1) subject matter that does not come within the subject matter of copyrights as specified by sections 102 and 103, including works of authorship not fixed in any tangible medium of expression; or

(2) any cause of action arising from undertakings commenced before January 1, 1978; or

(3) activities violating legal or equitable rights that are not equivalent to any of the exclusive rights within the general scope of copyright as specified by section 106.

§ 102. SUBJECT MATTER OF COPYRIGHT: IN GENERAL

(a) Copyright protection subsists, in accordance with this title, in original works of authorship fixed in any tangible medium of expression, now known or later developed, from which they can be perceived, reproduced, or otherwise communicated, either directly or with the aid of a machine or device. Works of authorship include the following categories:

(1) literary works;
(2) musical works, including any accompanying words;
(3) dramatic works, including any accompanying music;
(4) pantomimes and choreographic works;
(5) pictorial, graphic, and sculptural works;
(6) motion pictures and other audiovisual works; and
(7) sound recordings.

(b) In no case does copyright protection for an original work of authorship extend to any idea, procedures, process, system, method of operation, concept, principle, or discovery, regardless of the form in which it is described, explained, illustrated, or embodied in such work.

§ 103. SUBJECT MATTER OF COPYRIGHT: COMPILATIONS AND DERIVATIVE WORKS

(a) The subject matter of copyright as specified by section 102 includes compilations and derivative works, but protection for a work employing preexisting material in which copyright subsists does not extend to any part of the work in which such material has been used unlawfully.

(b) The copyright in a compilation or derivative work extends only to the material contributed by the author of such work, as distinguished from the preexisting material employed in the work, and does not imply any exclusive right in the preexisting material. The copyright in such work is independent of, and does not affect or enlarge the scope, duration, ownership, or subsistence of, any copyright protection in the preexisting material.

§ 106. EXCLUSIVE RIGHTS IN COPYRIGHTED WORKS

Subject to sections 107 through 118, the owner of copyright under this title has the exclusive rights to do and to authorize any of the following:

(1) to reproduce the copyrighted work in copies or phonorecords;

(2) to prepare derivative works based upon the copyrighted work;

(3) to distribute copies or phonorecords of the copyrighted work to the public by sale or other transfer of ownership, or by rental, lease, or lending;

(4) in the case of literary, musical, dramatic, and choreographic works, pantomimes, and motion pictures and other audiovisual works, to perform the copyrighted work publicly; and

(5) in the case of literary, musical, dramatic, and choreographic works, pantomimes, and pictorial, graphic, or sculptural works, including the individual images of a motion picture or other audiovisual work, to display the copyrighted work publicly.

APPENDIX II

THE PRELIMINARY DRAFT TEXT (1963)

§ 19. PRE-EMPTION WITH RESPECT TO OTHER LAWS

(a) On and after the effective date of this act, all rights in the nature of copyright in works for which copyright protection is available under sections 1 and 2, whether created before or after that date and whether published or unpublished, shall be governed exclusively by this title. Thereafter, no person shall be entitled to copyright, to literary or intellectual property rights, or to any equivalent legal or equitable right in any such work under the common law or statute of any State.

(b) Nothing in this title shall annul or limit any rights or remedies under the law of any State:

(1) With respect to material for which copyright protection is not available under sections 1 and 2;

(2) With respect to any cause of action arising from undertakings commenced before the effective date of this act;

(3) With respect to activities constituting breaches of trust, invasion of privacy, or deceptive trade practices including passing off and false representation.

APPENDIX III

COMPARATIVE TEXTS

PRELIMINARY DRAFT

§ 19. PRE-EMPTION WITH RESPECT TO OTHER LAWS

(a) On and after the effective date of this act, all rights in the nature of copyright in works for which copyright protection is available under sections 1 and 2, whether created before or after that date and whether published or unpublished, shall be governed exclusively by this title. Thereafter, no person shall be entitled to copyright, to literary or intellectual property rights, or to any equivalent legal or equitable right in any such work under the common law or statute of any State.

(b) Nothing in this title shall annul or limit any rights or remedies under the law of any State:

(1) With respect to material for which copyright protection is not available under sections 1 and 2;

(2) With respect to any cause of action arising from undertakings commenced before the effective date of this act;

(3) With respect to activities constituting breaches of trust, invasion of privacy, or deceptive trade practices including passing off and false representation.

1964 BILL

§ 19. PRE-EMPTION WITH RESPECT TO OTHER LAWS

(a) On and after January 1, 1967, all rights in the nature of copyright in works that come within the subject matter of copyright as specified by sections 1 and 2, whether created before or after that date and whether published or unpublished, are governed exclusively by this title. Thereafter, no person is entitled to copyright, literary property rights, or any equivalent legal or equitable right in any such work under the common law or statutes of any State.

(b) Nothing in this title annuls or limits any rights or remedies under the law of any State with respect to:

(1) unpublished material that does not come within the subject matter of copyright as specified by sections 1 and 2;

(2) any cause of action arising from undertakings commenced before January 1, 1967;

(3) activities violating rights that are not equivalent to any of the exclusive rights within the general scope of copyright as specified by section 5, including breaches of contract, breaches of trust, invasion of privacy, defamation, and deceptive trade practices such as passing off and false representation.

1965 BILL

§ 301. PRE-EMPTION WITH RESPECT TO OTHER LAWS

(a) On and after January 1, 1967, all rights in the nature of copyright in works that come within the subject matter of copyright as specified by sections 102 and 103, whether created before or after that date and whether published or unpublished, are governed exclusively by this title. Thereafter, no person is entitled to copyright, literary property rights, or any equivalent legal or equitable right in any such work under the common law or statutes of any State.

(b) Nothing in this title annuls or limits any rights or remedies under the law of any State with respect to:

(1) unpublished material that does not come within the subject matter of copyright as specified by sections 102 and 103;

(2) any cause of action arising from undertakings commenced before January 1, 1967;

(3) activities violating rights that are not equivalent to any of the exclusive rights within the general scope of copyright as specified by section 106, including breaches of contract, breaches

of trust, invasion of privacy, defamation, and deceptive trade practices such as passing off and false representation.

1967 HOUSE BILL

§ 301. PRE-EMPTION WITH RESPECT TO OTHER LAWS

(a) On and after January 1, 1969, all rights in the nature of copyright in works that come within the subject matter of copyright as specified by sections 102 and 103, whether created before or after that date and whether published or unpublished, are governed exclusively by this title. Thereafter, no person is entitled to copyright, literary property rights, or any equivalent legal or equitable right in any such work under the common law or statutes of any State.

(b) Nothing in this title annuls or limits any rights or remedies under the common law or statutes of any State with respect to:

(1) unpublished material that does not come within the subject matter of copyright as specified by sections 102 and 103, including works of authorship not fixed in any tangible medium of expression;

(2) any cause of action arising from undertakings commenced before January 1, 1969;

(3) activities violating rights that are not equivalent to any of the exclusive rights within the general scope of copyright as specified by section 106, including breaches of contract, breaches of trust, invasion of privacy, defamation, and deceptive trade practices such as passing off and false representation.

1975 SENATE BILL

§ 301. PRE-EMPTION WITH RESPECT TO OTHER LAWS

(a) On and after January 1, 1978, all legal or equitable rights that are equivalent to any of the exclusive rights within the general scope of copyright as specified by section 106 in works of authorship that are fixed in a tangible medium of expression and come within the subject matter of copyright as specified by sections 102 and 103, whether created before or after that date and whether published or unpublished, are governed exclusively by this title. Thereafter, no person is entitled to any such right or equivalent right in any such work under the common law or statutes of any State.

(b) Nothing in this title annuls or limits any rights or remedies under the common law or statutes of any State with respect to—

(1) subject matter that does not come within the subject matter of copyright as specified by sections 102 and 103, including works of authorship not fixed in any tangible medium of expression; or

(2) any cause of action arising from undertakings commenced before January 1, 1978; or

(3) activities violating legal or equitable rights that are not equivalent to any of the exclusive rights within the general scope of copyright as specified by section 106, including rights against misappropriation not equivalent to any of such exclusive rights, breaches of contract, breaches of trust, trespass, conversion, invasion of privacy, defamation, and deceptive trade practices such as passing off and false representation.

APPENDIX IV

PART I., THE JUSTICE DEPARTMENT LETTER (pp. 1–7)

Department of Justice
Washington, D.C. 20530
July 27 1976

Honorable Robert Kastenmeier
Chairman, Subcommittee on Courts,
Civil Liberties and the Administration of Justice
Committee on the Judiciary
House of Representatives
Washington, D.C. 20515

Dear Mr. Chairman:

On May 8, 1975, Deputy Assistant Attorney General Irwin Goldbloom represented this Department before your Subcommittee on Courts, Civil Liberties and the Administration of Justice during hearings on H.R. 2223, a bill "For the general revision of the Copyright Law, title 17 of the United States Code, and for other purposes."

For a number of reasons, which will be discussed separately below, we would like to supplement the Department's earlier testimony.

I.

Because we were principally concerned with the many changes which the bill would make to the existing law of copyright, we did not discuss an issue which we now believe should be brought to your attention. In our view, the function and structure of the proposed Copyright Royalty Tribunal, which would be established by a new chapter 8 to title 17, raises possible constitutional questions.

Proposed section 803 would authorize the Register of Copyrights to appoint a Copyright Royalty Tribunal consisting of three persons named by the American Arbitration Association. Section 801 would authorize this Tribunal to make determinations concerning the adjustment of copyright royalty rates specified by sections 111 and 115 and to make changes in the royalty rate, or the revenue basis on which the royalty fee is assessed, or both, to assure a reasonable royalty fee. The Tribunal would also determine in certain circumstances the distribution of the royalty fees deposited with the Register under sections 111 and 116. Section 111 concerns secondary transmission; section 115 and 116 concern phonorecords and coin-operated phonorecord players.

A final determination of the Tribunal in any proceeding for adjustment of a statutory royalty would be required by section 806 to be transmitted to the Secretary of the Senate and the Clerk of the House for reference to the Judiciary Committees. Proposed section 807 provides that either House of Congress may veto the "recommended royalty adjustment" by adopting a resolution of disapproval within ninety days. Proposed section 809 would attempt to limit judicial review of a final determination of the Tribunal to situations where the determination was procured by fraud, where partiality or corruption of any member of the panel was evident, or where any member of the panel was guilty of any misconduct which may have prejudiced a party.

The absence of meaningful standards for the Tribunal's decision making, the Tribunal's transient and inexpert membership, its lack of continuity in establishing policy and precedent, and the very restricted judicial review provision, taken together, raise questions whether petitioners before the Tribunal can be assured of due process of law.

Moreover, the Tribunal, with its administrative (rate-making) and judicial (dispute resolution) functions, would be lodged within the Library of Congress, an arm of the Congress, thereby raising separation of powers questions. Both executive and judicial prerogatives may be jeopardized by placing within the exclusive control of Congress powers which are not legislative in nature. Indeed, separations of powers questions have already been raised with respect to the existing location of the Copyright Office within the legislative branch. See Brylawski, "The Copyright Office: A Constitutional Confirmation," 44 *Geo. Wash. L. Rev.* 1 (1976).

Furthermore, in our view, the one-House veto mechanism raises questions concerning Article I, section 7, of the Constitution which prescribes the procedures by which the Congress legislates. The Constitution has created a process whereby both Houses and the President have a role in creating legislation and mentions no procedure whereby one House can take actions which have the force of law.

II.

On February 19, 1976, the Senate passed S. 22, the Senate omnibus copyright reform bill, making certain changes to section 301. We believe that these changes have anticompetitive implications which should be called to your attention.

Section 301 would provide that the federal Copyright Act would preempt all state regulation of rights in the nature of copyright protection. However, certain exceptions to complete preemption would be made by subsection (b) of section 301. The Senate-passed bill made two significant additions to the exceptions, both of which are opposed by this Department. These additions seemingly allow (1) protection under the theory of misappropriation, and (2) less preemption than the committee intended with respect to state law regarding sound recordings made prior to 1972.

A. MISAPPROPRIATION

Paragraph (3) of section 301(b) would exempt from preemption, state common law or statutory rights that are not equivalent to the exclusive rights granted by the Copyright Act. The Copyright Act would grant rights such as the exclusive right to make copies of the copyrighted work (Section 106). In addition to the rights that paragraph (3) previously specifically listed as non-equivalent rights (e.g., breach of contract and breach of trust) the committee has now added "rights against misappropriation not equivalent to any of such exclusive rights. . . ." The committee report accompanying the bill asserts that there is a need for this provision because "state law should" be able to permit the misappropriation theory to apply. S. Rep. 94–473, 94th Cong., 1st Sess. 116 (1975) (hereinafter, "Senate Report").

This Department is concerned that inclusion of the above quoted phrase in section 301 would sanction use of the highly anticompetitive "misappropriation" theory, and may defeat the underlying purpose of the preemption section.

1. *The Misappropriation Doctrine Is Anticompetitive.* This Department strongly opposes allowance of monopolies based on the theory of "misappropriation." This term is not defined in the proposed Act, but the concept apparently stems from the much-criticized decision of the Supreme Court in *International News Service v. Associated Press,* 248 U.S. 215 (1918) (hereinafter, the "INS" case). In *INS,* the Supreme Court held that the defendant news service committed an unlawful act of unfair competition by copying the plaintiff's uncopyrighted published news stories from east coast newspapers and wiring them to west coast subscribing newspapers. The Court found that even though the plaintiff would have had no rights against the public, who were entitled or privileged to copy the articles, nonetheless the defendant had "misappropriated" the published work done by the plaintiff and was therefore liable to the plaintiff. The Court's theory was that the defendant's conduct was unlawful because it sought to "reap where it has not sown" (248 U.S. at 239). This unjust enrichment theory could be used broadly to prohibit the copying of uncopyrighted published materials, the manufacture by others of unpatented goods, the use by a doctor of a surgical technique developed by another doctor, or the use of an advertising technique which another has developed at his own expense. The effect of the theory is boundless—it is potentially applicable each time a person engages in conduct that imitates some work that was developed at another's expense.

The courts generally have declined [1] to follow the suggestion in

[1] *See* 2 R. Callmann, Unfair Competition, Trademarks & Monopolies, § 60.2 at 505, 507 (3d ed. 1975).

the *INS* case that the traditional unfair competition doctrine be expanded to cover so-called "misappropriation." [2] See, e.g., *G. Ricordi & Co. v. Haendler*, 194 F.2d 914, 916 (2d Cir. 1952); *National Comics Pub., Inc. v. Fawcett Pub., Inc.*, 191 F.2d 594, 603 (2d Cir. 1951); *RCA Mfg. Co. v. Whiteman*, 114 F.2d 86, 90 (2nd Cir.), cert. denied, 311 U.S. 712 (1940); *Cheney Bros. v. Doris Silk Corp.* 35 F.2d 279, 280 (2d Cir. 1929), cert. denied, 281 U.S. 728 (1930). Indeed, District Judge Wyzanski once stated his belief that the Supreme Court would follow the Brandeis dissent in *INS* and overrule *INS* if given the opportunity. *Triangle Pub., Inc. v. New England Newspaper Pub. Co.*, 46 F. Supp. 198, 204 (D. Mass. 1942). This view is supported by the recent *Sears* and *Compco* decisions,[3] in which the Supreme Court reversed decisions from a court of appeals that prohibited copying of unpatented products, without even attempting to distinguish *INS*. See also *Columbia Broadcasting System, Inc. v. DeCosta*, 377 F.2d 315, 318 (1st Cir.), cert. denied, 389 U.S. 1007 (1967), in which the court found both that *INS* was no longer authoritative, since it occurred before *Erie R.R. Co. v. Tompkins*, 304 U.S. 64 (1938),[4] and that it was overruled by *Sears* and *Compco*.

The New York State courts, in a series of cases beginning with appropriation of news and artistic productions, retrieved the "misappropriation" theory of *INS* from innocuous desuetude and gradually extended the doctrine into the area of unfair competition in the sale of ordinary merchandise.[5] The *INS* doctrine has also been codified in the New York General Business Law (§ 368-d). The bulk of authority elsewhere in the United States, however, is against the recognition of "misappropriation" as an independent basis for recovery in imitation cases (*West Point Mfg. Co. v. Detroit Stamping Co.*, 222 F.2d 581, 598–99 [6th Cir. 1955] [misappropriation is "contrary to the great weight of authority"]).

This Department supports the position taken in the foregoing majority line of cases, and opposes any attempt to limit nondeceptive copying of uncopyrighted or unpatented subject matter by the general

[2] The *INS* decision predates Erie R.R. Co. v. Tompkins, 304 U.S. 64 (1938), and is thus no longer binding on federal courts.

[3] Sears, Roebuck & Co. v. Stiffel Co., 376 U.S. 225 (1964); Compco Corp. v. Day-Brite Lighting, 376 U.S. 234 (1964).

[4] Under *Erie*, federal courts are to apply local law to non-federal causes of action.

[5] Cases reviewed in KAPLAN & BROWN, CASES ON COPYRIGHT, UNFAIR COMPETITION, AND OTHER TOPICS 614–19 (2d Ed. 1974).

public. We believe that sound policy reasons underlie the weight of authority that opposes the *INS* "misappropriation" doctrine.

The "misappropriation" theory is vague and uncertain. The "misappropriation" provision of section 301 does not indicate what it is that is not to be appropriated. It may extend beyond an appropriation of the forms or styles of ordinary merchandise to include an appropriation of mere ideas, or technology or other know-how long in the public domain. Neither the *INS* case, other cases, nor proposed paragraph (3) adequately defines the conduct prohibited, or establishes any standard for distinguishing improper, as opposed to proper, copying.[6]

The "misappropriation" doctrine may be used contrary to copyright and antitrust policies to sustain perpetual monopolies over printed matter, and contrary to patent and antitrust policies to sustain perpetual monopolies over alleged inventions which do not qualify for patent protection. In the *Sears* and *Compco* cases, noted above, the Supreme Court set aside such grants and held the states to be without power to block off from the public the non-deceptive copying of an unpatentable article. The Court held this in the ground that such grants contravene the federal patent statutes and constitutional provisions.

Furthermore, imitation is the life-blood of competition. Mere commercial copying is neither unlawful, nor immoral; instead it is often a commercial and economic necessity. Copying very often supports and promotes competition—it spurs further invention and innovation, permits newcomers to enter markets, and generally, by bringing forward functionally equivalent products and services, is a necessary condition for the competitive forces of the marketplace acting to lower prices, satisfy consumer demand, and allocate production optimally.

2. *Preemption Would Be Nullified.* Paragraph (3), as noted above, lists causes of action, such as for breach of contract, that are specifically identified in the introductory phrase as giving "rights that are not equivalent to any of the exclusive rights," that would be granted by section 106 of the proposed Copyright Act. These are causes of action different in nature from that for copyright infringement (see Senate Report, p. 115). Apparently what is meant is that, for example, one may sue to enjoin reproduction of an uncopyrighted

[6] Such vague language, of course, may present serious due process problems under the United States Constitution. *See* United States v. Cardiff, 344 U.S. 174 (1952); United States v. Evans, 333 U.S. 483 (1948).

book if there is a contract between the parties prohibiting the defendant from reproducing it. Thus, reproducing the literary expression itself may be prohibited under a cause of action for breach of contract.

Similarly, paragraph (3) exempts from preemption "rights against misappropriation not equivalent to any of such rights" specified in section 106. This apparently would permit states to prohibit the reproduction of the literary expression itself under a "misappropriation" theory. "Misappropriation" would stand in the place of breach of contract as a cause of action in the book example above. Any copying of copyrightable subject matter that has not been federally protected could be prohibited under the amorphous theory of "misappropriation."

The Senate Report states (p. 116) that reproduction of "the literary expression" itself should be preempted and should not be able to be prohibited under the "misappropriation" theory; yet that is what inclusion of the term "misappropriation" in paragraph (3) would prohibit. The preemption sought by the omnibus Copyright Act revision bill would be nullified by paragraph (3).

While "misappropriation" is almost certain to nullify preemption, any of the causes of action listed in paragraph (3) following the phrase "as specified by section 106" may be construed to have the same effect. For example, a court could construe the copying of an uncopyrighted, published book to be an invasion of the author's right to privacy, i.e., the right to keep the control of the publication of his book privately to himself. In order to more clearly delineate the courts the area to be preempted, we recommend striking the specific causes of action listed in paragraph (3) so as to amend that paragraph to preempt only: "(3) activities violating legal or equitable rights that are not equivalent to any of the exclusive rights within the general scope of copyright as specified by section 106."

3. *Recommendation.* For the reasons discussed, this Department recommends that section 301(b)(3) be amended as suggested above.

PART II. LEGISLATIVE AND ADMINISTRATIVE DEVELOPMENTS

I. UNITED STATES OF AMERICA AND TERRITORIES

511. *U.S. Department of Justice.* 28 CFR Part 0. Seizure and

forfeiture of materials under copyrights act. Final rule. [Order No. 766–78.] *Federal Register*, vol. 43, no. 31 (Feb. 14, 1978), p. 6228.

This order adds the copyright act to the list of Federal statutes under which the Criminal Division of the Justice Department may bring civil penalty actions as a result of the criminal provisions in the new law (17 U.S.C. 509).

512. *U.S. Library of Congress, Copyright Office.* 37 CFR Part 202. Deposit requirements-motion pictures. Interim regulations. [Docket RM 78–3.] *Federal Register*, vol. 43, no. 58 (Mar. 24, 1978), pp. 12320–4.

This notice of interim amendments to regulations in 37 C.F.R. S202.19–202.20 allows public comment while permitting immediate effect by making available a special agreement for published motion pictures which would: (1) provide for the return of the copy of the work to the depositor under certain conditions, and (2) establish certain rights and obligations of the Library of Congress with respect to the copies of these works.

513. *U.S. Library of Congress, Copyright Office.* Implementation of the Privacy Act of 1974. Systems of Records and Notice of Proposed Routine Uses. [Docket No. RM 77–13.] *Federal Register*, vol. 42, no. 233 (Monday, Dec. 5, 1977), pp. 61574–61585.

A listing of Privacy Act systems of records of the Copyright Office, including system location, categories of individuals covered by the system, authority for maintenance of the system, routine use of records maintained in the system, including categories of users and purposes of such uses, storage, retrievability, safeguards, and record access procedure.

NATIONAL SECOND PRIZE

Fair Use: Evidence of Change in a Traditional Doctrine

MARY S. LAWRENCE

UNIVERSITY OF OREGON SCHOOL OF LAW

THE exclusive right to their writings which the Constitution empowers Congress to secure to authors[1] has frequently been likened to a monopoly.[2]

> [T]he Constitution takes the unusual course of expressly sanctioning a gain by private persons. Authors, musicians, painters are among the greatest benefactors of the race. So we incline to protect them. Yet the very effect of protecting them is to make the enjoyment of their creations more costly and hence to limit the possibility of that enjoyment especially by persons of slender purses. Moreover, a monopoly, here as always, makes it possible for the wares to be kept off the market altogether.[3]

A definition of statutory copyright, however, cannot end with this analogy. The rights of the copyright holder are

[1] U.S. Const. art. 1, § 8, cl. 8.

[2] *See, e.g.*, Ringer, *The Demonology of Copyright*, PUBLISHERS WEEKLY, 26 at 28–30, Nov. 18, 1974; CONG. REC. H10880 (daily ed. Sept. 22, 1976) (remarks of Rep. Drinan). RCA Mfg. Co. v. Whiteman, 114 F.2d 86, 88 (2d Cir.), *cert. denied* 311 U.S. 712 (1940); 2 Blackstone's COMMENTARIES 405, as quoted in Hudon, *The Copyright Period: Weighting Personal Against Public Interest*, 49 A.B.A.J. 759 (1963).

[3] Chafee, *Reflections on the Law of Copyright: I*, 45 COLUM. L. REV. 503, at 507 (1945).

circumscribed by the Constitution: by the Copyright Clause itself and, at least implicitly, by the First Amendment.

The structure of the constitutional clause from which congressional authority to grant copyright protection derives makes clear that the exclusive rights granted to authors are to be limited not only in time but also by the overriding objective of "promot[ing] the progress of Science and the useful Arts." [4] Both legislative history and judicial interpretation attest to the precedence granted public benefit over reward of the copyright holder.[5] First Amendment limitations on the "quasi-monopolistic" [6] aspects of copyright, although only infrequently voiced by the courts,[7] are implicit in some holdings of noninfringement.[8] Right of reasonable access to information,[9] premised on the First Amendment, is

[4] U.S. CONST. art. 1, § 8, cl. 8. *See* Richards, *The Value of the Copyright Clause in Construction Copyright Law*, 2 HASTINGS CON. L. Q. 221 (1975).

[5] H.R. REP. No. 2222, 60th Cong., 2d Sess. 9 (1909); Remarks of Rep. Drinan, H10880; Rep. E. W. Pattison (D. N.Y.), Congressional Copyright Committee member, in a speech given before the Association of American Publishers, as reported in 8 INFORMATION HOTLINE (Science Associates) July-Aug. 1976; United States v. Paramount Pictures, Inc., 334 U.S. 131, 158 (1948); Berlin v. E. C. Publications, Inc., 329 F.2d 541, 543–44 (2d Cir. 1964); Rosenfield, *The Constitutional Dimension of "Fair Use" in Copyright Law*, 50 N.D.L. 790, 801–2 (1975) [hereinafter cited as Rosenfield]. *Cf.* Richards, *supra* note 4.

[6] A. LATMAN, COPYRIGHT LAW REVISION, Studies for Comm. on Judiciary, Subcomm. on Patents, Trademarks, and Copyrights, 86th Cong., 2d Sess., Study No. 14 at 15 (Comm. Print 1960) [hereinafter cited as LATMAN].

[7] *See, e.g.*, Walt Disney Productions, Inc. v. Air Pirates, 345 F. Supp. 108 (N.D. Cal. 1972).

[8] *See, e.g.*, Rosemont Enterprises, Inc. v. Random House, Inc. 366 F.2d 303, 309 (2d Cir. 1966) *cert. denied*, 385 U.S. 1009 (1967), in which it is stated: "the public is being deprived of an opportunity to become acquainted with the life of a person endowed with extraordinary talents . . . narration [of Hughes' story] ought to be available to a reading public. . . . Thus, in balancing the equities at this time . . . the public interest should prevail over the possible damage to the copyright owner." *See also* the concurring opinion of Lumbard J. at 311. Similarly, *see* Berlin v. E. C. Publications, Inc. 329 F.2d 541, 545 (2d Cir. 1964) on the social importance of parody. For a discussion of the First Amendment and parody, *see Parody, Copyrights, and the First Amendment*, 10 U.S.F. L. REV. 564 (1976).

[9] *See generally*, Rosenfield, *supra* note 5, 790; *Parody, Copyrights, and the First Amendment, supra* notes 573–85; M. NIMMER, COPYRIGHT § 9.2 (1976 [hereinafter cited as NIMMER]; Comment, *Copyright Fair Use*, 1969 DUKE L.J. 73, at 96–7 (1969).

consonant with the underlying public benefit boundaries of copyright privilege.[10]

The "monopoly" granted the copyright holder by statute is therefore necessarily qualified, and it has not stood free from further encroachment. Fair use permits the appropriation of a copyrighted work without the consent of the copyright holder by a judicially created doctrine, subjecting the copyrighted work to "the right of all persons into whose possession [it] comes to make 'fair use' of it." [11]

Fair use may be viewed as a minor invasion of constitutionally authorized rights, permissible because based on reasonableness [12] and minimal injury to the copyright holder's privilege.[13] On the other hand, an even more basic reason for the acceptability of the doctrine is its essential compatibility with the constitutional principle of copyright, the furtherance of public benefit. Inherent in the fair use doctrine, even if not invariably effected by its application, are the promotion of knowledge and dissemination of information. The codification of fair use in the 1976 Copyright Statute [14] acknowledges, if only tacitly, this consistency with Article I, section 8 of the U.S. Constitution. Furthermore, even though determination of public interest has not characterized most fair use decisions, recent instances of increased judicial reliance, explicit and implicit, on a public interest rationale in

[10] For a discussion of copyright as privilege, *see* Rosenfield, *supra* note 5, 791–2.

[11] Yankwich, *What Is Fair Use?* 22 U. CHI. L. R. 203, 204 (1954) [hereinafter cited as Yankwich].

[12] For comments on fair use as "an equitable rule of reason," see H.R. REP. NO. 83, 90th Cong., 1st Sess. (1967); H.R. REP. NO. 1476, 94th Cong., 2d Sess. 65 (1976); S. Wagner, *Copying and the Copyright Bill. Where the New Revision Stands on "Fair Use,"* PUBLISHERS WEEKLY, Oct. 18, 1976 at 28.

[13] U.S. Copyright Office, Copyright Law Revision, 87th Cong., 1st Sess., REPORT OF THE REGISTER OF COPYRIGHTS ON THE GENERAL REVISION OF THE U.S. COPYRIGHT LAW 24 (Comm. Print 1961). "['Fair use'] eludes precise definition; broadly speaking, it means that a reasonable portion of a copyrighted work may be reproduced without permission when necessary for a legitimate purpose *which is not competitive* with the copyright owner's market for his work . . ." *Id.*

[14] 17 U.S.C. §§ 101 *et seq.* (1976).

fair use analysis may reflect an emerging shift in emphasis in the doctrine, an evolution which codification could both accelerate and intensify.

DEFINITION AND BASIS OF FAIR USE

The doctrine of fair use developed in the United States as the American judicial counterpart of the English concept of "fair dealing," which attempted "to reconcile what courts recognized as the dual purposes of [the Copyright Statute of Anne]: [15] to reward the author and to stimulate other authors to produce for the benefit of society." [16]

> The term apparently originated in 1810 when, in the case of *Wilkins v. Aikin*, Lord Eldon contrasted what he called "fair quotation" with the taking of the "whole or part"—meaning a substantial or material part—of another's work. In isolating this concept that only the taking of a substantial part is infringement, the English judges, through a process of semantic evolution, came to refer to an appropriation not substantial enough to infringe as "fair use." In 1878, Lord Hatherley in *Chatterton v. Cave* said that "if the quantity taken be neither substantial nor material, if, as it has been expressed by some Judges, a 'fair use' only be made of the publication, no wrong is done and no action can be brought. . . ." [17]

The impossibility of adequately defining fair use has been frequently commented upon. In the leading case, *Folsom v. Marsh*,[18] often cited as "the source of the fair use doctrine" [19] in the United States, Mr. Justice Story noted that

[15] Copyright Act of 1709, 8 Anne c. 19 (1710).

[16] COMMENT, *Copyright Fair Use—Case Law and Legislation*, 1969 DUKE L.J. 73, 74–75 (1969).

[17] Crossland, *The Rise and Fall of Fair Use: The Protection of Literary Materials against Copyright Infringement by New and Developing Media*, 20 S.C.L. REV. 153, at 158–9 (1968) [hereinafter cited as Crossland].

[18] 9 F. Cas. 342 (C.C.D. Mass. 1841) (No. 4,901).

[19] Stevenson, *The Doctrine of Fair Use as it Affects Libraries*, 63 L. LIB. J. 254, 257 (1970).

cases involving the concept of "justifiable use . . . approach nearer than any other class of cases . . . the metaphysics of the law, where the distinctions are . . . subtle and refined, and sometimes, almost evanescent."[20] Definitional difficulty has led to a pragmatic approach to the doctrine;[21] fair use is seen as a question of fact[22] to be determined on a case-by-case basis. The "quicksilver concept of fair use"[23] is delineated in terms of the criteria evolved by the courts.

The factors set forth by Mr. Justice Story in 1841, variously paraphrased, are still applied.

> [Q]uestion[s] of piracy often depend upon a nice balance of the comparative use made in one of the materials of the other; the nature, extent, and value of the materials thus used; the objects of each work; and the degree to which each writer may be fairly presumed to have resorted to the same common sources of information, or to have exercised the same common diligence in the selection and arrangement of the materials. . . . We must often, in deciding questions of this sort, look to the nature and objects of the selections made, the quantity and value of the materials used, and the degree in which the use may prejudice the sale, or diminish the profits, or supersede the objects of the original work. Many mixed ingredients enter into the discussion of such questions.[24]

The four criteria incorporated in the 1976 Copyright Statute are their most recent reiteration.

> In determining whether the use made of a work in any particular case is a fair use the factors to be considered shall include—
>
> 1) the purpose and character of the use, including whether such use is of a commercial nature or is for nonprofit educational purposes;
>
> 2) the nature of the copyrighted work;

[20] *Id.* at 344.

[21] *See* Crossland, *supra* note 17, at 158–61, 181–89, for a summation of the leading definitional statements.

[22] *See, e.g.*, Peter Pan Fabrics, Inc. v. Martin Weiner Corp., 274 F.2d 487 (2d Cir. 1960); Mathews Conveyor Co. v. Palmer-Bee Co., 135 F.2d 73 (6th Cir. 1943); Holdredge v. Knight Publishing Co. 214 F. Supp. 921 (S.D. Cal. 1963).

[23] Marvin Worth Productions v. Superior Films Corp., 319 F. Supp. 1269, 1274 (S.D.N.Y. 1970).

[24] Folsom v. Marsh, 9 F. Cas. at 343–44 and 348.

3) the amount and substantiality of the portion used in relation to the copyrighted work as a whole; and

4) the effect of the use upon the potential market for or value of the copyrighted work.[25]

In contrast with this continuous tradition of judicial criteria,[26] there is no general agreement on the source of judicial power to apply the doctrine or the judicial theory on which it is based. Fair use can be considered "a technical infringement which is nevertheless excused" or as no infringement because outside the realm of copyright.[27] In general, fair use is most often seen as a defense to a charge of infringement.[28]

Fair use has been said to derive from the implied consent of the copyright proprietor.[29] But this explanation has been rejected as "fictitious and unsuited for a rational system of jurisprudence," [30] with the exception of a few limited uses, and is scarcely compelling in the face of an infringement charge to which fair use is claimed as a defense.

The rationale of implied consent may be related to the theory that "custom is *per se* 'fair use.' " [31] Customary practice was a factor emphasized by the U.S. Court of Claims in *Williams and Wilkins* in its finding of fair use. "The fact that photocopying by libraries of entire articles was done with hardly any (and at most very minor) complaint until about 10 or 15 years ago, goes a long way to show . . . that there was at least a time when photocopying, as then

[25] 17 U.S.C. § 107 (1976).

[26] For an elaboration of this judicial continuity, *see* Yankwich, *supra* note 11, at 209–12.

[27] LATMAN, *supra* note 6, at 6. See LATMAN for an extensive review of fair use theory and development.

[28] *Copyright—Fair Use Doctrine*, 23 ALR 3rd 139, 154; NIMMER, *supra* note 9, at § 145.

[29] Sampson and Murdock Co. v. Seaver-Radford Co., 140 F. 539, 541 (1st Cir. 1905). *See* Yankwich, *supra* note 11, at 214.

[30] Crossland, *supra* note 17, at 166.

[31] Rosenfield, *Customary Use as "Fair Use" in Copyright Law*, 25 BUFFALO L. REV. 119 (1975) [hereinafter Rosenfield, *Customary Use*].

carried on, was 'fair use.' "[32] Not all fair use is necessarily customary, however; "novel use which is a departure from custom may be embraced within the doctrine if it meets the established judicial criteria."[33]

The basis for designating incidental or minimal use as fair may lie in the equity principle of *de minimus non curat lex.*[34] On the other hand, fair use may be no more than a test used by courts "to bring some order out of the confusion surrounding the question of how much can be copied."[35]

The source of the doctrine was recently explicitly ascribed to the Constitution by the Solicitor General of the United States.

MR. BORK: . . . fair use, after all, is basically a constitutional doctrine. It asks whether a rigid conceptualized application of the Copyright Act would in fact retard the progress of science as a useful art. And when I address myself to this question, I am talking about what would happen to medical research and what is not happening to petitioner despite his claims. I am talking about fair use.

QUESTION: Are you suggesting that Congress would be constitutionally obligated to incorporate a doctrine of fair use into the copyright law?

MR. BORK: That is debatable. I have seen it debated both ways, Mr. Justice Rehnquist. I don't know that I need to—well, I—

QUESTION: I thought you said a moment ago that fair use was a constitutionally—

MR. BORK: The courts have derived their power to evoke a doctrine of fair use from the constitutional value, the constitutional principle.[36]

[32] Williams and Wilkins Co. v. United States, 487, F.2d 1345, 1356 (Ct. Cl. 1973), *aff'd. by equally divided Court,* 420 U.S. 376 (1975) (per curiam); *see also* Karll v. Curtis Pub. Co., 39 F. Supp. 836, 837 (E.D. Wisc. 1941).

[33] Crossland, *supra* 17, at 168.

[34] *Id.* at 166–67; Note, *Legal Protection for the Author,* 14 H.D.L. 443, at 447 (1939).

[35] Note, 14 N.D.L. at 449.

[36] Exchange between U.S. Solicitor General Robert N. Bork and Mr. Justice Rehnquist, oral argument of Dec. 6, 1974, before the U.S. Supreme Court in Williams and Wilkins Co. v. United States, as reported in 7 INFORMATION NEWS AND SOURCES, 35, 38 (Feb. 1975). For a discussion of this exchange, *see* Rosenfield, *supra* note 5.

Although both the doctrine *per se* and the policy it effectuates arose independent of the U.S. Constitution, and although the direct origins of judicial power to develop and apply the doctrine are not so unambiguous as the Solicitor General's statement implies, the general effect of the fair use doctrine has been to carry out the purpose clause of congressional constitutional copyright authority.

Largely unacknowledged in fair use decisions, this essential parallelism with constitutional copyright policy may nevertheless provide the unspoken jurisprudential basis of the doctrine. Thus the evolution of the doctrine in the United States was recently attributed to its implicit constitutional nexus by the U.S. Court of Claims.

> [T]he development of "fair use" has been influenced by some tension between the direct aim of the copyright privilege to grant the owner a right from which he can reap financial benefit and the more fundamental purpose of the protection "To promote the Progress of Science and the useful Arts." [37]

Few fair use decisions incorporate such direct reference to constitutional values. Courts have rested their holdings on principles of equity and reasonableness,[38] placing primary emphasis on the analysis of factors on a case-by-case basis. A determination of public interest is not one of the usually listed factors on which courts rely; nor has public interest been unwaveringly "dispositive on whether a particular use [was] fair." [39] Yet modern decisions have cited public interest not only as an underlying philosophical reason for application of the doctrine but also as one of the specific criteria against which courts are to measure infringing use. "[I]n passing upon particular claims of infringement

[37] Williams and Wilkins, 487 F.2d at 1352. *See also* Rosemont Enterprises, 366 F.2d 303, 307 (2d Cir. 1966).

[38] Schulman, *Fair Use and the Revision of the Copyright Act*, 53 Iowa L. Rev. 832 (1968); Crossland, *supra* note 17, at 164.

[39] Rosenfield, *supra* note 5, at 802.

[courts] must occasionally subordinate the copyright holder's interest . . . to the greater public interest in the development of art, science and industry." [40]

Whether the privilege [fair use] may justifiably be applied to particular materials turns initially on the nature of the materials, *e.g.*, whether their distribution would *serve the public interest in the free dissemination of information* and whether their preparation requires some use of prior materials dealing with the same subject matter.[41] (Emphasis added.)

The significance of the omission of the public interest factor in the 1976 statutory criteria is unclear (see discussion below), as is the eventual effect of the omission on any developing tendency by the courts to rely explicitly on such a criterion.

TYPES OF FAIR USE AND PUBLIC INTEREST ANALYSIS

Any attempt at a logical classification of fair use is complicated by the wide variety of instances in which fair use has been found, together with the courts' *ad hoc* balancing process. It is possible, however, to examine those general areas of infringement for which a finding of fair use based on furthering public interest is the most expectable: scholarly works, news, reviews and criticism, burlesque and parody, use by educators and libraries.

SCHOLARLY WORKS

Scholarly works have been found subject to the privilege of reasonable appropriation because otherwise "writers of books would be deprived of the proper growth in knowledge, and from taking advantage of the position to which the earlier

[40] Berlin v. E. C. Publications, Inc., 329 F.2d 541, 544 (2d Cir. 1964).

[41] Rosemont Enterprises Inc. v. Random House, Inc., 366 F.2d 303, 307 (2d Cir. 1966), *cert. denied* 385 U.S. 1009 (1967).

writers had carried the science under consideration." [42] Generally speaking, the doctrine allows writers of scientific, medical, legal, historical, and biographical works "to use even the identical words" of copyrighted works.[43] Absence of independent effort on the part of the defendant user is often a decisive factor.[44] Whatever benefit might accrue to the public, the doctrine traditionally has not extended to copying *substantial* portions either verbatim or by paraphrase.[45] This restriction is experiencing erosion, however; for example, one recent decision declared that in the case of historical works, "copying must be . . . more substantial to constitute infringement." [46]

NEWS

Although news as such is not copyrightable, appropriations of a reporter's precise language, deductions, and comments constitute infringement.[47] In contrast, "public interest in having the fullest information available on the murder of President Kennedy" when little or no injury was incurred by the copyright owners, was dispositive in finding fair use.[48]

REVIEWS AND CRITICISM

The application of the doctrine of fair use to reviews and

[42] West Pub. Co. v. Edward Thompson Co., 169 F. 833, 866 (E.D.N.Y. 1909). *See also* Baker v. Selden, 101 U.S. 99, 103 (1879); Sampson and Murdock Co. v. Seaver-Radford Co., 140 F. 539, 541 (1st Cir. 1905). For a discussion of scholarly works, *see* Yankwich, *supra* note 11 at 205–7; Crossland, *supra* note 17, at 168–71.

[43] Thompson v. Gernsback, 94 F. Supp. 453, 454 (S.D.N.Y. 1950).

[44] List Pub. Co. v. Keller, 30 F. 772 (C.C.S.D.N.Y. 1887); Holdredge v. Knight Publishing Corp., 214 F. Supp. 921 (S.D. Cal. 1963).

[45] Meredith Corp. v. Harper and Row, Publishers, Inc., 378 F. Supp. 686 (S.D.N.Y.), *aff'd*, 500 F.2d 1221 (2d Cir. 1974); *see* LATMAN, *supra* note 6, at 10–11 for comment on decisions in the law book field in which substantial copying was the basic issue.

[46] Gardner v. Nizer, 391 F. Supp. 940, 943, *modified*, 396 F. Supp. 63 (S.D.N.Y. 1975).

[47] Chicago Record-Herald Co. v. Tribune Ass'n., 275 F. 797, 799 (7th Cir. 1921).

[48] Time Inc. v. Bernard Geis Assoc., 293 F. Supp. 130, 146 (S.D.N.Y. 1968).

criticism may be based as much on the benefit which accrues to the copyright holder, author, or publisher as on the benefit to the public. Reviewers "may fairly cite largely from the original work . . . for purposes of fair and reasonable criticism." [49] As with scholarly works, the amount taken has been held determinative.

> Reviewers may take extracts sufficient to show the merits, or demerits of the work, but they cannot so exercise the privilege as to supersede the original book. Sufficient may be taken to give a correct view of the whole; but the privilege of making extracts is limited to those objects, and cannot be exercised to such an extent that the review shall become a substitute for the book reviewed.[50]

Substantial appropriation for commercial purposes which masquerades as criticism, therefore, is not fair use.[51]

PARODY

Parody and satire, art forms of long tradition, pose peculiar problems of potential infringement since their success depends upon their ability to "recall or conjure up" the identity of the object of the satire.[52] The Second Circuit Court of Appeals has found "parody and satire . . . deserving of substantial freedom—both as entertainment and as a form of social and literary criticism." [53] Cases which had previously found infringement based on substantial similarity were unduly restrictive of a socially valuable art form, the Court suggested. In one of the best known of such prior cases, the *Benny* case, the Federal District Court of the Southern District of California had declared that

> The attempt to defend against copyright infringement by the claim that the infringing work was "merely a parody or burlesque" is not

[49] Folsom v. Marsh, 9 F. Cas. 342, 343 (C.C.D. Mass. 1841) (No. 4,901).

[50] Lawrence v. Dana, 15 F. Cas. 26, 60 (No. 8,136) (C.C.D. Mass. 1869).

[51] For a discussion of the right of comment and criticism *see* Crossland, *supra* note 17 at 171–74. For a discussion of permissible amount, *see* Yankwich, *supra* note 11 at 207–9.

[52] Berlin v. E. C. Publications, Inc., 329 F.2d 541, 544 (2d Cir. 1964).

[53] *Id.* at 545.

new. Such an attempt has been the subject of several decisions and has been disposed of, not by determining whether the alleged infringing use was parody or burlesque, but by ascertaining whether it amounted to a taking of substantial, copyrightable material. In other words, *a parodized or burlesqued taking is treated no differently from any other appropriation.*[54] (Emphasis added.)

The District Court in *Benny* also rejected the test of reduction in demand for the plaintiff's work, the determinative factor in the well-known *Mutt and Jeff* parody case.[55] In affirming the lower court's decision in the *Benny* case, the Ninth Circuit Court of Appeals stressed the factor of "wholesale copying" and the copyright proprietor's sole right "to make any other version of the work that he desires.[56] . . . Counsel have not disclosed a single authority, nor have we been able to find one, which lends any support to the proposition that wholesale copying and publication of copyrighted material can *ever* be fair use." [57] (Court's emphasis.)

The Supreme Court's equally divided decision of the *Benny* case, coupled with the District Court's apparent modification of its approach in a subsequent parody decision,[58] "indicates the uncertainty that exists" in the application of fair use in this area.[59] It can be argued that, whereas the *Benny* courts relied on strict traditional analysis, the reasoning of the Second Circuit reflects a shift toward a public interest standard for fair use.

[54] Loew's Inc. v. Columbia Broadcasting System, Inc., 131 F. Supp. 165, 176–77 (S.D. Cal. 1955), *aff'd sub nom.* Benny v. Loew's Inc., 239 F.2d 532 (9th Cir. 1956), *aff'd by an equally divided Court,* 356 H.S. 43 (1958).

[55] Hill v. Whalen & Martell, Inc., 220 F. 359 (S.D.N.Y. 1914).

[56] 239 F.2d at 536–37.

[57] *Id.* at 536, *quoting* Leon v. Pacific Telephone and Telegraph Co., 91 F.2d 484, 486 (9th Cir. 1937).

[58] Columbia Pictures Corp. v. Nat'l Broadcasting Co., Inc., 137 F. Supp. 348 (S.D. Cal. 1955).

[59] LATMAN, *supra* note 6, at 10; for a discussion of the parody cases, *see* NIMMER, *supra* note 9, at § 145; Note, *Parody, Copyrights, and the First Amendment* 10 U.S. L. REV. 564 (1976); Note, *Burlesque of Literary Property as Infringement of Copyright* 31 N.D.L. 46 (1955).

EDUCATIONAL USE

Few cases have centered on educational use as fair use. Far from endorsing a public interest analysis, the two most often cited cases in this area found liability despite the nonprofit educational purpose of the infringement. In *Macmillan Co. v. King*, the distribution by an economics teacher of mimeographed outlines of a copyrighted work to a small group of students was held an infringement of the author's right to make any other versions of the work.[60] The distribution was considered "a publication" by the *Macmillan* court, a finding which the *Williams and Wilkins* decision repudiated. "To the extent that *Macmillan Co. v. King* . . . may possibly suggest that 'publication' can occur through simple distribution to a very small restricted group, for a special purpose, we think the opinion goes too far." [61]

In *Wihtol v. Crow*, a high school and church choir director was held liable for copyright violation for the distribution of forty-eight duplicated copies of an arrangement he had made of a copyrighted song. The reviewing court rejected the trial court's finding of fair use based on innocent intent, without considering the fact that the use was clearly nonprofit.[62]

The 1976 statute, as finally amended, includes as one of its criteria a consideration of whether use is commercial or for nonprofit educational purposes. (*See* discussion below.) Under the statute, therefore, a different analysis would certainly obtain, a fact that may augur a shift in the balancing of fair use criteria to favor the advancement in the public interest of nonprofit education over the protection of the copyright holder's exclusive right to reproduce the work. The

[60] Macmillan Co. v. King, 223 F. 862 (D. Mass. 1914).
[61] 487 F.2d at 1352 n. 11.
[62] Wihtol v. Crow, 309 F.2d 777 (8th Cir. 1962).

implications of such a change could be sufficiently far-reaching as to alter radically copyright of educational materials.

LIBRARY USE

As with educational use, few cases have dealt with library use of copyrighted materials. Until the advent of reprography, little possibility of library infringement existed. Probably the most important fair use case in recent times, *Williams and Wilkins*,[63] grew out of library photoduplication. The defendant libraries, the National Library of Medicine (NLM) and the National Institutes of Health (NIH), distributed photocopies of articles from the plaintiff's medical journals free of charge, NLM through an interlibrary loan program and NIH primarily to researchers employed by the National Institutes of Health. In 1970, NIH copied 85,744 articles, and NLM 93,746 articles.[64] Articles were duplicated in their entirety. Both libraries are nonprofit government-operated institutions. In an opinion resting on a number of interlinked criteria, the Court of Claims held such use fair, a decision later affirmed by an equally divided Supreme Court. The case is of particular significance for the present discussion because of its articulation of the constitutional dimension of fair use[65] and for its reliance on a public interest analysis.

The reasoning of the Court of Claims took a multifaceted approach to one of the key fair use tests: the extent to which the alleged infringement replaces or diminishes the demand for the copyrighted work.[66] Competitive effect is, of course,

[63] 487 F.2d 1345 (Ct. Cl. 1973), *aff'd*, 420 U.S. 376 (1975).

[64] 487 F.2d at 1355, n. 15.

[65] *Id.* at 1352.

[66] Report of the Register of Copyrights, *supra* note 13, at 24. "[T]he actual decisions bearing upon fair use, if not always their stated rationale, can best be explained by looking to the central question of whether the defendant's work tends to diminish or prejudice the potential sale of the plaintiff's work. This determination must be made not by comparing the media in which the two works may appear, but rather in terms of the function of each work regardless of media."

most easily discerned in commercial terms, but commercial use by the defendant has not in the past precluded the defense of fair use. Success as a "money-maker" if not a "best seller" of a book "designed . . . and sold . . . for commercial gain" has been held "no reason to conclude that it should be denied the benefits of the fair use doctrine" when the book was "a serious . . . account of great historical interest." [67] In contrast, the commercial nature of the defendant's use in an advertisement of three sentences from a medical treatise was decisive in the denial of fair use despite total lack of competition.[68] Nor has use for nonprofit purposes ensured a finding of fair use,[69] as the educational use cases discussed above illustrate. In *Williams and Wilkins*, however, the Court of Claims stressed the nonprofit nature of the institutions and of their practices, practices which "[o]n both sides—library and requester—[were] untainted by any commercial gain from the reproduction. . . . There has been no attempt to misappropriate the work of earlier scientific writers for forbidden ends, but rather an effort to gain easier access to the material for study and research. . . ." [70]

Closely related to its emphasis on the nonprofit nature of the defendant libraries' use was the court's focus on the "personal individual" nature of the library patron's use. Despite the large numbers of articles duplicated, "the personal, individual focus is still present. The reader who himself makes a copy does so for his own personal work needs, and individual work needs are likewise dominant in the reproduction programs of the two medical libraries. . . ." [71]

[67] Meeropol v. Nizer, 361 F. Supp. 1063, 1068 (S.D.N.Y. 1973).

[68] Henry Holt and Co., Inc. v. Liggett & Myers Tobacco Co., 23 F. Supp. 302 (E.D. Pa. 1938).

[69] Associated Music Publishers, Inc. v. Debs Memorial Radio Fund, Inc., 46 F. Supp. 829 (S.D.N.Y. 1942), *aff'd*, 141 F.2d 852 (2d Cir. 1944).

[70] 487 F.2d at 1354. *See* Rosenfield, *Customary Use, supra* note 31, at 122–25.

[71] 487 F.2d at 1355. *See also* n. 16 at 1355. For a discussion of the "individual focus" factor, *see* Note, *Williams and Wilkins Co. v. U.S.: Library Photocopying*

Here, the court may be echoing the generally held notion that "private use is completely outside the scope and intent of restriction by copyright."[72] The extensive duplication permitted, however, marks a departure from prior fair use decisions and can be seen as indicative of a shift in the development of the doctrine toward explicit endorsement of copying for private use by certain classes of persons whose ultimate goal is to benefit the public, in this instance through medical research. The revised copyright statute validates this private use privilege for teachers in nonprofit schools and goes beyond the *Williams and Wilkins* court to include library users in general.[73]

Central to the court's reasoning was the great benefit which accrues to the public from medical research, and the potential injury which would befall medicine and the public good if the court held the libraries' practice an infringement.[74] Such an analysis reflects the court's espousal of a constitutional theory of fair use and, at the less abstract, produces the burden the court placed on the plaintiff, a burden which some critics have found an unfortunate departure from prior case law.

The plaintiff's failure "to prove its assumption of eco-

of Copyrighted Materials, 1974 UTAH L. REV. 127, 133 (1974); Rosenfield, *Customary Use, supra* note 31 at 125–27.

[72] LATMAN, *supra* note 6, at 11–12, quoting Shaw, *Publication and Distribution of Scientific Literature,* 17 COLLEGE AND RESEARCH LIBRARIES 294, 301 (1956); *Cf.* NIMMER, *supra* note 9, § 145 at 654–55. "There is no reported case on the question of whether a single handwritten copy of all or substantially all of a protected work made for the copier's own private use is an infringement or fair use. If such a case were to arise the force of custom might impel a court to rule for the defendant on the ground of fair use. . . . [H]owever . . . the handwritten copy would serve the same function as the protected work, and would tend to reduce the exploitation value of such work." NIMMER at 656.3.

[73] 17 U.S.C. § 108 (a), (d) (1976); H.R. REP. No. 1476, 94th Cong., 2d Sess. 68 (1976). For a discussion of limited duplication for a limited number of recipients, *see* Comment, *Photocopying and Copyright Law,* 63 KY. L.J. 256, 259–61 (1975).

[74] Williams and Wilkins, 487 F.2d at 1356.

nomic detriment, in the past or potentially for the future,"[75] weighed heavily with the reviewing Court of Claims. In reversing the trial commissioner's inference "that the extensive photocopying has resulted in some loss of revenue to plaintiff" through loss of subscriptions, the court asserted that it could not "mechanically assume such an effect, or hold that the amount of photoduplication proved here 'must' lead to financial or economic harm. This is a matter of proof and plaintiff has not transformed its hypothetical assumption, by evidence, into a proven fact."[76]

In contrast, prior case law has held "an action will lie even if no damage be shown."[77] According to a major authority,

> [The *Williams and Wilkins*] court fell into error by confusing the issues of damage and liability. It is often difficult for a plaintiff to prove actual damages as against a given defendant. Far from this justifying a defense of fair use, failure to prove damages will in the usual case give rise to a minimum statutory damages liability. It is only when the general dissemination of an allegedly infringing work by all potential defendants, and without limitation as to the number of reproductions, and volume of users would still not adversely affect the plaintiff's potential market that a conclusion of fair use may be justified.[78]

In addition, the court's analysis may indicate a shifting to the plaintiff of the burden of proof "to prove any claimed detrimental effect on his potential market."[79] It should be noted with respect to the *Williams and Wilkins* plaintiff that the impact of photoduplication by libraries on publishing,

[75] *Id.* at 1359.

[76] *Id.* at 1357, 1359.

[77] Leon v. Pacific Telephone and Telegraph Co., 91 F.2d 484, 487 (9th Cir. 1937).

[78] NIMMER, *supra* note 9, § 145 at 655.

[79] Note, *Photocopying as Fair Use—Williams and Wilkins Co. v. U.S.*, 24 BOSTON COLL. IND. & COMM. L. REV. 141, 147–50 (1975); for a discussion of the burden of proof in copyright cases as it relates to the constitutional dimension of fair use, *see* Richards, *The Value of the Copyright Clause in Construction of Copyright Law*, 2 HASTINGS CON. L. Q. 221 (1975).

particularly the effect on the publication of periodicals, has been the subject of much comment and dispute. Some studies suggest that

[T]he financial incentive to write has not been affected measurably by copying machines. Nor have publishing interests in general suffered any serious monetary losses because of photocopying, a factor that should promote information production. But . . . the situation is not static, and it is the potential use of photocopying, more than any other single factor, that concerns copyright owners.[80]

The potential effect of this aspect of the *Williams and Wilkins* analysis may extend beyond difficulties of proof in cases of alleged infringement by photoduplication. A constitutional basis for the fair use doctrine may impel the placing of an almost insurmountable burden on plaintiff.

Without its constitutional dimension and protection, fair use has been relegated to the status of an affirmative defense, with the user being required to carry the burden of proof that the use was not an actionable infringement. Thus, the whole defense of the public interest and constitutional right is thrown on the alleged infringer. Significant procedural effects attach to the legal conclusions that copyright is merely a statutory privilege whereas fair use has constitutional protection. Once fair use has been properly vested with its appropriate constitutional status, the burden of proof shifts to the copyright proprietor to prove that an alleged infringement is not protected as a fair use. . . .[81]

Although the *Williams and Wilkins* court did not explicitly adopt this reasoning, such a rationale may inhere in its

[80] Henry, *Copyright, Public Policy, and Information Technology*, 183 SCIENCE 384, 390 (Feb. 1, 1974); Line and Wood, *The Effect of a Large-Scale Photocopying Service on Journal Sales*, J. DOCUMENTATION 234 (Dec. 1975). *See also* NIMMER, *supra* note 9, § 145 n. 211, for a list of recent significant studies on this issue; L. H. HATTERY and G. BUSH, REPROGRAPHY AND COPYRIGHT LAW (1964); COPYRIGHT—THE LIBRARIAN AND THE LAW, Bureau of Library and Information Science Research, Rutgers Univ. (1972); N. HENRY, COPYRIGHT, INFORMATION TECHNOLOGY, PUBLIC POLICY, 2 vol. (1976). For an annotated bibliography and source materials, *see* G. BUSH, TECHNOLOGY AND COPYRIGHT (1972).

[81] Rosenfield, *supra* note 5 at 804.

attribution of constitutional values to fair use and in its weighing of the interests of the plaintiff publisher against detriment to medical research if the court held the libraries' practice an infringement.[82] Few plaintiffs could show a sufficient countervailing interest to meet this test, which has been likened to "balancing the interest of a particular author in his novel against the public's interest in literature generally."[83] Ironically, so extreme an outcome of raising fair use to a constitutional level would entail the virtual demise of copyright protection for certain classes of works in the name of public benefit in opposition to the express authority granted the Congress to promote science and the arts *by means of copyright.*

Less dramatic, but nevertheless equally extreme in its implication for radical change in fair use case law, is the *Williams and Wilkins* court's sanction of entire-work copying. Courts have, since the earliest cases, considered the substantiality of the appropriation a basic factor in determining fair use. Generally speaking, incidental use has been permitted,[84] whereas "wholesale copying" is deemed an infringement.[85] While originally assuming that permissible copying extended only to an insignificant portion of protected material, the doctrine was later expanded to allow more substantial reproduction "where such copying was clearly in the public interest."[86] The *Williams and Wilkins* validation of entire-work duplication may be no more than a logical extension of this development.

The foregoing brief survey of those classes of use for which a public policy basis seems most predictable illustrates that

[82] 487 F.2d 1359.

[83] NIMMER, *supra* note 9, § 145, at 656.1 (1976).

[84] Karll v. Curtis Pub. Co., 39 F. Supp. 836 (E. D. Wis. 1941); Shapiro, Bernstein and Co. v. P. F. Collier and Son Co., 26 U.S.P.Q. 40 (S.D.N.Y. 1934); Broadway Music Co. v. F-R Pub. Corp., 31 F. Supp. 817 (S.D.N.Y. 1940).

[85] Benny v. Loew's Inc., 239 F.2d 532, 536.

[86] Meredith Corp. v. Harper and Row, 378 F. Supp. 686, 689 (S.D.N.Y. 1974), *aff'd,* 500 F.2d 1221 (2d Cir. 1974).

at least some decisions rest on such a consideration. Of these, the most outstanding, *Williams and Wilkins*, may be the least representative, given its unique circumstances and limited holding. Sufficient other evidence exists, nevertheless, to suggest an incipient transformation of the doctrine. Whether the future contours of the fair use doctrine emerge substantially different from their traditional form will depend to a great extent on the effect of its recent codification.

STATUTORY FAIR USE

Under the 1976 revised Copyright Statute, the copyright holder has exclusive rights to reproduce the work; to prepare derivative works; to distribute copies and, in the case of designated art forms, to display and perform the work.[87] The two sections which immediately follow restrict the exclusivity of these rights: the first, by fair use, *per se*, and the second, by separate statutory recognition of a specific form of fair use, namely, library reproduction.

Section 107, the fair use section, enumerates the purposes for which use is to be considered fair and specifies the factors courts are to consider in a determination of fair use. The extent to which the statutory enumeration of criteria will impair the flexibility of the doctrine is uncertain. The stated legislative intent is to leave the development of the doctrine to the courts.[88]

The statute "endorses the general scope and purpose of the fair use doctrine," without intending to change, narrow or enlarge it in any way. The drafters disclaimed "any disposition to freeze the doctrine especially during a period of technological change."[89]

[87] 17 U.S.C. § 106 (1976).

[88] H.R. Rep. No. 1476, 94th Cong., 2d Sess. 66 (1976).

[89] *Id. See* Schulman, *supra* note 38, for a discussion of dangers arising from statutory enumeration.

The statute enumerates the purposes for which use may be considered fair: criticism, comment, news reporting, teaching (including multiple copies for classroom use), scholarship, or research. With the exception of the specification of "teaching (including multiple copies for classroom use)," these uses fall within the established perimeters of the doctrine. The list is not intended to be restrictive; the language reads "purposes, such as . . . ;" furthermore, the committee reports make plain that "the singling out of some instances to discuss in the context of fair use is not intended to indicate that other activities would or would not be beyond fair use." [90] Although parody and burlesque are unmentioned in the statute, "use in a parody of some of the content of the work parodied" appears in the Register's list of uses which both the House and Senate Reports quote with approval.[91]

Since questions of fair use arise in an "endless variety of situations and combinations of circumstances," formulation of exact rules was deemed impossible.[92] The statute, therefore, repeats the four basic criteria usually applied by the courts: the purpose and character of the use, the nature of the copyrighted work, the amount and substantiality of the appropriation, and the effect of the use on the potential market for or value of the copyrighted work.[93] A dispositive determination of public benefit is not included. One explanation

[90] S. Rep. No. 473, 94th Cong., 1st Sess. 63 (1975).

[91] *Id.* 6 at 61; H.R. Rep. No. 1476 at 65. "[Q]uotation of excerpts in a review or criticism for purposes of illustration or comment; quotation of short passages in a scholarly or technical work, for illustration or clarification of the author's observations; use in a parody of some of the content of the work parodied; summary of an address or article, with brief quotations, in a news report; reproduction by a library of a portion of a work to replace part of a damaged copy; reproduction by a teacher or student of a small part of a work to illustrate a lesson; reproduction of a work in legislative or judicial proceedings or reports; incidental and fortuitous reproduction, in a newsreel or broadcast, of a work located in the scene of an event being reported." Report of the Register of Copyrights, *supra* note 13, at 24.

[92] H.R. Rep. No. 1476, *supra* note 88 at 6.

[93] 17 U.S.C. § 107 (1976).

may be that inclusion in the statute implicitly confers on fair use the constitutional purpose of copyright. The drafters in their discussions made clear that the justification for copyright lies in its promotion of the public good through the growth of knowledge and dissemination of information and that conflicting claims are to be measured by this standard.[94]

The statute does, however, incorporate some aspects of judicial public interest analysis of fair use. Moreover, it significantly enlarges traditional fair use boundaries with the library reproduction section and the inclusion of nonprofit educational purposes in fair use criteria, expansions in conformity with public policy development of the doctrine.

EDUCATIONAL USE

The House Committee amended the first of the criteria enumerated in the statute, which originally read "the purpose and character of the use" [95] in order to state explicitly that this factor includes a consideration of "whether such use is of a commercial nature or is for non-profit educational purposes." According to the Committee's report, however, the amendment is not intended to place a not-for-profit limitation on educational use of copyrighted material. "It is an express recognition that, as under the present law, the commercial or non-profit character of an activity, while not conclusive with respect to fair use, can and should be weighed along with other factors in fair use decisions." [96] So stated, the nonprofit criterion is a natural outgrowth of prior fair use reasoning. In application, however, the nonprofit factor may signal a more dramatic shift. First, it requires different

[94] Remarks of Rep. Drinan (D. Mass.), CONG. REC.—HOUSE, H10880 (Sept. 22, 1976); speech of Rep. E. W. Pattison (D.N.Y.), INFORMATION HOTLINE, *supra* note 5.

[95] S. 22 § 107(1); S. REP. No. 473, *supra* note 90 at 5.

[96] H.R. REP. No. 1476, *supra* note 88 at 66.

results in teacher use cases such as the two discussed above. Even more significant, a noncommercial purpose is obligatory for noninfringing library duplication [97] and under the educational guidelines which accompany the statute.

In a departure from prior case law, the statute specifies as fair use multiple copies for classroom use. This inclusion represents a House amendment to the earlier Senate version of the statute in response to what has been called "one of the most difficult questions" [98] the drafters faced. Educators feared that "because of the vagueness and ambiguity of the bill's treatment of the doctrine of fair use, they [might] subject themselves to liability for unintentional infringement of copyright . . ." [99] The House amendment "is a recognition that, under the proper circumstances of fairness, the doctrine can be applied to reproductions of multiple copies for the members of a class." [100] Educators had pressed for a clear legislative blanket exemption, but this the House Committee rejected.

> The Committee also adheres to its earlier conclusion, that "a specific exemption freeing certain reproductions of copyrighted works for educational and scholarly purposes from copyright control is not justified." At the same time the Committee recognizes, as it did in 1967, that there is a "need for greater certainty and protection for teachers." In an effort to meet this need, the Committee has not only adopted further amendments to section 107, but has also amended section 504(c) to provide innocent teachers and other non-profit users of copyrighted material with broad insulation against unwarranted liability for infringement.[101]

[97] 17 U.S.C. § 108(a)(1) (1976).

[98] Remarks of Mr. Kastenmeier, CONG. REC.—HOUSE, H10875 (daily ed. Sept. 22, 1976); for a discussion of some of the basic points raised by educators, *see* MacLean, *Education and Copyright Law: An Analysis of the Amended Copyright Revision Bill and Proposals for Statutory Licensing and a Clearinghouse System*, 20 ASCAP COPYRIGHT L. SYMP. 1 (1972).

[99] Remarks of Mr. Skubitz, CONG. REC., *id.*

[100] H. REP. No. 1476, *supra* note 88 at 66. *See also* S. REP. No. 476, *supra* note 95 at 63.

[101] H. REP. No. 1476, *supra* note 88 at 66–67.

When the move for a special educational exemption failed, educators agreed "to discuss in earnest" [102] with authors and publishers guidelines on how the fair use section would work in practice. The resulting guidelines apply to not-for-profit educational institutions and cover books and periodicals only. Under the guidelines, which conform in most respects to the comments of the Senate Report of 1975,[103] a single copy of

A. A chapter from a book;
B. An article from a periodical or newspaper;
C. A short story, short essay or short poem, whether or not from a collective work;
D. A chart, graph, diagram, drawing, cartoon or picture from a book, periodical, or newspaper

may be made for a teacher's own use in "scholarly research or . . . in teaching or preparation to teach a class." [104] This first use is in accord with the traditional principle of scholarly use; the second and third constitute a clear instance of private use by a specified category of persons for public benefit, in keeping with the private use emphasis of *Williams and Wilkins* discussed above. The endorsement of copying *for use in teaching* enlarges the scope of fair use; furthermore, notwithstanding the distinction, noted in the Senate Report, between an entire work and an excerpt,[105] this section sanctions

[102] Wagner, *supra* note 12 at 29; for a discussion of "the limited educational exemption" proposed by educators, *see* Comment, *Copyrights: Concurrence, Revision and Photocopying*, 79 Dick L. Rev. 260, 292–93 (1975).

[103] S. Rep. No. 473, *supra* note 90 at 62–65.

[104] H.R. Rep. No. 1476, *supra* note 88 at 68.

[105] During the consideration of this legislation there has been considerable discussion of the difference between an "entire work" and an "excerpt." The educators have sought a limited right for a teacher to make a single copy of an "entire" work for classroom purposes, but it seems apparent that this was not generally intended to extend beyond a "separately cognizable" or "self-contained" portion (for example a single poem, story, or article) in a collective work. and that no privilege is sought to reproduce an entire collective work (for example, an encyclopedia volume, a periodical issue) or a sizable integrated work published as an entity (a novel, treatise, monograph. and so forth).

the use of copies of complete works in teaching, a definite extension of past application of the doctrine. The often salient factor of lack of independent effort on the part of the infringer was apparently not considered.

The guidelines establish three basic criteria for multiple classroom copies, which "in any event" may not exceed one copy per pupil per course. Copying must meet three tests: spontaneity and brevity; cumulative effect; and inclusion in each copy of a copyright notice.[106]

Educators had voiced concern over the impracticability of applying for permissions.[107] The spontaneity test allows copying if "[t]he inspiration and decision to use the work and the moment of its use of maximum teaching effectiveness are so close in time that it would be unreasonable to expect a timely reply to a request for permission." [108] This test, together with that of cumulative effect, precludes the common practice of distributing duplicated copies of the same work in subsequent school terms without permission.

The first element of the spontaneity test requires that the copying be made "at the instance and inspiration of the individual teacher." [109] Under this requirement, protection against infringement does not extend to copying if "required or suggested by the school administration . . . as part of a general plan." [110] Educators objected to this restriction "on pre-planned activity" especially as it related to the role of teacher supervisors and educational specialists.[111] In clarification, the House Committee explained that, although

---

With this limitation, and subject to the other relevant criteria, the requested privilege of making a single copy appears appropriately to be within the scope of fair use. S. REP. No. 473, *supra* note 90 at 64.

[106] H.R. REP. No. 1476, *supra* note 88 at 68.

[107] Remarks of Mr. Skubitz, CONG. REC.—HOUSE, at H10875 (Sept. 22, 1976).

[108] H.R. REP. No. 1476, *supra* note 88 at 69.

[109] *Id.*

[110] S. REP. No. 473, *supra* note 90 at 63. *See also* CONG. REC.—HOUSE, at H10875 (Sept. 22, 1976).

[111] MacLean, *supra* note 98 at 9–10.

spontaneity does not preclude consultation with supervisors and specialists, the prohibition against copying "directed by higher authority" still holds.[112]

The need for teachers to copy current news items for classroom instruction was acknowledged by the Senate Committee.[113] The spontaneity criterion allows for this practice. In addition, the definition of cumulative effect accords "current news periodicals and newspapers and current news sections of other periodicals" special exempt status.[114]

The test of spontaneity is coupled with that of brevity. The guidelines "define" brevity in specific quantitative terms with respect to various genres. Multiple copying of the following for classroom use will meet the requirement of brevity:

(i) Poetry: (a) A complete poem if less than 250 words and if printed on not more than two pages or, (b) from a longer poem, an excerpt of not more than 250 words.

(ii) Prose: (a) Either a complete article, story or essay of less than 2,500 words, or (b) an excerpt from any prose work of not more than 1,000 words or 10% of the work, whichever is less, but in any event a minimum of 500 words.

[Each of the numerical limits stated in "i" and "ii" above may be expanded to permit the completion of an unfinished line of a poem or of an unfinished prose paragraph.]

(iii) Illustration: One chart, graph, diagram, drawing, cartoon or picture per book or per periodical issue.

(iv) "Special" works: Certain works in poetry, prose or in "poetic prose" which often combine language with illustrations and which are intended sometimes for children and at other times for a more general audience fall short of 2,500 words in their entirety. Paragraph "ii" above notwithstanding such "special works" may not be reproduced in their entirety; however, an excerpt comprising not more than two of the published pages of such special work and con-

[112] Remarks of Mr. Katzenmeier, CONG. REC.—HOUSE at H10875 (Sept. 22, 1976).

[113] S. REP. NO. 473, *supra* note 90 at 64.

[114] H.R. REP. NO. 1476, *supra* note 88 at 69.

taining not more than 10% of the words found in the text thereof, may be reproduced.[115]

Here, the guidelines apply two traditional and now statutorily mandated tests of fair use, namely, the amount and substantiality of the material used and the nature of the copyrighted work. The result, however, diverges from judicial antecedents. The permissible copying in its entirety of a short poem, short story, or essay, expands the perimeters of fair use. In like fashion, the quantitative specificity of the guidelines departs from prior judicial case-by-case balancing. To the extent that such detailed measurements of liability become embedded in the doctrine, fair use analysis and the very nature of the concept will undergo transformation.

That multiple classroom copying meets the combined requirement of spontaneity and brevity is not sufficient to ensure nonliability under the guidelines. The test of cumulative effect must also be met. This criterion applies both to the amount of the individual copyrighted collective work duplicated and to the number of times any such multiple copying may take place for one course during a school term. Copying is permissible when for only one course in the school in which the copies are made. No more than nine instances of multiple copying for one course in one term is allowed. Selections from any one author must be limited to one short poem, article, or story, or two excerpts, per term. No more than three selections from any collective work is allowed in any one school term.[116] Here again, the guidelines set a specificity that the judicial fair use standards eschew.

Basically, the thrust of the limitations on classroom copying is to protect the copyright holder's interest in marketing his work by preventing its replacement with classroom copies. Even before the "nonprofit educational purposes" language

[115] *Id.* at 68–69.
[116] *Id.* at 69.

had been added to the fair use section, the Senate had pointed out the importance of the fourth statutory factor, "the effect of the use on the potential market for or value of" the copyrighted work.[117] The guidelines, therefore, prohibit copying of consumables, such as workbooks, and copying to create, replace, or substitute for collective works like anthologies. Copying may not substitute for purchase of books or periodicals. Further, the same item may not be copied by the same teacher from term to term.[118]

These provisions acknowledge, as *Williams and Wilkins* did not, that "[i]solated instances of minor infringements, when multiplied many times, become in the aggregate a major inroad on copyright that must be prevented." [119] If the provisions are granted judicial acceptance, they may avert the potential undermining of traditional copyright concepts that

[117] This factor must almost always be judged in conjunction with the other three criteria. With certain special exceptions (use in parodies or as evidence in court proceedings might be examples) a use that supplants any part of the normal market for a copyrighted work would ordinarily be considered an infringement. As in any other case, whether this would be the result of reproduction by a teacher for classroom purposes requires an evaluation of the nature and purpose of the use, the type of work involved, and the size and relative importance of the portion taken. Fair use is essentially supplementary by nature, and classroom copying that exceeds the legitimate teaching aims such as filling in missing information or bringing a subject up to date would go beyond the proper bounds of fair use. S. REP. No. 473, *supra* note 90 at 65.

[118] The guidelines state that "(A) Copying shall be used to create or to replace or substitute for anthologies, compilations or collective works. Such replacement or substitution may occur whether copies of various works or excerpts therefrom are accumulated or reproduced and used separately.

"(B) There shall be no copying of or from works intended to be "consumable" in the course of study or of teaching. These include workbooks, exercises, standardized tests and test booklets and answer sheets and like consumable material.

"(C) Copying shall not

(a) substitute for the purchase of books, publishers' reprints or periodicals;

(b) be directed by higher authority;

(c) be repeated with respect to the same item by the same teacher from term to term.

"(D) No charge shall be made to the student beyond the actual cost of the photocopying." H.R. REP. No. 1476, *supra* note 88 at 69–70.

[119] S. REP. No. 473, *supra* note 90 at 65.

a simple balancing of the general public interest in nonprofit education against the interests of a single individual almost inevitably entails.

Guidelines similar in scope and underlying rationale have also been drawn up for educational uses of music.[120] These take into consideration some of the problems peculiar to that field. Emergency copying to replace purchased copies is allowed for an imminent performance, provided replacements are subsequently purchased. Otherwise, copying for the purpose of performance is prohibited even if for nonprofit performance. This restriction is consistent with the holding in *Wihtol v. Crow*,[121] discussed earlier. As with books and periodicals, copying of an entire performance unit is permissible for the private scholarly use of the teacher or for use in preparation to teach a class; copying an out-of-print work is also allowed. Beyond these uses, the provisions protect the composer's potential market. Entire work duplication which substitutes for the purchase of music constitutes an infringement.

It is important to note that, although written at the urging of the Chairman of the Judiciary Subcommittee,[122] these fair use guidelines for educators were not written by a legislative committee. Nor are they the product of an administrative agency to whose expertise the courts frequently defer.[123] Each represents the compromise agreement on "minimum standards of educational fair use,"[124] of a committee of affected parties. The music education guidelines "represent the understanding of the Music Publishers' Association of the United States, Inc., the National Music Publishers Association, Inc., the Music Teachers National Association, the Mu-

[120] H.R. REP. No 1476, *supra* note 88 at 70–72.
[121] Wihtol v. Crow, 309 F. 2d 777 (8th Cir. 1962).
[122] H.R. REP. No. 1476, *supra* note 88 at 67.
[123] *See, e.g.,* Mourning v. Family Publications Service, Inc. 411 U.S. 356, 369 (1973).
[124] H.R. REP. No. 1476, *supra* note 88 at 68, 70.

sic Educators National Conference, the National Association of Schools of Music, and the Ad Hoc Committee on Copyright Law Revision."[125] The classroom copying guidelines for nonprofit educational institutions were approved by the Ad Hoc Committee (made up of forty-one educational organizations); Author-Publisher Group; Authors League of America; Association of American Publishers, Inc.;[126] and the National Education Association.[127] The approval was not unanimous, however. In the view of the American Association of University Professors, the guidelines "contradict the basic concept of fair use," and "would seriously interfere with . . . the effective operation of higher education." The Association questioned the validity of the suggestion that the guidelines be binding on any other than the agreeing parties.[128] In the

[125] Cong. Rec.—House, at H10875 (Sept. 22, 1976).

[126] H.R. Rep. No. 19476, *supra* note 88 at 70.

[127] Cong. Rec.—House, at H10876 (Sept. 22, 1976).

[128] *Id. at* H10880. Excerpts from Letter of May 25, 1976, to Chairman Kastenmeier from the American Association of University Professors. As scholars and teachers who both produce and use copyrighted materials, we appreciate and approve the recognition of the needs of the scholar and university teacher reflected in Sections 107 and 504 of S. 22 as recently amended by your Subcommittee. In Section 504, the mandatory remission of statutory damages for teachers acting in good faith constitutes a recognition of the function of the scholar and teacher. More significantly, by its references to "teaching (including multiple copies for classroom use), scholarship, or research," and in the distinction recognized between commercial and non-profit uses, Section 107 as presently drafted is an articulate statement of the general principle of fair use on which courts and others may build a comprehensive framework for the educational uses of copyrighted material.

However, these salutary and progressive provisions in the Bill would be undermined by the proposed Guidelines if, as is apparently contemplated by the parties who submitted them to you, they were to become a significant part of the legislative history of Section 107 as a result of incorporation in your Committee Report. We recognize, of course, the right of any given groups mutually to agree upon the terms and conditions by which they, and those they actually represent, will be guided in conforming to a statute such as this. To suggest, however, that such agreements should be binding upon *other* persons or groups or should, through incorporation in a committee report, be given weight in the interpretation of the statute generally, is quite a different matter. Consequently, these Guidelines—agreed to recently by author and publisher representatives and some members of the education community but with no representation from our Association—have caused us deep dismay. They would

same vein, the Association of American Law Schools criticized the guidelines as so restrictive of fair use "as to make it almost useless for classroom teaching," and declared a preference for allowing the courts "to delineate . . . where to draw the lines on abuses of the fair-use doctrine." [129]

In response to these criticisms, the legislative history stresses that the guidelines set forth *minimum* standards of educational fair use.

> The purpose of the following guidelines to *state the minimum* and not the maximum standards of educational fair use under Section 107. . . . The parties agree that the conditions determining the extent of permissible copying for educational purposes may change in the future; that certain types of copying permitted under these guidelines may not be permissible in the future, and conversely that in the future

---

seriously interfere with the basic mission and effective operation of higher education and with the purpose of the Constitutional grant of copyright protection, which is designed to promote, not hinder, the discovery and dissemination of knowledge. These proposed Guidelines, notwithstanding the insistence that they represent only minimum standards, and despite other disclaimers, ultimately resort to the language of prohibition (see Section III). In so doing, they contradict the basic concept of fair use and threaten the responsible discharge of the functions of teaching and research."

[129] *Id.* Excerpts from Letters to Chairman Kastenmeier from the Association of American Law Schools, May 26, 1976. "Our substantive objections to the guidelines are spelled out in the letters of Professors Raskind and Gorman to you. They are in essence that the guidelines restrict the doctrine of fair use so substantially as to make it almost useless for classroom teaching purposes. Requiring a law school teacher to meet all three tests of brevity, spontaneity and cumulative effect stifles the use of copyrighted material for classroom purposes. The draft guidelines are based on the principle, with which most people would agree, that copying should not substitute generally for purchase of a copyrighted work. The effect of the draft guidelines before you, however, is to stifle dissemination of material rather than encourage purchasing or licensing of it. The realities of classroom teaching and the economics of our students are such that they cannot purchase or pay royalties on works other than the standard text and case books that are used as the major resources in classroom teaching. Thus the teacher's choice is not between purchasing and copying; it is between copying and not using. The vague and restrictive nature of the draft guidelines leaves the teacher with no assurance of safety in the fair-use doctrine and will result in sharply curtailing the use of copyrighted works in the classroom. We would prefer that the courts be allowed to delineate, within the well-phrased current draft of the statute, where to draw the line on abuses of the fair-use doctrine."

other types of copying not permitted under these guidelines may be permissible under revised guidelines.[130]

The House Committee accepted the guideline provisions as "a reasonable interpretation of [fair use] minimum standards." [131] The Conference Committee accepted them "as part of their understanding of fair use. . . ." [132] The extent to which the courts will adopt the guidelines is unclear. The legislative history of the statute voices approval not only of the educational guidelines but of judicial case-by-case adaptation of the doctrine.[133]

LIBRARY PUBLICATION

Libraries are subject to the fair use doctrine under Section 107, but the particular problems of libraries and archives are dealt with separately in Section 108.[134] Photocopying by libraries, considered one of the "most troublesome" issues faced by the legislative drafters, is noninfringing use under Section 108 "as long as such photocopying is not systematic"

[130] H.R. Rep. No. 1476, *supra* note 88 at 68, 70, 72, *See also* remarks of Chairman Kastenmeier, Cong. Rec.—House, at H10880 (Sept. 22, 1976).

[131] H.R. Rep. No. 1476, *supra* note 88 at 72.

[132] Conference Report, H.R. Rep. No. 1733, 94th Cong. 2d Sess. 70 (1976). "The conferees accept as part of their understanding of fair use the Guidelines for Classroom Copying in Not-for-Profit Educational Institutions with respect to books and periodicals appearing at pp. 68–70 of the House Report (H. Rept. No. 94–1476 as corrected at p. H10727 of the Congressional Record for September 21, 1976), and for educational uses of music appearing at pp. 70–71 of the House report, as amended in the statement appearing at p. H10875 of the Congressional Record for September 21, 1976. The conferees also endorse the statement concerning the meaning of the word 'teacher' in the guidelines for books and periodicals, and the application of fair use in the case of use of television programs within the confines of a nonprofit educational institution for the deaf and hearing impaired, both of which appear on p. H10875 of the Congressional Record of September 22, 1976."

[133] H.R. Rep. No. 1476, *supra* note 88 at 66.

[134] 17 U.S.C. § 108(f)(4) (1976); Cong. Rec.—House, at H10878.

and does not constitute "a substitute for purchase or subscription." [135]

All permissible library duplication is subject to the requirement of copyright notice.[136] Each copy made for users must include notice of copyright.[137] In addition, the "library [must display] prominently, at the place where orders are accepted, and [must include] on its order form, a warning of copyright in accordance with requirements that the Register of Copyrights shall prescribe by regulation." [138] A library can allow unsupervised use of reproducing equipment maintained on its premises without incurring liability, if the equipment displays a notice that the making of a copy may be subject to the copyright law.[139]

Section 108 specifies the conditions under which a library may make single copies of copyrighted material. It is not an infringement for a library, or any of its employees, to duplicate in facsimile form and distribute *one* copy or phonorecord of a work provided the reproduction or distribution is made without any purpose of direct or indirect commercial advantages and the collections of the library are open to the public.[140]

The noncommercial advantage stipulation

> is intended to preclude a library or archives in a profit-making organization from providing photocopies of copyrighted materials to

[135] Remarks of Chairman Kastenmeier, CONG. REC.—HOUSE, at 10874 (Sept. 22, 1976).

[136] 17 U.S.C. § 108(f)(1) (1976).

"(f) Nothing in this section—

> (1) shall be construed to impose liability for copyright infringement upon a library or archives or its employees for the unsupervised use of reproducing equipment located on its premises: *Provided*, That such equipment displays a notice that the making of a copy may be subject to the copyright law."

[137] *Id. at* § 108(a)(3).

[138] *Id.* at § 108(d)(2), (e)(2).

[139] *Id.* at § 108(f)(1).

[140] *Id.* at § 108 (a).

employees engaged in furtherance of the organization's commercial enterprise, unless such copying qualifies as a fair use, or the organization has obtained the necessary copyright licenses. A commercial organization should purchase the number of copies of a work that it requires, or obtain the consent of the copyright owner to the making of the photocopies.[141]

The practical implications for libraries in profit-making institutions of this provision were clarified in the House Report.[142] Generally speaking, libraries in for-profit institutions are prohibited from making photocopies "when there is direct or indirect commercial gain resulting from the *reproduction or distribution* of the photocopy *itself*, as distinct from any ultimate profit-making motivation behind the enterprise in which the library is located."[143] Isolated, spontaneous duplication by such libraries, even if given to employees, is covered by Section 108; the key is whether the purpose of the distribution is to substitute for subscriptions or purchases.[144] Reproduction of published works to replace copies that are damaged, deteriorating, lost, or stolen is permitted if the library, after a reasonable effort, deter-

[141] S. Rep. No. 473, *supra* note 90 at 67.

[142] Under Section 108, a library in a profit-making institution, such as the research and development departments of chemical, pharmaceutical, automobile, and oil corporations, the library of a proprietary hospital, the collections owned by a law or medical partnership, etc., cannot

"(a) use a single subscription or copy to supply its employees with multiple copies of material relevant to their work; or

"(b) use a single subscription or copy to supply its employees, on request, with single copies of material relevant to their work, whehe the arrangement if "systematic" in the sense of deliberately substituting photocopying for subscription or purchase; or

"(c) use "interlibrary loan" arrangements for obtaining photocopies in such aggregate quantities as to substitute for subscriptions or purchase of material needed by employees in their work.

"Moreover, a library in a profit-making organization could not evade these obligations by installing reproducing equipment on its premises for unsupervised use by the organization's staff."

H.R. Rep. No. 1476, *supra* note 88 at 74–75.

[143] Letter to members of the Medical Library Association, Inc., Aug. 13, 1976; *see* H.R. Rep. No. 1476, *supra* note 88 at 75.

[144] H.R. Rep. No. 1733, *supra* note 132 at 74.

mines that an unused replacement cannot be obtained at a fair price.[145] Similarly, out-of-print works, including phonorecords, may be reproduced in their entirety at the request of the user provided that it is established that a copy cannot be obtained at a fair price.[146] Both provisions protect the potential market of the copyright holder.

Subsection (d) of Section 108 authorizes the reproduction of an entire article, but *no more than one such article* or other contribution to a copyrighted collection or periodical issue. The duplication of *a small part of* any other copyrighted work is also permitted. The copy may be made by the library where the user makes the request or through an interlibrary loan.[147] These provisions maintain the entire-copy expansion of traditional fair-use doctrine of *Williams and*

[145] 17 U.S.C. § 108(c) (1976); S. REP. No. 473, *supra* note 95 at 68; H.R. REP. No. 1476, *supra* note 88 at 75–76.

[146] The Senate Report places the burden of establishing unavailability on the user. "Subsection (e) authorizes the reproduction and distribution of a copy of a work, with certain exceptions, at the request of the user of the collection if the *user* has established that an unused copy cannot be obtained at a fair price." S. REP. No. 473, *supra* note 95 at 68 (emphasis added). The language of the section, however, indicates that the responsibility falls on the library. It is further required that: "(1) the copy or phonorecord becames the property of the user, and the library or archives has had no notice that the copy or phonorecord would be used for any purpose other than private study, scholarship, or research; and

"(2) the library or archives displays prominently, at the place where orders are accepted, and includes on its order form a warning of copyright in accordance with requirements that the Register of Copyrights shall prescribe by regulation." 17 U.S.C. § 108(3) (1976).

[147] "(d) The rights of reproduction and distribution under this section apply to a copy, made from the collection of a library or archives where the user makes his or her request or from that of another library or archives, of no more than one article or other contribution to a copyrighted collection or periodical issue, or to a copy or phonorecord of a small part of any other copyrighted work, if—

"(1) the copy or phonorecord becomes the property of the user, and the library or archives has had no notice that the copy or phonorecord would be used for any purpose other than private study, scholarship, or research; and

"(2) the library or archives displays prominently, at the place where orders are accepted, and includes on its order from a warning of copyright in accordance with requirements that the Register of Copyrights shall prescribe by regulation." *Id.* at § 108(d).

Wilkins, at least with respect to the duplication of entire articles from periodicals for private use. The reach of the section, and with it, implicitly, the scope of *Williams and Wilkins,* is limited, however, by the prohibitions of Section (g).

The Senate version of Section (g), which reads as follows:

> (g) The rights of reproduction and distribution under this section extend to the isolated and unrelated production or distribution of a single copy or phonorecord of the same material on separate occasions, but do not extend to cases where the library or archives, or its employee:
>
> (1) is aware or has substantial reason to believe that it is engaging in the related or concerted reproduction or distribution of multiple copies or phonorecords of the same material, whether made on one occasion or over a period of time, and whether intended for aggregate use by one or more individuals or for separate use by the individual members of a group; or
>
> (2) engages in the systematic reproduction or distribution of single or multiple copies or phonorecords of material described in subsection (d),[148]

"provoked a storm of controversy, centering around the extent to which the restrictions on 'systematic' activities would prevent the continuation and development of interlibrary networks and other arrangements involving the exchange of photocopies."[149] The House Committee, in response, and "after thorough consideration" added to Section 108(g)(2) the proviso:

> *Provided,* that nothing in this clause prevents a library or archives from participating in interlibrary arrangements that do not have, as their purpose or effect, that the library or archives receiving such copies or phonorecords for distribution does so in such aggregate quantities as to substitute for a subscription to or purchase of such work.[150]

[148] S. Rep. No. 473, *supra* note 90 at 6–7.
[149] H.R. Rep. No. 1476, *supra* 88 at 77–78.
[150] *Id.* at 78; 17 U.S.C. § 108(g)(2) (1976).

In addition, the Committee amended Section 504(c) to "insulate librarians from unwarranted liability" and added Subsection (i) to Section 108[151] to provide for further studies by the Register of Copyrights at five-year intervals "to report on the practical success of the section . . . and to make recommendations for any needed changes."[152]

The House amendment left still unresolved the precise meaning of "such aggregate quantities as to substitute for a subscription to or purchase of such work."[153] That task fell to the newly founded National Commission on New Technological Uses of Copyrighted Works (CONTU).[154] Guidelines interpreting this provision were adopted by CONTU after "lengthy consultations" with author-publisher groups and the library community[155] in time for last-minute qualified adoption by the Conference Committee.

The Committee endorsed the guidelines as a reasonable

[151] *Id.*; 17 U.S.C. § 108(i) (1976).

[152] H.R. REP. No. 1733, *supra* note 132 at 71.

"Five years from the effective date of this Act, and at five-year intervals thereafter, the Register of Copyrights, after consulting with representatives of authors, book and periodical publishers, and other owners of copyright materials, and with representatives of library users and librarians, shall submit to the Congress a report setting forth the extent to which this section has achieved the intended statutory balancing of the rights of creators, and the needs of users. The report should also describe any problems that may have arisen, and present legislative or other recommendations, if warranted." 17 U.S.C. § 108(i) (1976).

[153] The Senate Report had provided a few illustrative examples:

"[I]f a college professor instructs his class to read an article from a copyrighted journal, the school library would not be permitted, under subsection (g), to reproduce copies of the article for the members of the class; . . .

"A library with a collection of journals in biology informs other libraries with similar collections that it will maintain and build its own collection and will make copies of articles from these journals available to them and their patrons on request. Accordingly, the other libraries discontinue or refrain from purchasing subscriptions to these journals and fulfill their patrons' requests for articles by obtaining photocopies from the source library." S. REP. No. 473, *supra* note 90 at 70.

[154] The Act of Dec. 31, 1976, Pub. L. No. 93–573, § 201, 88 Stat. 1873, established in the Library of Congress a National Commission on New Technological Uses of Copyrighted Works.

[155] H.R. REP. No. 1733, *supra* note 132 at 71.

interpretation of the "substitution for a subscription" proviso but stressed that the guidelines are not determinative in themselves, particularly since "they deal with an evolving situation that will . . . require their continuous reevaluation and adjustment." [156]

These guidelines, together with those governing educational use, have been heralded by an agency of the United Nations, the World Intellectual Property Organization, as a means of halting "indiscriminate copying by libraries and schools." [157] They place a clear restriction on the extensive duplication that the *Williams and Wilkins* court found fair, and as such will retard, if not halt, the almost limitless enlargement of fair use augured by that decision. Nevertheless, like their counterparts in education, the library guidelines modify traditional fair use analysis in their emphasis on quantitative specificity, a feature undoubtedly mandated by practical necessity.

The library guidelines do not embrace periodicals "the issue date of which is more than five years prior to the date when request for the copy thereof is made. . . . The meaning of the proviso to subsection 108(g)(2) in such case[s] is left to future interpretation." [158] Generally speaking, the guidelines provide that a library requesting photocopies of articles from periodicals through interlibrary loan may receive within one year *five* photocopies from a single periodical to which it does not subscribe. The filled request of a *sixth* copy from the same periodical within one calendar year constitutes an infringement.[159]

[156] *Id.* at 71.

[157] Mitgang, *New Copyright Law Held a Boon for the U.S.*, N.Y. Times, Oct. 10, 1976 at 17.

[158] H.R. Rep. No. 1733, *supra* note 132 at 72.

[159] As used in the proviso of subsection 108(g)(2), the words ". . . such aggregate quantities as to substitute for a subscription to or purchase of such work" shall mean:

"(a) with respect to any given periodical (as opposed to any given issue of a periodical), filled requests of a library or archives (a "requesting entity") within

The five-copy limit also applies to filled requests for copies of works other than periodicals, such as requests for poetry or fiction from a copyrighted anthology.[160] As with periodicals, the guideline limitations on anthology duplication apply only to those published within five years prior to the request. It has been suggested, however, that, without a longer period of protection, authors of literary works "might lose some of the anthology rights market." It was agreed that, should empirical evidence develop that "interlibrary traffic" adversely affects the sale of anthology rights, the guidelines would be reevaluated.[161]

The onus of record-keeping falls on the requesting library.[162] The supplying library may not fill a request unless it is "accompanied by a representation . . . that the request was made in conformity with these guidelines." The requesting entity can obviate the five-copy limit if it has in force or has entered an order for a subscription to a periodical.[163]

Like the educational guidelines, the library guidelines represent a compromise, "an appropriate statutory balancing of the rights of creators, and the needs of users." [164] Similar questions arise about the acceptance of each of the guidelines by the courts, although the legislative creation of

---

any calendar year for a total of six or more copies of an article or articles published in such periodical within five years prior to the date of the request." *Id.* at 72. It may be particularly important to stress that liability arises with the sixth copy since some accounts of the CONTU guidelines have used the confusing expression "up to six copies." *See* Winkler, *A Sweeping Revision of the Copyright Laws*, CHRONICLE FOR HIGHER EDUCATION 1 (Oct. 4, 1976).

[160] H.R. REP. No. 1733, *supra* note 132 at 73.

[161] S. Wagner, *House Passes S. 22, CONTU Offers Photocopy Guides*, PUBLISHERS WEEKLY 30, Oct. 4, 1976.

[162] "The requesting entity shall maintain records of all requests made by it for copies or phonorecords of any materials to which those guidelines apply and shall maintain records of the fulfillment of such requests, which records shall be retained until the end of the third complete calendar year after the end of the calendar year in which the respective request shall have been made." H.R. REP. No. 1733, *supra* note 132 at 73.

[163] *Id.*

[164] S. REP. No. 473, *supra* note 90 at 70.

CONTU may lend the library guidelines greater force. The legislation anticipates inevitable changes in technology by the provision for five-year evaluative review [165] and by explicit recognition of the possibility of the creation of new systems to replace current interlibrary loan practices.[166] Such flexibility in approach is consistent with judicial application of fair use principles. Similarly, the general purpose of the periodic review which is to ensure "the intended statutory balancing of the rights of creators and the needs of users" [167] is a continuation of traditional analysis. On the other hand, it is not impossible that the formulation of guidelines has set a precedent so that the future development of the doctrine of fair use may fall largely into the hands of a quasi-regulatory agency with concomitant modifications in judicial influence over its evolution.

CONCLUSION

The doctrine of fair use, a judicially created concept, is intrinsically congruent with the constitutional values of copyright law. Although ostensibly in derogation of the copyright holder's exclusive rights granted under former copyright legislation, the fundamental principles on which fair use rests are not at variance with the constitutionally designated purpose of copyright legislation. Further, despite the continuing similarity for over 100 years of the criteria by which courts decide whether use is fair, the judiciary has recently displayed a tendency to rely on constitutional rationale in applying the doctrine. The revised statute's codification of fair use reflects the doctrine's inherent constitutional basis.

Modifications of the doctrine's traditional emphasis are discernible in explicit endorsement of entire-work copying

[165] 17 U.S.C. § 108(i) (1976).
[166] H.R. Rep. No. 1733, *supra* note 132 at 72.
[167] H.R. Rep. No. 1476, *supra* note 88 at 78.

for private use in both recent case law and the revised statute. Technological change has forced adjustments in the time-honored test based on the substantiality of the amount appropriated, but a trend toward permitting more than insignificant copying had already begun outside the realm of photoduplication. The *Williams and Wilkins* decision may have been but an extreme application of this gradual shift. The provisions of the revised statute adopt this tendency by designating some entire-work copying noninfringing. Moreover, the permitted duplication, in most cases, serves the same function as the original, a departure from traditional fair use principles. But statutory acceptance of this radical expansion is qualified; permissible entire-work copying is restricted to limited purposes and stops short of the wholesale copying the *Williams and Wilkins* court found to be fair use.

Although the criterion of the amount of the copyrighted work used retains some of its viability under the statute, the test underwent a marked transformation in character during the codification of the doctrine. The quantitative specificity by which the guidelines interpret fair use is more akin to agency regulation than to the amorphous judicial criteria of fair use. Specific rules for general classes of use are set forth in place of particularized case-by-case balancing. The periodic review of Section 108 buttresses this regulatory characteristic and may signal the future diminution of *judicial* development of the doctrine.

In accompaniment with these changes in the substantiality of appropriation criterion and, to a certain extent, because of them, greater weight has been placed on the always important test of impairment of the value of the copyrighted work. Moreover, one strand of this latter test has received increasing emphasis: it has recently been seen less in terms of invasion of the copyright holder's exclusive right to make other versions of the work and more as a decrease in his financial reward from the present version. The restrictions of the guidelines designed to protect the market for the copyrighted work reflect this emphasis, as did the analysis of the *Williams and Wilkins* court.

The designation in the statute of certain favored uses is a continuation of judicial practice. Despite legislative disclaimers on the conclusiveness of nonprofit use, however, the noncommercial nature of the use may assume greater significance than in prior case law. When applied in conjunction with a growing emphasis on constitutional dimensions of fair use, this factor must weigh heavily toward finding nonprofit use fair. Both recent judicial decisions and legislative history demonstrate the enhanced importance accorded the public's right of access to copyrighted works. It is, for example, the declared legislative intent of the new copyright statute "to maximize artistic endeavors while protecting the public from unwarranted restrictions on access to creative works." [168] While such emphasis on public benefit may represent no more than an inconsequential variation in the national concept of copyright and therefore imply no impending fundamental alteration in traditional fair use balancing, it may well portend the eventual emergence of the fair use doctrine as a means of ensuring the American public expanded free access to the works of creative artists in their entirety.

[168] CONG. REC.—HOUSE, at H10880 (Sept. 22, 1976). "At every intersection the committee sought, with great diligence, to resolve the differences in a manner which would maximize artistic endeavors while protecting the public from unwarranted restrictions on access to the creative works."

NATIONAL THIRD PRIZE

Performance Rights in Sound Recordings: How Far to the Horizon?

H. CRAIG HAYES

UNIVERSITY OF NORTH CAROLINA SCHOOL OF LAW

It don't look all that far, no
No more than thirty mile
But I set out thirty years ago
Been walkin' all that while . . .[1]

WHEN an interpretive singer records a song written by another, and it is played by a broadcasting station or other commercial user, *what* is being publicly performed? Is it the song itself, the singer's interpretive rendition of the song, or both? Mick Jagger, who got his start by imitating classic rhythm and blues stylists, would surely argue that it is "The Singer, Not The Song." In fact, he has a copyright in a song by that name.

Current copyright law in the United States grants a performance right to the composer of the song itself; however, when played by a broadcaster or other commercial user, only "the song" embodied in the sound recording is being publicly performed.[2] But why do we buy a record album or attend a

[1] From "How Far to the Horizon?" by Jesse Winchester; copyright 1974, Fourth Floor Music, Inc. (ASCAP).
[2] 17 U.S.C. § 1(e) (1970).

specific concert if not to listen to the performer take that same melody and create an ingenious series of highly sophisticated harmonic extensions, intricate voicings, and impassioned improvisations that weave into a tapestry of deeply emotional sounds—to hear the singer, the instrumentalists, or the orchestra perform, play, or sing that song? Both the song itself and the singer's creative and expressive interpretation of that song, when in the form of a sound recording, deserve protection against unfettered commercial use.

The purpose of this paper is to examine the legal and equitable considerations inherent in granting federal copyright protection in the form of a performance right to the record producers and to the performing artists whose creative efforts are embodied in a sound recording.

It is a traditional copyright concept that one who uses another's creative work for profit must pay the creator of that work. The exclusive right of a copyright owner to authorize the public performance of his creative work is known as a "performance right." Not every creative work eligible for copyright protection is capable of being performed; for this reason, the term is usually in reference to literary, dramatic, or musical works. The Copyright Act of 1909 generally grants the composer of a musical composition the right to control the reproduction, distribution, adaptation, and commercial performance of the musical work.[3] Therefore, the holder of a copyright in a musical composition could prohibit public performance of his music for profit whether by musicians performing live or, with the advent of radio, by broadcast of a sound recording containing that music.[4]

When the 1909 Act was passed, the record industry was just beginning. Musicians played before live audiences, and the music could be heard again only by one's attending another performance. The aural performance was simul-

[3] 17 U.S.C. § 1(a), (b), (e) (1970).
[4] 17 U.S.C. § 1(e).

taneously visual—"live" meant seeing as well as hearing, similar to the presentation of drama through the theater.

The congressional power to grant exclusive rights to holders of copyright is derived from Article 1, Section 8, Clause 8 of the Constitution: "To promote the Progress of . . . the useful Arts, by securing for limited Times to Authors . . . the exclusive Right to their respective Writings. . . ." [5] The constitutional provision respecting copyright contemplates exclusive protection of "Writings" of "Authors."

> These terms have not been construed in their narrow literal sense but, rather, with the reach necessary to reflect the broad scope of constitutional principles. While an "author" may be viewed as an individual who writes an original composition, the term, in its constitutional sense has been construed to mean an "originator," or "he to whom anything owes its origin." [6]

In a similar fashion, the word "writings" "may be interpreted to include any physical rendering of the fruits of creative intellectual or aesthetic labor." [7] Congress has the power to determine at any time whether a "particular category of 'writings' is worthy of national protection and the incidental expenses of federal administration. . . ." [8]

The history of our federal copyright law shows that, as technology has expanded and necessitated new areas worthy of protection, Congress has eventually responded with protection to new classes of "writings." [9] Whenever an artistic

[5] U.S. Const. art. I, § 8, cl. 8.

[6] Goldstein v. California, 412 U.S. 546, 561 (1973) *quoting in part* Burrow-Giles Lithographic Co. v. Sarony, 111 U.S. 53, 58 (1884).

[7] Goldstein, 412 U.S. at 561, *citing* Trade-Mark Cases, 100 U.S. 82, 94 (1879).

[8] Goldstein, 412 U.S. at 559.

[9] The first congressional copyright statute governed only books, maps, and charts. Act of May 31, 1790, ch. 15, 1 Stat. 124. In 1802, prints were added. Act of April 29, 1802, c. 36, 2 Stat. 171. In 1831, musical compositions were added to the list of protected works. Act of Feb. 3, 1813, ch. 16, 4 Stat. 463. In 1865, photographs and photographic negatives were added. Act of Mar. 3, 1865, ch. 123, 13 Stat. 540. In 1870, the list was expanded to include paintings, drawings, chromos, statuettes, statuary, and models or designs of fine art. Act of July 8, 1870, ch. 230, 16 Stat. 198. In the 1909 Copyright Revision, Congress provided

or intellectual concept existing in the heart, the mind, or the eye of a creator becomes embodied in a form or medium of expression that is tangible, original, discernible, and capable of reproduction commercially for profit, Congress may grant copyright protection.

SOUND RECORDINGS: A LONG TIME COMING

Only recently has federal copyright protection been expanded to include sound recordings. Although a massive revision of the Copyright Law was already in motion to amend title 17 of the United States Code in its entirety, it was determined that the creation of a limited copyright in sound recordings should not await action on the general revision bill. Consequently, the Sound Recording Amendment of 1971 was enacted to provide federal statutory protection to sound recordings fixed and published between February 15, 1972 (the effective date), and January 1, 1975 (the expiration date).[10] It was thought that, by putting a terminal date on the legislation, a determination of whether it should be extended permanently could be judged on the basis of actual experience. The Amendment granted a limited copyright for sound recordings, held generally by the record company,[11] but it protected only against copying by unauthorized duplication, "pirating." This amendment became an effective weapon against record and tape pirates who, by

---

eleven categories of works to be protected. Act of March 4, 1909, ch. 320, 35 Stat. 1075. In 1912, the list of categories was expanded to include motion pictures. Act of Aug. 24, 1912, ch. 356, 37 Stat. 488. Finally, in 1971, the list of categories was amended to include sound recordings. Pub. L. No. 92–140, 85 Stat. 391 (1971).

[10] Pub. L. No. 92–140, 85 Stat. 391 (1971). *See* M. Nimmer, Copyright, § 109.2 (1972).

[11] The owner of copyright in sound recordings is generally the record company, or alternatively, the producer named on the label. For the purposes of this paper, the terms *record company* and *record producer* are synonymous.

directly copying the records and tapes, thereby avoided the high costs of recording and its inherent economic risks. The constitutionality of this amendment was upheld by a three-judge court in *Shaab v. Kliendienst.*[12] On the last day of 1974, the expiration date was struck out, and the criminal penalties for commercial piracy were strengthened against manufacture, use, or sale of unauthorized copies of sound recordings fixed after February 15, 1972.[13]

The Copyright Act of 1976, a general revision of the copyright law which becomes effective January 1, 1978, with minor exceptions continues this limited federal protection of sound recordings fixed on or after February 15, 1972.[14] Sound recordings that are fixed before February 15, 1972, have no federal copyright protection against unauthorized duplication, but the majority of states have enacted some form of protection under common law principles of unfair competition or by specific criminal antipiracy statutes.[15] The Supreme Court upheld the constitutionality of the California antipiracy statute as applied to sound recordings fixed prior to that date in the *Goldstein* case.[16]

Such protection under the guise of state law with respect to pre-1972 recordings is limited by section 301(c) of the Copyright Act of 1976 to a period ending February 15, 2047, which is seventy-five years after the February 15, 1972, date

[12] 345 F. Supp. 589 (D.D.C. 1972).

[13] Pub. L. No. 93–573, 88 Stat. 1873 (1974).

[14] Pub. L. No. 94–558, 90 Stat. 2541 (amending 17 U.S.C. in its entirety) (1976) [hereinafter cited as ACT].

[15] *See, e.g.*, ARIZ. REV. STAT. ANN. § 13–1024 (Supp. 1973); CAL. PENAL CODE ANN. § 653 h (West 1970); FLA. STAT. ANN. § 543.041 (1972); N.Y. GEN. BUS. LAW § 561 (McKinney 1968); N.C. GEN. STAT. §§ 14–432 to 14–437 (ch. 1279) (Sess. Laws 1974); TENN. CODE ANN. §§ 39–4244 to 39–4250 (ch. 166) (Supp. 1971); TEX. REV. CIV. STAT. ANN. art. 9012 (Supp. 1974).

In addition, eighteen other states have enacted similar legislation. *See* Bard and Kurlantzick, *A Public Performance Right in Sound Recordings: How to Alter the System Without Improving It*, 43 GEO. WASH. L. REV. 152, 155 n. 9 (1974).

[16] Goldstein, 412 U.S. 546 (1973).

when federal copyright protection first became available for sound recordings.[17] During that period continued state law protection is available to the owner of copyright in a sound recording, coupled with the new Act's codification of existing case law creating federal civil and criminal remedies.[18] Again, the distinction must be made between the owner of the copyright in a sound recording and the owner of copyright in the underlying musical composition.

PERFORMERS: LOST IN AN OZONE OF AMBIGUITY

What is the legal status of the musical performing artist? Unless he is also the composer of the musical composition his rights are limited to his ability to contract. His aim is to create and play music and to share this creative experience with the listening audience. Is the promotion and progress of the musical arts being retarded by the denial of the performing artist's right to profit from the use of his recorded performance? The sound recording is the *only* copyrightable work the commercial use of whose performance cannot be controlled by the performer. Certainly an important aspect of our inquiry into proprietary rights in a performance is the *use* of that performance. Ethics and equity are important also, but economic exploitation and commercial use of a recorded performance to the benefit of those not involved in the creative process is unconscionable.

Copyright has long been concerned with the visual, what can be seen, as contrasted to what can be heard, a practice derived from the constitutional reference to "writings."[19] Is the visual any more creatively intelligible than the aural?

[17] ACT at § 301(a), (c) (1976).
[18] ACT at § 501, §§ 502–505 (1976).
[19] U.S. CONST. art. I, § 8, cl. 8.

Sound is the basic form of communication for all animals—mammals, birds, reptiles alike. Should the creator of sound in the form of an improvisational rendition or performance embodied in a sound recording be distinguished from the owner or the person having the power to exploit that creation?

What are the competing values and interests that emerge from an analysis of the copyright status of sound recordings? We want to encourage, promote, and maximize artistic endeavor and, correspondingly, intellectual and social development by granting a limited monopoly in the form of copyright protection to those creative individuals. On the other hand, it is fundamental to our democratic society to provide free access to certain forms of communication without unwarranted public restrictions placed on the consuming public—the viewers, readers, and listeners. But any such concern of free access should be directed toward the consuming public, not in favor of those who exploit the creative work through whatever vehicle of mass communication. We certainly will always find pure nonprofit, educational, or social uses where exemption from copyright infringement will be necessary, and the benefit of free access to the consuming public will clearly outweigh any economic detriment to the copyright holder. But even so, in such situations, we should proceed with extreme caution and tread very lightly indeed.

THE NEW COPYRIGHT LAW

As the twentieth century steadily advances in the area of the entertainment media, new forms and uses of creative works seem to appear in the marketplace every day. In the Copyright Act of 1976 Congress saw the possibility of ever-expanding forms and uses of creative expression brought about by scientific and technological development. Their purpose was neither to limit the scope of copyrightable technology nor "to allow unlimited expansion into areas . . .

outside the present congressional intent."[20] Section 102 of the Act defines the general area of subject matter to be protected as subsisting in "original works of authorship fixed in any tangible medium of expression, now known or later developed, from which they can be perceived, reproduced, or otherwise communicated, either directly or with the aid of a machine or device."[21]

As a basic prerequisite to copyright protection, section 102 perpetuates the existing requirement that a work be fixed in a "tangible medium of expression," and adds that this medium may be one "now known or later developed."[22]

Under the first sentence of the definition of "fixed" in section 101, a work would be considered "fixed in a tangible medium of expression" if there has been an authorized embodiment in a copy or phonorecord, and if that embodiment "is sufficiently permanent and stable" to permit the work "to be perceived, reproduced, or otherwise communicated for a period of more than transitory duration." The second sentence makes clear that, in the case of "[a] work consisting of sounds, images, or both, that are being transmitted," the work is regarded as fixed if a fixation is being made at the same time as the transmission.[23]

"Live" broadcasts, such as live performances of music, that are reaching the public in unfixed form but are simultaneously being recorded (on videotape, film, etc.) are therefore subject to statutory protection against unauthorized reproduction or retransmission of the broadcast. If the performance is first taped or filmed, and then subsequently transmitted to the public, the recorded work would be analogous to a motion picture, subject to statutory protection. In addition,

[20] H.R. Rep. No. 1476, 94th Cong., 2d Sess. 51 (1976) [hereinafter cited as H.R. Rep. No. 1476].

[21] Act at § 102(a) (1976).

[22] H.R. Rep. No. 1476 at 52.

[23] Act at § 101 (1976).

[i]f the program content is transmitted live to the public while being recorded at the same time, the case would be treated the same; the copyright owner would not be forced to rely on common law rather than statutory rights in proceeding against the infringing user of the live broadcast.[24]

Whereas section 5 of the Copyright Act of 1909 specified fourteen separate classes of works eligible for registration,[25] section 102 of the Act of 1976 lists seven broad categories which the concept of "works of authorship" is said to "include." [26] The use of the word "include," as defined in section 101, makes plain that such a list is "illustrative and not limitative," [27] and that, with respect to the general area of copyrightable subject matter, "original works of authorship" should be sufficiently flexible "to free the courts from rigid or outmoded concepts of the scope of particular categories." [28]

In addition to sound recordings, section 102 specifically includes "pantomimes and choreographic works" in the categories of the works of authorship.[29]

DANCE

Choreography has been accepted and integrated into television, theater, and motion pictures and has become a valuable part of the entire entertainment industry. Even musicians have sufficiently utilized choreographic routines to complement their performances, as elements of both music and drama are grafted into one creative expression. Choreography consists of "a specific pattern of body movements, performed by dancers . . . , which conveys thought, drama, or emotion to an audience." [30] Choreographic work in the

[24] H.R. Rep. No. 1476 at 52.
[25] 17 U.S.C. § 5 (1970).
[26] Act at § 102(a) (1976).
[27] *Id.* at § 101.
[28] H.R. Rep. No. 1476 at 53.
[29] Act at § 102 (1976).
[30] Ordway, *Choreography and Copyright*, 15 ASCAP Copyright L. Symp. 172 (1967).

context of copyright relates to both the dance itself, as conceived by the author and performed for the audience, and the graphic representation of the dance itself as recorded in some concrete form. The Laban system is a dance notation system which consists of scoring the dance in a manner similar to that used for music through the use of symbols and lines, accompanied by a detailed textual description of the dance movements. Other choreographic works have been recorded on film or videotape, and although economically unfeasible, film or video recordation is a perfectly acceptable form of registration for choreographic works or pantomime.[31]

The exclusive right to perform the copyrighted work publicly is the most important right to the holder of copyright in a choreographic work or pantomime, since such works, like dramatic and musical works, are created with the intention to perform publicly. The 1976 Act grants the exclusive right to publicly perform and display the copyrighted work to literary, musical, dramatic, and choreographic works, pantomimes, motion pictures and other audiovisual works,[32] subject to specific limitations.[33] Choreography, as well as pantomime, then, is an expression of an author's interpretive style, an emotional impression representing an original creation of authorship. As such, it is analogous to an interpretive performance by a musician: both are original works of authorship and should be granted exclusive rights when reduced to a tangible form or medium of expression.

LIVE PERFORMERS—REPLACED BY THEIR OWN RECORDINGS

With the advent of sound recordings and the emergence of

[31] *Id.* at 173–74.
[32] ACT at § 106(4), (5) (1976).
[33] ACT at §§ 107–118 (1976).

the broadcasting industry, a vast new frontier appeared. Transcribed performances on the sound recording began to compete with live performances; eventually, the sound recording completely replaced the live musician in radio broadcasting. Television broadcasters, night clubs, theaters, taverns, discotheques, stage plays, dance companies, and many other former markets for live musicians have turned to the sound recording as the catalyst in their respective economic and cultural experiments.

During the jazz era in the thirties and forties, it wasn't uncommon for musicians to walk into a studio off the street, record an all-star session of improvisational magnificence, receive a payment of a rather insignificant amount, and never realize another cent off their creation. And yet, 40 years later, when that record has been played 40 million times, still there is no proprietary status attached to the all-star cast of "mere performers," whose talents were utilized to make the composer's creative sketches come alive.

JUDICIAL EFFORTS

The first case to attach a recognizable common law property right to a performer's recorded work was *Waring v. WDAS Broadcasting Station, Inc.*[34] There, the Supreme Court of Pennsylvania enjoined broadcast of recordings which bore the legend "not licensed for radio broadcasting," holding that, although the sale of phonographic records would normally destroy whatever common law rights there might be in a performance, the restrictive legend on the records created an equitable servitude which preserved the performer's right and prevented the work from falling into the public domain.[35]

[34] 327 Pa. 433, 194 A. 631 (1937).

[35] The validity of an equitable servitude on chattels such as sound recordings was challenged in 1939 by the North Carolina General Assembly, who immedi-

The Court was careful to distinguish between the underlying musical composition and the performers' contribution to it "of novel intellectual or artistic value." [36]

Just three years later a similar case arose in the Second Circuit. In *RCA Mfg. Co. v. Whiteman,*[37] Judge Learned Hand, writing for the court, found that such a restrictive statement on the records could not prevent the performance embodied in the recording from passing into the public domain upon sale of the records, which divested common law rights in the performance. Judge Hand was careful to distinguish between the abandonment of rights in the musical composition and the *performance* of that composition.[38] The implication was that a performer had a common law copyright in his recorded performance, but only if the records were not distributed or sold. There were a number of decisions involving such common law property rights and theories of unfair competition following the *Waring* and *Whiteman* decisions.[39]

---

ately passed a statute which prohibited any rights to further restrict the use of sound recordings sold for use within North Carolina, N. C. GEN. STAT. § 66–28 (1939 e. 113); S. C. CODE § 66–101 (1942); FLA. STAT. §§ 543.02–.03 (1943). This was in response to Waring v. Dunlea, 26 F. Supp. 338 (E.D.N.C. 1939), in which a federal district court in North Carolina enjoined a local station from unlicensed broadcasting of similar recordings. *See also,* Baer, *Performer's Rights to Enjoin Unlicensed Broadcast of Recorded Renditions,* 19 N.C. L. REV. 202 (1941).

Contra, California has just recently enacted a statute providing for a mandatory payment to the artist (creator) of a work of fine art (painting, sculpture, drawing) of 5% of the sale price, whenever such work of fine art is sold and the seller resides in California or the sale takes place in California. If the seller or agent is unable to locate the artist, the money is transferred to the state Arts Council. CAL. CIVIL CODE § 986 (1976).

[36] 327 Pa. 433, 441, 194 A. 631, 639 (1937).

[37] 114 F.2d 86 (2d Cir.), *cert. denied,* 311 U.S. 712 (1940).

[38] 114 F.2d at 86, 88.

[39] *See e.g.,* Ettore v. Philco Television Broadcasting Corp., 229 F.2d 481 (2d Cir.), *cert. denied,* 351 U.S. 926 (1958); Capitol Records, Inc. v. Mercury Records Corp., 221 F.2d 657 (2d Cir. 1955); Man v. Warner Bros. Inc., 317 F. Supp. 50 (S.D.N.Y. 1970); Granz v. Harris, 98 F. Supp. 906 (S.D.N.Y.

Fred Waring and Paul Whiteman were directors of the National Association For The Performing Arts (NAPA), which helped initiate the first congressional attempt at drafting a bill in support of a performance right, without success.[40] In the summer of 1939, a copyright for the performers and a separate copyright for the recorders of sound recordings was considered by the Shotwell Committee for the Study of Copyright.[41] Such recognition was still a bit premature for reconciling the serious conflicts of interest arising in this field.[42] Again in 1947, an attempt to introduce a bill was reported adversely by a subcommittee of the House Judiciary Committee.[43]

There was a general reluctance to grant a proprietary right to performers under the law of copyright. Does the performer express an original intellectual creation in his interpretive performance? In *Supreme Records v. Decca Records,* Judge Yankwich offered this suggestion: "it is my view that before a musical arrangement may be protected as a right against a competitor, it must have a distinctive characteristic, aside from the composition itself, of such character that any person hearing it would become aware of the distinctiveness of the arrangement." [44]

1951), *aff'd and modified,* 198 F.2d 585 (2d Cir. 1952); Waring v. Dunlea, 26 F. Supp. 338 (E.D.N.C. 1939); Capitol Records, Inc., v. Erickson, 2 Cal. App. 3d 526, 82 Cal. Rptr. 798 (Ct. App. 1969), *cert. denied,* 398 U.S. 960 (1970); Lennon v. Pulsebeat News, Inc., 143 U.S.P.Q. 309 (Sup. Ct. N.Y. 1964); Gieseking v. Urania Records, Inc., 17 Misc. 2d 1034, 155 N.Y.S. 2d 171 (Sup. Ct. 1956); Metropolitan Opera Assn. v. Wagner-Nichols Recording Corp., 199 Misc. 786, 101 N.Y.S. 2d 483 (Sup. Ct. 1950).

[40] H.R. 10632, 74th Cong., 2d Sess. (1936); H.R. 5375 75th Cong., 1st Sess. (1937).

[41] 84 Cong. Rec. 14799 (1939).

[42] Cong. Rec. 63, 78 (1940).

[43] H.R. Rep. No. 1270, 80 Cong., 1st Sess. (1947); 93 Cong. Rec. 15 at D406 (1947). *See also,* Chafee, *Reflections on the Law of Copyright: II,* 45 Colum. L. Rev. 719, 735–37 (1945).

[44] 90 F. Supp. 904, 908 (S.D. Cal. 1950).

In 1955, the Court of Appeals for the Second Circuit, in *Capitol Records, Inc., v. Mercury Records,*[45] held that the sale of phonograph records did not destroy the common law rights in the performances embodied in the recording. Both the majority opinion and the dissent found that the performance of a musical composition to be a "writing of an author" under the constitutional clause, but not under the Copyright Act of 1909. Judge Learned Hand wrote a well-reasoned dissenting opinion:

> I also believe that the performance or rendition of a "musical composition" is a "Writing" . . . separate from, and additional to, the "composition" itself. It follows that Congress could grant the performer a copyright upon it, provided it was embodied in a physical form capable of being copied. The propriety of this appears, when we reflect that a musical score in ordinary notation does not determine the entire performance, certainly not when it is sung or played on a stringed or wind instrument. Musical notes are composed of a "fundamental note" with harmonic overtones which do not appear on the score. There may indeed be instruments—e.g. percussive—which do not allow any latitude, though I doubt even that; but in the vast number of renditions, the performer has a wide choice, depending upon his gifts, and this makes his rendition pro tanto quite as original a "composition" as an "arrangement" or "adaptation" of the score itself, which § 1(b) makes copyrightable. Now that it has become possible to capture these contributions of the individual performer upon a physical object that can be made to reproduce them, there should be no doubt that this is within the Copyright Clause of the Constitution.[46]

Finally, the Supreme Court, in the *Goldstein* decision indicated that recordings of artistic performances may be "writings" within the reach of Clause 8;[47] coupled with the inclusion of sound recordings in the Copyright Act of 1976,[48] the decision renders any further attack on the constitution-

[45] 221 F.2d 657 (2d Cir. 1955).
[46] *Id.* at 664.
[47] 412 U.S. at 562.
[48] ACT, at §§ 106, 114 (1976).

ality of sound recordings as copyrightable subject matter redundant.

LEGISLATIVE EFFORTS

Performers continued to lobby Congress, and at various times amendments were introduced, again with little success.[49] As legislative momentum was gaining on copyright revision, performance rights in sound recordings were included as part of the general revision bill considered by the Senate Committee on the Judiciary during the 93rd Congress.[50]

Senator Hugh Scott proposed that public performance of sound recordings be subject to a compulsory or voluntary licensing system, generally based on gross receipts of the commercial user, and this proposal was a major issue in the Senate consideration of the revision bill.[51] It was reported favorably by the Senate Committee on the Judiciary [52] and the Senate Committee on Commerce,[53] only to be later withdrawn from section 114 of the full revision bill, again as a compromise, in order not to jeopardize passage of the comprehensive revision so desperately needed. Instead Senator Scott reintroduced the proposal as a separate bill, the *Performance Rights Amendment of 1975*,[54] in the 94th Congress with a simultaneous proposal in the House by Representative George Danielson.[55]

[49] S. 597, 90th Cong., 1st Sess. (1967). *See also, Copyright Law Revision, Hearings on S. 597 Before the Subcommittee of Patents, Trademarks, and Copyrights of the Senate Committee on the Judiciary*, 90th Cong., 1st Sess. 540, 1244 (1967); S. Amendment No. 9 to S. 543, 91st Cong., 1st Sess. (1969); *see generally*, Diamond, *Sound Recordings and Copyright Revision*, 53 IOWA L. REV. 839 (1968).

[50] S. 1361, 93rd Cong. 1st Sess. § 114 (1973).

[51] S. 1361, 93rd Cong., 1st Sess. § 114 (1973).

[52] S REP. No. 983 93rd Cong., 2d Sess. (1974).

[53] S. REP. No. 1035, 93rd Cong., 2d Sess. (1974).

[54] S. 1111, 94th Cong., 1st Sess. (1975).

[55] H.R. 5345, 94th Cong., 1st Sess. (1975).

Public hearings were held in July 1975, pursuant to S. 1111 by the Subcommittee of Patents, Trademarks, and Copyrights of the Senate Committee on the Judiciary. Statements and discussions included the history and efforts to obtain performance rights, the benefits of such legislation to backup and orchestral musicians, and the obligation and economic ability of the broadcasting industry to pay the proposed royalty.[56]

In particular, concern was expressed for the encouragement and development of those performing artists falling outside of the commercially successful categories. Narrative recordings, indigenous American Folk music, symphonic, operatic, and other music in the area of the fine arts, suffer from an extremely poor marketplace.[57] In fact, it was revealed that the music profession, as a whole, was highly unemployed and among the lowest paid professions in the country; according to the 1970 census, America's musicians carried a median income of $4,668, and the Unions indicated that more than 80% of their membership is generally unemployed.[58]

An amendment with respect to sound recordings could not be easily constructed within the limits and scope of the 1909 Act. The priority of the cable television issue, the status of library photocopying, the extent of fair use exemptions, and other "thorny" problems inherent in the general revision bill, accentuated by the absolute urgency and necessity of expediting its passage, moved the issue of performance rights in sound recordings back on the legislative clock once again. A compromise proposal was suggested to provide time for the

[56] S. Rep. No. 1, 94th Cong., 1st Sess. 47–68 *passim* (1975).

[57] S. Rep. No. 1, 94th Cong., 1st Sess. 9, 23–25 (1975) (Statements of Nancy Hanks, Chairman, National Endowment For the Arts; Sanford Wolff, on behalf of the American Federations of Musicians and Television and Radio Artists, AFL-CIO).

[58] S. Rep. No. 1, 94th Cong., 1st Sess. 31 (1975).

Register of Copyrights to study and consider the economic conflicts of interest.

NEW STATUS FOR SOUND RECORDINGS

Section 114 of the Act of 1976 expressly denies any right of performance with respect to sound recordings.[59] Instead, 114(d) directs the Register of Copyrights:

> [A]fter consulting with representatives of owners of copyrighted material, representatives of the broadcasting, recording, motion picture, entertainment industries, and arts organizations, representatives of organized labor and performers of copyrighted material, [to] submit to the Congress [on January 3, 1978] a report setting forth recommendations as to whether this section should be amended to provide for performers and copyright owners of copyrighted material any performance rights in such material.[60]

In preparation of this report, the Copyright Office published Notice of Inquiry in the *Federal Register*[61] on April 27, 1977, intending to elicit public comment, views, and information relating to legislative recommendations or alternatives. Public Hearings were held at the Copyright Office on July 6 and 7, 1977, and again in Beverly Hills, California, on July 26–28, 1977. These hearings were beneficial and appropriate forums for securing responses, economic data, and public comment from the major interested parties. The Copyright Office will retain an independent team of economic consultants to analyze the major economic considerations. The Report of the Register of Copyrights, if favorable, should stimulate legislative action toward resolving this issue.

[59] ACT at § 114 (1976).
[60] ACT at § 114 (d) (1976).
[61] 42 Fed. Reg. 21527–21528 (April 27, 1977); 42 Fed. Reg., 28191 (June 2, 1977). More than 120 comment letters had been received by the General Counsel of the Copyright Office by the time of the first Public Hearings on July 6, 1977.

THE INTERNATIONAL ARENA

An increasing number of talented and successful musicians have recently emerged from countries such as England, France, Japan, Australia, Canada, Mexico, Brazil, Austria, Poland, Czechoslovakia, Hungary, Sweden, Germany, West Africa, and Jamaica. The 1975 *Downbeat Magazines' Readers and Critics Jazz Poll*[62] reflects this international roster of talent with representatives from Europe, Africa, and Central and South America.

International practice with respect to payment of performance royalties is not consistent. However, most of the major music producing countries, other than the United States, do have domestic laws specifying performance royalties.[63] In some countries individual performers have a specific right to remuneration when broadcast commercially, whereas in other countries that do not grant legal rights, performers nevertheless do participate in royalties on the basis of voluntary sharing arrangements with the record producer.[64] In the United Kingdom, Ireland, Spain, and Italy, the law grants performance rights to record producers alone, but the record producers have sharing arrangements on a voluntary basis with performers.[65] In West Germany, on the other hand, the law gives performance rights to the performers, with a share to be paid producers.[66] In Japan, the four Scandinavian

[62] DOWNBEAT—MUSIC HANDBOOK '76: THE DEFINITIVE REFERENCE BOOK 66074 (1976).

[63] *Copyright Law Revision, Hearings on H.R. 2223 Before the Subcommittee on Courts, Civil Liberties, and the Administration of Justice of the House Committee on the Judiciary*, 94th Cong., 1st Sess. 1346 (1975). ("General Survey on the Legal Protection of Performers," submitted by Theo Bikel, President, Actor's Equity Association) [hereinafter cited as *Hearings on H.R. 2223*].

[64] Generally, in the context of copyright, the record company and the record producer are synonymous, *supra* n. 11.

[65] *Hearings on H.R. 2223, supra* n. 63 at 1343.

[66] S. REP. No. 1, 94th Cong. 1st Sess. 60 (1975) (Statement of the Record Industry Association of America, "International Producers of Phonograms and Videograms: General Survey of the Legal Protection of Sound Recordings As At December 31, 1974").

countries, and Czechoslovakia, national law grants performance rights to both record producer and performers.[67] In France, Belgium, and The Netherlands, the law does not specifically recognize performance rights in records, but broadcasting organizations nevertheless make payments to the record producers.[68] Such protection in other countries of the world is predominant.[69]

England has granted copyright protection to sound recordings since the British Copyright Act of 1911, classifying them as musical works, except that the term is limited to fifty years from the making of the matrix recording.[70] British performers were protected by the criminal law against unauthorized recording, filming, or broadcasting of their performances; however, only the record producer receives royalties from public performance of the sound recordings, leaving the performer to bargain for voluntary sharing arrangements.[71]

THE ROME CONVENTION

The United Kingdom was a signatory to the *International Convention for the Protection for Performers, Producers of Phonograms and Broadcasting Organizations* done at Rome, Italy, in 1961, known as the Rome Convention on Neighboring Rights.[72] The central provision regarding protection of

[67] *Hearings on H.R. 2223, supra* n. 63, at 1347–51 (1975).

[68] S. Rep. No. 1, 94th Cong. 1st Sess. 60 (1975).

[69] S. Rep. No. 1, 94th Cong., 1st Sess. 60 (1975). (The report lists 37 countries in which the law grants performance rights to performers and/or record producers.)

[70] *Copyright Act*, 1911, 1&2 Geo. 5 c. 46, § 19(1), *as amended by Copyright Act*, 1956 4 & 5 Eliz. 2, c. 74, § 12(3), 1956.

[71] *Performers' Protection Acts*, 1958–72, 6&7 Eliz. 2, c. 44 §§ 4(1), 5(1) (1958–1972).

[72] U.N.T.S. 43 (31 Dec. 1976). Ratification or Accession by: Austria, Brazil, Chile, Colombia, Congo, Costa Rica, Czechoslovakia, Denmark, Ecuador, Fiji, Federal Republic of Germany, Guatemala, Italy, Luxembourg, Mexico, Niger, Paraguay, Sweden, and the United Kingdom [hereinafter cited as Rome Convention].

performance rights in sound recordings under the Rome Convention is article 12, which reads:

> If a phonogram, published for commercial purposes, or a reproduction of such phonogram, is used directly for broadcasting or for any communication to the public, a single equitable remuneration shall be paid by the user to the performers, or to the producers of the phonograms, or to both. Domestic law may, in the absence of agreement between these parties, lay down the conditions as to the sharing of this remuneration.[73]

Article 12 contemplates some type of mutual agreement between performers and record producers regarding the sharing of this remuneration, with payment for use of the recordings to be made by the broadcasters or other commercial users.[74] However, any contracting state to the Convention may make a reservation declaring that it will limit or refuse to apply the protection granted by article 12 to phonograms whose producers are not nationals of other contracting states.[75] This allows contracting states to grant protection to other states on the basis of reciprocity. Phonograms are defined as "any exclusively aural fixation of sounds of a performance or of other sounds."[76] Though the designation "performers" is defined in terms of literary or artistic works,[77] article 9 allows any contracting state to extend the protection provided for in this Convention to artists who do not perform literary or artistic works, perhaps opening the door to allow protection of athletes, circus performers, daredevils or other "performers" who make considerable economic and personal sacrifice.[78]

[73] Rome Convention, *supra* n. 72, art. 12.
[74] *Id.* (Also called "neighboring rights" or "secondary use rights.")
[75] *Id.*, at art. 16, § 1(a)(iii), (iv). (A contracting party may either limit or not apply article 12 to its own nationals also. *Id.* at § 1(a)(i), (ii)).
[76] *Id.* at art. 3.
[77] *Id.*
[78] *Id.* at art. 9. (Such protection may not be found within the law of copyright, however.)

The Rome Convention on Neighboring Rights is extremely important in principle because it speaks in terms of the individual performing artist and of the necessity of compensation or remuneration to that individual artist. It would be a great benefit to the progress of the arts in this country for the United States to adhere to the Rome Convention. Record producers in this country are denied performance royalties from abroad. As one record company executive testified, "in Denmark, payment is made only for the performance of recordings originating in Denmark itself or in a country which grants reciprocal rights to recordings of Danish origin. As a result, no payment is made for the use of U.S. recordings there." [79]

The United States is the world's largest producer of sound recordings, yet many nations deny payments to American artists and record companies while continuing to use and exploit our music for their commercial benefit, because our country offers no reciprocal right. Should foreign commercial use of American produced sound recordings be unrestricted, undefined, and ignored when it is the most popular in the world? If this country were to follow the precedent of other nations in paying such royalties, more money would flow into this country than would flow out and thereby contribute positively to the balance of international payments.

Canada recently abandoned performance royalty payments to record producers and performers, primarily because most payments were being remitted to United States recording artists and producers while there was no reciprocity for Canadian artists in the United States. This state of affairs was aggravated by the fact that the majority of record manufacturers in Canada are subsidiaries of, or associated with,

[79] *Copyright Law Revision, Hearings on S. 597 Before the Subcommittee on Patents, Trademarks, and Copyrights of the Committee on the Judiciary, supra* note 49 at 508 (Statement of Sidney Diamond).

American firms.[80] There is an interrelationship between the Rome Convention on Neighboring Rights and the 1971 Geneva Anti-Piracy Convention, the latter an agreement which does impose a treaty obligation on the United States with respect to sound recordings originating in other countries.[81] This convention entered into force in the United States on March 10, 1974.[82]

ECONOMIC CONSIDERATIONS

If the idea of performance royalties is at least accepted on principle, then the method of implementing or establishing an effective licensing system can always be worked out. Major economic objections have been advanced by the broadcasting industry, background music services, and other commercial users, claiming that the creation of a performance royalty would impose a serious financial burden upon such users. This basic argument has effectively blocked legislative consideration of performance royalties in sound recordings for more than thirty years.

There are indeed many technical and economic difficulties inherent in any system of compulsory licensing; however, any number of ways of implementing a license system are feasible. One possibility is for Congress to accept the principle but delay the implementation until an effective licensing procedure can be worked out. This would encourage voluntary licensing during the deliberation period. Another possibility would be to put a terminal date on the legislation,

[80] S. Rep. No. 1, 94th Cong., 1st Sess. 60 (1975).

[81] 25 U.S.T. 309, T.I.A.S. 7808 (1974). The other ratifying or acceding countries include: Argentina, Australia, Brazil, Ecuador, Fiji, Finland, France, West Germany, Guatemala, Hungary, Kenya, Luxembourg, Mexico, Monaco, New Zealand, Panama, Spain, Sweden, and the United Kingdom (and certain territories).

[82] *Id.*

similar to what was done in the Sound Recording Amendment of 1971.[83] This would allow a future Congress to decide whether permanent legislation is warranted, based upon an observation of the actual experience.[84]

Considerable economic data on the operation and financial condition of the broadcasting industry, particularly radio broadcasting, were submitted to the 93rd Congress in 1974.[85] Analysis by the Senate Committee on the Judiciary indicated a consistent growth in the pretax profits of radio stations in representative large, medium, and small markets and also indicated that 75% of the commercial time of radio stations is devoted to the playing of sound recordings.[86] This led to the inclusion of a performance royalty in sound recordings, subject to a compulsory license, in section 114 of the former revision bill,[87] later deleted in compromise.[88]

"DON'T TOUCH THAT DIAL . . ."

The commercial use of any sound recording by radio broadcasters builds audiences, increases advertising revenues, and creates profits. Recorded music is the primary programming material used to secure audiences and generate revenues. In order for listeners to remain "glued to that dial," it is necessary for radio stations to play high-quality music between commercials. Radio broadcasters pay for virtually every other form of programming they employ, including

[83] Pub. L. No. 92–140, 85 Stat. 391 (1971), *amended by* Pub. L. No. 93–573, 88 Stat. 1873 (1974).

[84] These suggestions were made by the Register of Copyrights, Barbara Ringer, in S. REP. No. 1, 94th Cong., 1st Sess. 17 (1975).

[85] S. REP. No. 983 on S. 1361, 93d Cong., 2d Sess. 141 (1974). *Contra, see* Bard and Kurlantzick, *A Public Performance Right in Recordings: How to Alter the System Without Improving It*, 43 GEO. WASH. L. REV. 152 (1974).

[86] S. REP. No. 983 on S. 1361, 93d Cong., 2d Sess. 141 (1974).

[87] *Id.* 24–29.

[88] S. 22, 94th Cong., 1st Sess. (1975). Later enacted into law, *supra* note 14.

news services, sports, dramatic shows, game shows, syndicated features, weather, commentaries, financial and business services, disc jockeys, and other radio personalities.[89] Yet they pay nothing for sound recordings, which furnish 75 percent of their programming.

Radio broadcasters argue that airplay of sound recordings yields substantial benefits secondarily to the record company and performers. Frequent radio airplay promotes the particular sound recording, generates sales, and enables the performing artist to realize additional compensation from personal appearances, concerts, etc.[90] This is undoubtedly true for some performers, but not for the vast majority. Many performers are successful in becoming local or regional hits, and obtain good regional airplay but otherwise have rather limited sales. Many recordings played on the air, particularly classical, folk, and the older recordings, have negligible sales and virtually no secondary market.

An analysis of the music programming of broadcasting stations in six major markets, in a survey done by the Cambridge Research Institute, indicates that of the advertising revenues earned by the playing of music, 55.8 percent were earned by the playing of "oldies,"[91] that is, records that have been out on the market for a number of years and are long past their period of significant sales. That same idea of promoting sales of records by radio airplay could be used by broadcasters to deny performance rights to composers and publishers who also benefit from airplay. Another significant factor is the typical practice of "Top-Forty" radio stations, who usually add to their playlists only songs which already show signs of significant sales and popularity

[89] S. REP. No. 1, 94th Cong., 1st Sess. 42 (1975).

[90] *Id.* at 77 (Statement of the National Association of Broadcasters) (1975).

[91] *Id.* 58–59 (Statement of the Recording Industry Association of America) (1975). *See also, Hearings on H.R. 2223, supra* n. 63 at 1421–22 (1975) (Statement of John D. Glover).

based on industry charts (*Billboard, Record World, Cash Box*). Add to this the fact that a Top-Forty radio station usually adds only five or six new songs to its program playlist each week, whereas about 135 single records and approximately 75 new albums, representing almost 900 recorded songs, are released weekly by the recording industry.[92] Many radio stations do not even announce the title or the artist of sound recordings played; others give that information only at infrequent intervals. In many ways, radio stations do not promote success but exploit what is already successful.

Record companies understandably take a substantial risk in recording the majority of performing artists. The breakeven point is the number of copies of a record that have to be sold in order to recoup the cost of making, packaging, and promoting the record. Based on 1972 figures, the average breakeven point for 33 RPM record albums was 61,000 units sold, and 77 percent failed to recover their costs.[93] For 45 RPM records, the breakeven point was 46,000 units sold, and 81 percent failed to recover their costs.[94] While the breakeven point for classical albums was only 22,000 units sold, an astounding 95 percent of all classical releases fail to recover their costs.[95] This indicates that the small percentage of records that do make any real profit must subsidize the vast majority of releases that fail.

In light of the broadcasters' present position against paying for the use of sound recordings, it is ironic to note what one broadcasting spokesman testified in 1975: "it is unreasonable and unfair to let [the cable television] industry ride on our backs, as it were, to take our product, resell it, and

[92] *Hearings on 2223*, *supra* n. 63 at 1320–21 (1975) (Statement of Recording Industry Association of America).

[93] *Id.* at 1316–17 (Exhibit 1).

[94] *Id.*

[95] *Id.*

not pay us a dime. That offends my sense of the way things ought to work in America."[96] If the cable television industry must pay for the use of programming created by others, so should the broadcasting industry pay for the use of sound recordings created by others.

Radio also provides the opportunity for private home taping of sound recordings directly off the air. Album-oriented radio stations, in their effort to appeal to the discriminating listening audience, prelist the titles and artists of sound recordings to be played, together with the exact time, and then play the entire album without commercial interruption and thereby encourage home taping. At current market prices for blank tapes, the private home taping enthusiast can record anywhere from two to three record albums at the cost of one. The estimated loss to record companies and artists—though virtually incalculable—is clearly high.[97] A subsidiary question is whether or not this might also indirectly encourage commercial record piracy. As blank tapes begin to outsell prerecorded tapes around the world, the blank tape industry is aware of pressures of some type of tax on software, with proceeds to go in part to composers, publishers, record companies, and performing artists now recorded off radio and from other sound recordings.[98]

INSTANT ENTERTAINMENT

Technological advances in electronics have created and will continue to create new areas of development. Highly sophisticated stereo and quadraphonic sound systems are commonplace for most successful discotheques and night clubs, not to mention the average consumer. Quality sound

[96] *Hearings on H.R. 2223, supra* n. 63 at 769 (1975) (Statement of Robert V. Evans).

[97] *The Blooming Blank Tape Market*, 89 BILLBOARD, No. 28, July 16, 1977, 48–69.

[98] *Id.* at 1.

systems are rapidly becoming as important to the average consumer as an automobile and often cost more. Certain trends in production and consumer buying patterns seem to be developing toward gradual disappearance of lower quality merchandise, accompanied by significant advancements in the high end (quality, cost).[99]

Videotape-cassette recorders are now moving into the United States retail pipeline, using both prerecorded and blank tapes.[100] Blank videotape cassettes enable the home viewer to record directly from televised broadcasts for videotape playback later at the viewer's discretion. The copyright and other legal problems inherent in videotape-cassette recording off the television are beyond the scope of this paper. The foreseeable possibility appears to be unlimited private home libraries of taped sound recordings, motion pictures, sports events, dramatic and musical performances, and other forms of entertainment. Prerecorded videotape cassettes, on the other hand, offer a new market to the performer and the consumer. The performing artist could visually and aurally record a musical performance, for example, and the consumer would receive the equivalent of a record album and a "live" concert all in one, with the ability to play back the recording continuously. The status of videotape-cassette recorders will no doubt be the subject of future legislative and judicial debate.

LIMITED EXCLUSIVE RIGHTS IN SOUND RECORDINGS

The exclusive rights of the owner in a sound recording are limited to the rights of reproduction, adaptation, and distribution.[101] The right of adaptation is limited to derivative works in which the actual sounds are "rearranged, remixed,

[99] *Id.* at 49.
[100] *Id.* at 57.
[101] ACT, *supra* n. 14 at § 114(a) (1976).

or otherwise altered in sequence," and does "not extend to the making or duplication of another sound recording that consists entirely of an independent fixation of other sounds, even though such sounds imitate or simulate those in the copyrighted sound recording." [102]

One of the fundamentals of our system of music education is that one must first learn to imitate before one can create. The composer (and the publisher) understandably would prefer to license the recording of as many "cover" versions of his song as possible. The more versions of a song actually recorded, the bigger the mechanical royalty payment to the composer [103] although, as any musician will testify, no one makes a living off royalties in the United States.[104]

The Copyright Act of 1976 expressly denies any right of performance to the owner of copyright in a sound recording.[105] It also provides a broad exemption for the use of sound recordings included in educational television and radio programs distributed or transmitted by or through public broadcasting entities.[106] The exemption was created to allow limited nonprofit use by educational institutions, religious services, governmental bodies, the blind or handicapped, and other nonprofit charitable or noncommercial groups.[107] Section 107 of the new Act allows the "fair use" of a copyrighted work, subject to certain restrictions, for such pur-

[102] *Id.* § 114(b).

[103] 17 U.S.C. § 1(e) (1970). Mechanical royalties are paid to the composer at the statutory rate of 2¢ for each authorized version of his song manufactured. This rate will be increased to 2¾¢ (or 12¢ per minute of playing time, whichever is longer) under the Act of 1976. ACT, *supra* note 14 at § 115(c) (2).

[104] *See, Hearings on H.R. 2223, supra* note 63 at 1646 (testimony of Marvin Hamlisch) (1975). Mr. Hamlisch, as the writer of the music to "The Way We Were," received all of $5,000, based on the mechanical rate of 2¢, for 1 million records sold. Presumably, his lyricist received the same amount, while the publisher received twice that amount. *Id.* at 1647.

[105] ACT, *supra* note 14 at § 114(a).

[106] *Id.* at § 114(b) (Public broadcasting entities are defined in § 118[g]).

[107] *Id.* § 110.

poses as news reporting, criticism, comment, scholarship, research, and classroom teaching.[108] Most of these limited uses are based upon nonprofit educational motives, and in no case will outright piracy for commercial profit be authorized.

One of the most important sections of the new copyright law is section 301, the preemption section, which states that "[o]n and after January 1, 1978, all legal and equitable rights equivalent to any of the exclusive rights within the scope of copyright . . . are governed exclusively by this title. Thereafter, no person is entitled to any such right or equivalent right . . . under the common law or statutes of any State."[109] With respect to sound recordings fixed before February 15, 1972, the states are free to provide any rights or remedies.[110]

Any efforts to enact a performance royalty into law must necessarily await the Report of the Register of Copyrights, due on January 3, 1978.[111] Perhaps remembering the purpose of promoting the progress of the useful arts, the Register of Copyrights, Barbara Ringer, so eloquently testified:

> Is it naive and unrealistic of me to hope that the commercial users of music should realize the benefit to their own interests of doing everything reasonably possible to promote the economic interests of those whose work is their business to purvey? Would it be too much to hope that, recognizing that they are all part of the same process, the users of copyrighted sound recordings could accept the principle of performance royalties, and could sit down with the performers and record makers to work out a reasonable compulsory licensing system? The alternative, no one need be told, is years more of wrangling in the legislative arena, with people pitted against each other who should be working together for their mutual profit.[112]

[108] *Id.* § 107.
[109] *Id.* § 301(a).
[110] *Id.* § 301(c) (subject to a period of 75 years, until February 15, 2047).
[111] *Id.* § 114(d).
[112] S. Rep. No. 1, 94th Cong., 1st Sess. (1975).

PERFORMANCE RIGHTS AMENDMENT OF 1977

Representative George Danielson introduced in the House of Representatives, on April 5, 1977, the Performance Rights Amendment of 1977.[113] This bill will receive no action until after the Report to Congress by the Register of Copyrights, presumably in the 95th Congress, 2nd session.

The Danielson bill, H.R. 6063, proposes to amend section 114 of the Copyright Act of 1976 to provide a compulsory license system for performance rights in sound recordings, similar in framework to the system contained under the former revision bill, S. 1361,[114] with some major changes. It grants the copyright owner of the sound recording [115] the exclusive right to perform publicly *all or any part* of the actual sounds fixed in the recording.[116]

PERFORMANCE RIGHTS DISTINCT

The exclusive right to perform publicly a copyrighted musical work by means of a *phonorecord*, and the exclusive right to perform publicly a *sound recording*, are separate and distinct rights under this title.[117]

[113] H.R. 6063, 95th Cong., 1st Sess. (1977). [hereinafter cited as *Amendment*].

[114] S. Rep. No. 983 on S. 1361, 93d Cong., 2d Sess. 24–29 (1974).

[115] *See* note 11 *supra*.

[116] *Amendment, supra* note 113 at VV, (1977) [Emphasis added.] The emphasized portion seems to expand the scope of the exclusive rights granted by § 106, which only grants "the right to perform publicly the copyrighted work." The addition of "any part of" eliminates any question of what constitutes a substantial taking and therefore also narrows the limits of fair use, as defined by § 107. This addition will probably be contested vigorously. Act, *supra* note 14 at § 106, 107 (1976).

[117] *Amendment, supra* note 113 at § 114(b) (1977). Phonorecords are material objects in which sounds are fixed, and from which the sounds can be perceived, reproduced, or otherwise communicated, either directly or with the aid of a machine or device; sound recordings are *works* that result from the fixation of a series of musical, spoken, or other sounds, but not including the sounds accompanying a motion picture or other audiovisual work, regardless of the nature of the material objects, such as disks, tapes, or phonorecords, in which they are embodied. Act, *supra* note 14 at § 101 (1976).

COMPULSORY LICENSE SYSTEM

Compulsory license rates for commercial users of sound recordings are to be computed on a per-use basis, a prorated basis, or a blanket basis, at the user's option.[118] The addition of a per-use basis would be advantageous to radio stations or other users who program long and extended cuts, that is, songs which are longer than the traditional two- to three-minute average. This basis would represent a numerical expression of the number of times a specific sound recording was broadcast. A prorated basis would allow a radio station to take into account the amount of time devoted to playing copyrighted sound recordings. If a station plays copyrighted sound recordings only 10 percent of their broadcast time, for example, background spots, commercials, news, etc., then a fraction of the blanket rate may be selected as an alternative in accordance with a standard formula that the Register of Copyrights shall prescribe by regulation.[119] This bill encourages voluntary negotiated licensing as a substitute for compulsory licensing and its administrative formalities, provided that the negotiated rate is not less than the applicable compulsory rate.[120] The record companies, performers, and copyright users affected are encouraged to establish a private nongovernmental entity to assume the collection and distribution functions otherwise to be performed by the Register of Copyrights.[121] Perhaps this endorsement will encourage the creation of a new and distinct performing rights society to collect and distribute performance royalties to performers.[122]

[118] *Amendment, supra* note 113 at § 114(c) (4).
[119] *Id.* § 114(c) (4) (A) (iii), (c) (4) (E).
[120] *Id.* (c) (4).
[121] *Id.* (f).
[122] ASCAP, BMI, and SESAC collect and distribute performance rights royalties for composers and publishers. Whether they wish to act for record producers and performers remains to be seen.

Under H.R. 6063, the following rates are applicable:

Radio stations with gross receipts of under $25,000 need pay no fee; those with gross receipts between $25,000 and $100,000 must pay $250 per year; those between $100,000 and $200,000 must pay $750 per year; and for those with gross receipts of more than $200,000 the fee is 1 percent of *net* receipts or prorated fraction thereof.[123]

Television stations with gross receipts of less than $1 million need pay no fee, those between $1 and $4 million must pay $750 per year; and those with gross receipts of more than $4 million must pay $1,500 per year.[124]

For background music services and other transmitters a yearly blanket rate of 2 percent of the gross receipts from subscribers or others who pay to receive the transmission is provided, with an alternative prorated amount when applicable.[125] All other users not otherwise exempted will have a blanket rate of $25 per year for each location at which copyrighted sound recordings are performed or an alternative prorated amount.[126]

EXEMPTIONS

Exemptions are provided for nonprofit educational, religious, or charitable use [127] (as defined by section 110), whereas public broadcasting entities (as defined by section 118) are not mentioned in the Danielson Bill. Owners of coin-operated phonorecord players (juke boxes) and cable systems [128] are exempt from liability under this section, although this raises questions in the case of cable television

[123] *Amendment, supra* note 113 at § 114(c) (4) (A) (i), (ii), (d).
[124] *Id.* (c) (4) (B) (i), (ii), (d).
[125] *Id.* (c) (4) (C).
[126] *Id.* (c) (4) (E).
[127] *Id.* (d). For a discussion of the scope of these exemptions, *see* Korman, *Limitations on the Right of Public Performance and Other Rights Under the 1976 Copyright Act*, 81 CURRENT DEVELOPMENTS IN COPYRIGHT LAW (C.C.H.) 103, 149–181 (1977).
[128] *Amendment, supra* note 113, § 114(d).

operators who originate their own local programming. Radio and television stations with gross receipts from sponsors of less than $25,000 and $1,000,000, respectively, are exempt from any liability, and background services and other users with gross receipts from subscribers or customers of less than $10,000 are expressly exempt from liability.[129]

In the absence of voluntary negotiations, collection and distribution of compulsory royalties is to be handled by the Register of Copyrights.[130] If the Register certifies the fact that a controversy concerning distribution of royalties under a compulsory license does exist, she shall then proceed to create a panel of the Copyright Royal Tribunal in accordance with section 803.[131] This is an adequate two-step administrative procedure.

An antitrust exemption is provided for claimants to agree among themselves about the proportioned division of compulsory license fees among them. This allows copyright owners (the record companies) and performers to lump their claims together and file them jointly or as a simple claim; alternatively, they may designate a common agent to receive payment on their behalf.[132] One half of all royalties to be distributed shall be paid to the copyright owners, and the other half shall be paid to the performers to be shared equally on a per capita basis;[133] neither may assign to the other this right to the royalties.[134] This is an extremely important provision designed to protect the performer from an otherwise inferior bargaining position.

Another antitrust exemption is provided to encourage copyright owners and performers to negotiate with the commercial users about the establishment of a private collection

[129] *Id.* (D) (1), (2), (3).
[130] *Id.* (c) (2) (B), (e) (1).
[131] *Id.* (e) (2).
[132] *Id.* (e) (1).
[133] *Id.* (e) (3) (A).
[134] *Id.* (e) (3) (B).

agency or a common agent for collection and distribution of licensing fees.[135] This is impelled by providing that distribution of royalties to claimants shall not take effect until one year after enactment of this legislation; during such time copyright owners, performers, and users are encouraged to voluntarily negotiate.[136]

Failure to record a notice of intention to obtain a compulsory license,[137] or to file a statement of annual account,[138] or to deposit the royalty [139] renders the public performance of sound recordings actionable as an infringement, subject to an injunction, damages, impounding and disposition of the infringing articles, and costs and attorney's fees.[140]

The definition of performers in the Danielson Bill includes musicians, singers, conductors, actors, narrators, and others whose performance of literary, musical, or dramatic work is embodied in a sound recording.[141] This opens the door to such possibilities as dramatic radio plays, narrative recordings, and other nonmusical recordings.

THE GREAT ZACCHINI

The Supreme Court recently discussed the state's power to protect the economic incentive of the performer against unauthorized broadcasts. In *Zacchini v. Scripps-Howard Broadcasting Co.*,[142] decided on June 28, 1977, the Court reasoned that the State of Ohio can, consistent with the First Amendment, impose liability on a television station for broadcast-

[135] *Id.* (f).
[136] *Id.*
[137] *Id.* (c) (2) (A).
[138] *Id.* (c) (2) (B).
[139] *Id.*
[140] *Id.* (c) (3).
[141] *Id.* (h) (2).
[142] 45 U.S.L.W. 4954 (June 28, 1977).

ing a videotaped newscast of a performer's entire act and thus infringing the performer's state law right to the publicity value of his own performance.[143] The performance was a 15-second "human cannonball" act in which the performer is shot from a cannon into a net some 200 feet away. The right of the publicity value of one's performance, recognized by Ohio, protected the performer's personal control over the unauthorized commercial display and exploitation of his personality and the exercise of his talents. The Court reasoned:

> Of course, Ohio's decision to protect petitioner's right of publicity here rests on more than a desire to compensate the performer for the time and effort invested in his act; the protection provides an economic incentive for him to make the investment required to produce a performance of interest to the public. This same consideration underlies the patent and copyright laws long enforced by this Court.[144]

The analogy to the goals of copyright law is focused on the right of the individual to reap the reward of his endeavors; when an entire performance is telecast, the First Amendment privilege accorded the press to report on newsworthy events does not immunize the broadcaster. The economic incentive of the artist is a fundamental concern, and protection is sometimes found at the common law.[145]

SUMMARY

A statutorily defined performance right in sound recordings could provide needed incentive to many diverse areas of the performing arts—instrumentalists, stylists, arrangers, sound engineers, narrators, dramatists, and experimental

[143] 47 Ohio St. 2d 224, 351 N.E. 2d 454 (1976).

[144] 45 U.S.L.W., *supra* note 142 at 4957.

[145] *See*, Lang, *Performance and the Right of the Performing Artist*, 21 ASCAP Copyright L. Symp. 68, 82–87 (1974); Nelson, *Jazz and Copyright: A Study in Improvised Protection*, 21 ASCAP Copyright L. Symp. 35, 44–58 (1974); *compare*, Liebig, *Style and Performance*, 17 Bull. Copyright Soc'y 40 (1970).

performers[146] of infinite variety would be protected against unauthorized secondary uses of their recordings. It could pave the way to new and innovative forms of radio broadcasting and could result in the availability of a much wider range of music to the consumer; classical, jazz, folk, experimental and esoteric recordings might prove less of an economic burden to the record company. Perhaps the consideration of a weighted formula or system of royalties in favor of the fine arts would compensate for their poor marketplace and the ever increasing expense necessary to stage an opera, ballet, or orchestral concert.[147] Classical performing artists are creative individuals who devote entire lives and inexhaustible amounts of energy, discipline, and fortitude to preserve a formal tradition; let us hope they do not become an endangered species.

A performance royalty would allow the small, independent record company with limited resources to recoup some of its recording costs. This could create a greater latitude in the selection of new performing artists. On the other hand, it might make it even harder for the independent to make the playlist on radio stations who might not want to incur the administrative costs. It will all depend on the public demand for the particular sound recording.

The record companies contribute in a creative sense by capturing and producing the sound recording independent of the actual performance embodied on the recording. They are responsible for the hiring of backup musicians, vocalists, arrangers, sound engineers, and technicians necessary to

[146] *See generally*, Goldstein, *Copyrighting the New Music*, 16 ASCAP Copyright L. Symp. 1 (1968); Keziah, *Copyright Registration for Aleatory and Indeterminate Musical Compositions*, 17 Bull. Copyright Soc'y 311 (1970); Savelson, *Electronic Music and Copyright Law*, 13 ASCAP Copyright L. Symp. 133 (1963).

[147] S. Rep. No. 1, 94th Cong. 1st Sess. 9 (1975) (Statement of Nancy Hanks, Chairman, National Endowment of the Arts).

achieve maximum acoustical perfection, electronically capturing, balancing, mixing, editing, and processing the sounds to make the final recording. The record company performs many diverse but integrated operations, analogous to the making of a motion picture.

Most record companies prefer to record the performer who is also composer of his own material; consequently, many strictly interpretive performers are denied the chance to record. Imposition of a guaranteed performance royalty would give record companies and performers an additional consideration; rather than record mediocre original material, performers might try other popular standard material and thereby decrease the number of repetitive and mundane "original" recordings released today in most major markets.

The large record companies concentrate most of their productive efforts on selecting and recording music designed to please the record-buying public. Most sound recordings are produced for large sales and quick return from a specialized consumer market (rock-and-roll, country, soul, disco, etc.). The record companies do not generally produce recordings designed exclusively for the radio listening audience—though there is an interrelationship, their goal is to sell records to be played on home systems. Let them "be compensated for the use of their records on the air, and they will be financially able to record for the benefit of [a much larger] listening audience which wants to *hear* good recorded music, but which does not necessarily *buy* records," that is, the radio listener.[148]

A mutual and cooperative effort between commercial users and record producers and performers will ensure better quality sound recordings for the public airways and maximum

[148] *Hearings on S. 507 Before the Subcommittee on Patents, Trademarks, and Copyrights of the Senate Committee on the Judiciary*, 90th Cong., 1st Sess. (testimony of Alan H. Livingston) (emphasis added).

promotion of the useful arts. Both the commercial users and the record producers have the same ultimate customer, the discriminating listener, who must in his discretion be satisfied before he will lend an ear. Whether it means buying an album or tape, paying admission to a concert, or simply turning on a particular radio station, it is the listener who must be satisfied. In the end, it is that listener who decides what sound recording is a hit and what is a failure, and it should be the universal goal of all producers, performers, and commercial users of sound recordings to give maximum service and satisfaction to his or her discriminating taste.

Is the recorded performance a "creative" entity in and of itself? If pantomimes, choreographic routines, photographs, and motion pictures are deemed worthy of exclusive rights, certainly a recorded interpretive performance as harmonically creative as John Coltrane's "My Favorite Things," or the electrifying perfection reached in the interpretation of the classics by Andres Segovia should be worthy also. For example, performers, and even writers, of traditional blues, and its derivative, jazz, have for too long been confined to back-alley bars and clubs and denied the exposure and remuneration that their "imitators" received. From its beginnings in the rural South, through its nurtured adolescence in the streets of New Orleans, throughout its domestic and international growth during the past five decades, this most precious national musical resource is the "grand-daddy" and the very cornerstone of the great musical-industrial complex as we know it today.[149] The echoes of every interpretive jazz and blues stylist of the past denied protection as a mere performer ring loud in our ears. Does this truly promote the

[149] *See generally*, FEATHER, PLEASURES OF JAZZ (1976); HENTOFF AND SHAPIRO, HEAR ME TALKIN' TO YA (1955); Countryman, *The Organized Musicians: II*, 16 U. CHI. L. REV. 239 (1949); Nelson, *Jazz and Copyright: A Study in Improvised Protection*, 21 ASCAP COPYRIGHT L. SYMP. 35 (1974).

progress of the art? Or does it result, as the Register of Copyrights has suggested, in the

> tragic . . . loss of a major part of a vital artistic profession and the drying up of an incalculable number of creative wellsprings. The effect of this process on individual performers has been catastrophic, but the effect on the nature and variety of records that are made and kept in release, and on the content and variety of radio programming, have been equally malign. Most of all it is the United States public that has suffered from this process.[150]

The effect of this "deafness" of the copyright laws to the status of performing artists is simple: it works as a disincentive; we are gradually losing our great interpretive performers. Virtuoso soloists and brilliant instrumentalists whose utterly flawless techniques are recorded should be entitled to performance royalties. Fundamentally, is there a difference between paying musicians to perform live and paying for the use of recorded performances by those very same musicians?

Given the substantial success of American-produced music in the international market, foreign performers are eager to move their musical business ventures to the United States. Ironically, most foreign performers have greater protection for their recorded performances against commercial use than their American counterparts.

Has the incentive in the hearts of our young composers and performers to create fresh and imaginative new works been replaced by a touch of vaudeville, incorporating outrageous costumes, laser lighting, drama, choreography, sophisticated electronic audio and visual equipment to embellish and augment an otherwise inferior creative effort?

We should listen to the echoes of the creative individuals whose faint cries of commercial exploitation by the gargan-

[150] S. Rep. No. 1, 94th Cong., 1st Sess. 15 (1975).

tuan advances of communications technology have been met by an inconsistency in the application of the law designed for their protection, at least on an equal status with that of their foreign musical brethren.

Music is the one great language of universal understanding, known by all who can hear its vibration, felt by all living beings with hearts able to feel the tides of emotion manifested in the presentation of a performer's dream, a bridge between otherwise conflicting ideologies.

> Look yonder, look yonder
> Look over there
> Ain't that a sight to see
> Just a few more miles to the blue horizon
> Oh lord, don't give up on me.[151]

ADDENDUM

In accordance with the mandate of § 114(d), on January 3, 1978, the Register of Copyrights submitted a comprehensive report on the status of performance rights in sound recordings, including the legislative history, the constitutional and legal issues, and testimony and comments representing current views on the subject in this country. Additionally, the report reviews and analyzes foreign systems for protection of performance rights in sound recordings, as well as the existing structure for international protection in the field, specifically the Rome Convention. The basic report also includes an "economic impact analysis" of the proposals for performance royalty legislation, prepared by an independent economic consultant under contract with the Copyright Office. This report is a comprehensive, unbiased, and

[151] From "How Far To The Horizon?" by Jesse Winchester, copyright 1974, Fourth Floor Music, Inc. (ASCAP).

objective study of the problem and strongly endorses the creation of a performance right in sound recordings.

On January 18, 1979, Representative George Danielson introduced H.R. 997, entitled "The Sound Recording Performance Rights Amendment," in the House of Representaives. This bill was referred to the Committee on the Judiciary and is currently pending in the Sub-Committee on Courts, Civil Liberties, and the Administration of Justice. The royalty rate structure and exemptions are precisely the same as the earlier H.R. 6063 (introduced by Representative Danielson on April 5, 1977), with an additional flat yearly rate of One Hundred Dollars ($100.00) per location chargeable to discotheques and other similar commercial users. Supporters of this bill expect the effective date of the legislation to be January 1, 1981.

NATIONAL FOURTH PRIZE

The Rise and Fall of Record Piracy

ROBERT T. MOWREY

SOUTHERN METHODIST UNIVERSITY SCHOOL OF LAW

Away to the cheating world go you
where pirates are all well to do
Gilbert & Sullivan
Pirates of Penzance

I. INTRODUCTION

THE music recording business is indeed an American success story. Sales of records and prerecorded tapes rose from $48 million in 1940 to nearly $200 million in 1950, $600 million in 1960, and a staggering $1.7 billion in 1970.[1] One author has suggested that the reason for this remarkable prosperity is the youthful emphasis on music and the increasing level of teenage affluence.[2] With "hit" recordings producing a disproportionate share of the profits,[3] the industry is able to subsidize the production of less profitable items such as classical music, opera, and religious recordings.[4] Large

[1] S. SHEMEL & M. KRASILOVSKY, THIS BUSINESS OF MUSIC xvii (rev. ed. 1971).

[2] *See* Comment, *Copyright Protection for Sound Recordings: Past Problems and Future Directions*, 19 ST. LOUIS U.L.J. 189, 190 (1974).

[3] Statement of Isabelle Marks, Assistant Secretary of Decca Records, *Hearings on S. 597 Before the Subcomm. on Patents, Trademarks, and Copyrights of the Senate Comm. on the Judiciary*, 90th Cong., 1st Sess., pt. 2, at 527 (1967).

[4] Statement of Clive J. Davis, Vice President and General Manager of CBS Records, *id.* at 516.

profits on "hit" records are essential since sound recording is becoming increasingly expensive.[5] Sophisticated recording equipment and techniques; specialized technicians; salaries of the artist, his musical accompanists, studio musicians, arrangers, and composers; royalties; and the length of the production process—all add up to the 50,000-to-75,000 dollar cost of producing a long-playing album, manufacturing and advertising expenses excluded.[6]

Although tape and record pirates [7] have been around almost as long as the sound recording industry itself,[8] it was not until the jelling of these factors, namely, the emergence

[5] *See generally* Brief for Recording Industry Association of America, Inc., as Amicus Curiae at 8–9, Goldstein v. California, 412 U.S. 546 (1973).

[6] *See* Capitol Records, Inc. v. Spies, 130 Ill. App. wd 429, 264 N.E. 2d 874, 875 (1970). It is not unusual for a recording company to risk up to $2 million in marketing a single record. *See* Note, *Copyright Protection of Sound Recordings*, 23 DRAKE L. REV. 449 (1974).

[7] Record piracy consists primarily of the unauthorized reproduction of musical performances from commercially available phonograph records and prerecorded magnetic tapes, and the subsequent sale of copies thus made in competition with the original recordings. *See, e.g.*, Comment, *Sound Recordings' Copyright: The Disc Dilemma*, 36 U. PITTS. L. REV. 887 (1975). Piracy is also known as "dubbing" or "disklegging." Piracy is distinguished from "counterfeiting" in that the latter involves not only the reproduction of the musical recording itself but also the duplication of the original record album or tape cartridge cover, including the legitimate manufacturer's name and trademark. This practice is expressly prohibited under 18 U.S.C. § 2318 (1970). *See* Appendix I. Although "bootlegging" is sometimes confused with "piracy," *see* Annotation, *Making, Selling, or Distributing Counterfeit or "Bootleg" Tape Recordings or Phonograph Records as Violation of Federal Law*, 25 A.L.R. FED. 207 (1975), the more commonly accepted view is that "bootlegging" involves either the surreptitious recording and reproduction of a live performance or the obtaining and distribution of previously unreleased recordings. *See* Kurlantzick, *The Constitutionality of State Law Protection of Sound Recordings*, 5 CONN. L. REV. 204 (1974). Counterfeiting and bootlegging are not discussed in this article.

[8] *See* Note, *Piracy on Records*, 5 STAN. L. REV. 433 (1953). *See also* Comment, *Record Piracy and Copyright: Present Inadequacies and Future Overkill*, 23 MAINE L. REV. 359 (1971). Piracy of sound recording devices, such as piano roll and phonograph records, began in the early 1900's. *See* Staff of Senate Comm. on the Judiciary Subcomm. on Patents, Trademarks, and Copyright, 96th Cong., 2d Sess., The Unauthorized Duplication of Sound Recordings 3 (Comm. Print. 1961) (Ringer, Study No. 26).

of the "hit" record coupled with spiraling production costs, that piracy has become a major economic threat to the music industry. Pirates purchase records, tapes, cartridges, and cassettes that have been manufactured and sold through the usual commercial channels by legitimate recording companies and make a master tape of the legitimate recordings by directly connecting a separate recorder to the playback unit.[9] Utilizing a matrix, metal disc-press "stamper" or a number of "tape slaves," the pirate mass-produces phonograph records or prerecorded magnetic tapes from this master tape recording.[10]

As is obvious, pirates circumvent a great portion of the costs of engaging in the recording business [11]—production costs are minimal and only the "hits" are pirated.[12] Not only are the recording companies hurt, but the artists suffer as well. Although some artists may not particularly dislike piracy since the practice aids in disseminating the artists' music to the public,[13] many artists are strongly opposed to the practice. Not only do pirates fail to pay royalties,[14] but

[9] *See* Comment, *supra* note 2, at 191–92.

[10] *See* Comment, *supra* note 7, at 888.

[11] *See* Liberty/UA, Inc. v. Eastern Tape Corp., 11 N.C. App. 20, 180 S.E.2d 414, *appeal dismissed*, 278 N.C. 702, 181, S.E. 2d 600 (1971).

[12] By only reproducing the "hits," the pirate is not limited to the reproduction of only one artist or even one record company; thus, he is able to combine an even more desirable consumer package than the record company. *See Hearings on S. 646 and H.R. 6927 Before Subcomm. No. 3 of the House Comm. on the Judiciary*, 92d Cong., 1st Sess. 78–79 (1971) (hereinafter cited as *1971 Hearings*).

[13] Record piracy is also advantageous to record collectors who are consequently able to buy recordings that are no longer available in regular commercial outlets and for which issuance by record companies for such limited potential sales is economically unfeasible. *See* Note, *Piracy on Records*, 5 STAN. L. REV. 433, 457 (1953).

[14] Barbara Ringer, the then Assistant Register of Copyright, seated during the hearings to the Sound Recording Act that "[n]ot all, but the great majority of unauthorized record producers do not pay this royalty. They just go ahead and take the chance. They are really operating outside the law. They are violating sections 1(e) and 101(e) of the copyright statute." *1971 Hearings* at 18. The

when the public purchases a pirated tape of a star and the quality is poor, the purchaser blames the artist, as well as the recording company.[15]

More than the music industry is harmed by piracy. The public is hurt also. Usually, as noted earlier, "pirate merchandise is of poor quality, so the sound is not as good as a legitimate recording." [16] Moreover, because "legitimate companies are hampered in their efforts to offer a wide selection of recordings, [they often fail] to meet the widely varying interests of the public. . . . Without the income from the big sellers that are pirated, the selection of recordings available to the public will decline." Third, "it is more difficult for recording companies to invest in new artists, new musicians and song writers, as well as classical orchestras, because of the income lost to the pirates. Pirates seldom pay taxes." It is estimated that 75 percent of pirate income is unreported.[17] Finally, law enforcement is affected by record and tape piracy. Not only does this blatant illegal activity contribute to the erosion of public respect for the law, but organized crime is also involved with piracy.[18]

As will be developed, recording piracy has flourished until recently without any great threat by copyright law. Until

---

Harry Fox Agency, which currently represents more than 3,000 music publishers, submitted a statement at the hearings, asserting that "[t]he vast majority of the illicit duplicators do not attempt to make any payment of copyright royalties. According to the records of the Agency, the only illicit duplicators making purported royalty payments are G&G Sales, Inc., . . . and Custom Recording Company." *Id.* at 95.

[15] Public Hearing on Tape Piracy, Statement of Herbie Mann Before Attorney General of State of New York, reported in 5 PERF. ARTS REV. 5, 12 (1974).

[16] Also, the equipment and materials used by pirates are rarely the same high quality as those used by legitimate companies. *See* Yarnell, *Recording Piracy is Everybody's Burden: An Examination of its Causes, Effects and Remedies*, 20 BULL. COPYRIGHT SOC'Y 234, 236 (1973). Some pirated tapes are, however, of superior quality to that of national brand tapes. *See 1971 Hearings* at 78–79.

[17] *See* Yarnell, *supra* note 16 at 236. *See also* Public Hearings on Tape Piracy, *Statement of Jules Yarnell before Attorney General of State of New York*, reported in 5 PERF. ARTS REV. 9, 16 (1974).

[18] Public Hearings on Tape Piracy, *supra* note 17, at 17.

enactment of the Sound Recording Act [19] passed by Congress in 1971, amending the Copyright Act [20] and extending federal protection against recording piracy, there was little protection afforded recordings other than through state criminal statutes and state unfair competition suits by record companies. Although the Sound Recording Act, as well as the Copyright Revision Act,[21] protect post-1972 recording, and state statutes protect pre-1972 recordings, piracy is still not dead. In August 1974, Jules Yarnell, director of the Anti-Piracy Intelligence Bureau, Recording Industry Association of America, Inc., remarked that more than $250 million worth of pirated product is sold each year in the United States.[22] In the 1971 legislative history of the Sound Recording Act, it was reported that the annual volume of piracy is in excess of $100 million.[23]

II. PROTECTION OF SOUND RECORDINGS PRIOR TO SOUND RECORDING ACT OF 1971

A. THE EXCLUSION OF SOUND RECORDINGS IN THE COPYRIGHT ACT OF 1909

The copyright clause of the Constitution grants Congress

[19] Act of October 15, 1971, Pub. L. No. 92–140, 85 Stat. 391. The act granted federal copyright protection for sound recordings made and published after February 15, 1972, and before January 1, 1975. *Id.* at § 3.

[20] 17 U.S.C. §§ 1 et seq. (1952).

[21] Act of October 19, 1976, Pub. L. No. 94–553, 90 Stat. 2541. This new law supersedes the Copyright Act of 1909, as amended, completely revamping Title 17, USC, Copyrights. To avoid confusion, all references are to the *prior* act unless specifically stated otherwise.

[22] Public Hearings on Tape Piracy, *Statement of Jules Yarnell before Attorney General of State of New York,* reported in 5 PERF. ARTS REV. 5, 16 (1974).

[23] H.R. REP. No. 487, 92d Cong., 1st Sess., *reprinted in* [1971] U.S. CODE CONG. & AD. NEWS 1566, 1567.

Despite the Sound Recording Amendment in 1971, record piracy in the

the power "[t]o promote the Progress of Science and useful Arts, by securing for limited Times to Authors and Inventors the exclusive Right to their respective Writings and Discoveries." [24] One of the first enactments of the first Congress was the Copyright Law of 1790,[25] yet it did not include musical compositions within its scope. When an act in 1831 [26] was passed protecting such works, it included protection only for published music, not for the performing right. The performing right was not recognized until 1897,[27] when an amendment to the copyright law encompassing all public performances of a copyrighted musical composition was passed.[28]

One year before passage of the Copyright Act of 1909,[29] the Supreme Court settled the question of whether the manufacture and sale of the perforated paper roll, that is, the player piano roll, constituted an infringement of the copyrighted musical composition that the roll would produce when inserted in a player piano.[30] The Court noted that there was an important distinction between musical scores that could be reproduced by a human performer and sound recordings that could be reproduced by a machine. Whereas the former were protectible "writings" within the meaning of the Constitution,[31] the latter were "parts of a machine

---

United States "continues to assume epidemic proportions. . . . Knowledgeable persons estimate that 30–40 per cent of all tape sales are made by record pirates." *A.B.A. Section of Patent, Trademark, and Copyright Law*, Comm. Reports 153 (1973). The estimate in 1971 was 25%. H.R. REP. NO. 487 at 2.

[24] U.S. CONST. art I, § 8, cl. 8. For a discussion of the early development of copyright law in England, *see* E. DRONE, THE LAW OF PROPERTY IN INTELLECTUAL PRODUCTIONS (1879).

[25] Act of May 31, 1790, ch. XV, 1 Stat. 124.

[26] Act of 1831, ch. XVI, 4 Stat. 436.

[27] Act of Jan. 6. 1897, ch. IV, 29 Stat. 481.

[28] *See generally* Cary, *The Common Law and Statutory Background of the Law of Musical Property*, 15 VAND. L. REV. 397 (1962).

[29] Act of March 4, 1909, ch. 320, 35 Stat. 1075, 17 U.S.C. §§ 1–215 (1952).

[30] White-Smith Music Publishing Co. v. Apollo Co., 209 U.S. 1 (1908).

[31] *See* note 24 *supra* and accompanying text.

which, when duly applied and properly operated in connection with the mechanism to which they are adapted, produce musical tones. . . . [W]e cannot think that they are copies within the meaning of the copyright act." [32] Because the Court viewed sound recordings as not being "copies" and hence unprotectible, "piano roll manufacturers were free to use copyrighted music without having to pay any royalties." [33]

Taking steps to ensure that this situation would not continue under the revised copyright act on which Congress was working at the time, composers and music publishers were largely responsible [34] for the insertion of language establishing the limited right "to make any arrangement or setting of it . . . in any system of notation or *any form of record* in which the thought of an author may be recorded and from which it may be read or *reproduced*. . . ." [35] This provision gave the copyright owner control over recordings of a musical work, since an unauthorized recording would be an infringement of one of the copyright owner's exclusive rights in the musical compositions.[36]

Moreover, this same section of the Act contained a clause protecting musical compositions by subjecting the recordings to a compulsory licensing provision.[37] Under this provision,

[32] 209 U.S. at 18. Previously in Burrows-Giles Lithographic Co. v. Sarony, 111 U.S. 53 (1884), the Supreme Court, in dictum, spoke of the copyright power as encompassing only "all forms of . . . *visible* expression." *Id.* at 58 (emphasis added).

Nimmer points out that the *Apollo* decision did *not* hold that sound recordings are not copyrightable—it merely held that a mechanical reproduction does not constitute a "copy" of the musical composition recorded in the reproduction, and was therefore a limitation on the bundle of rights which might be claimed by a copyright owner of a musical composition. M. NIMMER, NIMMER ON COPYRIGHT § 25.3 (1976) [hereinafter cited as NIMMER].

[33] *See* Diamond, *Copyright Problems of the Phonograph Record Industry*, 15 VAND. L. REV. 419, 420 (1962).

[34] *Id.*

[35] 17 U.S.C. § 1(e) (1952) (emphasis added).

[36] *See* Diamond, *supra* note 33, at 420.

[37] 17 U.S.C. § 1(e) (1952). *See also* the original 17 U.S.C. § 101(e)

once the composer permitted his composition to be recorded, he had to allow any other person to make a similar use of such composition upon notification of the user's intention and payment to the copyright holder of a two-cent royalty for each record reproduced.[38]

The only party granted protection under the Copyright Act of 1909 was the composer. He was deemed the true "author" of the musical composition as opposed to performers who "author" the recorded performance and record manufacturers who "author" the production of the sound recording.[39] Most important for purposes of this article, the Copyright Act of 1909 did not extend federal protection to actual sound recordings.[40] This omission was not an oversight. As noted in the House Committee's analysis of the 1909 version of the Copyright Act:

> It is not the intention of the committee to extend the right of copyright to the mechanical reproductions [records] themselves, but only to give the composer or copyright proprietor the control, in accordance with the [compulsory licensing] provisions of the bill, of the manufacture and use of such devices.[41]

(1952), still effective for recordings fixed prior to February 15, 1972, which provides that when the owner of a copyrighted musical composition (i.e., sheet music) permits others to make mechanical reproductions, any unauthorized reproduction or other infringement can be enjoined and damages as specified in § 1(e) can be obtained, but no criminal actions can be initiated.

[38] *See* Comment, *supra* note 7, at 890. For the various issues surrounding § 1(e), *see* Diamond, *supra* note 33, at 420–29. *See generally* NIMMER, *supra* note 32 at § 108.4.

[39] *See* Comment, *The Sound Recording Act of 1971: An End to Piracy on the High C's?*, 40 GEO. WASH. L. REV. 964, 966–67 (1972). The 1976 Copyright Revision Act does not protect performers either. Performers have turned to contracts with record manufacturers and state common law for protection. *See generally*, Waxman, *Performance Rights in Sound Recordings*, 52 TEX. L. REV. 42 (1973); Comment, *The Twilight Zone: Meanderings in the Area of Performers' Rights*, 9 U.C.L.A. L. REV. 819 (1962).

[40] *See generally* Chafee, *Reflections on the Law of Copyright*, 45 COLUM. L. REV. 719 (1945).

[41] H.R. REP. No. 2222, 60 Cong., 2d Sess. 7–9 (1909). Nine bills were intro-

Moreover, the courts have held that the scope of the term "writings" in the Act is more narrow than the same term in the Constitution and that, even though a copyright in a sound recording is within the scope of possible congressional protection, such protection was not available under the Act.[42]

Two reasons have been submitted for this intentional omission of Congress in 1909. The first reason is historical: Congress was reacting to the situation which had developed prior to the Supreme Court's 1908 decision in *White-Smith Music Publishing Co. v. Apollo Co.*[43] In anticipation of the *Apollo* decision, Aeolian Music Company, the leading piano roll manufacturer, attempted to dominate the recording industry by contracting with almost all the members of the Music Publishers Association for exclusive recording rights in their musical compositions.[44] Congress feared that giving the proprietor of the copyright in the musical composition a copyright interest in the mechanical reproduction itself would open the door for large recording companies to buy up the rights to these reproductions and thereby create a "musical trust" that would unduly hamper the dissemination of recorded music.[45]

Second, constitutional questions about whether sound recordings could be considered as "writings" of an "author"

---

duced prior to the Act's passage—none contained any provision recognizing a copyright in sound recordings. *See* Staff of Senate Comm. on the Judiciary Subcomm. on Patents, Trademarks, and Copyrights, 86th Cong., 2d Sess., *The Unauthorized Duplication of Sound Recordings* 47 (Comm. Print 1961) (RINGER, Study No. 26) [hereinafter cited as RINGER].

[42] *See, e.g.*, Capitol Records, Inc. v. Mercury Records Corp., 221 F.2d 657 (2d Cir. 1955). *See also* Mazer v. Stein, 347 U.S. 201 (1954). *See generally* NIMMER, *supra* note 32, at § 12.

[43] 209 U.S. 1 (1908). *See* notes 30–33 *supra* and accompanying text.

[44] H.R. REP. No. 2222, 60th Cong., 2d Sess. 4–6 (1909); H.R. REP. No. 7083, 59th Cong., 2d Sess. 9 (1908). *See* Comment, *supra* note 7, at n. 26.

[45] *See* Comment, *Goldstein v. California and the Protection of Sound Recordings: Arming the States for Battle with the Pirates*, WASH. & LEE. L. REV. 604, 609 (1974).

hindered their inclusion in the 1909 Act.[46] With but one early exception [47] the courts over the years since the inception of the 1909 Act uniformly assumed that sound recordings were not copyrightable.[48] In the acclaimed case of *Capitol Records, Inc. v. Mercury Records Corp.*,[49] the court held that, although sound recordings were expressly omitted from the original Act, they are capable of copyright under the Constitution. In *Shaab v. Kleindienst*,[50] the court upheld the constitutionality of the Sound Recording Act of 1971, finding sound recordings to be copyrightable under the Constitution. Although some older authority is *contra*,[51] the Supreme Court in *Goldstein v. California* [52] recognized, albeit *in dictum*, that "recordings of artistic performances may be within the reach of [the Constitution]." [53]

The upshot of this development is that the actual sound recording did not receive federal protection until the Sound Recording Amendment in 1971. Until recently the regulations of the Copyright Office stated: "[A] phonograph record or other sound recording is not considered a 'copy' of the compositions recorded on it, and is not acceptable for copy-

[46] *See* Hearings on Pending Bills to Amend and Consolidate the Acts Respecting Copyright Before the Senate and House Committees on Patents, 60th Cong., 1st Sess. 265–67, 273–81, 359–60 (1908). *See generally* Copyright Society of the U.S.A., Studies on Copyright, The Meaning of "Writings" in the Copyright Clause of the Constitution (Study No. 3, Fisher ed. 1963).

[47] Fonotipia Ltd. v. Bradley, 171 E. 951 (C.C.E.D. N.Y. 1909).

[48] R.C.A. Mfg. Co., Inc., v. Whiteman, 114 F.2d 86 (2d Cir. 1940); Jerome v. Twentieth Century-Fox Film Corp., 67 F. Supp. 736 (S.D.N.Y. 1946), *aff'd*, 165 F.2d 784 (2d Cir. 1948); Waring v. WDAS Broadcasting Station, Inc., 327 Pa. 433, 194 A. 631 (1937); *See generally* Nimmer *supra* note 32 at § 35.2.

[49] 221 F.2d 657 (2d Cir. 1955).

[50] 345 F. Supp. 589 (D.D.C. 1972). *See also* United States v. Bodin, 375 F. Supp. 1265 (W.D. Okla. 1974).

[51] *See* People v. Strassner, 299 N.Y. 325, 87 N.E. 2d 280 (1949). *See also* United States v. Alpers, 338 U.S. 680 (1950).

[52] 412 U.S. 546 (1973).

[53] *Id.* at 562. *See* Note, *Protection of Sound Recordings Under the Proposed Copyright Revision Bill* 51 Minn. L. Rev. 746, 747–48 (1967). *See generally* Comment, *supra* note 39, at n. 11.

right registration. Likewise, the copyright office does not register claims to exclusive rights in mechanical recordings themselves, or in the performances they reproduce."[54]

B. DEVELOPMENT OF STATE LAW PROTECTION TO COMBAT RECORDING PIRACY

In the absence of federal statutory protection, varying remedies were developed by state courts to protect sound recordings from unauthorized duplication. Such common law theories as right of privacy,[55] interference with contractual relations,[56] injury to reputation and moral rights,[57] interference with employer-employee relations, and *quantum meruit*[58] were employed to grant protection.[59] These doctrines have been labeled "extrinsic" because their primary thrust is to protect rights other than copyright;[60] their effect upon the copyright is therefore a tangential one. The two most successful and widely accepted theories were the common law doctrines of common law copyright and unfair competition.[61] Although courts have sometimes confused the

[54] J. Taubman, *Performing Arts Management and Law* 148 (1972), *citing* 37 C.F.R. § 202.8(b) (1959).

[55] Waring v. WDAS Broadcasting Station, Inc., 327 Pa. 433, 456, 194 A. 631, 642 (1937) (*concurring opinion*). *See generally* Gieseking v. Urania Records, Inc., 17 Misc. 2d 1034, 155 N.Y.S.2d 171 (Sup. Ct. 1956); Nimmer, *The Right of Publicity*, 19 LAW & CONTEMP. PROB. 203 (1954).

[56] Metropolitan Opera Ass'n v. Wagner-Nichols Recorder Corp., 199 Misc. 756, 101, N.Y.S.2d 483, 498–99 (Sup. Ct. 1950), *aff'd*, 279 App. Div. 632, 107 N.Y.S.2d 795 (1951).

[57] Granz v. Harris, 198 F.2d 585, 590 (2d Cir. 1952) (Frank, J., *concurring*).

[58] Peterson v. KMTR Radio Corp., 18 U.S.L.W. 2044 (Cal. Super. Ct., July 7, 1949).

[59] *See* Note, *The Future of Record Piracy*, 38 BROOKLYN L. REV. 406, 421–24 (1971).

[60] *See* Goldstein, *Federal System Ordering of the Copyright Interest*, 69 COLUM. L. REV. 49 (1969). These theories have received little acceptance in the courts as a basis for granting copyright-related state law relief. *See* Comment, *supra* note 45, at n. 36.

[61] *See* Comment, *Performers' Rights and Copyright: The Protection of Sound Recordings from Modern Pirates*, 59 CALIF. L. REV. 548, 550 (1971).

concepts and used them interchangeably,[62] the theories are separate, with the better reasoned decisions maintaining the distinction. Another source of protection has been state antipiracy penal statutes. The statutes are of fairly recent origin and represent an outgrowth of the protection earlier afforded by the states in civil actions.[63]

1. *Protection Under Common Law Copyright.* Often referred to as "the right of first publication," the doctrine of common law copyright protects an author's proprietary interests in his works prior to publication.[64] Under this doctrine an author has exclusive control over the first publication of his work and may prevent publication entirely.[65] To qualify for such a copyright the work must satisfy three requirements: (1) the expression of the work must be developed beyond the point of merely an abstract idea; (2) the work must be original with its author; and (3) the work must be unpublished.[66] Since works capable of statutory copyright must also satisfy the first two conditions, it follows that all works capable of statutory copyright protection are likewise protected under common law copyright provided only that such works are unpublished.[67] Once a work is published

[62] *See, e.g.,* Waring v. Dunlea, 26 F. Supp. 338 (E.D.N.C. 1939); Metropolitan Opera Ass'n, Inc. v. Wagner-Nichols Recorder Corp., 199 Misc. 786, 101 N.Y.S.2d 483 (Pup. Ct. 1950), *aff'd,* 279 App. Div. 632, 107 N.Y.S.2d 795 (1951).

It has been suggested that courts have confused the two concepts because both involve property rights. *See* Waxman, *supra* note 39, at 51. Moreover, confusion by the courts was facilitated by the fact that a single party could assert rights based on both theories. *See* Comment, *supra* note 45, at n. 38.

[63] *See* Kurlantzick, *The Constitutionality of State Law Protection of Sound Recordings.* 5 CONN. L. REV. 204, 207 (1972).

[64] *See* Estate of Hemingway v. Random House, Inc., 23 N.Y.2d 341, 244 N.E.2d 250, 296 N.Y.S.2d 771 (1968).

[65] *See* Chamberlain v. Feldman, 300 N.Y. 135, 139, 89 N.E.2d 863, 865 (1949).

[66] NIMMER, *supra* note 32 at § 11.

[67] *Id.* 17 U.S.C. § 2 (1952) specifically preserves common law rights in unpublished works by providing that "nothing in this title shall be construed to annul or limit the right of the author or proprietor of an unpublished work, at common law or in equity, to prevent the copying, publication, or use of such unpublished work without his consent, and to obtain damages therefor."

the common law copyright is extinguished by the act of public dedication.[68]

Although the protection of common law copyright hinges on the definition of "publication," the term is not defined in the Copyright Act of 1909.[69] Nimmer points out that the relevant decisions indicate that

> publication occurs when by consent of the copyright owner, the original or tangible copies of a work are sold, leased, loaned, given away, or otherwise made available to the general public, or when an authorized offer is made to dispose of the work in any such manner even if a sale or other such disposition does not in fact occur.[70]

If the definition of publication applied by state courts permits the author to exploit his work commercially without having that exploitation constitute publication, the author is completely protected by common law copyright of unlimited duration.[71]

Although the court in *Waring v. WDAS Broadcasting Station*[72] was concerned with the unauthorized broadcasting of records rather than the record piracy issue of unauthorized reproduction, the decision represents restricted application of the nonpublication doctrine. In holding that common law

[68] *See* Cary, *The Common Law and Statutory Background of the Law of Musical Property*, 15 VAND. L. REV. 397, 401–05 (1962) for a complete discussion of the development of common law rights in this area.

[69] The Act does define "date of publication" as "the earliest date when copies of the first authorized edition were placed on sale, sold, or publicly distributed. . . ." 17 U.S.C. § 26 (1952). However, it has been held consistently that this section merely specifies the time at which the statutory copyright, if any, begins running and that it does not define publication itself. "Apparently, a definition of publication was intentionally omitted because of the difficulty of defining the term with respect to works of art where no copies are reproduced." NIMMER, *supra* note 32 at § 49, n. 41, citing Hearings on S. 6330 and H.R. 19853, 59th Cong. 1st Sess. 71 (1906).

[70] NIMMER, *supra* note 32, § 49 at 194–95 (emphasis deleted).

[71] In contrast the copyright clause of the Constitution mandates that Congress may grant copyright protection only for "limited times." *See* text accompanying note 24, *supra*. *See also* Comment, *supra* note 45, at 614.

[72] 327 Pa. 433, 194 A. 631 (1937).

rights in a recording are not divested by publication,[73] the court made a spurious distinction between publication of the musical composition and the sound recording. While the prevailing state rule that sale or distribution of records does not divest the common law protection in the sound recording was gradually developing,[74] Judge Learned Hand, writing for the Second Circuit in *RCA Manufacturing Co. v. Whiteman*,[75] stated that, even if each phonorecord bears a specific restriction, its sale or distribution constitutes a publication divesting any copyright protection. He could "see no reason why the same acts that unconditionally dedicate the common law copyright in works copyrightable under the act, should not do the same in the case of works not copyrightable."[76]

Disagreeing with the federal rule as set forth in *Whiteman*, a New York state court in *Metropolitan Opera Association v. Wagner-Nichols Recorder Corp.*[77] granted an order restraining the defendant from making an unauthorized recording of a radio broadcast. Although primarily basing the decision on unfair competition, the court noted that "the performance of operas by Metropolitan Opera and their broadcast over the network of American Broadcasting cannot be deemed a general publication"[78] which divests the plaintiffs of their property rights in the performances.

In the leading case of *Capitol Records v. Mercury Records*

[73] The court's reasoning in *WDAS* is not entirely clear regarding common law protection, since the court emphasized that the restriction Waring put on each record created an equitable servitude. The court also relied upon the theory of unfair competition. *Id. See also* Waring v. Dunlea, 26 F. Supp. 338 (E.D.N.C. 1939), in which the court, in a less than cogent manner, held that a legend appearing on the record restricting broadcasts to a specific program rendered their commercial distribution a nondivestitive limited publication.

[74] *See* Waxman, *supra* note 39, at 56.

[75] 114 F.1d 86 (2d Cir.), *cert. denied*, 311 U.S. 712 (1940).

[76] *Id.* at 89.

[77] 199 Misc. 786, 101 N.Y.S.2d 483 (Sup. Ct. 1950), *aff'd*, 279 App. Div. 632, 107 N.Y.S.2d 795 (1951).

[78] 199 Misc. at 793, 101 N.Y.S.2d at 494.

Corp.,[79] the Second Circuit held that state law, not federal, should govern the determination of when sound recordings are "published." The majority claimed that because Congress had chosen not to include sound recordings as copyrightable works, federal law did not apply.[80] In overruling the earlier *Whiteman* decision, the court noted that New York's law was set forth in *Metropolitan Opera*[81] and that, under *Erie R.R. v. Tompkins*,[82] federal courts were bound to follow state substantive law in diversity cases.[83] Although the holding of *Capitol Records* makes clear that the sale of phonograph records of performances by musical artists does not constitute a "publication" which would result in the loss of any common law rights,[84] the court's reasoning has been highly criticized.[85]

Judge Hand's dissent in *Capitol Records* came as no surprise, since the majority was overruling his *Whiteman* deci-

[79] 221 F.2d 657 (2d Cir. 1955).

[80] *Id.* at 662.

[81] Because neither *Metropolitan Opera* nor *Capitol Records* distinguished performances from duplication rights in sound recordings, no recent cases have tested the *Capitol Records* court's assertion that *Metropolitan Opera* overruled *Whiteman*. Although one court has so recognized, Ettore v. Philco Television Broadcasting Corp., 229 F.2d 481, 488 (3rd Cir.), *cert. denied*, 351 U.S. 926 (1956), Nimmer questions the *Capitol Records* court's assertion. *See* NIMMER, *supra* note 32 at § 51.2.

[82] 304 U.S. 64 (1938).

[83] 221 F.2d at 662. It would appear that *Whiteman* is still the federal rule and thus applies in federal cases not based on diversity. *See* Comment, *The Sound Recording Act of 1971: An End to Piracy on the High C's?*, *supra* note 39, at n. 44. The federal policy of defining the sale of a record as a publication is also found in Copyright Office Circular 56 entitled "Copyright for Sound Recordings." This circular, issued after the Sound Recording Act, states that "[p]ublication generally means the sale, placing on sale, or public distribution of copies of the sound recording."

[84] This holding was adopted by a New York state court the next year. *See* Gieseking v. Urania Records, Inc., 17 Misc.2d 1034, 155 N.Y.S.2d 171 (Sup. Ct. 1956).

[85] *See* NIMMER, *supra* note 32 at § 51.2; Kaplan, *Performer's Right and Copyright: The Capitol Records Case*, 69 HARV. L. REV. 409, 425–28 (1956); Comment, *The Twilight Zone: Meanderings in the Area of Performers' Rights*, 9 U.C.L.A. L. REV. 819, 827 (1962).

sion. He agreed with his brethren that sound recordings are "writings" capable of copyright under the Constitution even though Congress had chosen not to include them in the Copyright Act. But he strongly disagreed with the majority when he argued in favor of total federal preemption, asserting that, because federal law exclusively governs "writings," it must also control the question whether an author has "published" his writings.[86] He realized that his view was harsh in that Congress had not provided copyright protection for phonorecords, but because the alternative was unlimited monopoly, he was satisfied his conclusion was just.[87] As one commentator has noted:

> Until Judge Hand's preemption theory raised its head again in the mid-1960's, the law seemed settled that state law defined the concept of publication, and the prevailing state law rule was that sale of phonorecords does not constitute a publication divesting the performer of common law copyright in his recorded performance.[88]

2. *Protection Under Unfair Competition.* Unlike copyright protection which depends upon originality or creativity, the tort of unfair competition "recognizes a property right in business assets acquired through the investment of time, money, and effort." [89] In an early New York case [90] in which

[86] 221 F.2d at 667.

[87] *Id.* Judge Hand was especially concerned about the possibility of "unlimited monopoly," since this ran directly contrary to the "limited times" language of the Constitution. *See* text accompanying note 24 *supra.*

[88] *See* Waxman, *supra* note 39, at 58. Not all state courts have jockeyed the definition of publication. These courts have realized the inherent fallacy in extending perpetual protection under common law copyright. *See* Shapiro, Bernstein & Co., Inc. v. Miracle Record Co., Inc., 91 F. Supp. 473 (N.D. Ill. 1950). *See also* McIntyre v. Double-A Music Corp., 166 F. Supp. 681 (S.D. Cal. 1958); Mills Music, Inc. v. Cromwell Music, Inc., 126 F. Supp. 54 (S.D.N.Y. 1954); Granz v. Harris, 98 F. Supp. 906 (S.D.N.Y. 1951), *modified,* 198 F.2d 585 (2d Cir. 1952).

[89] *See* Waxman, *supra* note 39, at 58.

A hodge-podge of practices fall under the general heading of unfair competition. See W. Prosser, Law of Torts 956–57 (4th ed. 1971). One court has noted: "The doctrine, as thus announced, has since, by process of growth, been

the defendants had produced exact duplicates of the plaintiff's records and sold them to the public, the court found the three traditional elements of a cause of action for unfair competition: first, there was *competition* because both parties were selling the same recordings; second, there was *misappropriation* of a business asset in the form of the recordings themselves; and third, there was "*passing off*" because the defendant was representing his records as those of the plaintiff, causing confusion among purchasers about the source of the goods.[91]

Whereas the element of passing off must be met to protect the copyright proprietor against counterfeiting,[92] pirates often label their products as duplications or reproductions of the original recording.[93] Thus, the expansion of unfair competition began in another early New York decision, *Fonotipia Ltd. v. Bradley*,[94] in which the court held that, although the defendant had made no attempt to pass off his records as those of the plaintiff, the element of "passing off" was no longer necessary to establish unfair competition.[95] In effect,

---

greatly expanded in its scope to encompass the schemes and inventions of the modern genius bent upon reaping where he has not sown." National Tel. Directory Co. v. Dawson Mfg. Co., 214 Mo. App. 683, 263 S.W. 483, 484 (1924).

[90] Victor Talking Machine Co. v. Armstrong, 132 F. 711 (C.C.D.N.Y. 1904). *See also* Pottstown Daily News Pub. Co. v. Pottstown Broadcasting Co., 411 Pa. 383, 388, 192 A.2d 657, 663 (1963).

[91] 132 F. at 712.

[92] Because counterfeiting includes imitation of trademarks or trade names, wrappers, labels, or containers, false marketing ("passing off") is not difficult to prove. As has been noted previously, however, counterfeiting is expressly prohibited by 18 U.S.C. § 2318 (1970). *See* note 7 *supra.*

[93] *See 1971 Hearings* 16; Comment, *The Sound Recording Act of 1971*, *supra* note 39, at 971. *But cf. Public Hearing on Tape Piracy*, Statement of Joel Schoenfeld before Attorney General of the State of New York, *reported in* 5 PERF. ARTS REV. 5, 8 (1974). In his testimony, Schoenfeld points out that, although the packaging of pirated records often looks cheaper, the pirate nonetheless attempts to demonstrate to the public that the recordings are legitimate.

[94] 171 F. 951 (C.C.E.D.N.Y. 1909).

[95] *Id.* at 964.

the court was widening the element of misappropriation in that equitable relief was granted without intentional deception.[96]

The elimination of the passing or "palming" off element was given further impetus in the Supreme Court's decision, *International News Service v. The Associated Press*.[97] In holding that the defendant competing news service could not distribute rewritten copies of plaintiff's news releases under its own name even though plaintiff's dispatches had previously been published, the Court commented:

> It is said that the [traditional] elements of unfair competition are lacking because there is no attempt by defendant to palm off its goods as those of the complainant, characteristic of the most familiar, if not the most typical, cases of unfair competition. . . . But we cannot concede that the right to equitable relief is confined to that class of cases.[98]

The *INS* decision greatly expanded the misappropriation doctrine in that the Court established an "unjust enrichment" theory: as long as the plaintiff's dispatches retained any commercial value, that is, a qualified "property" right, the misappropriation theory could be used to enjoin the defendant.[99]

The broadest application of *INS*[100] is found in *Metro-*

[96] The court held that equitable relief should be granted whenever one party gains a commercial advantage by appropriating the salable properties of another's product or idea. *Id.*

It might be noted here that both torts of unfair competition and common law copyright law do not hinge on a showing of good or bad faith. *See* United Drug Co. v. Obear-Nester Glass Co., Ill F.2d 997, 999 (8th Cir.), *cert. denied*, 311 U.S. 665 (1940). Therefore, liability for unfair competition is generally not subject to a defense of good faith. *See generally* R. CALLMAN, UNFAIR COMPETITION, TRADEMARKS, AND MONOPOLIES 175 (3d ed. 1970).

[97] 248 U.S. 215 (1918).

[98] *Id.* at 241–42 (citation omitted).

[99] *See* Waxman, *supra* note 39, at 59.

[100] Many subsequent cases have confined *INS* to its facts. *See, e.g.*, Cable Vision, Inc. v. KUTV, 335 F.2d 348, 352 n. 5 and accompanying text (9th Cir. 1964); RCA Mfg. Co. v. Whiteman, 114 F.2d 86 (2d Cir.), *cert. denied*, 311

politan Opera Association, Inc. v. Wagner-Nichols Recorder Corp.,[101] in which the court, albeit *in dicta*, purported to hold that neither passing off nor direct competition is required to establish unfair competition.[102] The court noted that all that was required was an "effort to profit from labor, skill, expenditures, name and reputation of others."[103] The strength of *Metropolitan Opera*'s holding is weakened, however, because the court found both the elements of competition and passing off to exist.[104]

C. THE SEARS-COMPCO DECISIONS AND AFTERMATH

Despite Judge Hand's dissent in *Capitol Records* urging that the Constitution's copyright clause preempted state pro-

U.S. 712 (1940); Cheney Bros. v. Doris Silk Corp., 35 F.2d 279, 280–81 (2d Cir. 1929). Other courts have, however, used the *INS* decision to broadly apply the misappropriation doctrine. *See, e.g.*, Pottstown Daily News Publishing Co. v. Pottstown Broadcasting Co., 247 F. Supp. 578 (E.D. Pa. 1965); Capitol Records, Inc. v. Mercury Records Corp., 109 F. Supp. 330 (S.D.N.Y. 1952), *aff'd*, 221 F.2d 657 (2d Cir. 1955); Metropolitan Opera Ass'n v. Wagner-Nichols Recorder Corp., 199 Misc. 786, 101 N.Y.S.2d 483 (Sup. Ct. 1950), *aff'd*, 279 App. Div. 632, 107 N.Y.S.2d 795 (1951).

[101] 199 Misc. 786, 101 N.Y.S.2d 483 (Sup. Ct. 1950), *aff'd*, 279 App. Div. 632, 107 N.Y.S.2d 795 (1951).

[102] 199 Misc. at 795, 101 N.Y.S.2d at 491–92. No claim was made that the defendant was actually competing with the plaintiff itself in the sale of records.

[103] 199 Misc. at 795, 101 N.Y.S.2d at 492.

[104] *See* Gieseking v. Urania Records, Inc., 17 Misc. 2d 1034, 155 N.Y.S.2d 171 (Sup. Ct. 1956). Though neither passing off nor direct competition was present, the court, citing the *Capitol Records* decision, which upheld *Metropolitan Opera*, denied a motion to dismiss based upon the theory of unfair competition.

The most significant resistance to the *INS–Metropolitan Opera* rationale was voiced by Judge Hand in RCA Mfg. Co., Inc. v. Whiteman, 114 F.2d 86 (2d Cir.), *cert. denied*, 311 U.S. 712 (1940). Although *Whiteman* was based on common law copyright protection, *see* notes 75–76 *supra* and accompanying text, Judge Hand rejected the alternative theory of unfair competition. He was unwilling to extend *INS* beyond its particular facts, and, in the absence of "palming off" or misleading the public, he could find no remedy for the plaintiff in the law of unfair competition. 114 F.2d at 90. *See also* Cheney Bros. v. Doris Silk Corp., 35 F.2d 279 (2d Cir. 1929) (earlier Hand decision limiting *INS* to its facts).

tection, most state courts continued to expand their protective authority under common law copyright or, more generally, because of its broadened possibilities, unfair competition.[105] Hand's dissent did, however, foreshadow the Supreme Court's treatment of the federal preemption question raised in the 1964 landmark companion cases of *Sears, Roebuck & Co. v. Stiffel Co.*[106] and *Compco Corp. v. Day-Brite Lighting, Inc.*[107] In the words of one author, "[b]oth cases presented the issue of whether a state could grant protection against copying, under the doctrine of unfair competition, to an item not protectible under the federal design patent statute."[108] Writing for the Court in both cases Justice Black stated:

> [W]hen an article is unprotected by a patent or a copyright, state law may not forbid others to copy that article. To forbid copying would interefere with the federal policy, found in Art. I, sec. 8, cl. 8, of the Constitution and in the implementing federal statutes, of allowing free access to copy whatever the federal patent and copyright laws leave in the public domain.[109]

[105] *See generally* Chapman, *The Supreme Court and Federal Law of Unfair Competition*, 54 TRADEMARK REP. 573 (1964).

[106] 376 U.S. 225 (1964).

[107] 376 U.S. 234 (1964). Both cases involved substantially identical facts. Each case involved a particular item, pole lamps in *Sears* and overhead lighting fixtures in *Compco*, the design of which had been registered for a federal design patent. Both actions were for infringment of these design patents by defendants who had manufactured virtually identical copies of the original items and who had sold them under their own names. And in both cases the lower courts had declared the design patent invalid but had nevertheless granted relief on the basis of the state law of unfair competition. The only appreciable factual distinction between the two cases was that, in *Compco*, there was evidence in the record indicating that there had been at least one incident in which a purchaser of the defendant's copy had been confused by its similarity to the original. *Id.* at 236–37. There was no such evidence of public confusion in the *Sears* case. However, the Court did not consider this difference significant and treated both cases as presenting the same issues. *Id.* at 237–38.

[108] *See* Comment, *Goldstein v. California and the Protection of Sound Recordings: Arming the States for Battle with the Pirates*, 31 WASH. AND LEE L. REV. 604, 627–28 (1974).

[109] 376 U.S. at 237.

The *Sears* and *Compco* decisions left the courts in judicial chaos. Read literally, the cases appeared to spell the end of protection against sound recording piracy by any authority except Congress. The cases seriously undermined protection afforded by common law copyright and unfair competition. Common law copyright was most seriously deterred, for although the *Sears* Court recognized that its decision would not affect copyright in unpublished writings,[110] the constitutional preemption theory espoused by the Court would require a federal definition of "publication," a state definition violating the supremacy clause.[111] Nimmer has noted that "[t]he states may not simply fashion their own peculiar definition of publication for sound recordings in order to avoid the thrust of federal preemption." [112] Unabashed by *Sears* and *Compco*, the New York state courts did not accept that the Supreme Court had precluded a state definition of publication if the alternative was denial of all rights in the work.[113]

[110] *Id.* at 231 n. 7. *See* 17 U.S.C. § 2 (1952). Application of the *Sears'* and *Compco's* preemption doctrine to common law protection for unpublished works has correctly been withheld. Edgar H. Woods Associates, Inc. v. Skene, 347 Mass. 357, 197 N.E.2d 886 (1964); Columbia Broadcasting System, Inc. v. Documentaries Unlimited, Inc., 42 Misc. 2d 723, 248 N.Y.S.2d 809 (Sup. Ct. 1964). *See generally* Comment, *Goldstein v. California: Validity of State Copyright Under the Copyright and Supremacy Clauses*, 25 Hast. L.J. 1196, 1205 (1974).

[111] Nimmer, *supra* note 32 at § 35.222.

[112] *Id. See also* Nimmer §§ 50.3, 51, and 59. *See* notes 64–88 *supra* and accompanying text.

[113] Capitol Records, Inc. v. Greatest Records, Inc., 43 Misc. 2d 878, 252 N.Y.S. 2d 553 (Sup. Ct. 1964); *accord*, Columbia Broadcasting Sys., Inc. v. Documentaries Unlimited, Inc., 42 Misc. 2d 723, 726, 248 N.Y.S.2d 809, 812 (Sup. Ct. 1964); *see* Columbia Broadcasting Sys., Inc. v. Cartridge City Ltd., 35 C.O. Bull. 87 (Sup. Ct. N.Y. 1966).

At least one commentator has contended that, in spite of *Sears'* and *Compco's* implication of federal preemption, it is "not unreasonable for lower courts to cling to the common law definition of publication," since otherwise "the sole result would be a diversion of profits to pirates unburdened by the expenses of producing the music." *See* Comment, *supra* note 61, at 562–65.

Moreover the dual decisions seemed to close the door to unfair competition. The Court in *Sears* held that the states could not prohibit under the doctrine of unfair competition the "copying" of inventions which, although eligible for federal patent protection, failed to meet the requisite standards for such protection.[114]

Motivated by their moral indignation at the pirates' practices, courts moved swiftly to distinguish *Sears* and *Compco* from common law misappropriation.[115] In the first record duplication case subsequent to *Sears* and *Compco*, *Capitol Records, Inc. v. Greatest Records, Inc.*,[116] the court distinguished the "copying" involved in *Sears* from the "misappropriation" involved in the unauthorized duplication in the case at hand. The distinction is that copying is a practice by "which a 'substantially identical' imitation"[117] is independently developed by the copier who "must himself expend labor and expense in its manufacture and production,"[118] whereas misappropriation involves the exact duplication of a work "by the odious act of stealing the actual investment

[114] 376 U.S. at 231–32. The *Compco* court did indicate that states could continue to prohibit the deceptive practice of "palming off" and that they could require proper labeling "or other precautions" to prevent customer confusion. *Id.* at 238–39.

[115] *See generally* Price, *The Moral Judge and the Copyright Statute: The Problem of* Stiffel *and* Compco, 14 ASCAP Copyright L. Symp. 90, 114 (1966).

[116] 43 Misc. 2d 878, 252 N.Y.S.2d 553 (Sup. Ct. 1964). For other cases maintaining the copying-misappropriation distinction, *see* Tape Indus. Ass'n of America v. Younger, 316 F. Supp. 340 (C.D. Cal. 1970); Capitol Records, Inc. v. Erickson, 2 Cal. App. 3d 526, 82 Cal. Rptr. 798, 164 U.S.P.Q. 465 (Dist. Ct. App. 1969); Baez v. Fantasy Records, Inc., 144 U.S.P.Q. 537 (Cal. Super. Ct. 1964); Capitol Records, Inc. v. Spies, 167 U.S.P.Q. 489 (Ill. App. Ct. 1970); CBS, Inc. v. Spies, 167 U.S.P.Q. 492 (Ill. Cir. Ct. 1970); Greater Recording Co., Inc. v. Stambler, 144 U.S.P.Q. 547 (Sup. Ct. N.Y. 1965); Liberty/U.A., Inc. v. Eastern Tape Corp., 11 N.C. App. 20, 180 S.E.2d 414 (1971).

[117] Comment, *Copyrights: States Allowed to Protect Works Not Copyrightable Under Federal Law*, 58 Minn. L. Rev. 316, 320 (1973).

[118] Note, *Copyright—New Light on Sears and Compco—State Copyright Laws Are Not Totally Preempted By the Copyright Act. Goldstein v. California, 412 U.S. 546 (1973)*, 5 Tex. Tech. L. Rev., 843, 846 (1974).

of time, money, effort and skill" [119] of the competitor.[120] Although this distinction has received impetus because of the failure of *Sears* and *Compco* to overrule the *INS* decision,[121] the distinction has been criticized by commentators, as well as courts, as being spurious because it rests upon the relative degree of technical proficiency and cost of the duplication process.[122]

Finally, courts have used various other theories to distinguish *Sears* and *Compco*. One such theory is the narrow exception of "palming off" carved out by the *Sears* and *Compco* Court.[123] Nimmer points out, however, that "palming off" in the *Compco* sense means "some *affirmative misrepresentation* by the defendant, and cannot arise merely by virtue of the fact that the public associates a given product with the plaintiff." [124] Other courts have purported to find statutory grounds within the Copyright Act itself for granting relief against pirates and have thereby provided protection while avoiding the preemption problem.[125] Finally, some courts have attempted to distinguish *Sears* and *Compco* on

[119] Comment, *supra* note 117, at 320.

[120] *See* Comment, *supra* note 7, at 899–900.

[121] *See* notes 97–99 *supra* and accompanying text. *But see* Columbia Broadcasting System, Inc. v. DeCosta, 377 F.2d 315, 318 (1st Cir. 1967), which held that *Sears* and *Compco* had overruled *International News Service*. One Texas court has held similarly to *DeCosta*. *See* Time-Saver Check, Inc. v. Deluxe Check Printers, Inc., 178 U.S.P.Q. 510 (N.D. Tex. 1973).

[122] *See* NIMMER, *supra* note 32 at § 35.224, Kurlantzick, *supra* note 7, at 215–16. *See also* International Tape Mfrs. Ass'n v. Gerstein, 344 F. Supp. 38, 51 (S.D. Fla. 1972); Columbia Broadcasting System, Inc. v. DeCosta, 377 F.2d 315 (1st Cir.), *cert. denied*, 389 U.S. 1007 (1967).

[123] *See* Capitol Records, Inc. v. Erickson, 2 Cal. App. 3d 526, 82 Cal. Rptr. 798 (1969).

[124] NIMMER, *supra* note 32 at § 35.223 (emphasis added). Compare note 91 *supra* and accompanying text.

[125] *See* Duchess Music Corp. v. Stern, 458 F.2d 1305 (9th Cir.), *cert. denied sub nom.* Rosner v. Duchess Music Corp., 409 U.S. 847 (1972), in which the court based its decision on a construction of the phrase "similar use," in 17 U.S.C. § 1(e) (1952). *See* Comment, *supra* note 45, at 631 n. 123. The *Duchess* doctrine is criticized by Nimmer. NIMMER, *supra* note 32 at § 108.4621.

the ground that they involved patent law only and were limited to the facts[126]—language to the contrary in *Sears* being disregarded.[127]

Common law copyright protection and the doctrine of unfair competition had given courts and commentators theoretical difficulties, if not practical ones, because the courts usually granted relief regardless of the theory or its application. *Sears* and *Compco* increased the difficulty of protecting plaintiffs under these theories. But even if *Sears* and *Compco* had not raised serious preemption questions, common law remedies were far from being adequate to control the burgeoning practice of record piracy. First, these varied approaches would cause a lack of uniformity among courts. Moreover, even if granted, an injunction against unauthorized duplication would prevent the pirate from duplicating only specific recordings of a plaintiff. Third, because of the relatively short life of most hit records, the real harm to the performer and manufacturer would already have been done before any remedy could be obtained. Finally, damages would be difficult to prove even if relief were granted.[128]

III. LEGISLATIVE ACTION TO PROTECT SOUND RECORDINGS

A. THE SOUND RECORDING ACT OF 1971

Between 1906 and 1951, thirty-one bills that would have provided some protection for sound recordings were defeated in Congress.[129] Although there was little direct opposition

[126] *See, e.g.,* Capitol Records, Inc. v. Greatest Records, Inc., 43 Misc. 2d 878, 252 N.Y.S.2d 553 (Sup. Ct. 1964). *See also* Pottstown Daily News Publishing Co. v. Pottstown Broadcasting Co., 247 F. Supp. 578, 580–81 (E.D. Pa. 1965).

[127] *See* Comment, *supra* note 2, at 199.

[128] *See* Comment, *supra* note 61, at 569 n. 139. *See also* Goldstein, *Copyrighting the New Music,* 17 BUFFALO L. REV. 355, 369 (1968).

[129] *See* Comment, *The War Against Record Piracy: An Uneasy Rivalry Between the Federal and State Governments,* 39 ALBANY L. REV. 87, 99 (1974).

to the principle of protecting sound recordings against unauthorized duplication, efforts failed largely because each segment of the entertainment industry attempted to maximize its own economic well-being.[130] In 1955 work began on legislation designed to revise the 1909 Act in its entirety which would include provisions to protect sound recordings. By 1970, even though Congress was reluctant to undertake extensive revision of the Act until the copyright problems raised by cable television were resolved,[131] the threat of record piracy to the economic stability of the recording industry became so overwhelming that the Departments of State, Justice, and Commerce, as well as the Librarian of Congress, joined with industry representatives to urge immediate passage of some form of legislation.[132]

The enactment of S. 646 [133] on October 15, 1971, marked the official recognition of a sound recording as a copyrightable work. As indicated in the legislative history, the purpose of the Sound Recording Act (SRA) was twofold: [134] first, the bill created "a limited copyright in sound recordings

[130] *Id.* There were also constitutional attacks in that some contended recordings were neither creative nor "writings." *See* notes 42–46 *supra* and accompanying text.

[131] *See* 1971 Hearings 11. *See* Comment, *The Sound Recording Act of 1971, supra* note 39, at n. 87.

[132] *Id.* at 9–16. Nimmer states that "[a]n additional reason for such enactment was to 'resolve' the problem of federal preemption under the *Sears-Compco* doctrine, which had pervaded, though not controlled, the attempts to combat record and tape piracy in the state courts." NIMMER, *supra* note 32 at § 35.1. *See also* H.R. REP. No. 487, 92d Cong., 1st sess., *reprinted in* [1971] U.S. CODE CONG. & AD. NEWS 1566.

Moreover, one writer points out that special impetus for the passage of the Sound Recording Act was provided by the participation of the United States in an international conference which met in 1971 to draft a treaty to combat record piracy worldwide. *See* Comment, *The Sound Recording Act of 1971, supra* note 39, at 978–79.

[133] Pub. L. No. 92–140, 85 Stat. 391 (1971). The amended provisions include: 17 U.S.C. §§ 1(f), 5(n), 19, 20, 26, 101(e) (Supp. 1976).

[134] H.R. REP., *supra* note 132, *reprinted in* [1971] U.S. CODE CONG. & AD. NEWS 1556, 1567.

[which made] unlawful the unauthorized reproduction and sale of copyrighted sound recordings"; second, the bill provided that persons using copyrighted musical works in recordings without authorization would be "subject to all the provisions of Title 17 [covering the] infringement of copyrights[135] and, in the case of willful infringement for profit, to criminal prosecution. . . ."[136] As a prerequisite for protection, the sounds must be embodied in a tangible medium in which the sounds are fixed[137] and from which the sound can be communicated directly or with the aid of a machine or device.[138]

Although the SRA does not contain a compulsory licensing provision permitting manufacturers engaged in the unauthorized reproduction of records and tapes "to copy the finished product, which has been developed and promoted through the efforts of the record company and the artists,"[139] the amendment does change the existing compulsory license provision.[140] Previously, record pirates were sometimes able to avoid liability by complying with this provision.[141] If pirates failed to comply with the provision, they

[135] *See* 17 U.S.C. §§ 501–510 (Supp. 1976).

[136] H.R. REP., *supra* note 132, *reprinted in* [1971] U.S. CODE CONG. & AD. NEWS 1566, 1577.

[137] *See Copyright for Sound Recordings*, Circular 56, Copyright Office (1973). The circular states that "a series of sounds constituting a sound recording is 'fixed' when that complete series is first produced in a final master recording that is later reproduced in published copies." *See also* NIMMER § 35.11 n. 11.

[138] *See* Circular 56, *supra* note 137. Distinguishing between sound recordings themselves and reproductions that are considered copies of the actual sound recordings, the SRA makes it clear that protection is afforded to the collection of sounds stored on the reproduction, rather than to the physical reproduction itself. *See* 17 U.S.C. §§ 1(e), 26 (1952 and Supp. 1976). *See also* Comment, *Sound Recording Act of 1971, supra* note 39, at 979–80.

[139] H.R. REP., *supra* note 134, *reprinted in* [1971] CODE CONG. & AD. NEWS 1566, 1569. *See* Comment, *supra* note 2, at 201.

[140] 17 U.S.C. § 101(e) (Supp. 1976). *See* Shaab v. Kleindienst, 345 F. Supp. 589 (D.D.C. 1972). *See also* Comment, *supra* note 129, at 100.

[141] *See* Schrader, *Sound Recordings: Protection Under State Law and Under the Recent Amendment to the Copyright Code*, 14 ARIZ. L. REV. 689, 713 (1972).

were subject to the possible remedies of an injunction and a statutory penalty of two cents per record. The owner of the copyright was allowed to recover three times the amount of the royalty if the infringer did not file the requisite notice of "intention to use." [142] Although no criminal action for piracy was provided before 1972, the SRA permits such actions for willful infringement for profit.[143] Because the SRA includes phonorecords in its list of copies [144] that are subject to infringement actions, the owner of the infringed copyright may recover both his damages and the profits of the infringer, or in the alternative, statutory damages ranging from $250 to $5,000.[145]

The SRA originally applied only to recordings fixed on or after February 15, 1972, that are also published and copyrighted before January 1, 1975.[146] Although it was hoped by the drafters of SRA that total copyright revision would be finalized by 1975, therefore making this legislation necessary only for a limited time period,[147] it became apparent that January 1, 1975, would come without the enactment of the general revision of the Copyright Act. The Sound Recording Act of 1974 [148] was enacted to expurgate the January 1, 1975, termination date for federal protection.

[142] *Id.*

[143] 17 U.S.C. § 104 (1952).

[144] 17 U.S.C. § 5(n) (Supp. 1976).

[145] *Id.* § 101(b). The copyright owner may also have impounded all the infringing copies and the equipment used to produce those copies, *id.* § 101(c), or destroyed, *id.* § 101(d). *See generally* Comment, *supra* note 129, at 100.

[146] H.R. Rep. *supra* note 132, *reprinted in* [1971] U.S. Code Cong. & Ad. News at 1566, 1566–67.

[147] *Id.* Another reason for this short time span was "to provide a period for further consideration of various alternatives for solving the problems in this area, before resorting to permanent legislative enactment." *Id.*

[148] Pub. L. No. 93–573, 88 Stat. 1973 (1974) (codified in scattered sections of 17 U.S.C.). The 1974 SRA did not pass without dissent. *See* 120 Cong. Rec., H 9976 (Oct. 7, 1974). The Department of State predicted "that a lapse in protection may trigger an increase in piracy and confront the industry with disastrous economic consequences." H.R. Rep. No. 93–1389, 93d Cong., 2d Sess. 3 (1974).

The significant problems with the SRA arose from the status of sound recordings fixed prior to 1972. Partially because of the "historical antipathy toward retroactive" legislation [149] and "the uncertain status of sound recordings under state law," [150] Congress specifically provided in the SRA that its terms shall not "be applied retroactively or be construed as affecting in any way any rights with respect to sound recordings fixed before the effective date of this Act." [151] Therefore, it was clear that Congress did not create any rights in existing recordings, leaving protection to the states.

As to the specific reasons Congress did not include pre-1972 recordings in the SRA, one can only speculate.[152] First, legislators may have thought there were too many practical problems with respect to recordings that were already in circulation, that is, bringing them into a scheme that made vesting of copyright depend upon notice and registration. But, as has been noted by one commentator, "these problems would not have been insuperable," [153] because those wishing to claim copyright in pre-1972 recordings could have been given a reasonable time to register their claims. Second, legislators may have thought that pre-1972 recordings were in the public domain and that it would simply not be a good idea to try to bring them into copyright.[154] Moreover, if the recordings were thought to be published, legislators may have thought themselves powerless to bring pre-1972 recordings back into copyright.[155] Finally, Congress may simply have

[149] Schrader, *supra* note 141, at 705.

[150] *Id. See also* Brown, *Publication and Preemption in Copyright Law: Elegiac Reflections on Goldstein v. California,* 22 U.C.L.A. L. Rev. 1022, 1041–43 (1975).

[151] Pub. L. No. 92–140, § 3, 85 Stat. 391 (1971).

[152] *See generally* Brown, *supra* note 50, at 1041–42.

[153] *Id.* at 1041.

[154] *See* notes 64–88 *supra* and accompanying text.

[155] In a recent trade secrets case, Chief Justice Burger commented: "[T]hat which is in the public domain cannot be removed therefrom by action of the States." Kewanee Oil Co. v. Bicron Corp., 416 U.S. 470, 481 (1974).

decided to leave these complex questions for resolution by state law.[156]

B. STATE STATUTES AND INTERPRETATION BY THE COURTS

The decision by Congress to exclude pre-1972 recordings from federal protection led to the proliferation of state anti-piracy statutes. At the time of the SRA's enactment, eight states had some type of statutory protection; [157] as of July 1974, twenty-six states had enacted such statutes.[158] These statutes confronted the identical preemption issues raised by the *Sears-Compco* decisions that state courts encountered in protecting the music industry in the post *Sears-Compco* period.[159] Unlike the courts, however, statutes "did not . . . have to talk about how they were doing it." [160] In defense of the Tennessee statute, the Attorney General of that state remarked that its statute was directed at "traffic in illicit and contraband property." [161] The Attorney General of New York declared that its statute was an "anti-larceny statute, whose enactment was within the state's police power." [162]

[156] Other aspects of the SRA are thoroughly discussed in Schrader. *supra* note 141; Comment, *The Sound Recording Act of 1971*, *supra* note 39; and, Note, *supra* note 6.

Additionally, the formal requirements of notice necessary to obtain a copyright are set forth in 17 U.S.C. § 19 (Supp. 1976). The notice, which must appear upon the publication of any reproduction of the sound recording in order to obtain protection, consists of "the letter *P* in a circle, the year of first publication of the sound recording, and the name of the owner of the copyright, . . . an abbreviation by which the name can be recognized, or a generally known alternative designation of the owner." *Id.*

[157] H.R. Rep. No. 487, 92d Cong., 1st Sess. 2 (1971).

[158] *See* State Laws Against Piracy of Sound Recordings: A Handbook for Enforcement and Prosecution (R IAA 1974).

[159] *See* notes 105–28 *supra* and accompanying text.

[160] Brown, *supra* note 150, at 1043.

[161] Brief for the Attorney-General of the State of Tennessee as Amicus Curiae at 1, Goldstein v. California, 412 U.S. 546 (1973).

[162] Brief for the Attorney-General of the State of New York as Amicus Curiae at 2, Goldstein v. California, 412 U.S. 546 (1973).

"It has been drawn," he said, "to prevent the theft of a particular type of property."[163] Other states have also defended the statutes on the basis of police power.[164]

Although technically not the equivalent of a copyright statute,[165] the ultimate effect of these statutes is identical. In general, these statutes prohibit the reproduction, distribution, or vendition of recordings whose sounds are duplicated without the consent of the owner of the original master recording.[166] An example of the language employed by many statutes is that of the Pennsylvania statute:

> It shall be unlawful for any person to:
> (1) knowingly transfer or cause to be transferred, directly or indirectly by any means, any sounds recorded on a phonograph record . . . tape . . . or other article on which sounds are recorded, with the intent to sell or cause to be sold . . . such article on which sounds are so transferred, without consent of the owner; or
> (2) manufacture, distribute or wholesale any article with the knowledge that the sounds are so transferred without consent of the owner.[167]

By their very language, these state statutes are equally applicable to post-1972 duplications. As such, a potential conflict exists with federal protection under the SRA since a sound recording covered by these state statutes never passes into the "public domain" and thereby loses its protection.[168] Because

[163] *Id.* at 6.

[164] *See* Brown, *supra* note 150, at 1043.

[165] By penalizing the "transfer" without the consent of the owner of sounds recorded on a phonograph record, the New York statute, N.Y. Gen. Bus. Law § 561 (McKinney 1968) artlessly attempted to avoid any suggestion that the "copying" of another's work was prohibited. It is interesting, however, that the "unauthorized copying of phonograph records did creep in as the caption of New York General Business Law § 561." Brown, *supra* note 150, at 1043.

[166] *See* Appendix II for a summary of the provisions of these various statutes.

[167] 18 Pa. Cons. Stat. § 4116(b) (1973). "Owner" is defined as "the person who owns the master phonograph record, master disc, master tape, master film or other device used for reproducing recorded sounds. . . ." *Id.* § 4116(a).

[168] Also, unlike the federal copyright provisions, no form of notice or registration is necessary to entitle sound recordings to the protection of the state statutes. *See* Dunaj, *Tape Piracy and Applicable Florida Criminal Laws*, 48 Fla. B. J. 338, 340 (1974).

of this apparent overlap, and the possibility of total federal preemption of the sound recording field in light of the SRA and the *Sears-Compco* doctrine, a court encounter was inevitable.[169]

Three significant cases emerged before the Supreme Court was finally to resolve the issues raised above. The first was the decision by a federal district court involving California's antipiracy statute, *Tape Industries Association of America v. Younger.*[170] Arguing the preemption theories of *Sears* and *Compco,* tape pirates sought declaratory and injunctive relief against enforcement of the California statute. The court denied plaintiffs relief, relying upon the distinction between copying and misappropriation to show that *Sears* and *Compco* were inapplicable.[171] In conclusion the court maintained "that [the California law] is a tolerable and permissible state regulation . . . and does not unconstitutionally intrude on the Federal policies enunciated in the Copyright Clause. . . ."[172]

In a case almost identical to *Younger,* a Florida federal district court reached a contrary result in *International Tape Manufacturers Association v. Gerstein.*[173] In noting that *Sears* and *Compco* may have "undermined the legality" of such theories as the copying-misappropriation theory relied upon in *Younger,*[174] the *Gerstein* court remarked: "[t]he focus of both *Sears* and *Compco* was the *artificial creation* [by state law] of patent or copyright protection afforded to [federally] unpatentable or uncopyrightable works, not the *manner* in which the works were reproduced."[175]

[169] *See generally* Comment, *supra* note 7, at 902–3.

[170] 316 F. Supp. 340 (C.D.Cal. 1970), *appeal dismissed,* 401 U.S. 902 (1971) (appeal dismissed for lack of jurisdiction). *See* CAL. PENAL CODE § 653h (West 1970).

[171] 316 F. Supp. at 350. *See* notes 115–22 *supra* and accompanying text.

[172] *Id.* at 351.

[173] 344 F. Supp. 38 (S.D. Fla. 1972). The Florida statute is similar to that of California's. Fla. Stat. Ann. § 543.041 (West 1973).

[174] *Id.* at 49.

[175] *Id.* at 51 (emphasis added).

The *Gerstein* Court also discussed the then recently enacted SRA.[176] The court took the position that, as to pre-1972 recordings, Congress did not intend to preempt relief granted by application of state law, because the language of the enacting clause "merely retained the status quo as existed prior to the enactment of the law."[177] The court went on to hold, however, that, although Congress may not have statutorily preempted state antipiracy laws as to pre-1972 recordings by the SRA, nevertheless such laws are preempted by the judicially created *Sears-Compco* doctrine.[178] Further, as to post-1972 recordings, the *Gerstein* court argued that there were two irreconcilable conflicts between state and federal statutes: first, federally granted protection was for a "limited time," that is, a fifty-six-year maximum duration, as opposed to the perpetual protection afforded by the Florida statute; and, second, the elaborate notice and registration requirements imposed by the federal copyright scheme were absent under the state formulation.[179]

The validity of the SRA was again before a federal court in *Tape Head Co. v. RCA Corp.*[180] With facts similar to *Younger* and *Gerstein*, the *Tape Head* court denied relief in refusing the plaintiff's contention that the SRA retroactively invalidated the state antipiracy law. Although as to this issue the *Gerstein* court had reached a like conclusion that the SRA did not change the status quo with respect to federal preemption for sound recordings prior to 1972, the *Tape Head*

[176] This issue, obviously, was not treated by the *Younger* Court, because the case was decided before the enactment of the SRA.

[177] 344 F. Supp. at 52. Nimmer takes a contrary view to *Gerstein*, arguing that the SRA in effect repealed the *Sears-Compco* doctrine. *See* NIMMER, *supra* note 32 at § 35.225. The Committee Reports did not discuss the effect of the SRA on federal preemption before 1972.

[178] 344 F. Supp. at 52.

[179] *Id.* at 54–55. The Court did imply that a state statute regarding post-1972 sound recordings could be drafted if carefully worded. *Id.* at 55. *See* Comment, *supra* note 45, at 634–35.

[180] 452 F.2d 816 (10th Cir. 1971).

court departed from the *Gerstein* argument that the *Sears-Compco* doctrine was controlling. In so doing, *Tape Head* followed the view that *Sears* and *Compco* did not require federal preemption even prior to enactment of the SRA.[181]

IV. THE SUPREME COURT RESPONDS: *GOLDSTEIN V. CALIFORNIA*

A. THE DECISION

In the landmark decision *Goldstein v. California*,[182] petitioners were charged with violating § 653(h) of the California Penal Code, the same statute involved in *Younger*, which makes record piracy a misdemeanor. The basic question raised in *Goldstein* was whether the states have the power to protect sound recordings fixed and published before 1972.[183] In a five-to-four decision, the Supreme Court answered the question affirmatively.

The Court first considered whether or not the constitutional grant of copyright power to Congress preempted all state power in that area. In concluding that it did not, the Court relied heavily upon passages from the Federalist Papers.[184] Asking itself whether the existence of such a power in the states be " 'absolutely and totally *contradictory* and *repugnant*' to the existence of a like one in Congress?"[185] the Court distinguished between items of local and national in-

[181] *Id.* at 819.

[182] 412 U.S. 546 (1973). The literature discussing the *Goldstein* decision is extensive. See articles and comments cited throughout this essay.

[183] The Court specifically stated that *Goldstein* did *not* concern the power of the states to protect post-1972 sound recordings. 412 U.S. at 552 n.7. Thus, the Court did not deal with this issue as *Gerstein* did. *See* note 179 *supra* and accompanying text.

[184] 412 U.S. at 552–58. The Federalist Papers were political pamphlets written to secure support for the proposed Constitution. CAHILL, JUDICIAL LEGISLATION (1952).

[185] 412 U.S. at 553, quoting *The Federalist No. 32*, at 241 (B. Wright ed. 1961) (A. Hamilton).

terest.[186] When the item is of "purely local importance," [187] concurrent exercise of power is constitutionally permissible, because the interest of the locale may dictate that the item be afforded a higher level of protection than that deemed necessary by congressional legislation.[188] As applied to the *Goldstein* factual setting, this reasoning is somewhat faulty because the practice of tapes and record piracy can hardly be viewed as merely a local matter.[189]

Assuming the states could grant copyright protection, the petitioners next claimed that the California statute was unconstitutional because it gave protection for an unlimited time, in violation of the "limited Times" restriction [190] in the copyright clause.[191] The Court rejected this argument, interpreting the limit on copyright protection to refer only to acts of Congress.[192] Although the Court reasoned that any harm of perpetual duration would be minimized because it would be confined to the borders of the state, the Court failed to consider the possibility of the effect of all fifty states' enacting antipiracy statutes without durational limits.

The Court then considered another challenge of the petitioners: whether the California statute violates the Supremacy Clause.[193] Analogizing sound recordings, which were not

[186] 412 U.S. at 556–58.

[187] *Id.* at 558.

[188] *Id.* at 557–58.

[189] *See* Comment, *supra* note 129, at 107.

[190] *See* text accompanying note 24 *supra.*

[191] 412 U.S. at 560–61.

[192] *Id.*

[193] *Id.* at 561. Because the Court construed the California statute as providing state *copyright* protection, the Court raised serious Supremacy Clause issues that it might have avoided if it had construed the statute as one providing unfair competition protection. Indeed, other courts analyzing the California statute previous to *Goldstein* held that its protection ran to the business interests of competitors, rather than to the owner's rights as against the public at large. *See, e.g.,* Tape Indus. Ass'n of America v. Younger, 316 F. Supp. 340, 351 (C.D. Cal. 1970); Capitol Records, Inc. v. Erickson, 2 Cal. App. 3d 526, 538, 82 Cal. Rptr. 798, 806 (Ct. App. 1969), *cert. denied,* 398 U.S. 960 (1970). *See generally* Comment, *Goldstein v. California—The Constitutionality of a State Copyright,* 1973 UTAH L. REV. 851, 860–61 (1973).

given federal protection until 1972, to technological advances in the arts such as photographs and motion pictures which were given federal protection soon after their respective popularization, the Court ruled that congressional failure to protect sound recordings did not necessarily mean that they are not within a constitutional "writing." [194] Although petitioners pointed to the express intention of Congress in 1909 not to extend protection to sound recordings,[195] the Court ruled that the congressional failure to protect sound recordings was neutral, notwithstanding the fact that it took the form of active rejection of protective legislation.[196]

In establishing that congressional failure to provide for federal protection does not create an implication of such federal preemption, the *Goldstein* court's most difficult task was in distinguishing the *Sears-Compco* doctrine.[197] Although the *Sears* and *Compco* opinions, albeit *in dicta*, had explicitly applied the *Sears-Compco* doctrine to the area of copyrights as well as patents,[198] the *Goldstein* Court nevertheless distinguished the earlier decisions on the ground that the doctrine there enunciated applies only when there is a failure of protection under the patent laws, not when such failure is found in the copyright laws.[199] The Court thus

[194] 412 U.S. at 561–62. *See* Shaab v. Kleindienst, 345 F. Supp. 589, 590 (D.D.C. 1972) (sound recordings generally considered to fall within the copyright clause).

[195] 412 U.S. at 563–64. *See* note 41 *supra* and accompanying text.

[196] 412 U.S. at 559.

[197] *Id.* at 567–70. *See* notes 105–14 *supra* and accompanying text.

[198] *See* text accompanying note 109 *supra.*

[199] 412 U.S. at 569–70. *See generally* NIMMER, *supra* note 32 at § 1.2. Additionally, the Court dismissed petitioners' contention that the sound recordings had been published. In a footnote, the Court made this significant remark: "We have no need to determine whether, *under state law*, these recordings had been published or what legal consequences such publication might have. *For purposes of federal law*, 'publication' serves only as a term of the art which defines the legal relationships which Congress has adopted under the federal copyright statutes. As to categories of writings which Congress has not brought within the scope of the federal statute, the term has no application. 412 U.S. at 570 n. 28 (Court's emphasis)."

avoided the copying-versus-misappropriation argument that had arisen after *Sears* and *Compco.*[200]

In his dissent, Justice Douglas forcefully argued that *Sears* and *Compco* had made it clear that federal policy in the copyright clause was to have "national uniformity in patent and copyright laws." [201] In upholding the strong federalist position of Learned Hand in *Capitol Records, Inc. v. Mercury Records Corp.*,[202] Douglas reaffirmed Hand's reasoning of the need for uniformity through preemption.[203]

Although Justice Marshall, in a separate dissent, agreed with the majority that the states remain free until Congress acts to protect "writings" that are not specifically covered in the Copyright Act, he did not agree that because pre-1972 sound recordings were not subject to federal copyright, they could be protected by the states.[204] In taking issue with the majority position that *Sears* and *Compco* are limited to their facts, Marshall stated that the rule of those two cases was that unless the failure to provide copyright protection for some classes of works could be shown to reflect permission for state regulation, then failure of Congress to act reflects a desire for free competition.[205] Realizing his position was harsh, he concluded that "we should not let our distaste for 'pirates' interfere with our interpretation of the copyright laws." [206]

[200] *See* notes 115–22 *supra* and accompanying text. The Court's failure to distinguish *Sears* and *Compco* on grounds other than merely patent versus copyright protection has been highly criticized. *See generally* NIMMER, *supra* note 32 at §§ 1.2, 35.225; Comment, *Goldstein v. California: Breaking Up Federal Copyright Preemption*, 74 COLUM. L. REV. 960 (1974).

[201] 412 U.S. at 573 *citing* 376 U.S. at 231, n. 7.

[202] 221 F.2d 657 (2d Cir. 1955). *See* notes 79–88 and accompanying text *supra.*

[203] 412 U.S. at 575. *See* H.R. REP. No. 92-487, 92d Cong., 1st Sess. at 13 (1971), in which the Department of Justice, in response to the SRA, stated that "extending copyright to reproduction of sound recordings is the soundest, and in our interpretation of *Sears* and *Compco*, the only way in which sound recordings should be protected."

[204] 412 U.S. at 576–79.

[205] *Id.* at 577–78.

[206] *Id.* at 579.

B. POST-*GOLDSTEIN* JUDICIAL ACTIVITY

Although *Goldstein* validated state protection for pre-1972 recordings, the infringement provisions of the federal copyright laws are more certain and often more stringent than the state remedies. Nevertheless, in a series of cases from the Third,[207] Fifth,[208] Ninth,[209] and Tenth [210] Circuits decided subsequent to *Goldstein*,[211] the courts held that the unauthorized duplication of sound recordings which were fixed prior to 1972 constituted an infringement of the copyright of the composer whose musical work is reproduced by the recording.[212]

The pattern of all four cases was nearly identical, involving the typical pirating of legitimate sound recordings. Unlike many other pirates, however, these pirates complied with the requirements of 17 U.S.C. § 1(e) (1952). This section provides that once a composer has licensed, either expressly or impliedly, a first use of his musical composition in sound recording, a compulsory license arises in favor of any other person who makes "*similar use* of the copyright work" provided he complies with two explicit conditions: the filing of notice of intent to use the copyrighted composition [213] and payment of statutory royalties.[214]

The courts concluded that the pirates had not become compulsory licensees entitled to reproduce and sell copies of

[207] Jondora Music Publishing Co. v. Melody Recordings, Inc., 506 F.2d 392, 395 (3d Cir. 1974), *cert. denied*, 421 U.S. 1012 (1975).

[208] Fame Publishing Co., Inc. v. Alabama Custom Tape, Inc., 507 F.2d 667, 669–70 (5th Cir.), *cert. denied*, 423 U.S. 841 (1975).

[209] Duchess Music Corp. v. Stern, 458 F.2d 1305, 1310 (9th Cir.), *cert. denied sub nom.* Rosner v. Duchess Music Corp., 409 U.S. 847 (1972).

[210] Edward B. Marks Music Corp. v. Colorado Magnetics, Inc., 497 F.2d 285, 288 (10th Cir. 1974), *cert. denied*, 419 U.S. 1120 (1975).

[211] *Duchess* was decided prior to *Goldstein*.

[212] *See generally* Messina, *The Tape Piracy Cases: Judicial Creation of a Federal Copyright Interest in Sound Recordings*, 17 BOSTON COLL. IND. & COMM. L. REV. 169 (1976). *See also* NIMMER, *supra* note 32 at § 108.4621.

[213] *See* 17 U.S.C. § 101(e) (Supp. 1976).

[214] *Id.* § 1(e) (1952).

the musical works, notwithstanding the pirates' attempts to comply with § 1(e). In focusing on the difference between "similar" and "identical" use, the courts reasoned that because tape pirates who duplicate the recordings of legitimate manufacturers thereby make an "identical" use of the underlying musical work, they are not in compliance with § 1(e) and infringe the composer's copyright.[215]

Although most courts and commentators have not criticized the desirable effects of halting the pirates' activity in these cases, the four courts' reasoning has been subject to legitimate criticism.[216] As discussed earlier, copyright protection was not granted to sound recordings until 1972.[217] Moreover, the express intention of the drafters of the 1909 Act was that such protection should not be given.[218] As the dissent in *Duchess* correctly noted,[219] these courts are condoning relief which is not authorized by the Copyright Act. By erroneously entangling the copyright protection for musical compositions under the compulsory licensing provision of the Act with the sound recordings in which they are incorporated, the courts are providing copyright protection for the records themselves.[220]

Further, the broad interpretation given by these courts to the composer's property interest via § 1(e) appears to be

[215] *Duchess Music*, 458 F.2d at 1310. *See* Fame Publishing, 507 F.2d at 669–70; *Jondora Music*, 506 F.2d at 395; *Marks Music*, 497 F.2d at 288.

[216] *See* NIMMER, *supra* note 32 at § 105.4621; Comment, *supra* note 212; Comment, *supra* note 7; Comment, *supra* note 129 at 110–11.

[217] *See* text accompanying note 133 *supra.*

[218] *See* text accompanying note 41 *supra.*

[219] 458 F.2d at 1311 (Byrne, J., dissenting).

[220] Courts relied heavily upon the 1912 New York case Aeolian Co. v. Royal Music Roll Co., 196 F. 926 (W.D.N.Y. 1912), to support their view that "similar use" creates an implied condition that a subsequent licensee may not duplicate the product of the efforts of a prior licensee. One court, however, in *Jondora Music*, attempted to depart from the reasoning of the others by construing an argument on the general "spirit" of the 1909 Act. 506 F.2d at 395–96. The heart of the argument, it seems, was that the *Jondora* court refused to believe that the drafters of the 1909 Act would permit the unethical and immoral practice of tape piracy.

contrary to *Goldstein,* which suggests a narrow definition of the composer's property interest.[221] In effect, these cases extend federal protection to pre-1972 recordings, an extension whose existence was not recognized by *Goldstein.*[222] Although these cases do not hold that federal copyright law preempts the states' role in regulating pre-1972 sound recordings, they do expand federal protection beyond what was recognized in *Goldstein.*[223]

C. *GOLDSTEIN* POSTSCRIPT

The *Goldstein* Court rejected the contention that the states must refrain from granting protection in certain areas merely because under the Constitution, Congress has the power to legislate in those particular areas. But, as one commentator has aptly noted, Goldstein has replaced *Sears* and *Compco* "as the nebulous guide to federal preemption in cases of record piracy." [224] That is, the impact of *Goldstein* lies primarily in its approval of state laws, common [225] or statu-

[221] *See* Messina, *supra* note 212 at 186–89. *See also* Comment, *Goldstein v. California: Validity of State Copyright Under the Copyright and Supremacy Clauses,* 25 HAST. L. J. 1196, 1214–18 (1974).

[222] 412 U.S. at 566.

[223] These four cases dealt only with the extension of federal *civil* liability to pirates of sound recordings fixed prior to 1972. The court in Heilman v. Levi, 391 F. Supp. 1106 (N.D. Wis. 1975), expanded the doctrine of these cases when it held that a pirate who duplicates a sound recording not directly eligible for federal copyright protection and who tenders the statutory royalties to the composition copyright holder is nevertheless *criminally* liable for willful infringement. *Id.* at 1113. Certainly, if Congress left the status of pre-1972 sound recordings "unattended," 412 U.S. at 570, a finding of federal criminal sanctions of pre-1976 recordings is inconsistent with *Goldstein. See* Messina, *supra* note 212, at 189–90.

[224] Comment, *supra* note 129, at 111.

[225] As indicated earlier in the text, *Goldstein* appears to have given the green light to the states to apply the misappropriation doctrine to protect interests not reached by federal law, *i.e.,* pre-1972 sound recordings. *See* note 200 *supra* and accompanying text. *See* GAI Audio of New York, Inc. v. Columbia Broadcasting Sys., Inc., 188 U.S.P.Q. 75 (Ct. Spec. App. Md. 1975) (recognized that "*Goldstein* permits state protection against record piracy by common law . . ." *Id.* at 61); Mercury Record Prod., Inc. v. Economic Consultants, Inc., 183 U.S.P.Q. 358 (Wis. 1974) (Wisconsin Supreme Court upheld protection under

tory, which extend full copyright protection to those writings not subject to a federal copyright.[226] In holding that the question of compatibility of state and federal remedies is purely a matter of congressional interest, the Court narrowed the preemption issue, abandoning the traditional boundary between state and federal protection, that is, publication.[227] Under *Goldstein,* therefore, the question of the validity of state copyright for classes of "writings" not covered by congressional protection remains open.[228]

V. GENERAL REVISION OF COPYRIGHT LAW

The signing of S.22 [229] on October 19, 1976, by President Gerald Ford represented the culmination of a program begun in 1955 under the supervision of the Copyright Office of the Library of Congress and a series of thirty-five extensive studies of major copyright issues.[230] The first major revision of the Copyright Act of 1909, the 1976 Act specifies that with certain exceptions, its provisions are to enter into force on January 1, 1978.[231] Although a thorough discussion of the new Act is beyond the scope of this article, certain portions are relevant to record piracy. Primarily the new Act retains all of the substantial elements of the SRA but incorporates several major innovations in protecting sound recordings.

---

unfair competition and *International News Service*); Columbia Broadcasting Sys. Inc. v. Newman, 184 U.S.P.Q. 18 (D.N.M. 1974) (recognition of unfair competition).

[226] *See* Comment, *supra* note 45, at 641.

[227] *See* note 199 *supra.*

[228] *See* Comment, *supra* note 129, at 113–16 for a good discussion of the arguments for and against federal preemption in this area.

[229] Act of October 19, 1976, Pub. L. No. 94–553, 90 Stat. 2541.

[230] *See* note 131 *supra* and accompanying text. *See also* Oct. 1976 *Announcement* in ML-134, Copyright Office (1976).

[231] 17 U.S.C. § 301(a) (hereinafter cited as NEW ACT).

A. SECTION 101: DEFINITIONS

In § 101 the definition of "phonorecords" and "sound recordings" is given.[232] The legislative history[233] reveals that

> copyrightable "sound recordings" are original works of authorship comprising an aggregate of musical, spoken, or other sounds that have been fixed in tangible form. The copyrightable work comprises the aggregation of sounds and not the tangible medium of fixation. Thus, "sound recordings" as copyrightable subject matter are distinguished from "phonorecords," the latter being physical objects in which sounds are fixed.[234]

Therefore, sound recordings are "clearly within the scope of 'writings of an author' capable of protection under the Constitution."[235]

B. SECTION 114: SCOPE OF EXCLUSIVE RIGHTS IN SOUND RECORDINGS

Section 114[236] of the Act retains the distinction between rights in a sound recording and rights in the musical composition or other work embodied in the recording.[237] Subsection (a) stipulates "that the exclusive rights of the owner of copyright in a sound recording are limited to the rights to reproduce the sound recording in copies or phonorecords, to prepare derivative works based on the copyrighted sound recording, and to distribute copies or phonorecords of the sound recording to the public."[238] Subsection (b) "makes

[232] *Id.* § 101. For the first time, the definition of "publication" is also included in the Act.

[233] H.R. REP. NO. 1476, 94th Cong., 2d Sess. (1976) (hereinafter cited as 1976 Report).

[234] 1976 Report at 55–56.

[235] *Id.*

[236] NEW ACT at § 114.

[237] *Id.* 114(c). *See* 1976 Report at 107.

[238] 1976 Report at 106. Whether to include a right of performance had been a highly controverted issue. Senator Hugh Scott argued strongly for the inclusion, but the Committee concluded "that the problem requires further study."

clear that statutory protection for sound recordings extends only to the particular sounds of which the record consists, and would not prevent a separate recording of another performance in which those sounds are imitated."[239]

C. SECTION 115: COMPULSORY LICENSE FOR MAKING AND DISTRIBUTING PHONORECORDS

Section 115, dealing with compulsory licensing, is a departure from the previous §§ 1(e) and 101.

> Subsection (a) of § 115 deals with three doubtful questions under the present law: (1) the nature of the original recording that will make the work available to others for recording under a compulsory license; (2) the nature of the sound recording that can be made under a compulsory license; and (3) the extent to which someone acting under a compulsory license can depart from the work as written or recorded without violating the copyright owner's right to make an "arrangement" or other derivative work.[240]

For present purposes the second question is the important one addressed by the statute. Section 115(a)(1) states in part:

> A person may not obtain a compulsory license for use of the work in the making of phonorecords duplicating a sound recording fixed by another, unless: (i) such sound recording was fixed lawfully; and (ii) the making of the phonorecords was authorized by the owner of copyright in the sound recording or, if the sound recording was fixed before February 15, 1972, by any person who fixed the sound recording pursuant to an express license from the owner of the copyright in the musical work or pursuant to a valid compulsory license for use of such work in a sound recording.

The Committee Report indicates that the basic intent of this portion of the statute is "to make clear that a person is not

---

Id. As a compromise, subsection (d) was added: "[A] report setting forth recommendations as to whether this section should be amended to provide for performers and copyright owners . . . any performance rights in copyrighted sound recordings." *Id.*

[239] 1976 Report at 106.

[240] *Id.* at 107.

entitled to a compulsory license of copyrighted musical works for the purpose of making an unauthorized duplication of a musical sound recording originally developed and produced by another."[241] In effect, the statute affirms the cases from the Third, Fifth, Ninth, and Tenth Circuits discussed earlier.[242] Although the statute may be subject to the same criticism discussed previously,[243] the attacks are somewhat obviated by the fact that Congress *is now* addressing pre-1972 sound recordings and thus *Goldstein* remains intact.

D. SECTION 301: PREEMPTION

Perhaps the most significant section of the new Act is § 301, which specifically reserves to Congress exclusive jurisdiction over the protection of sound recordings. Describing § 301 as "one of the bedrock provisions of the bill,"[244] the Committee remarks:

> Common law copyright protection for works coming within the scope of the statute would be abrogated, and the concept of publication would lose its all-embracing importance as a dividing line between common law and statutory protection and between both of these forms of legal protection and the public domain.[245]

The Committee gives four reasons for substituting a single federal system for the present "anachronistic, uncertain, impractical, and highly complicated dual system."[246] First, a single system will provide national uniformity; second, a single system will abrogate "publication" as the demarcation of federal protection versus state protection; third, the dis-

[241] *Id.* at 108.

[242] *See* notes 207–23 *supra* and accompanying text. The Committee further stated: "It is the view of the Committee that such was the original intent of the Congress in enacting the 1909 Copyright Act. . . ." The Committee cited the four circuit court cases, specified in notes 207–10 *supra.* 1976 Report at 108.

[243] *See* notes 216–20 *supra* and accompanying text.

[244] 1976 Report at 129.

[245] *Id.* Thus, the Committee is in harmony with *Goldstein. See* note 199 *supra* and accompanying text.

[246] 1976 Report of 129.

tortion of the "limited Times" provision of the Constitution, in that state common law protection is perpetual, will be eliminated; and fourth, a uniform national copyright system will improve international dealings in copyrighted material.[247] Under § 301, the statute applies to all works created after January 1, 1978, regardless of whether they are ever published or disseminated.[248]

The Committee indicates that § 301 is drafted so as to "foreclose any conceivable misinterpretation of its unqualified intention that Congress shall act preemptively, and to avoid the development of any vague borderline areas between State and Federal protection." [249] The report goes on to state that, "[r]egardless of when the work was created and whether it is published or unpublished, disseminated or undisseminated, in the public domain or copyrighted under the Federal Statute, the States cannot offer it protection equivalent to copyright." [250] Thus, the uncertainties of *Goldstein* are answered.

On the other hand section 301(b), a necessary counterpart to 301(a), reminds us that there still remains a lingering problem of determining what is, and what is not, protected by federal copyright. Thus, *Goldstein* lives but its emphasis has shifted. The Committee remarks:

> [S]ection 301(b) explicitly preserves common law copyright protection for one important class of works: works that have not been "fixed in any tangible medium of expression." Examples would include choreography that has never been filmed or notated, an extemporaneous speech, "original works of authorship" communicated solely through conversations or live broadcasts, and a dramatic sketch or musical composition improvised or developed from memory and without being recorded or written down.[251]

[247] *Id.* at 129–30.

[248] Section 303 deals with works created but not published or copyrighted before January 1, 1978.

[249] 1976 Report at 130.

[250] *Id.* at 130–31.

[251] *Id.* at 131.

The Committee is particularly concerned with § 301(b)(3), a general area that is left unaffected by preemption: "violations of rights that are not equivalent to any of the exclusive rights under copyright." This clause is meant to protect the evolving common law rights of "privacy," "publicity," and trade secrets, as well as the general laws of defamation and fraud "as long as the causes of action contain elements, such as an invasion of personal rights or a breach of trust or confidentiality, that are different in kind from copyright infringement." [252] False labeling, fraudulent representation, passing off, and misappropriation are also preempted if the right is not within the general "scope of the copyright statute." [253]

Finally, as to the problem of pre-1972 recordings, the Committee reached a compromise. The statute does not grant "perpetual protection under state law" as urged by the Department of Justice, but it does permit state protection until February 15, 2047, when federal protection will go into effect.[254]

VI. CONCLUSION

The development of efforts to combat tape and record piracy has been long and tedious. The initial failure of Congress to protect sound recordings under the federal copyright laws did not hinder courts from granting protection against the practice of piracy. *Sears* and *Compco* remind us that, even in the face of federalism at its high point, courts are loath not to afford protection to injured plaintiffs. When Congress finally did act in 1971, it did not do so sufficiently,

[252] *Id.* at 132.

[253] *Id. See* New Act § 706. The Committee specifically recognizes the misappropriation exception of *International News Service* but limits it to its facts.

[254] *See id.* § 301(c). *See also* 1976 Report at 133.

It should also be noted that the new Act's infringement penalties are tougher than those in the 1909 Act. *See* New Act §§ 501 *et seq.*

giving rise to the landmark *Goldstein* decision. Now that the Copyright Revision Act has been enacted, the troublesome questions raised by *Goldstein* regarding sound recordings have been answered.[255] Although tape piracy was still on the rise immediately following the Sound Recording Act of 1971,[256] the all-out war by the Copyright Act of 1976 should dictate its eventual fall.

[255] *But cf.* notes 251–53 and accompanying text *supra.*
[256] *See* notes 22–23 and accompanying text *supra.*

APPENDIX

State	*Effective Date*	*Type of Offense*	*Penalties Imposed*	*Scope of Coverage*
ARIZONA Criminal Code Sec. 13–1052	August 15, 1972	Misdemeanor	Fine of not more than $300 and/or imprisonment of not more than 6 months	Unlawful to knowingly manufacture, distribute or retail a recording whose sounds are transferred without the owner's consent
ARKANSAS Criminal Offenses Chapter 4617	February 12, 1971	Misdemeanor	Fine of not less than $50 nor more than $250	Same as the above
CALIFORNIA Penal Code 65311	November 13, 1968	Misdemeanor	Fine of not more than $500 and/or imprisonment of not more than 6 months	Same as the above
CONNECTICUT General Statutes Public Act 74–160	October 11, 1974	Misdemeanor	Fine of not more than $1,000 and/or imprisonment for not more than one year. Subsequent offense—fine of up to $2,000 and/or not more than one year imprisonment	Unlawful to knowingly manufacture, distribute, sell or advertise for sale a recording whose sounds have been transferred without the owner's consent. Unlawful to rent or make available equipment for such transfers.
FLORIDA Chapter 543 Section 543–041	October 1, 1971	Misdemeanor	Fine of not more than $500 or imprisonment of not more than 60 days	Same as the above

State	*Effective Date*	*Type of Offense*	*Penalties Imposed*	*Scope of Coverage*
INDIANA Code 1971, 3517 Ch. 7 Secs. 1–3 (1974)	July 1, 1974	Misdemeanor/ Felony	1st offense up to $2,000 and/or up to 1 year imprisonment. Subsequent offense—fine up to $5,000 and/or 1–10 years imprisonment	Unlawful to knowingly manufacture, distribute or retail a recording whose sounds are transferred without the owner's consent
KENTUCKY KRS Chap. 434	June 20, 1974	Misdemeanor	Fine of up to $1,000 or double the amount of gain from the commission of the offense, whichever is greater, or imprisonment for up to 60 days, and fine of up to $1,000, and police may confiscate recordings produced in violation of this act	Same as the above and Unlawful to knowingly sell or distribute recordings not bearing the name and address of the transferrer of sounds
LOUISIANA Revised Statute Section 14.223	January 1, 1973	Misdemeanor	1st offense—up to $1,000. Subsequent offense—up to $2,000	Unlawful to knowingly manufacture, distribute or retail a recording whose sounds are transferred without the owner's consent
MARYLAND Annotated Code Article 27 § 467A	July 1, 1973	Misdemeanor	1st offense—up to $2,500 and/or up to 1 year's imprisonment. Subsequent offense—up to $10,000 fine and/or up to 3 years imprisonment	Same as the above, and it is also unlawful to knowingly distribute or retail any sound recording which does not bear the actual name and street address of the transferrer of sound

MASSACHUSETTS General Law Chapter 266, Section 143	October 31, 1973	Misdemeanor	Fine of not more than $5,000 or imprisonment for not more than 1 year	Unlawful to knowingly manufacture, distribute or sell recordings whose sounds are transferred without the owner's consent
MINNESOTA Chapter 579 Laws of 1973	August 1, 1973	Felony	1st offense—up to $25,000. Subsequent offense—up to $100,000 fine and/or imprisonment of not more than 3 years	Same as the above
MISSISSIPPI Senate Bill 2105	July 1, 1974	Misdemeanor	1st offense—up to $100 and/or up to 30 days imprisonment. Subsequent offense—up to $500 and/or 6 months imprisonment	Unlawful to knowingly manufacture, distribute, retail or advertise a recording whose sounds are transferred without the owner's consent. It is also unlawful to knowingly manufacture, distribute or sell any recording not bearing the actual name and street address of the transferrer as well as the name of the actual performer
NEBRASKA 683 (Signed 2/25/74)	July 12, 1974	Misdemeanor	Fine of up to $1,000 and/or 6 months imprisonment	Unlawful to knowingly manufacture, distribute or sell a recording whose sounds are transferred without the owner's consent

State	*Effective Date*	*Type of Offense*	*Penalties Imposed*	*Scope of Coverage*
NEVADA Chapter 636 Laws of 1973	July 1, 1973	Felony	1st offense—fine of not more than $5,000 and/or imprisonment for not less than 1 year nor more than 6 years. Subsequent offense—fine of not more than $5,000 and/or imprisonment for not less than 1 year nor more than 10 years	Same as the above
NEW HAMPSHIRE Revised Statutes Chapter 352-A	November 1, 1973	Prohibited Conduct	Owner of recorded device has cause of action for treble compensatory damages and/or injunctive relief	Prohibited to knowingly manufacture, distribute, or retail a recording whose sounds are transferred without the owner's consent and/or which does not bear the manufacturer's name and address
NEW MEXICO Laws of 1974 Chapter 89	May 15, 1974	Misdemeanor/ Felony	Felony for manufacturers and distributors—up to $5,000 and/or 1 year imprisonment. Misdemeanor for retailers.	Unlawful to knowingly manufacture, distribute or sell a recording whose sounds are transferred without the owner's consent.
NEW YORK General Business Law § 560–1	September 1, 1967	Misdemeanor	Fine of not more than $1,000 and/or imprisonment of up to one year	Unlawful to knowingly manufacture, distribute or sell a recording whose sounds are transferred without the owner's consent

NORTH CAROLINA Chapter 14, General Statutes, Article 56A	**January 1, 1975**	Misdemeanor	Fine of up to $500 and/or imprisonment of up to 6 months	Unlawful to knowingly manufacture, distribute or sell unauthorized duplications of sound recordings or to record live concerts without permission. Unlawful to manufacture, distribute or sell recordings not bearing the true name of the manufacturer
OHIO Criminal Code §§ 2913. 31–2	**January 1, 1974**	Felony (4th Degree)	Fine of not more than $2,500 and/or imprisonment for not less than 6 months nor more than 5 years	Unlawful to fraudulently (1) forge writing of another (2) possess a writing known to be a forgery (3) practice deception in reproducing a phonographic record or tape
OREGON Chapter 747 Laws of 1973	**October 5, 1973**	Misdemeanor	Fine not to exceed $500 and/or imprisonment for not more than 6 months	Unlawful to knowingly manufacture, distribute, retail or advertise for sale any sound recording which is duplicated without the consent of the owner of the original master recording
PENNSYLVANIA Title 18, Section 4116	**October 18, 1971**	Misdemeanor—to knowingly retail or possess for purpose of retailing. Felony—to knowingly manufacture, dis-	Confiscation of pirated recordings and: 1st offense—fine of not more than $25,000 and/or imprisonment of not less than 1 year nor more than 3 years. Sub-	Unlawful to knowingly manufacture, distribute or retail a recording whose sounds are transferred without the owner's consent and/or which does not bear the true

State	*Effective Date*	*Type of Offense*	*Penalties Imposed*	*Scope of Coverage*
		tribute or wholesale sound recordings duplicated without the consent of the owner	sequent offense—fine of not more than $100,000 and/or imprisonment of not less than 3 years nor more than 10 years	name of the manufacturer.
TENNESSEE Crim. Off. § 39–4244–50	July 1, 1971	Same as above	Same as above	Unlawful to knowingly manufacture, distribute or retail
TEXAS Penal Code 1137r-§ 1–4	June 14, 1971	Misdemeanor/ Felony	1st offense—fine of not more than $2,000. 2nd offense—fine of not more than $25,000 and/or imprisonment for not more than 5 years	Same as above
UTAH Chap. 17 Laws of Utah, 1973	May 8, 1973	Misdemeanor	Fine not to exceed $299 and/or imprisonment up to 6 months	Same as the above, as well as to rent or make available equipment for such transfers
VIRGINIA Code Sections 59.1–41.1 through 59.1–41.6	July 1, 1972	Misdemeanor	Fine not to exceed $500 and/or imprisonment up to 1 year	Unlawful to knowingly manufacture, distribute or retail without consent of the owner and/or does not bear the name of the manufacturer
WASHINGTON Chapter 100, 3rd Ext. Sess., Law of 1974 (signed 2/17/74)	July 25, 1974	Misdemeanor	Fine not to exceed $1,000 and/or up to 1 year imprisonment plus confiscation of tapes	Same as the above

NATIONAL FIFTH PRIZE TIE

Originality in Art Reproductions: "Variations" in Search of a Theme

GREGG OPPENHEIMER

BOALT HALL SCHOOL OF LAW
UNIVERSITY OF CALIFORNIA AT BERKELEY

I. THE REQUIREMENT OF "DISTINGUISHABLE VARIATION"

A. INTRODUCTION: ORIGINALITY IN ART REPRODUCTIONS

ONE of the most basic tenets of the law of copyright is that protection is offered only to "original" works.[1] This "originality" requirement is of a different nature from the "novelty" requirement of patent law; to be "original," a work need not be strikingly different from works produced previously by others, so long as it "owes its origin to the author, i.e., is independently created, and not copied from other works." [2]

Since 1909, when Congress first saw fit to include "reproductions of a work of art" [3] among the classes of copyrightable works,[4] the courts have been struggling to resolve the

[1] M. NIMMER, COPYRIGHT 32 (1976). [hereinafter cited as NIMMER]

[2] NIMMER *supra* note 1 at 34. *See generally* NIMMER 32–34.

[3] 17 U.S.C. § 5(h). (1970).

[4] The application for registration shall specify to which of the following classes the work in which copyright is claimed belongs:

paradox thus thrust upon them—the notion that a work of art could be a "reproduction," yet be "original." [5]

In 1951, *Alfred Bell & Co. Ltd. v. Catalda Fine Arts, Inc.*,[6] offered a solution to this apparent paradox by requiring for copyrightability that the "author" of the reproduction merely contribute "something recognizably 'his own' " to the copied work of art, a "variation" on which to plant the judicial stamp of originality.[7]

However, *Bell v. Catalda*'s solution to the originality paradox gave rise to a difficult line-drawing problem: exactly *how much* and *what kind* of "variation" is required in order to qualify for copyright as a reproduction of a work of art?

Bell v. Catalda did not provide a clearcut answer. The case was an action for infringement of copyrights covering mezzotint engravings of several paintings by old masters. The

---

"(a) Books, including composite and cyclopedic works, directories, gazetteers, and other compilations.

(b) Periodicals, including newspapers.

(c) Lectures, sermons, addresses (prepared for oral delivery).

(d) Dramatic or dramatico-musical compositions.

(e) Musical compositions.

(f) Maps.

(g) Works of art; models or designs for works of art.

(h) Reproductions of a work of art.

(i) Drawings or plastic works of a scientific or technical character.

(j) Photographs.

(k) Prints and pictorial illustrations including prints or labels used for articles of merchandise.

(l) Motion-picture photoplays.

(m) Motion pictures other than photoplays.

(n) Sound recordings.

"The above specifications shall not be held to limit the subject matter of copyright as defined in section 4 of this title, nor shall any error in classification invalidate or impair the copyright protection secured under this title." 17 U.S.C. § 5 (1970).

[5] Congress left little in the form of legislative history to resolve this paradox. The House Report on the General Revision Bill of 1909 merely states "Section 5 refers solely to a classification made for the convenience of the copyright office and those applying for copyrights." H.R. Rep. No. 2222, 60th Cong., 2d Sess. 9 (1909).

[6] 191 F.2d 99 (2d Cir. 1951).

[7] *Id.* at 102–3.

district court observed that the engravings were "fairly realistic" and "quite . . . satisfactory reproduction[s]" of the original oil paintings.[8] In rejecting the defendants' claim that the copyrights were invalid, Judge Frank observed for the Second Circuit Court of Appeals that each engraver had added something of "his own" to the old masters, without explaining precisely what that "something" was.[9] The court, citing an earlier decision, laid down the following standard:

> [A] "copy of something in the public domain" will support a copyright if it is a "distinguishable variation"; . . . All that is needed to satisfy both the Constitution and the statute is that the "author" contributed something more than a "merely trivial" variation, something recognizably "his own." Originality in this context "means little more than a prohibition of actual copying." No matter how poor artistically the "author's" addition, it is enough if it be his own.[10]

The requirement of merely a "distinguishable variation," taken from the 1927 case of *Gerlach-Barklow Co. v. Morris & Bendien, Inc.*[11] appears to be a slight retreat from Judge Frank's statement some six years before *Bell v. Catalda,* that copyright demanded "some *substantial,* not merely trivial, originality. . . ."[12] *Bell v. Catalda* has thus been interpreted as imposing a very modest originality requirement.[13]

[8] Alfred Bell & Co. v. Catalda Fine Arts, Inc., 74 F. Supp. 973, 975 (S.D.N.Y. 1947), *aff'd,* 191 F.2d 99 (2d Cir. 1951).

[9] Alfred Bell & Co. v. Catalda Fine Arts, Inc., 191 F.2d 99, 103, 104 (2d Cir. 1951).

[10] *Id.* at 102, *citing* Bleistein v. Donaldson Lithographing Co., 188 U.S. 239 (1903).

[11] 23 F.2d 159, 161 (2d Cir. 1927). It is not clear whether *Gerlach-Barklow* involved a "reproduction of a work of art." Since the painting involved in that case had merely taken its "theme" from an earlier work of art, the case may stand for little more than the familiar rule that copyright requires originality only in a work's expression, not in its underlying idea or theme. Baker v. Selden, 101 U.S. 99, 102–103 (1879).

[12] Chamberlin v. Uris Sales Corp., 150 F.2d 512, 513 (2d Cir. 1945) (emphasis added).

[13] NIMMER, *supra* note 1 at 93. *Contra,* Kuddle Toy, Inc. v. Pussycat-Toy Co., Inc., 183 U.S.P.Q. 642, 658 (E.D.N.Y. 1974), discussed in the text accompanying note 137 *infra.*

Later cases based the distinction between "merely trivial" variations and "distinguishable" ones on such diverse factors as the "skill, judgment, and labor" involved in creating the reproduction, the nature of the motivation behind creation of the variations, the presence or absence of artistic "creativity" in the variations, and whether the variations would be sufficient to bar a hypothetical infringement claim by the author of the underlying work.

A recent case, *L. Batlin & Son, Inc. v. Snyder* [14] appears to raise the standard once again from merely "distinguishable" variation to "substantial" variation,[15] while simultaneously suggesting a startling alternative to the traditional originality requirement: copyright protection for certain complex art reproductions lacking even trivial variations from their respective underlying works of art, falling within what the Second Circuit Court of Appeals has called a "category of exactitude." [16]

It is the purpose of this essay to analyze the merits of each of the many tests utilized by the courts in determining the copyrightability of art reproductions [17] and to propose a comprehensive standard designed to facilitate such a determination. The scope of the essay is limited to works of "visual art" (*e.g.*, paintings, sculptures, drawings), as opposed to those contemporary art forms which feature tactile or aural sensations as well.

B. ORIGINALITY COUNTERPARTS: "INTELLECTUAL LABOR" AND "CREATIVITY"

1. *Intellectual Labor*

The Supreme Court, in the 1879 *Trademark Cases*,[18] con-

[14] 536 F.2d 486 (2d Cir. 1976).

[15] *Id.* at 491.

[16] *Id.* at 492.

[17] The new Copyright Revision Act, Pub. L. No. 94-553, § 101, 90 Stat. 2541 (1976), uses the term "art reproductions" instead of "reproduction of a work of art." The two terms are used interchangeably in this essay.

[18] 100 U.S. 82 (1879).

strued the Copyright Clause [19] to encompass only such "writings" as are "*original*, and are founded in the creative powers of the mind. The writings which are protected are *the fruits of intellectual labor* embodied in the form of books, prints, engravings, and the like." [20] The case involved a federal trademark statute which granted exclusive rights in distinctive symbols to the first party to adopt and register them, regardless of how old or well known the symbol might be. Applying this principle, the Court held that, since the rights granted by the statute were "founded on priority of appropriation" rather than "any work of the brain," congressional power to enact such a statute could not be based on the Copyright Clause.[21]

Despite the apparent use of the term "intellectual labor" in the *Trademark Cases* to clarify the *originality* requirement of the Copyright Clause, Professor Nimmer states in his treatise that

> It is important to distinguish between the requirement of originality and the requirement of intellectual labor. . . . The doctrine of originality stems from the Copyright Clause's use of the term "authors" and refers to *independent creation.* Intellectual labor, on the other hand, suggests an absolute standard, albeit a highly minimal one, of creativity.[22]

This view seems unfounded, since the Supreme Court's entire discussion of the reasons trademarks are not necessarily "the fruits of intellectual labor" was based on the fact that a trade-

[19] 100 U.S. at 94.

[20] 100 U.S. at 94; *cf.* Goldstein v. Cal., 412 U.S. 546, 561 (1973) ("the fruits of creative intellectual or aesthetic labor").

[21] 100 U.S. at 94. Contrary to what Professor Nimmer contends, the case did *not* hold that "a trademark did not constitute a writing and hence could not claim copyright protection." NIMMER, *supra* note 1 at 19. It merely held that since *not every* trademark protected by the trademark statute was an *original* writing (the fruits of intellectual labor), the statute was too broad in coverage to be based solely on the Copyright Clause. No opinion was tendered on the question of the copyrightability of those individual trademarks that *were* "the fruits of intellectual labor."

[22] NIMMER, *supra* note 1 at 19–20 (emphasis added).

mark "may be, and generally is, the *adoption* of something *already in existence. . . .*" [23] In other words, a trademark need not be the product of "independent creation" by the registrant. Nothing in the Court's discussion suggests an absolute standard of creativity.[24] Consequently, the "intellectual labor" requirement should be regarded as an alternative phrase for "originality of authorship," rather than an independent constitutional prerequisite for copyright.

2. *Creativity*

a. *In Works of Art Generally*

The statement in the *Trademark Cases* that the Copyright Clause encompasses only those writings which "are original, and founded in the creative powers of the mind" [25] raises two questions: (1) is there an independent constitutional requirement of "creativity" for copyright? and (2) if so, how is "creativity" defined?

Although courts have discussed the "creativity" requirement, either by itself [26] or in conjunction with a discussion of the originality requirement,[27] it is sometimes difficult to tell whether anything other than a work's originality has in fact been examined by the court. The source of some of these judicial discussions of "creativity" is a Copyright Office regula-

[23] Trademark Cases, 100 U.S. 82, 94 (1879).

[24] Although the "intellectual labor" requirement was mentioned in later cases which excluded original descriptive labels and advertisements from copyright protection, Higgins v. Keuffel, 140 U.S. 428, 431 (1891), J. L. Mott Iron Works v. Clow, 82 F. 316, 318 (7th Cir. 1897), copyrightability was denied, owing to the purpose for which the intellectual labor was expended, rather than to any failure to meet an absolute standard of creativity. The line of reasoning barring "mere advertisements" from copyright protection on this basis was subsequently rejected by the Supreme Court. Jeweler's Circular Pub. Co. v. Keystone Pub. Co., 281 F. 83, 87 (2d Cir. 1922). *See also* Bleistein v. Donaldson Lithographing Co., 188 U.S. 239, 242–43 (1903).

[25] 100 U.S. 82, 94 (1897).

[26] *See, e.g.*, Tennessee Fabricating Co. v. Moultrie Mfg. Co., 421 F.2d 279, 281 (5th Cir. 1970).

[27] Gardenia Flowers, Inc. v. Joseph Markovits, Inc., 280 F. Supp. 776, 781–82 (S.D.N.Y. 1968).

tion describing the category "Works of Art": "In order to be acceptable as a work of art, the work must embody some creative authorship in its delineation or form." [28] However, since these regulations do not mention "originality" as a separate requirement for works of art, this reference to "creative authorship" may in fact mean nothing more than "originality."

Professor Nimmer is of the opinion that creativity and originality are independent requirements for copyright; he has partially defined them, as well: "Where creativity refers to the nature of the work itself, originality refers to the nature of the author's contribution to the work." [29] This dichotomy was expressly approved in *Gardenia Flowers, Inc. v. Joseph Markovits, Inc.*,[30] a case which demonstrates the tenuous distinction between the two concepts. *Gardenia Flowers* involved the copyright in arrangements of plastic artificial flowers. After quoting Nimmer's formulation of the "creativity" requirement, the court proceeded to find creativity lacking because the claimant had *copied* the plastic arrangements from natural and cloth flower arrangements he had seen on a trip to Italy.[31] Creativity was missing because the claimant "did not create anything *new*" [32] as contrasted with the material previously known to him. This sounds suspiciously like a discussion of *originality*,[33] a conclusion buttressed by the court's inability to add anything new in its subsequent discussion of the originality requirement: "Much of the same reasoning which led this court to the determination that plaintiff's corsages were devoid of creativity applies with equal force to its claim of originality." [34]

The source of Professor Nimmer's separate standard of ab-

[28] 37 C.F.R. § 202.10(b) (1976).
[29] NIMMER, *supra* note 1 at 86.2.
[30] 280 F. Supp. 776, 781 (S.D.N.Y. 1968).
[31] *Id.* at 779–80.
[32] *Id.* at 781.
[33] *See* text accompanying note 60 *infra.*
[34] 280 F. Supp. at 782.

solute creativity in works of art is said to be "a matter of definition." [35] That is, if a work displayed no creativity, it would not be "art," and hence it could not claim copyright as a "work of art." It is difficult to see how such a standard could function effectively. Courts have generally abstained from assuming the role of art critic, and with good reason. As Mr. Justice Holmes explained in *Bleistein v. Donaldson Lithographing Co.:*

> It would be a dangerous undertaking for persons trained only to the law to constitute themselves the final judges of the worth of pictorial illustrations, outside of the narrowest and most obvious limits. At the one extreme some works of genius would be sure to miss appreciation. Their very novelty would make them repulsive until the public had learned the new language in which their author spoke. It may be more than doubted, for instance, whether the etchings of Goya or the paintings of Manet would have been sure of protection when seen for the first time. At the other end, copyright would be denied to pictures which appealed to a public less educated than the judge. Yet if they command the interest of any public, they have a commercial value—it would be bold to say they have not an aesthetic and educational value—and the taste of the public is not to be treated with contempt. It is an ultimate fact for the moment, whatever may be our hopes for a change. That these pictures had their worth and success is sufficiently shown by the desire to reproduce them without regard to plaintiffs' rights.[36]

This "hands off" policy is still the prevailing standard for judging the artistic creativity of all types of works of art; and with the surprising assortment of objects that have gained acceptance as true art forms ("pop" or otherwise) in the last two decades, even the "most obvious limits" of the term "work of art" have all but disappeared. Indeed, it would be unrealistic to say that any original work of graphic design, no matter how simple or unfamiliar, could not arguably be

[35] Nimmer, *supra* note 1 at 85.
[36] 188 U.S. 239, 251–52 (1903).

regarded as a "work of art" by some segment of the population.[37]

The unworkability of a separate "artistic creativity" requirement is reflected by the dearth of cases denying copyrightability on this ground to works registered as "works of art." On only two occasions have courts expressly done so. One of these cases was *Gardenia Flowers, Inc. v. Joseph Markovits, Inc.*,[38] discussed *supra,* which in fact used the term "creativity" as a synonym for originality, the court's statements to the contrary notwithstanding. The only other case was *Bailie v. Fisher*,[39] which involved a cardboard star with a circular center (for insertion of a photograph) and with folding flaps which permit it to stand erect. In a *per curiam* opinion, the D.C. Circuit Court of Appeals applied the standard, "a thing is a work of art if it appears to be within the historical and ordinary conception of the term art," concluding, "[a] cardboard star which stands because of folded flaps does not fall within that conception." [40] It is suggested that the court erred in applying the above standard, in that it conflicts with the spirit of *Bleistein, supra.*[41]

Thus artistic creativity has been virtually eliminated as a meaningful hurdle for works when copyright protection as "works of art" is sought.

b. In Art Reproductions

The reasoning of *Bleistein v. Donaldson Lithographing*

[37] NIMMER, *supra* note 1 at 86.1.

[38] 280 F. Supp. 776 (S.D.N.Y. 1968).

[39] 258 F.2d 425 (D.C. Cir. 1958).

[40] *Id.* at 426.

[41] The D.C. Court took the quoted standard from Rosenthal v. Stein, 205 F.2d 633, 635 (9th Cir. 1953), in which it was invoked to illustrate that a work satisfying such a standard *remained* a "work of art" for copyright purposes despite the fact that it has been put to a functional use. *See also* Mazer v. Stein, 347 U.S. 201, 218 (1954). The phrase was merely intended to be broad enough to encompass the works at issue in *Rosenthal* (sculptured figures of dancers), *not* as a minimal standard to be met by *all* works claiming copyright as "works of art."

Co.[42] provides just as effective an argument against judicial examination of the degree of artistic creativity displayed by the author's contributions in the case of an art reproduction. However, the first regulations of the Copyright Office under the 1909 Act, issued in 1910 and still in effect at the time of the *Bell v. Catalda* decision, seemed to require just such an independent "creative" contribution: "*Reproductions of works of art.* This term refers to such reproductions (engravings, woodcuts, etchings, casts, etc.) as contain in themselves an artistic element distinct from that of the original work of art which has been reproduced." [43]

In view of the examples given by the regulation, it is quite possible that the art reproductions category was meant by the Copyright Office (for whose convenience the categories were created [44]) to encompass only those art reproductions produced in an artistic medium different from that of the underlying work. Pre-existing works of art reproduced in the same medium with "distinguishable variations" could be copyrighted as derivative "works of art" [45] rather than art reproductions.[46] This appears to be the line of reasoning followed by the district court in *Bell v. Catalda*,[47] which found this separate "artistic element" satisfied by "the handling of the painting in another medium to bring out the engraver's conception of the total effect of the old master." [48] The Court of Appeals, however, chose to *ignore* the difference in artistic medium, emphasizing instead the mezzotints' "substantial departures from the paintings." [49] Thus *Bell v. Catalda* seems

[42] 188 U.S. 239 (1903).

[43] R. Bowker, Copyright 223–24 (1912).

[44] *See* note 5 *supra.*

[45] 17 U.S.C. § 7 (1970).

[46] *See* Nimmer, *supra* note 1 at 92.2 n. 350.

[47] Alfred Bell & Co. v. Catalda Fine Arts, Inc., 74 F. Supp. 973 (S.D.N.Y. 1947), *aff'd*, 191 F.2d 99 (2d Cir. 1951).

[48] 74 F. Supp. at 976.

[49] Alfred Bell & Co. v. Catalda Fine Arts, Inc., 191 F.2d 99, 105 (2d Cir. 1951).

to have dispensed with the "separate artistic element" requirement for the art reproduction category, making originality, the presence of a "distinguishable variation," the sole controlling standard.[50]

In 1959, the regulations themselves were changed[51] to reflect the *Bell v. Catalda* approach: "Reproductions of works of art (Class H). This class includes published reproductions of existing works of art in the *same or different medium*, such as a lithography, photoengraving, etching or drawing of a painting, sculpture, or other work of art."[52]

3. *Copyrightability v. Infringement*

The many cases decided since *Bell v. Catalda*[53] that have found sufficient originality for copyright in art reproductions on the basis of perceived differences in graphic elements have failed to articulate any sharp dividing line between "trivial" and "distinguishable" variations. Most of the opinions do little more than cite *Bell v. Catalda*'s rejection of any requirement that the reproduction be "strikingly unique or novel"[54] and describe the particular variations involved before concluding that they satisfy the modest requirements of the *Bell* "test."[55]

The rare cases which have denied copyright protection to art reproductions for lack of originality, however, have gone

[50] *See* text accompanying note 10 *supra.* For a discussion of whether a change in medium alone can itself qualify as a "distinguishable variation," *see* text accompanying notes 137–149 *infra.*

[51] 40 FED. REG. 4956 (1959).

[52] 37 C.F.R. § 202.11 (1976) (emphasis added); note that under the Nimmer view artistic creativity is required in an art reproduction, but it is automatically supplied by the creativity "inherent in the underlying work of which it is a reproduction." NIMMER, *supra* note 1 at 95.

[53] 191 F.2d 99, 105 (2d Cir. 1951).

[54] *Id.* at 102.

[55] *See, e.g.,* Puddu v. Buonamici Statuary, Inc., 450 F.2d 401, 402 (2d Cir. 1971); Peter Pan Fabrics, Inc. v. Dixon Textile Corp., 280 F.2d 800, 802 (2d Cir. 1960); Peter Pan Fabrics, Inc. v. Dan River Mills, Inc. 295 F. Supp. 1366, 1368 (S.D.N.Y. 1969).

further to provide some explanation of how they reached that result. In *Gardenia Flowers, Inc. v. Joseph Markovits, Inc.*,[56] the court gave this explanation of its conclusion that plaintiffs' plastic corsages lacked originality as compared with pre-existing cloth corsages: "Applying the standard in *Sieff v. Continental Auto Supply*,[57] . . . that '. . . sameness or similarity is determined by the eye of the ordinary observer,' it cannot be said that plaintiff's works represent anything new."[58] Whatever the correctness of the *Gardenia Flowers* result, the appropriateness of the test used by the court is questionable. The "ordinary observer sameness" test applied in that case is the traditional test for infringement rather than copyrightability.[59] As Judge Friendly once explained, there is a considerable difference between the two issues:

> The tests for eligibility for copyright and avoidance of infringement are not the same. Originality sufficient for copyright protection exists if the "author" has introduced any element of novelty as contrasted with the material previously known to him. Introduction of a similar element by the copier of a copyrighted design will not avoid liability for infringement if "the ordinary observer, unless he set out to detect the disparities, would be disposed to overlook them, and regard their aesthetic appeal as the same."[60]

Stated in another way, while the mere alteration of detail will not be a defense to an action for infringement of a copyrighted work, the same change in the detail of a public do-

[56] 280 F. Supp. 776 (S.D.N.Y. 1968).

[57] 39 F. Supp. 683, 688 (D. Minn. 1941).

[58] 280 F. Supp. at 782.

[59] Sieff v. Continental Auto Supply, 39 F. 683, 688 (D. Minn. 1941), which the *Gardenia* court cited for the test, also used it to gauge the originality of a reproduction, but *Sieff* took the test from Falk v. Donaldson, 57 F. 32 (C.C.S.D.N.Y. 1893). *Falk* stated the test not as a standard of copyrightability, but rather as a test of whether an alleged infringer had copied a copyrighted photograph's protected "expression" or merely its unprotected "ideas." *Falk* at 35.

[60] Puddu v. Buonamici Statuary, Inc., 450 F.2d 401, 402 (2d Cir. 1971).

main work of art may well produce a copyrightable art reproduction.[61]

This sound result stems from the different purposes of the two types of determinations. The infringement test is designed to determine whether the "substantial copying" necessary for infringement has occurred.[62] Such "substantial copying" will *necessarily* be present in any art reproduction seeking copyright protection.[63] The issue in the copyrightability cases is not the extent of the unavoidable similarities between the art reproduction and its underlying work of art but rather the extent of their differences.

Gardenia Flowers[64] is not the only case to overlook the above distinction. In *L. Batlin & Son, Inc. v. Snyder,*[65] the court remarked that the differences between appellant's copyrighted "Uncle Sam Bank" and an antique model in the public domain were

> by all appearances, minor. *Similarities include, more importantly,* the appearance and number of stripes on the trousers, buttons on the coat, and stars on the vest and hat, the attire and pose of Uncle Sam, the decor on his base and bag, the overall color scheme, the method of carpetbag opening, to name but a few.[66]

There is a second reason for the inappropriateness of the infringement test in the copyrightability context: its reliance upon the perceptions of the "ordinary observer." In infringe-

[61] "This is a method which might permit copyright if done of some subject in the public domain, but it was here used to copy a copyrighted subject . . ." Alfred Bell & Co. v. Catalda Fine Arts, Inc., 74 F. Supp. 973, 977 (S.D.N.Y. 1947), *aff'd,* 191 F.2d 99 (2d Cir. 1951).

[62] *See* Cook, *infra* note 94 at 69.

[63] *See* Nimmer, *supra* note 1 at 92.2, 167.

[64] 280 F. Supp. 776 (S.D.N.Y. 1968).

[65] 536 F.2d 486 (2d Cir. 1976).

[66] *Id.* at 489 (emphasis added); consider all the similarities that could have been listed in Alfred Bell & Co. v. Catalda Fine Arts, Inc., 191 F.2d 99 (2d Cir. 1951), in which engravings of oil paintings were granted copyright protection.

ment cases, the "ordinary observer" standard is appropriate because it is his approval upon which both the author and infringer rely for their economic gain. Suppose minuscule "variations" in the alleged infringing work, discoverable only by expert witnesses, would bar an infringement claim, despite the fact that "the ordinary observer, unless he set out to detect the disparities, would be disposed to overlook them, and regard their aesthetic appeal as the same." [67] Copyists would then be free to produce not-quite-exact copies which the public would be just as willing to buy as the original copyrighted work. Such a severe reduction in the economic incentives provided by copyright protection might result in a reduction of artistic output by authors.

In the context of copyrightability, however, there is no similar competition for the eye of the "ordinary observer" between author (of the underlying work) and copyist (author of the reproduction). Since the underlying work is in the public domain, its author has no protectible rights to be threatened by the grant of copyright in the reproduction.[68] The relevant interests in such a determination are the public's and the copyist's. Moreover, these interests do not conflict; the question for the court is not whether the copyist has violated the public's rights in the underlying work (an impossibility, since anyone may copy a public domain work) but whether he should be entitled to enjoin others from copying his contributions.[69]

Since the copyright in a reproduction of a work of art protects only those elements that are original with the copy-

[67] *See* text accompanying note 60 *supra.*

[68] An art reproduction is a form of derivative work. NIMMER, *supra* note 1 at 92.2. As such it may be based on either a public domain work, or a copyrighted work used with the permission of the copyright proprietor. 17 U.S.C. § 7 (1970). In the latter case, the author of the underlying work retains protectable rights, but he is stopped from asserting them against the copyist.

[69] For a standard which would protect the interests of such would-be copyists, *see* text accompanying notes 78–85 *infra.*

right claimant,[70] granting such a copyright will not take the underlying work out of the public domain. Those "ordinary observers" who consider it identical in "aesthetic appeal" to the underlying work can still purchase copies of the latter, without paying a premium for the copyist's copyrighted "variations." The author of the reproduction seeks his economic rewards not from them but from those not-so-ordinary observers who find his contributions worth the higher price. In short, since neither "ordinary observers" nor any interests dependent on their patronage are affected by the determination of copyrightability, the use of the "ordinary observer" standard is improper.[71]

4. *Why Exclude "Trivial" Variations?*

One may well ask at this point why the courts, in testing for originality, should ignore "trivial" variations. So long as the claimant can point to a difference between his reproduction and the underlying work of art, why not allow that difference the protection of copyright? Since the copyright will protect only the "trivial variations" in the reproduction,[72] is granting such minimal protection merely a waste of time, or is there some more serious potential harm involved? The Second Circuit Court of Appeals recently put the answer this way: "To extend copyrightability to minuscule variations would simply put a weapon for harassment in the hands of mischievous copiers intent on appropriating and monopolizing public domain work." [73] Anyone has the right to reproduce any public domain work of art—either by copying from

[70] Millworth Converting Corp. v. Slifka, 276 F.2d 443 (2d Cir. 1960); NIMMER, *supra* note 1 at 95, 169.

[71] The "ordinary observer" standard was used in Chamberlin v. Uris Sales Corp., 150 F.2d 512, 513 (2d Cir. 1945). As previously noted, however, that case imposed a requirement of *substantial* variation, a standard that was relaxed somewhat by the same court in *Bell v. Catalda*; *see* notes 9–13 *supra* and accompanying text.

[72] *See* text accompanying note 70 *supra*.

[73] L. Batlin & Son, Inc. v. Snyder, 536 F.2d 486, 492 (2d Cir. 1976).

the original work itself, or by working from a copyrighted art reproduction—so long as he avoids copying the protected "variations."[74] However, the right to copy public domain works, indirectly, through the latter method, would be virtually destroyed if copyright protection were granted to variations so trivial that they might be overlooked and copied unintentionally, exposing the innocent copyist to the risk of an infringement action. Since access to many original works of art is impracticable for most, those works would be effectively taken out of the public domain.

This was the court's concern in the early case of *Snow v. Laird*,[75] in which the plaintiff sought to regain a monopoly on a photograph of his which had entered the public domain. He etched into the negative a small cane in the hand of one of the figures in the photograph and then obtained a copyright on the altered photograph. The court held the copyright invalid, remarking that "To declare that by such a change a photograph, engraving, or other style of picture, which has become public property, may be made a proper subject of copyright, would be to encourage deceit and extortion in a manner impressively illustrated by the facts of this record."[76]

The concern that the author's variations may have been overlooked by a copyist explains the courts' reluctance to apply in art reproduction cases the sort of estoppel argument often invoked against alleged infringers who challenge as "trivial" the creativity or artistic worth of the copyrighted work of art which they have copied: "If it has merit and value enough to be the object of piracy, it should also be of sufficient importance to be entitled to protection."[77]

[74] Millworth Converting Corp. v. Slifka, 276 F.2d 443, 445 (2d Cir. 1960).

[75] 98 F.813 (7th Cir. 1900).

[76] *Id.* at 817.

[77] Henderson v. Tompkins, 60 F.758, 765 (C.C.D. Mass. 1894); *see also* Bleistein v. Donaldson Lithographing Co., 188 U.S. 239, 252 (1903); Hoague-Sprague Corp. v. Frank C. Meyer Co., 31 F.2d 583, 584 (E.D.N.Y. 1929).

5. *A Proposed Standard for Originality in Art Reproductions*

The foregoing discussion suggests that the definition of "merely trivial variations" in art reproductions ought to encompass no more than is required to protect the would-be copyist of public domain works of art.[78] Any broader definition would conflict with the copyright law's requirement of only minimal originality.[79] It follows that if a court finds that there is little danger that would-be copyists of the art reproduction in question would overlook the disparities, it should classify such disparities as "distinguishable variations" possessing sufficient originality for copyright.

The presence of the copyright notice [80] is of key importance. The person who wishes to copy a public domain work of art indirectly, by means of a reproduction which bears such a notice, should be expected to look for any variations in the reproduction, so that he can omit them from his copy. The very existence of copyright protection for "art reproductions" suggests that he should not be entitled to assume that a copyrighted reproduction contains only those variations which are obvious at first glance.[81] Contrast the perceptions of the "ordinary observer"—one who is interested only in similarity of overall "aesthetic appeal" and who has *not* "set out to detect the disparities." [82]

[78] In the case of art reproductions made from copyrighted works of art with permission, *supra* note 68, the definition should encompass no more than is required to protect licensed would-be copyists of the underlying copyrighted work of art.

[79] *See* text accompanying note 13 *supra.*

[80] 17 U.S.C. §§ 10, 19 (1970).

[81] *Cf.* Alfred Bell & Co. v. Catalda Fine Arts, Inc., 74 F. Supp. 973, 976 (S.D.N.Y. 1947), *aff'd,* 191 F.2d 99 (2d Cir. 1951) (in which the court noted that "small photographs of the mezzotints reproduced in half-tone are so difficult to tell apart that a photo of one is sometimes used to advertise another," and even with the mezzotints themselves before it, the strongest language the court could muster to describe the differences was to call them "noticeable").

[82] *See* text accompanying note 60 *supra.*

The proposed standard is both objective and subjective. Since the usual context of such a determination is an action for infringement of the copyright in the reproduction, the court should find the copyright invalid only if it determines both (1) that would-be copyists of the reproduction who set out to detect the variations could not reasonably be expected to find them without great difficulty and (2) that the alleged infringer in the case at bar was not himself aware of the presence of the variations when he copied the reproduction.[83] Thus the alleged infringer must allege that he reasonably considered the reproduction to be an identical copy of the public domain work in order to prevail.[84] Where it is shown that he chose to copy the reproduction due to its improvements over the original, he should be estopped from asserting that those variations are too "trivial" to support a copyright.[85]

Applying such a standard to the reproduction at issue in *L. Batlin & Son, Inc. v. Snyder*[86] yields a conclusion different from that reached by the court in that case, in which the copyright in a plastic replica of an antique metal "Uncle Sam Bank" was invalidated. The plastic version featured a different shape and texture for Uncle Sam's carpetbag, as well as the substitution of *leaves* for *arrows* clutched by the eagle on the antique metal bank.[87] Such distinct and noticeable variations, though possibly "not perceptible to the casual observer,"[88] should reasonably have been detected with little difficulty by appellee Batlin, who was familiar with the public domain version. Thus, the proposed standard would

[83] *See* Ziegelheim v. Flohr, 119 F. Supp. 324, 327–28 (E.D.N.Y. 1954).

[84] *But cf.* L. Batlin & Son, Inc. v. Snyder, 536 F.2d 486, 488 (2d Cir. 1976) (appellee considered the plastic reproduction "an *almost* identical copy" of the antique bank).

[85] Ziegelheim v. Flohr, 119 F. Supp. 324, 326–28 (E.D.N.Y. 1954); *see also* cases cited at note 77 *supra*.

[86] 536 F.2d 486 (2d Cir. 1976).

[87] *Id.* at 489.

[88] *Id.*

result in the validation of the copyright in the reproduction.

II. INVISIBLE FACTORS IN THE ORIGINALITY DETERMINATION

A. SKILL, LABOR, AND JUDGMENT

1. *In General.* Courts often base their findings about the originality of art reproductions on nonvisual factors. One such factor is the degree of "skill, labor, and judgment" involved in the works' creation.[89] Perhaps the earliest mention of "skill, judgment, and labor" as a criterion for originality was made in the context of literary works by Mr. Justice Story in the 1845 case of *Emerson v. Davies* [90]: "He, in short, who by his own skill, judgment, and labor, writes a new work, and does not merely copy that of another, is entitled to copyright therein." This was but a proper statement of the established principle that originality for copyright requires merely independent creation, not novelty.[91]

Much the same language was applied to artistic works in *Bell v. Catalda*,[92] when Judge Frank quoted with approval a commentator's observation that "an engraver is almost invariably a copyist, but . . . his work may still be original in the sense that he has employed skill and judgment in its production." [93]

While the "skill and judgment" test may function well in testing the originality of literary works, it is considerably

[89] *See, e.g.*, L. Batlin & Son, Inc. v. Snyder, 536 F.2d 486, 491 (2d Cir. 1976); Millworth Converting Corp. v. Slifka. 276 F.2d 443, 445 (2d Cir. 1960); Alva Studios, Inc., v. Winninger, 177 F. Supp. 265, 266 (S.D.N.Y. 1959).

[90] 8 F.Cas. 615, 619 no. 4436 (C.C.D. Mass. 1845).

[91] *See* note 2 *supra* and accompanying text.

[92] 191 F.2d 99 (wd Cir. 1951).

[93] *Id.* at 104–105 n. 22, quoting W. Copinger, The Law of Copyrights 46 (7th ed. 1936).

less useful in the field of visual arts. The copyright in a literary work does not protect the physical appearance of the work—pages of a book, printed with groups of letters. These are but symbols. It is only the train of creative expression *represented* by those symbols which is granted copyright protection. The fact that a copy of a literary work does not physically resemble the original is irrelevant. So long as the author's choice and arrangement of symbols is maintained, the protected portion of the work will have been accurately copied.[94] Since skill and judgment are necessary in the choice and arrangement of words in a literary work, but not in the production of an accurate copy, they serve as accurate benchmarks of originality in literature.

However, the copyright in a work of art, unlike the literary copyright, *does* protect its physical appearance. The brush strokes of pigment on canvas are not symbolic—they are the work itself.[95] Artistic skill and judgment are required of the artist not only in his choice and arrangement of the features of his work (his original intellectual concept)[96] but also in the transformation of his ideas into tangible form. Here, in contrast to the literary field, the exercise of skill and judgment is not the antithesis of "slavish copying." Indeed, such skill is often a prerequisite for the production of an accurate copy.[97]

Thus, the use of the "skill and judgment" test to determine originality in the context of the visual arts is inappropriate; it fails to differentiate between the product of original intellectual conception and the product of "actual copying."[98]

[94] *See* Cook, *The Fine Arts: What Constitutes Infringement,* 13 ASCAP COPYRIGHT L. SYMP. 65, 80–81 (1964).

[95] *Id.*

[96] This component may be called "creative skill and judgment." *See* Thomas Wilson & Co. v. Irving J. Dorfman Co., 433 F.2d 409, 411 (2d Cir. 1970).

[97] *See* Bleistein v. Donaldson Lithographics Co., 188 U.S. 239, 250 (1903); Cook, *supra* note 94, at 81.

[98] *See* text accompanying note 10 *supra.*

In fact, since in the visual arts "the closer to exact duplication of the original, the greater skill demonstrated,"[99] this test may yield exactly the opposite of the desired result.

The "artistic skill and judgment" test, though ill suited to the task of sorting out mere copies from reproductions with independently created original contributions, does serve to distinguish the crude or mechanical copy from the more artistically executed one. Such a distinction, however, is not a valid one for purposes of copyrightability. *Bell v. Catalda*[100] flatly rejected the contention that the doctrine of patent law which excludes the results of ordinary skill should be applicable to copyright, noting that the degree of skill involved is immaterial in copyright law.[101]

Furthermore, as a practical matter, such a distinction is of doubtful merit. The judiciary is no better equipped to judge the degree of artistic skill and judgment required to produce a particular graphic work than it is to judge the artistic merit of the work itself.[102]

The logical extreme in the use of the "artistic skill and judgment" test was reached in *Alva Studios, Inc. v. Winninger*,[103] a case that demonstrates the inherent inconsistency of the test with the "distinguishable variation" requirement of *Bell v. Catalda*.[104] In *Alva Studios*, the plaintiff was granted

[99] Andrews, *Copyrighting Reproductions of Physical Objects*, 12 ASCAP Copyright L. Symp. 123, 146 (1963).

[100] 191 F.2d 99 (2d Cir. 1951).

[101] *Id.* at 102.

[102] *See* text accompanying note 36 *supra*; the very inappropriateness of the test may lead a court to refuse to accept even a clear showing of artistic skill. L. Batlin & Son, Inc., v. Snyder, 536 F.2d 486 (2d Cir. 1976). involved a commercial artist who had made sketches from a public domain bank in the figure of Music Sam and then, working from the sketches, carved a clay model of the bank in reduced size with a few alterations. Judge Oakes observed that, while the artist had demonstrated "physical skill," his work did not show "true artistic skill" and thus was insufficient to render the work copyrightable. *Id.* at 491.

[103] 177 F. Supp. 265 (S.D.N.Y. 1959).

[104] *See* text accompanying note 10 *supra*.

a copyright in an exact scale model of a public domain sculpture, in deference to the great artistic skill and effort required to create the reproduction.[105]

The Second Circuit Court of Appeals recently characterized the rationale of the *Alva Studios* holding in the following manner: "The court, indeed, found the *exact replica* to be so *original, distinct,* and *creative* as to constitute a work of art in itself."[106]

2. *In Photographs.* The judicial preoccupation with "skill and judgment" in the art reproduction cases is in apparent contrast to the prevailing view as to the universal copyrightability of another sort of "reproduction"—the photograph. The level of "skill and judgment" employed by photographers seeking copyright protection for their work is generally considered immaterial.[107] The Supreme Court, in the famous 1884 case of *Burrow-Giles Lithographic Co. v. Sarony,*[108] held constitutional the extension of copyright protection to artistically conceived photographs, leaving undecided the question of whether the common snapshot possessed the requisite originality for copyright.[109] For years courts "spent a good deal of time conjuring up all sorts of wondrous artistic skills embodied in the photographs in suit."[110] Judge Learned Hand, however, in *Jewelers' Circular Publishing Co. v. Keystone Publishing Co.*[111] expressed the conclusion that "no photograph, however simple, can be unaffected by the personal influence of the author. . . ."[112] Today, unlike art reproductions, almost any photograph may

[105] 177 F. Supp. 265, 266–67 (S.D.N.Y. 1959).

[106] L. Batlin & Son, Inc. v. Snyder, 536 F.2d 486, 491 (2d Cir. 1976) (emphasis added).

[107] NIMMER, *supra* note 1 at 99.

[108] 111 U.S. 53 (1884).

[109] *Id.* at 56–59

[110] Gorman, *Copyright Protection for the Collection and Representation of Facts,* 12 ASCAP COPYRIGHT L. SYMP. 30, 64 (1963).

[111] 274 F. 932 (S.D.N.Y. 1921), *aff'd,* 281 F. 83 (2d Cir. 1922).

[112] 274 F. at 934.

claim copyright protection, regardless of the degree of skill or judgment involved in its production.[113]

This distinction in the treatment of the two classes of works may be more illusory than real, however. Skill and judgment in art reproductions is generally considered by the courts only when there is a real question as to the sufficiency of graphic variation between the reproduction and its underlying work of art.[114] In contrast, almost all of the photograph cases involved pictures of three-dimensional objects or scenes, as to which there was clearly no close physical resemblance between photograph and real-life subject.[115] *Burrow-Giles* considered only the claim that no photographer should be considered an "author" of his photographs for copyright purposes, since a photograph is a "mere mechanical reproduction of the physical features or outlines of some object, animate or inanimate" rather than the embodiment of any intellectual conception of the photographer.[116] It was only this limited claim that was rejected in *Burrow-Giles* and the later photograph cases. There was no discussion of the very different idea that a photograph might be unoriginal owing to a lack of graphic variation from its subject.

B. UNINTENTIONAL VARIATIONS

At the opposite end of the spectrum from those variations requiring skill and judgment are those created unintentionally. Should such inadvertent variations be protected by copyright? The question was first raised in *Chamberlin v. Uris Sales Corp.*,[117] in which Judge Frank, after characterizing plaintiff's variations as "some inadvertent defects in shad-

[113] NIMMER, *supra* note 1 at 99.
[114] *See* text accompanying note 180 *infra*.
[115] *See* Andrews, *supra* note 99, at 141–42; for discussion of photographs of two-dimensional subjects, *see* text accompanying notes 153–165 *infra*.
[116] 111 U.S. 53, 59 (1884).
[117] 150 F.2d 512 (2d Cir. 1945).

ing," [118] remarked that "If one made an unintentional error in copying which he perceived to add distinctiveness to the product, he might perhaps obtain a valid copyright on his copy, although the question would then arise whether originality is precluded by lack of intention. That question we need not consider." [119]

In *Bell v. Catalda,* however, Judge Frank observed that "lack of intention" was *not* fatal to copyrightability: "A copyist's bad eyesight or defective musculature, or a shock caused by a clap of thunder, may yield sufficiently distinguishable variations. Having hit upon such a variation unintentionally, the 'author' may adopt it as his and copyright it." [120] He was no doubt persuaded by the enormous proof problems that would be created if inadvertent elements of works of art were excluded from copyright protection.[121]

The philosophy underlying the Copyright Clause [122] is encouragement of the production of literary and artistic works through the incentive of potential gain.[123] Judge Frank did not explain how this philosophy applies to authorship by accident, where incentives can play no part. Yet he found support for his conclusion in patent cases involving accidental discoveries.[124] The rationale of the accidental dis-

[118] *Id.* at 513.
[119] *Id.*
[120] 191 F.2d 99, 105 (2d Cir. 1951).
[121] "It is not easy to ascertain what is intended and what inadvertent in the work of genius: That a man is color-blind may make him a master of black and white art; a painter's unique distortions, hailed as a sign of his genius, may be due to defective muscles." Chamberlain v. Uris Sales Corp., 150 F.2d 512, 513 n. 4 (2d Cir. 1945).
[122] U.S. Const. art. I, § 8, cl. 8.
[123] Mazer v. Stein, 347 U.S. 201, 219 (1945).
[124] Alfred Bell & Co. v. Catalda Fine Arts, Inc., 191 F.2d 99, 105 n. 25 (2d Cir. 1951); *see e.g.* Diamond Rubber Co. v. Consol. Rubber Tire Co., 220 U.S. 428, 435–36 (1911); Nichols v. Minnesota Mining & Mfg. Co., 109 F.2d 162, 165 (4th Cir. 1940); Radiator Specialty Co. v. Buhot 39 F.2d 373, 376 (3d Cir. 1930); Byerly v. Sun Co., 184 F. 455, 456–57 (3d Cir. 1911); New Wrinkle, Inc. v. Fritz, 45 F. Supp. 108, 117 (W.D.N.Y. 1942).

covery cases appears to be that in order "to promote the Progress of Science and useful Arts,"[125] the government must not only encourage invention—it must also encourage inventors to make their discoveries available to the public (which an inventor might be less inclined to do if barred from patent protection for his accidental discovery).[126] Since this incentive rationale applies equally to copyright, Judge Frank's conclusion that inadvertence is no bar to copyrightability seems correct.

C. "FUNCTIONAL" MOTIVATIONS

Still another "invisible" factor considered important by at least one court in its determination of copyrightability is the *motivation* underlying the creation of the art reproduction's "original" variations: should variations inspired by commercial constraints and considerations of mass manufacture (as opposed to aesthetic reasons) be eligible for copyright protection? The case of *L. Batlin & Son, Inc. v. Snyder*[127] suggests that they should not be. In discussing the alleged variations between an antique metal "Uncle Sam Bank" and appellant's copyrighted plastic version, the court made much of the fact that none of the variations "had any purpose other than the functional one of making a more suitable (and probably less expensive) figure in the plastic medium."[128] One of the differences was that "the eagle on the front of the platform in the metal bank is holding arrows

[125] U.S. CONST. art. I, °, cl. 8.

[126] "Nor does it detract from its merit that it is the result of experiment and not the instant and perfect product of inventive power. . . . [I]f he has added a new and valuable article to the world's utilities, he is entitled to the rank and protection of an inventor. . . . This satisfies the law, which only requires as a condition of its protection that the world be given something new and that the world be taught how to use it." Diamond Rubber Co. v. Consol. Rubber Tire Co., 220 U.S. 428, 435–36 (1911).

[127] 536 F.2d 486 (2d Cir. 1976).

[128] *Id.* at 489.

in his talons while in the plastic bank he clutches leaves, this change concededly having been made, however, because 'the arrows did not reproduce well in plastic on a smaller size.' "[129]

The suggestion that commercial or "functional" motivations may be fatal to an art reproduction's prospects for copyright protection appears to conflict with the holding of *Mazer v. Stein.*[130] In that case the Supreme Court rejected a similar contention in holding that when an artist becomes a designer for a manufacturer, he does not lose the protection of copyright for his work.[131] While *Mazer* dealt with works of art as a whole rather than "variations," its reasoning seems equally applicable in both contexts.

A hypothetical case demonstrates further difficulties with the *Batlin* distinction. Suppose that the artist copying the antique metal bank had *inadvertently* sculpted leaves instead of the original arrows. Such inadvertence would not bar copyrightability,[132] and while the reproduction problem with the arrows would still be solved, the "functional purpose" objection to the variation would be absent. The variation would thus be copyrightable. Does it make any sense to deny copyright protection to the very same variation simply because the artist happened to recognize a practical reason for making it? It is suggested that it does not.[133]

[129] *Id.*

[130] 347 U.S. 201 (1954).

[131] *Id.* at 218.

[132] *See* text accompanying notes 117–126 *supra.*

[133] *See* L. Batlin & Son, Inc., v. Snyder, 536 F.2d 486, 493 (2d Cir. 1976) (Meskill, J., dissenting); *see also* Soptra Fabrics Corp. v. Stafford Knitting Mills, Inc., 490 F.2d 1092, 1094 (2d Cir. 1974), in which the court discussed "functional variations" in textile designs: "The embellishment or expansion of the original design 'in repeat,' so as to broaden the design and thereby cover a bolt of cloth, together with beginning the pattern in a particular way so as to avoid showing an unsightly joint when the pattern is printed on textiles on a continual basis, constitutes modest but sufficient originality so as to support the copyright."

III. WHEN IS A "DIFFERENCE" NOT A "VARIATION"?

Ordinarily the only question in determining the originality of an art reproduction is whether or not the "variations" contributed by the author of the reproduction are too "trivial" to be afforded copyright protection.[134] Occasionally, however, courts are presented with the more fundamental question of whether an alleged copyrightable contribution may properly be called a "variation" at all. For example, consider a replica of a public domain statue which differs from the original only in that the reproduction, unlike the original, is hollow. Clearly, this difference is not a "variation" for copyright purposes; since it cannot be visually detected, the nature of the work's interior is not a part of the work's "expression." Similar questions relating to differences in medium, material, size, and dimensionality continue to face the courts, and the way in which such questions are handled can have wide ramifications in the law of copyright.

A. DIFFERENCE IN MEDIUM

1. *In General.* What is the result if an artist creates an art reproduction not by deliberately adding something "recognizably his own"[135] to a public domain work of art but by creating as close and realistic a reproduction as is possible in a different medium? Does the "distinguishable variation" requirement of *Bell v. Catalda*[136] mean that the copyrightability of such a reproduction must be judged solely by the extent to which the artist missed his mark? Such a conclusion would be a misinterpretation of *Bell v. Catalda,* according to the recent case of *Kuddle Toy, Inc. v. Pussycat-Toy:*[137]

[134] *See* text accompanying note 10 *supra.*
[135] *Id.*
[136] *Id.*
[137] 183 U.S.P.Q. 642, 658 (E.D.N.Y. 1974).

> The mezzotint [in *Bell v. Catalda*] was a transformation of the original oil painting into a different medium of artistic presentation and of that transformation only the copyright owner was the author. . . .
>
> When *Bell v. Catalda* is subdued to its facts, it is seen that it has nothing to do with limited "originality"; every line of the mezzotint was "original" with the engravers. It has nothing to do with imperfect or variant copying; it was a copy and the plaintiffs were the authors of an independently copyrightable copy where copying itself required new and genuine "authorship."

Although this interpretation appears to conflict with the statement in *Bell v. Catalda* that "Originality in this context means little more than a prohibition of actual copying,"[138] it has much to commend it. To understand this, one must distinguish between two distinct components of the copyrightable "expression" of a work of art: (1) the total visual effect of the work on the observer and (2) the graphic means or "medium" through which the work achieves that effect.[139]

The mezzotint engravers in *Bell v. Catalda* copied not only the "ideas" of the oil paintings but their "total effect" as well.[140] The same situation occurred in *Millworth Converting Corp. v. Slifka*,[141] in which the plaintiff captured not only the "idea" of a public domain embroidery design but also its "three-dimensional effect."[142] What was *not* copied in either case, however, was the graphic means or "medium"

[138] *See* text accompanying note 10 *supra*.

[139] The term "medium" is used here to mean "That through or by which anything is accomplished, conveyed. or carried on; an intermediate means or channel; instrumentality; . . . ." WEBSTER'S NEW INTERNATIONAL DICTIONARY OF THE ENGLISH LANGUAGE 1528 (2d ed. 1960), rather than the material, such as plastic or metal, of which its work is composed; *compare* Alfred Bell & Co. v. Catalda Fine Arts, Inc., 74 F. Supp. 973, 976 (S.D.N.Y. 1947), *aff'd*, 191 F.2d 99 (2d Cir. 1951) *with* Doran v. Sunset House Distrib. Corp. 197 F. Supp. 940, 944–45 (S.D. Cal. 1961), *aff'd*, 304 F.2d 251 (9th Cir. 1962) *and* L. Batlin & Son, Inc. v. Snyder, 536 F.2d 486, 489 (2d Cir. 1976).

[140] Alfred Bell & Co. v. Catalda Fine Arts, Inc., 74 F. Supp. 973, 976 (S.D.N.Y. 1947), *aff'd*, 191 F.2d 99 (2d Cir. 1951).

[141] 276 F.2d 443 (2d Cir. 1960).

[142] *Id.* at 444.

through which the "effect" was conveyed to the observer. In *Bell v. Catalda,* the "due degrees of light and shade [in the mezzotints were] produced by different lines and dots . . ." These were "means very different from those employed by the painter or draughtsman from whom [the engravers copied.]"[143] In *Millworth,* the plaintiff developed "an arrangement of varying colors that would give on a flat surface something of the three-dimensional effect of embroidery."[144]

The "total visual effect" of these reproductions may reveal only "trivial" differences from that of their underlying works of art. Indeed, that is the whole idea of such reproductions. However, closer examination [145] in such cases of the graphic means or "medium" employed to achieve that effect will reveal the "distinguishable variations" that copyright requires.[146]

This view is consistent with the protection afforded by the copyright in such a reproduction.[147] As the district court in *Bell v. Catalda* pointed out, the treatment in another medium could "itself be copied by photography," the method used by the infringers.[148] The court's implication was that if the infringers had instead chosen a medium, such as pen and ink, by which the "total visual effect" of the oil paintings could be copied from the mezzotints, without copying the engravers' treatment in the mezzotint medium, then there would have been no infringement.

This copyrightable "treatment in another medium" must

[143] Alfred Bell & Co. v. Catalda Fine Arts, Inc., 191 F.2d 99, 104–05 n. 22 (2d Cir. 1951).

[144] 276 F.2d at 444.

[145] *See* text accompanying notes 78–88 *supra.*

[146] Note that a change in graphic medium, while one way of satisfying the originality requirement in art reproductions, is no longer the only way; *see* text accompanying notes 44–52 *supra.*

[147] *See* Millworth Converting Corp. v. Slifka, 276 F.2d. 443 (2d Cir. 1960).

[148] Alfred Bell & Co. v. Catalda Fine Arts, Inc., 74 F. Supp. 973, 976 (S.D.N.Y. 1947), *aff'd,* 191 F.2d 99 (2d Cir. 1951).

be distinguished, however, from the uncopyrightable *idea* of reproducing the work of art in such a medium. The copyright in *Bell v. Catalda* did not prevent anyone from independently engraving a mezzotint from the same oil painting, so long as the scheme of lines and dots in the copyrighted mezzotint was not also copied in the process.[149]

Doran v. Sunset House Distributing Co.[150] has been criticized by Professor Nimmer for reaching a contrary result in holding that the mere *idea* of converting a public domain Santa Claus figure into a three-dimensional plastic form constituted copyrightable originality where "plaintiffs were the first to reproduce the traditional character in this particular form and medium." [151] However, the Court of Appeals, in affirming the *Doran* decision, seems instead to have correctly relied on, and limited copyright protection to, the originality of the graphic elements of the three-dimensional plastic Santa Claus.[152]

2. *In Photographic Art Reproductions.* Whether photographically reproducing a work of art constitutes a copyrightable change of medium should theoretically depend on the presence or absence of "distinguishable variation" in the graphic elements of the photograph, just as is the case with other modes of reproduction.[153] This question is complicated, however, by the potential availability of copyright protection for such a reproduction under the alternate category of "photographs." [154]

[149] *Id.* at 976–77; NIMMER, *supra* note 1 at 93–94.
[150] 197 F. Supp. 940 (S.D. Cal. 1961), *aff'd,* 304 F.2d 251 (9th Cir. 1962).
[151] *Id.* at 944; NIMMER, *supra* note 1 at 93–94.
[152] Sunset House Distrib. Co. v. Doran, 304 F.2d 251, 252 (9th Cir. 1962); NIMMER, *supra* note 1 at 94 n. 358. *But see* L. Batlin & Son, Inc. v. Snyder, 536 F.2d 486, 491 (2d Cir. 1976), which appears to hold uncopyrightable not only the *idea* of a change in medium but also the actual graphic variations "such as might occur in the translation to a different medium."
[153] *Supra* note 10 and accompanying text.
[154] 17 U.S.C. § 5(j) (1970).

As noted previously, the present state of the law is that almost any photograph qualifies for copyright, without regard to its aesthetic value or the skill and judgment required to create it.[155] A photograph of a three-dimensional work of art is clearly copyrightable under standards applicable to either "art reproductions" or "photographs"; the "distinguishable variation" required of "art reproductions" is fulfilled in such a work by the reduction of a three-dimensional object to a two-dimensional representation.[156] The "originality" requirement applicable to "photographs" is satisfied "by virtue of the photographers' personal choice of subject matter, angle of photograph [and] lighting. . . ."[157]

A photograph of a two-dimensional work of art, however, might be uncopyrightable as an "art reproduction" because of its lack of graphic variation from the original work, while still possibly qualifying for copyright as a "photograph" owing to the special judicial gloss that has been placed on the latter category.[158]

The only "photograph" case dealing with the copyrightability of photographs of two-dimensional subjects is *Jeweler's Circular Publishing Co. v. Keystone Publishing Co.*,[159] in which Judge Learned Hand stated that all photographs are copyrightable, including those involved in the case, which were merely photographs of illustrations of jewelers' trademarks:

> *Burrow-Giles Co. v. Sarony* [160] . . . left open an intimation that

[155] *See* text accompanying notes 107–116 *supra.*

[156] Gardenia Flowers, Inc. v. Joseph Markovits, Inc., 280 F. Supp. 776, 782 (S.D.N.Y. 1968); *see also* note 115 *supra* and accompanying text.

[157] NIMMER, *supra* note 1 at 99.

[158] *See* text accompanying notes 159–61 *infra; but cf.* NIMMER, *supra* note 1 at 100 (offering the view that, while possibly uncopyrightable as a "photograph," such a work "could probably claim copyright protection as a 'reproduction of a work of art.' ").

[159] 274 F. 932 (S.D.N.Y. 1921), *aff'd*, 281 F. 83 (2d Cir. 1922).

[160] 111 U.S. 53 (1884).

some photographs might not be protected. . . . I think that, even as to these, *Bleistein v. Donaldson Lithographic Co., supra,* rules, because no photograph, however simple, can be unaffected by the personal influence of the author, and no two will be absolutely alike. Moreover, this all seems to me quite beside the point, because under section 5(j) photographs are protected, without regard to the degree of "personality" which enters into them. At least there has been no case since 1909 in which that has been held to be a condition. The suggestion that the Constitution might not include all photographs seems to me overstrained. Therefore, even if the cuts be deemed only photographs, which in these supposed cases they are, still I think that they and the illustrations made from them may be protected.[161]

To the extent that Judge Hand based his conclusion on the absence of an express originality requirement for "photographs" in the Copyright Act, this reasoning seems unacceptable. The courts have clearly demanded a showing of originality in other works seeking copyright protection, despite the similar absence of an express originality requirement.[162] As for the claim that no two photographs of a two-dimensional illustration will be exactly alike, this conclusion is equally untenable.

Therefore, it is submitted that a photographic art reproduction which lacks distinguishable variation from the underlying work of art should be uncopyrightable, whether it is called a "photograph" or a "reproduction of a work of art." [163] Such a uniform originality requirement for the two overlapping categories seems consistent with Congress's intention that the classes of copyrightable works enumerated in

[161] 274 F. at 934–35.

[162] NIMMER, *supra* note 1 at 99. ". . . the courts have uniformly inferred the requirement [of originality] from the fact that copyright protection may only be claimed by 'authors,' or their successors in interest." NIMMER at 32.

[163] Indeed, photography of two-dimensional subjects seems to be a perfect example of a mode of copying that is both "mechanical" *and* "slavish." *See* NIMMER, *supra* note 1, at 10.2. *But cf.* Alfred Bell & Co. v. Catalda Fine Arts, Inc., 191 F.2d 99, 103 n. 13 (noting with approval Judge Hand's remarks as to the copyrightability of photographs).

the Copyright Act [164] be used solely for administrative convenience.[165]

B. DIFFERENCE IN SIZE

An even more troublesome question is whether a mere difference in *size* between a work of art and its reproduction can constitute a copyrightable variation. This was the question in *Alva Studios, Inc. v. Winninger*,[166] which held that an exact one-half-scale reproduction of Rodin's "Hand of God," a sculpture in the public domain, demonstrated sufficient originality for copyright.[167] Although the decision rested largely on the skill required to create the reproduction,[168] Professor Nimmer, in approving of the decision, has noted that its correctness depends upon the change in scale being regarded as a "distinguishable variation." [169]

A change in size should not qualify as a "distinguishable variation" in the graphic elements of a work of art. The most fundamental objection to the *Alva Studios* result is that it is difficult to understand how an exact scale model can be considered anything more than a "slavish copy," whose maker cannot properly claim to be an "author" entitled to copyright protection.[170]

A work's size is no more a part of its copyrightable expression than its location or its orientation in space is. As Mr. Justice Story stated in *Emerson v. Davies*: [171] "In truth, every author [172] . . . has a copyright in the plan, arrange-

[164] 17 U.S.C. § 5 (1970).

[165] *Supra* notes 4–5.

[166] 177 F. Supp. 265 (S.D.N.Y. 1959).

[167] *Id.* at 267.

[168] *Id.; see also* text accompanying notes 80–106 *supra.*

[169] NIMMER, *supra* note 1 at 94 n. 359 (Supp. 1976).

[170] L. Batlin & Son, Inc. v. Snyder, 536 F.2d 486, 490 (2d Cir. 1976); NIMMER, *supra* note 1 at 10.2.

[171] 68 F.Cas. 615, No. 4436 (C.C.D. Mass. 1845).

[172] While Mr. Justice Story referred specifically only to authors of books, the statement is equally applicable to "authors" of all types of works. NIMMER, *supra* note 1 at 166.

ment and combination of his materials . . ."[173] The characteristic of "size" that differentiates it from a work's other elements is that it can be changed in the most extreme manner, and yet it will always leave the author's copyrighted "plan, arrangement and combination of materials" intact. Like "position" and "location," "size" is merely a relative term. It exists solely as a definition of the relationship of a work of art to the physical world that surrounds it. Altering the size of a work of art may normally result in a noticeable difference, but if all of the surrounding objects were removed, the difference in size would be difficult to detect.[174] On the other hand, if we were to include the surrounding objects in our visual examination in order to justify regarding a change in size as a "distinguishable variation," then why would a work of art not undergo an equally distinguishable variation when placed in a different room, or when turned upside down?

Ultimately, though, the most powerful reason to deny copyright protection to a variation in size is the problem that would otherwise be created in defining the scope of such a copyright's protection. How could such a copyright be infringed? Remember that copyright protects only the author's original "expression" and not his "ideas."[175] If someone were to see a copyrighted one-half-scale reproduction of a public domain sculpture and thereafter copy the "one-half-scale" idea by sculpting his own one-half-scale reproduction from the original public domain sculpture, surely he could not be considered an infringer of the copyright in the first reproduction; but if the variation in size were considered

[173] 68 F.Cas. at 619.

[174] Note that, without the surrounding objects, the same visual effect as a change in size could be accomplished by moving the object closer to or farther away from the observer.

[175] *See, e.g.*, Mazer v. Stein, 347 U.S. 201, 217 (1954).

"expression" rather than "idea," such a conclusion would be unavoidable.[176]

Alva Studios avoided such a result by basing its infringement finding on the fact that the alleged infringer "actually copied" the one-half-scale reproduction, strongly implying that if he had instead worked from the public domain sculpture (even after seeing the copyrighted one-half-scale reproductions) the infringement claim would have failed.[177] This view, however, cannot be reconciled with the principle of copyright law that an artist who knowingly duplicates the copyrighted elements of a graphic work is an infringer, regardless of whether the copyrighted work is physically present before the artist's eyes at the time the duplication takes place.[178]

In short, the fact that there is no acceptable way to define infringement for a copyright which protects only a variation in size compels the conclusion that size should not be regarded as part of the "expression" of a work of art at all.

C. THE "CATEGORY OF EXACTITUDE"

The Second Circuit Court of Appeals, in its opinion in the recent case of *L. Batlin & Son, Inc. v. Snyder*,[179] gave a different interpretation to the *Alva Studios* holding. The court began by alluding to the possibility that there might be "a point in the copyright law pertaining to reproductions at which sheer artistic skill and effort can act as a substitute for the requirement of substantial variation . . . ,"[180] and then distinguished *Alva Studios* from the situation in *Batlin:*

The complexity and exactitude there involved distinguishes that

[176] *See* NIMMER 94.
[177] 177 F. Supp. at 268.
[178] Gross v. Seligman, 212 F. 930, 931 (2d Cir. 1914).
[179] 536 F.2d 486 (2d Cir. 1976).
[180] *Id.* at 491; for a criticism of this "artistic skill" approach, *see* text accompanying notes 89–106 *supra*.

case amply from the one at bar. As appellants themselves have pointed out, there are a number of trivial differences or deviations from the original public domain cast iron bank in their plastic reproduction. Thus concededly the plastic version is not, and was scarcely meticulously produced to be, an exactly faithful reproduction. Nor is the creativity in the underlying work of art of the same order of magnitude as in the case of the "Hand of God. . . ." [181]

Thus, the court seems to have rejected Professor Nimmer's view that the size reduction in *Alva Studios* was a "distinguishable variation," [182] regarding the case instead as one granting copyright protection to the meticulous and skilled production of an *exact* replica of a highly creative public domain work of art.[183] The court phrased this basis for copyright protection as an *alternative* to the requirement of originality: "Thus appellants' plastic bank is neither in the category of exactitude required by *Alva Studios* nor in a category of substantial originality. . . ." [184] Granting copyright to an unoriginal work was justified, according to the court, by the public benefit that would accrue from the precise, artistic reproduction of such a unique and rare sculpture to which adequate public access is a problem.[185]

This "category of exactitude" theory of copyright is squarely in conflict with the constitutional requirement of originality implied by the term "authors," used by the Copyright Clause.[186] Indeed, the theory conflicts with the *Batlin* court's own statement that "Absent a genuine difference between the underlying work of art and the copy of it for which protection is sought, the public interest in promoting progress in the arts—indeed the constitutional demand, *Chamberlin v. Uris Sales Corp., supra*—could hardly be served." [187]

[181] 536 F.2d at 491–92.
[182] NIMMER, *supra* note 1 at 94 n. 359 (Supp. 1976).
[183] *See* text accompanying note 106 *supra*.
[184] 536 F.2d at 492.
[185] *Id.*
[186] U.S. CONST. art. I. § 8, cl. 9; *see also* NIMMER, *supra* note 1 at 32.
[187] 536 F.2d at 492.

IV. CONCLUSION

The treatment that the courts have given the issue of the copyrightability of art reproductions has been inconsistent at best. This aspect of the law of copyright is sorely in need of a standard less vague than the requirement of "more than a 'merely trivial' variation,"[188] which courts may find to be satisfied or not, on an *ad hoc* basis. This essay has suggested that such a standard of originality for art reproductions ought not to be more rigorous than is necessary to effectuate the policy favoring free circulation of public domain works of art—a policy that would be fully protected by a criterion based on a reasonable inspection of the reproduction by a would-be copyist.[189] Such a test would allow the courts to reasonably discriminate between original and unoriginal works without resort to such questionable factors as "skill and judgment,"[190] the perception of the ordinary observer,[191] or "categories of exactitude."[192]

THE GENERAL REVISION

The new Copyright Revision Act[193] eliminates the status of "reproductions of a work of art" as a separate category, introducing the term "pictorial, graphic, and sculptural works,"[194] which term is "intended to comprise everything

[188] *E.g.*, L. Batlin & Son, Inc. v. Snyder, 536 F.2d 486, 490 (2d Cir. 1976); Alfred Bell & Co. v. Catalda Fine Arts, Inc., 191 F.2d 99, 103 (2d Cir. 1951).

[189] *See* text accompanying notes 72–88 *supra*.

[190] *See* text accompanying notes 89–116 *supra*.

[191] *See* text accompanying notes 56–71 *supra*.

[192] *See* text accompanying notes 179–187 *supra*.

[193] Pub. L. No. 94–553 (Oct. 19, 1976), now codified at 17 U.S.C. §§ 101 *et seq.*

[194] ". . . Works of authorship include the following categories:

(1) literary works;
(2) musical works, including any accompanying words;
(3) dramatic works, including any accompanying music;
(4) pantomimes and choreographic works;
(5) pictorial, graphic, and sculptural works;

now covered by classes (f) through (k) of section 5 in the present statute. . . ."[195] This consolidation of such categories as "reproductions of a work of art"[196] and "photographs"[197] may have the salutary effect of eliminating the unwarranted differences in treatment sometimes afforded visual works by the courts, depending on the category in which a particular work is considered.[198]

However, the elimination of the separate status of the "reproductions of a work of art" category,[199] which status carried with it the strong implication that Congress intended to require for copyright no more than slight variation from the work "reproduced,"[200] may have the effect of raising the level of originality required for *all* derivative works, from "distinguishable variation" to "substantial variation," a trend already foreshadowed, even under the present statute, by the decision in *L. Batlin & Son, Inc. v. Snyder.*[201]

---

(6) motion pictures and other audiovisual works; and

(7) sound recordings."

Id. at § 102(a).

[195] S. Rep. No. 473, 94th Cong., 1st Sess. 53 (1975); *see also* note 4 *supra.*

[196] 17 U.S.C. § 5(h) (1970).

[197] 17 U.S.C. § 5(j) (1970).

[198] *See* text accompanying notes 153–165 *supra; see also* S. Rep. No. 473, 94th Cong., 1st Sess. 52 (1975), which states that the list of categories in § 102 "sets out the general area of copyrightable subject matter, but with sufficient flexibility to free the courts from rigid or outmoded concepts of the scope of particular categories."

[199] Although no longer a separate category, the term "art reproductions" is retained in the definition of "pictorial, graphic, and sculptural works." Pub. L. No. 94–553, § 102 (Oct. 19, 1976).

[200] Alfred Bell & Co. v. Catalda Fine Arts, Inc., 191 F.2d 99, 100 (2d Cir. 1951).

[201] 536 F.2d 486, 491 (2d Cir. 1976).

NATIONAL FIFTH PRIZE TIE

Is Notice Necessary? An Analysis of the Notice Provisions of the Copyright Law Revision

ELLYN SUE ROTH

GEORGE WASHINGTON UNIVERSITY
NATIONAL LAW CENTER

THE symbol ©, followed by a name and date, may not be as familiar in a few years as it is today. The strict copyright notice requirements of the statute enacted in 1909 have been relaxed by the General Revision of Copyright Law.[1] Signed into law by President Ford on October 19, 1976, the new act represents more than two decades of research and study on proposals to revise our copyright law. The goals of the change were to provide for technological innovations, eliminate ambiguities in the law, and bring the law more in line with copyright statutes in foreign countries.[2] One of the Revision's highlights is the provisions on notice.[3]

[1] Pub. L. No. 94–553, amending title 17 of the United States Code; it codified S. 22, 94th Cong., 1st Sess. (January 15, 1976) and H.R. 2223, 94th Cong., 1st Sess. (January 28, 1975).

[2] The first major step toward Revision was taken in 1955, when Congress authorized and appropriated funds for the copyright office to begin a comprehensive study of the law and proposals for change; *see* S. REP. No. 473, 94th Cong., 1st Sess. 47–50 (1975).

[3] Since 1924, Congress has held hearings on the various proposals to liberalize

Prompted by the problems caused by the notice requirement in the former law (summarized in the first section of this essay), the drafters of the new statute sought to lighten the burden on creators of works. At the same time, however, they had to consider the desire for notice on the part of users of works. This balancing resulted in a set of provisions (outlined in the second part of this paper) which retain the notice but eliminate many of the technicalities. However, the new provisions (as analyzed in the final part of this paper) have not satisfied the needs of either side and have created new problems. *Thus, this writer contends that, rather than compromise, the best solution to the problems would have been an elimination of the notice requirement.*

PART ONE—1909 STATUTE

"The copyright notice is the most important requirement for obtaining copyright in a work that is to be published."[4] This statement of the Copyright Office reflects the necessity, under the former statute, for published works to bear the prescribed notice. Publication[5] with notice secured statutory copyright.[6] Moreover, publication without notice or with

---

the notice provisions of the 1909 statute. *See* SUBCOMMITTEE ON PATENTS, TRADEMARKS AND COPYRIGHTS OF THE SENATE COMMITTEE ON THE JUDICIARY, 86th Cong., 2d Sess., COPYRIGHT LAW REVISION STUDIES, *Study No.* 7 (Comm. Print 1960) [hereinafter cited as *Study No.* 7].

[4] Copyright Office, Library of Congress, *The Copyright Notice,* Cir. 3 (February 1976).

[5] "The date of publication" is defined in the former statute as the date on which "copies of the first authorized edition were placed on sale, sold, or publicly distributed by the proprietor of the copyright or under his authority, . . ." 17 U.S.C. § 26 (1909); *see also* Regulations of the Copyright Office, 37 CFR § 202.2 (as amended, 1972) (hereinafter cited as *Regulations*).

[6] 17 U.S.C. § 10 (1909) provides: "Any person entitled thereto by this title may secure copyright for his work by publication thereof with the notice of copyright required by this title; and such notice shall be affixed to each copy thereof published or offered for sale in the United States by authority of the copyright proprietor, except in the case of books seeking ad interim protection under section 22 of this title." *See generally* H. HOWELL, HOWELL'S

inadequate notice resulted in the forfeiture of the copyright.[7] Thus, omission of the notice or of any required element,[8] a defect in any element,[9] or improper placement of the no-

COPYRIGHT LAW (4th ed. A. Latman 1962), 70–86 (hereinafter cited as HOWELL).

[7] Mifflin v. R. H. White Co., 190 U.S. 260 (1903); Holmes v. Hurst, 174 U.S. 82 (1899); Stuff v. E. C. Publications, Inc., 342 F.2d 143 (2d Cir. 1965); *see also Regulations*, *supra* note 5.

Generally, a greater amount of dissemination of the work was required before a court would hold that divestitive publication (publication without notice which would place the work in the public domain) had taken place than when the proper notice had been affixed and plaintiff asserted sufficient publication to secure the copyright (investitive publication). American Visuals Corp. v. Holland, 239 F.2d 740, 743 (2d Cir. 1956); *see* notes 23–32, *infra* and accompanying text.

[8] For example, the omission of the symbol of "c in a circle" as prescribed by § 19 of the Act, was held to have invalidated the notice. Kramer Jewelry Creations v. Capri Jewelry, Inc., 143 F. Supp. 120 (S.D.N.Y. 1956).

Under 17 U.S.C. § 19 (1909), the notice consisted of three elements: (1) the word "copyright," the abbreviation 'copr.," or the "c in a circle." The last symbol was not allowed until 1954. Pub. L. No. 83–743, 68 Stat. 1030 (1954). (2) "accompanied by the name of the copyright proprietor," and (3) the year of publication if the work was a printed literary, musical, or dramatic work. *See* definition of "date of publication," *supra* note 5.

An alternate (optional) form of notice was further provided under the same section for works in Classes (f) through (k) (generally, graphic and artistic works). The notice needed only two elements: (1) "c in a circle" and (2) "accompanied by the initials, monogram, mark or symbol of the copyright proprietor: *Provided*, that on some accessible portion of such copies or of the margin, back, permanent base, or pedestal, or of the substance on which such copies shall be mounted, his name shall appear."

However, despite this allowance of the optional form, the insertion of the year date was necessary to secure protection in countries who are in the universal copyright convention. 17 U.S.C. § 9(c) amending 17 U.S.C. § 9; *see* Circular 3, *supra* note 4; H. KAPLAN and B. BROWN, JR., CASES ON COPYRIGHT, UNFAIR COMPETITION, AND OTHER TOPICS BEARING ON THE PROTECTION OF LITERARY, MUSICAL AND ARTISTIC WORKS 146 (1960).

[9] While extremely minor variations, such as the order of the elements, inclusion or exclusion of commas or of the word "by" before the name of the proprietor, did not invalidate the notice, anything more, including the letter "c" in a triangle or square instead of a circle, would. M. NICHOLSON, A MANUAL OF COPYRIGHT PRACTICE FOR WRITERS, PUBLISHERS AND AGENTS 137 (2d ed. 1956); *see also Regulations*, *supra*, note 5.

An illegible notice would be invalid. Deward & Rich, Inc. v. Bristol Savings & Loan Corp., 120 F.2d 537, 540 (4th Cir. 1941); HOWELL, *supra* note 6 at 85. However, it was sufficient if the notice would be seen by the naked eye, even if close examination was required. Prestige Floral, Societe Anonyme v.

tice[10] caused the work to be placed in the public domain.

The requirement that notice be a condition precedent to the securing of statutory copyright, a provision not found in the copyright laws of most foreign countries,[11] has been a part of our law since 1802.[12] Earlier courts tended to interpret the provisions narrowly.[13] However, sensitive to the harsh results of forfeiture on these technical grounds, later courts were much more liberal. The view of many recent courts was that deliberate copyists should not be relieved of liability merely because of a slight deviation from the letter of the law.[14] Under this theory of substantial compliance, notice was sufficient if it informed a person who was "looking for the truth" and who desired "to avoid infringement" that the work was copyrighted.[15]

California Artificial Flower Co., 201 F. Supp. 287, 291 (S.D.N.Y. 1962); Trifari, Krussman & Fishel, Inc. v. Charel Co., 134 F. Supp. 551, 554 (S.D.N.Y. 1955).

[10] 17 U.S.C. § 20, *as amended by* Act of October 15, 1971, Pub. L. No. 92–140, 85 Stat. 391, set forth the location of the notice as follows:

Book or other printed publication: on the title page or page immediately following

Periodical: on the title page, on the first page of the text, or under the title heading

Musical Work: on the title page or on the first page of music

Sound recording: "on the surface of reproductions" or "on the label or container in such manner and location as to give reasonable notice of the claim of copyright."

See cases cited under *Position, infra.*

[11] *See Study No. 7, supra* note 3 at 26–27; *see also* HOWELL, *supra* note 6 at 70.

[12] Before that time, notice was given by the publication of the record of copyright registration in a newspaper. Register of Copyright, 87th Cong., 1st Sess., COPYRIGHT LAW REVISION, PART ONE: *Report on the General Revision of the U.S. Copyright Law,* 61 (Comm. Print 1961) [hereinafter cited as PART ONE].

[13] Note, *Copyright Law Revision—Copyright Notice, Governmental Ownership of Copyright, and the Manufacturing Clause* 52 IOWA L. REV. 1121 (1967); *Study No. 7, supra* note 3 at 11.

[14] For example, National Comics Publications, Inc., v. Fawcett Publications, Inc., 191 F.2d 594 (2d Cir. 1951A; Peter Pan Fabrics, Inc. v. Martin Weiner Corp., 274 F.2d 487 (2d Cir. 1969).

[15] Fleischer Studios, Inc. v. Ralph A. Freundlich, Inc., 73 F.2d 276 (2d Cir. 1934), *cert. denied,* 294 U.S. 717 (1935) (failure to add "inc." to the name held not to be fatal to the notice); *see also* Shapiro, Bernstein & Co. v. Jerry Vogel Music Co., 161 F.2d 406 (2d Cir. 1946), *cert. denied,* 331 U.S. 820

Yet despite this judicial trend, the requirement of notice remained. Under that provision, copyrights were still lost through omission of notice or improper notice.[16] The reason for the failure to comply by so many creators? One New York attorney who specialized in copyright law summed up the situation during the hearings on Revision as follows: ". . . except in the most conventional cases, no one is quite certain of the adequacy of the notice to comply with the statute." [17] This confusion was compounded by the fact that those who needed to fulfill the statute's requirements were artists, authors, photographers, and musicians, and other creative people—not businessmen and lawyers. As such, they lacked the knowledge of both the necessity of notice and its proper means of affixation.[18] Furthermore, copyright was often lost through no fault of the author when, for example, the notice was misprinted.[19] Whatever the reason for the improper notice, it was clear that even the most sophisticated publications, such as law reviews,[20] were published with a wide range of mistakes regarding the notice,[21] and thus the copyright was invalidated. The following are some of the main problems encountered: [22]

(1947) (Notice held valid despite a mistake in the date and an implied attribution of authorship of both music and lyrics of a song to the composer when, in fact, the composer wrote only the music).

[16] For example, Verney Corp. v. Rose Fabric Converters Corp., 87 F. Supp. 802 (S.D.N.Y. 1949) (omission of notice on each repetition of a design); Goes Lithographing Co. v. Apt Lithographic Co., 14 F. Supp. 620 (S.D.N.Y. 1936) (omission of name).

[17] *Hearings on H.R. 4347, 5680, 6831, and 6835, Before Subcommittee No. 3 of the House Committee on the Judiciary*, 89th Cong., 1st Sess., Ser. 8 at 1701 (1965).

[18] *Id.* at 1194; *see also* Sheehan, *Why Don't Fine Artists Use Statutory Copyright?* 22 Bull. Copyright Soc'y 242, 272 (1975).

[19] *Study No. 7, supra* note 3 at 60.

[20] *Id.* at 61.

[21] *See Regulations, supra* note 5; *see also* A Manual of Copyright Practice, *supra* note 9 at 139–140.

[22] *See generally*, Cary, *The Quiet Revolution in Copyright: The End of the "Publication" Concept*, 35 Geo. Wash. L. Rev. 652 (1967).

PUBLICATION

Under the former law, publications with proper notice divested common law copyright and, at the same time, invested statutory copyright.[23] Since publication without proper notice simply divested the copyright and left the proprietor with no statutory protection, the need for notice was essential. The major problem in this area was the difficulty in defining divestitive publication. As a result of inconsistent judicial holdings, the concept became ambiguous and confusing.

The source of confusion was the interpretation of the exception to divestitive publication: limited publication. That is, if the work was distributed to a selected group of people for a limited purpose, without the right of further distribution, the lack of notice did not cause the work to fall into the public domain.[24] However, what constituted limited publication was uncertain. In the landmark case of *Ferris v. Frohman,*[25] the Supreme Court held that the public performance of a play was not a publication, either divestitive or investitive. This theory, which was later applied to broadcasts, speeches, and movies,[26] was expanded in situations where the public's interest in the work was of prime importance. For example, in *King v. Mister Maestro, Inc.*[27] the oral delivery of Dr. King's "I Have a Dream" speech was held not to be a publication. Moreover, the advance distribution of the printed text of that speech in the press constituted a limited publication. The court blurred the line between common law and statutory copyright when it stated: "The public interest in the news value of the author's work may cut across

[23] Wheaton v. Peters, 33 U.S. (8 Pet.) 591 (1834); in fact, the main purpose of publication had been to "separate the domain of common-law copyright, administered by the states, from that of statutory copyright," administered chiefly by the federal courts. KAPLAN & BROWN, *supra* note 8 at 101.

[24] White v. Kimmell, 193 F.2d 244, 246–47 (9th Cir. 1952).

[25] 223 U.S. 424 (1912).

[26] KAPLAN & BROWN, *supra* note 8, at 101.

[27] 224 F. Supp. 101 (S.D.N.Y. 1963).

or postpone his rights, but that is not to say that it extinguishes them. . . ." [28]

Despite this stretching of the limited publication theory, many copyrights in works of art were forfeited by public exhibition of those works. It was generally agreed that the holdings did not give artists adequate notice of the law on this point.[29] *American Tobacco Co. v. Werckmeister* [30] held that a general publication did not occur when a work of art was displayed. However, in *Letter Edged in Black Press, Inc. v. Public Building Commission of Chicago,*[31] a case 63 years later, Picasso's monumental sculpture in the Chicago Civic Center was held to be in the public domain after the small model (maquette) of the sculpture had been displayed to the press. The press had been allowed to take and publish photographs of the maquette. Since the small model was thus placed in the public domain, the sculpture, which the court held to be a mere copy of the smaller version, was also put in the public domain. The court in the latter case distinguished the former on the basis that in *American Tobacco,* no copying was permitted in the gallery in which the work of art was shown, whereas, in *Letter Edged,* the showing was unrestricted.

As stated previously, the law was extremely unclear. Furthermore, it had been widely criticized as inequitable. For example, what was the significant difference between a telecast of a play and a display of art? [32] While both seemed to accomplish the same purpose, lack of copyright notice in one situation, but not the other, forfeited the rights in the work.

[28] *Id.* at 107–08, quoting dissent in Public Affairs Associates, Inc. v. Rickover, 284 F.2d 262, 273 (1960), *rev'd* 369 U.S. 111 (1962).

[29] Kunstadt, *Can Copyright Law Effectively Promote Progress in the Visual Arts?* 23 BULL. COPYRIGHT SOC'Y 233, *246* (1976); *see also* Jonakait, *Do Art Exhibitions Destroy Common-Law Copyright in Works of Art?* 19 ASCAP COPYRIGHT L. SYMP. 81 (1971).

[30] 207 U.S. 284 (1907).

[31] 320 F. Supp. 1303 (N.D. Ill. 1970A).

[32] KAPLAN & BROWN, *supra* note 8.

ERROR IN NAME

The first problem with regard to the copyright proprietor's name was the sufficiency of the name. Technically, anything less than the complete and full name of the copyright proprietor would be inadequate.[33] However, some courts were more lenient than the statute seemingly allowed. The absence of "Inc." from the name of a company, for instance, did not invalidate the notice.[34] Similarly, the copyright owner's trade name, rather than the official corporate name, was held to be adequate,[35] even when, as in another case, the trade name had, in fact, been subsequently changed.[36] The rationale for these decisions was that the trade names on the notices in question would reveal the identity of the proprietors to all interested persons.[37] A further extension of this reasoning is in the *National Comics* case,[38] in which the court would not allow the "Superman" comic strips under consideration to be forfeited merely because the technically wrong corporation was named in the notice. There both the named corporation and the actual one had had the same officers, directors, and shareholders, and therefore, the same interests. Thus, here, as in other notice issues, the judicial opinions were somewhat liberal. However, in order to ensure such protection for the author's copyright, that liberal doctrine needed codification.

The second problem with regard to the proprietor's name in the notice arose, to a great extent, in relation to periodicals. If an article was published in a periodical without notice

[33] 17 U.S.C. § 19 (1909), *supra* note 8.

[34] Fleischer Studios, Inc. v. Ralph A. Freundlich, Inc., 73 F.2d 276 (2d Cir. 1934).

[35] Scarves by Vera, Inc. v. United Merchants and Manufacturers, Inc., 173 F. Supp. 625, 628 (S.D.N.Y. 1959).

[36] Doran v. Sunset House Distributing Corp., 197 F. Supp. 940, 945–46 (S.D. Cal. 1961).

[37] *See* notes 35 and 36, *supra*.

[38] National Comics Publications, Inc. v. Fawcett Publications, 191 F.2d 594 (2d Cir. 1951).

but later published with proper notice when that same article was published in book form, the question was whether the notice of the entire periodical (in the name of the publisher of the periodical) was sufficient to secure or hold the copyright in the contribution. The answer was often no. Although an assignee of the copyright proprietor who had been assigned all of the rights in the work could publish the work in his name,[39] magazine publishers were not always assignees of the authors of the contributions. Sufficient evidence was needed to show that the publisher had been assigned the rights to copyright the work, and not merely to publish it.[40] That is, a "mere licensee" could not have acquired the right to take out the copyright in his name.[41] Thus, when a court held that the name in the notice was that of a "licensee" and not the "absolute proprietor," the copyright was forfeited.[42]

This well-established doctrine was, however, recently questioned. The court in *Goodis v. United Artists Television, Inc.*,[43] citing the then-upcoming revision of the copyright law, refused to follow the strict, yet often harsh, logic of former courts. That case held that the notice in the magazine publisher's name would protect the copyright in a novel which had been previously serialized in the magazine without notice in the installments themselves. Although the publisher had not, in fact, owned all the rights in the novel, the court would not apply the doctrine of indivisibility (*partial* assignments of copyrights are invalid) there, where the author,

[39] 17 U.S.C. § 32 (1909) provides: "When an assignment of the copyright in a specified book or other work has been recorded the assignee may substitute his name for that of the assignor in the statutory notice of copyright prescribed by this title."

[40] Mifflin v. R. H. White Co., 190 U.S. 260 (1903).

[41] Dam v. Kirk LaShelle Co., 175 F. 902 (2d Cir. 1910); Morse v. Fields, 127 F. Supp. 63, 64–65 (S.D.N.Y. 1954).

[42] For example, Mifflin v. R. H. White Co. 190 U.S. 260 (1903); Egner et al. v. Schirmer Music Co., 139 F.2d 398 (1st Cir. 1943), *cert. denied*, 322 U.S. 730 (1944).

[43] 425 F.2d 397 (2d Cir. 1970).

who was the plaintiff, would otherwise have been deprived "of the fruits of his creative effort." [44] The court reflected the views of many who were critical of the strict notice requirements when it said: "To require full proprietorship by the initial publisher would too often provide a trap for the unwary author who had assumed the publisher would attend to copyrighting the work in his behalf." [45] Although the author was protected from the trap in that situation, only legislative enactment could secure protection.

ERROR IN DATE

For printed literary, musical, or dramatic works, the statute required the notice to include the year of publication.[46] Under a strict interpretation of the statute, an incorrect date would invalidate the notice. However, whether the error proved fatal apparently depended upon whether the date were antedated (earlier than the actual date of publication) or postdated.[47] Antedated notices were usually held valid; [48] the twenty-eight year copyright term [49] was, under such circumstances, held to have begun on the date in the notice.[50] Thus, the rationale for the validity of the notice despite the wrong date was that the public was not hurt by the error and, in fact, profited from the error since the monopoly on the copyright would be that much shorter.[51]

In contrast, postdating of a notice was, for the most part,

[44] *Id.* at 400.
[45] *Id.* at 402.
[46] 17 U.S.C. §§ 19, 26, notes 5 and 9 *supra; see also The Copyright Notice, supra* note 4.
[47] *See generally* Howell, *supra* note 6 at 76–77.
[48] Callaghan v. Meyers, 128 U.S. 17, 657 (1888); Basevi v. Edward O'Toole Co., 26 F. Supp. 41 (S.D.N.Y. 1939); Shapiro, Bernstein & Co. v. Jerry Vogel Music Co., 161 F.2d 406 (2d Cir. 1946), *cert. denied*, 331 U.S. 820 (1947).
[49] *See* 17 U.S.C. § 24 (1909).
[50] *See* cases cited note 4 *supra*.
[51] *Id.*

deemed fatal[52] on the basis that the copyright would be claimed longer than was allowed. The problem with such a result was that it is not uncommon for a work bearing a new year date to be published before the turn of the year.[53] More recent cases, however, granted relief from the potentially drastic consequences. Thus, in one case, a postdating of four or five months was said to be a minor error which did not harm the public, in view of the total potential duration of fifty-six years.[54] In the absence of an intention to extend the statutory period or of fraudulent intent, such a mistake, said the court, should not cause the copyright to be lost.[55] In a later case, the notice was held valid despite the appearance of two different dates on two parts of the copyrighted object, one of those dates being two years later than the actual publication.[56] The date was not "so affirmatively misleading as to justify invalidating the copyright."[57]

Another issue arising with regards to postdating was that of new matter. The date of publication of a new edition of a work was to be inserted in the notice.[58] However, authors ran the risk that the work would contain no new matter and thus held to be postdated.[59] As a result, some authors and publishers used both the date of the original publication and publication of the new edition.[60]

[52] Baker v. Taylor, 2 F. Cas. 478 (No. 782) (C.C. S.D.N.Y. 1848); HOWELL, *supra* note 6 at 76.

[53] HOWELL, *supra* note 6 at 76.

[54] Advisers, Inc. v. Wiesen-Hart, Inc., 238 F.2d 706, 708 (6th Cir. 1956), *cert. denied*, 353 U.S. 949 (1957).

[55] *Id.*

[56] Prestige Floral, Societe Anonyme v. California Artificial Flower Company, Inc. 201 F. Supp. 287, 292 (S.D.N.Y. 1962).

[57] *Id.* at 292.

[58] *See* 17 U.S.C. § 7 (1909).

[59] *See* Wrench v. Universal Pictures Co. 104 F. Supp. 374, 378 (S.D.N.Y. 1952) (if the story originally published in 1944 had been republished in 1948 without change, it would have fallen into the public domain).

[60] HOWELL, *supra* note 6 at 78.

Here, again, despite some lenient judicial opinions, authors continually risked forfeiture of their works on the basis of an improper date.

POSITION

Authors encountered three basic problems in complying with the notice requirements regarding position of the notice. The first was the position of the elements of the notice; the Act required that first element be "accompanied by" the name and the date.[61] This term was ambiguous. It was unclear whether a name located a few inches from the rest of the notice satisfied the requirement. The courts often allowed such placement as long as it gave reasonable notice of the proprietor's identity.[62]

The second issue arose when a work contained more than one part. The plaintiff might consider the entire unit as the copy and thus affix notice once.[63] However, a court often thought differently. Thus, although notice on one part of a three-component Santa Claus outfit,[64] on one earring,[65] and on one side of a blouse which had the designs on front and back [66] were allowed, the courts were generally stricter in the area of repetitive designs. Notices were held invalid where each strip of Christmas wrapping paper had a notice but each of the twelve repetitions of the design did not; [67]

[61] 17 U.S.C. § 19 (1909). *See* note 8 *supra.*

[62] Harry Alter Co. v. Graves Refrigeration, Inc., 101 F. Supp. 703, 704–05 (N.D. Ga. 1951); Glenco Refrigeration Corp. v. Raetone Commercial Refrigerator Corp., 149 F. Supp. 691, 692 (E.D. Pa. 1957).

[63] 17 U.S.C. § 10, *supra* note 6, required the affixation of notice "to each copy."

[64] Doran v. Sunset House Distributing Corp., 197 F. Supp. 940, 947 (S.D. Cal. 1961).

[65] Boucher v. DuBoyes, Inc. 253 F.2d 948, 949 (2d Cir. 1958), *cert. denied,* 357 U.S. 936 (1958).

[66] Scarves by Vera, Inc. v. United Merchants and Manufacturers, Inc., 173 F. Supp. 625, 628 (S.D.N.Y. 1959).

[67] DeJonge v. Breuker & Kessler Co., 235 U.S. 33, 36 (1914).

where each piece of fabric containing eight squares had a notice, but each square, which contained a cluster of roses and was slightly different from every other, did not have a notice;[68] and in other similar cases.[69] One court acknowledged the technical nature of these holdings and the resulting inconsistency: in wide designs, a notice had to be given only once; however, in designs using a repetition of form for aesthetic value, the copyright could be lost through lack of notice on each repetition.[70]

Actual notice to the copyist was, for the most part, irrelevant in the decisions on repetitive designs,[71] just as it was irrelevant in decisions on the location of the notice.[72] A number of copyrights were lost because a court decided that the notice was located on a page which was something other than the "title page or the page immediately following."[73] Such a requirement created a great deal of difficulty in complying with the statute. For example, one New York attorney asked, "Where is the title page of a newspaper . . . or a magazine?"[74] It was likely that a court might give an answer different from that on which a plaintiff had counted.

Another question was the proper location of notice on graphic and artistic works.[75] For those works, the location was not specifically set forth.[76] It was perhaps for that reason or because the optional form was allowed for such

[68] H. M. Kolbe Co. v. Armgus Textile Co., 279 F.2d 555, 556 (2d Cir. 1960).

[69] Verney Corp. v. Rose Fabric Converters Corp., 87 F. Supp. 802 (S.D.N.Y. 1949).

[70] H. M. Kolbe Co. v. Armgus Textile Co., 279 F.2d 555, 557 (2d Cir. 1960).

[71] *Id.*

[72] *See* note 10 *supra.*

[73] Deward & Rich, Inc. v. Bristol Savings and Loan Corp., 120 F.2d 537, 539 (4th Cir. 1941); *see also* Booth v. Haggard, 184 F.2d 470 (8th Cir. 1950); United Thrift Plan, Inc. v. National Thrift Plan, Inc., 34 F.2d 300 (E.D.N.Y. 1929).

[74] *Hearings, supra* note 17 at 1711.

[75] 17 U.S.C. § 5 (1909): works in classes (f) through (k).

[76] The location is impliedly set forth in 17 U.S.C. § 19 (1909): ". . . Provided,

works[77] that the courts took the view that the notice was properly placed as long as it would give a potential copyist notice that the copyright existed.[78] The most radical decision in this area was that of *Peter Pan Fabrics, Inc. v. Martin Weiner, Corp.*,[79] which held that notice located on the selvage of cloth, cut off by the buyer of the cloth when the buyers use the material to make clothing, was valid. The court so held despite plaintiff's knowledge that the notice would be cut and despite the fact that the ultimate purchasers would not receive notice of the copyright. Thus, although the public would not be reasonably apprised of the notice, the court switched the burden to the "deliberate copyist" to prove an absence of actual notice. However, such protection for the proprietor was unusual.

WORKS PUBLISHED ABROAD

The unanswered question here was whether works first published abroad without the copyright notice required by our law could subsequently secure United States copyright.[80] An early court held no,[81] but a later court held yes.[82] However, the latter holding was the opposite of the view of the

---

that on some accessible portion of such copies or of the margin, back, permanent base, or pedestal, or of the substance on which such copies shall be mounted, his name shall appear."

[77] *Id.*

[78] Coventry Ware, Inc. v. Reliance Picture Frame Co., 288 F.2d 193 (2d Cir.), *cert. denied,* 368 U.S. 818 (1961) (notice appearing on the back of wall plaques complied with statute); Scarves by Vera, Inc. v. United Merchants and Manufacturers, Inc., 173 F. Supp. 625 (S.D.N.Y. 1959) (notice sewn into a side seam adjacent to the bottom opening of the garment held sufficient); Trifari, Krussman & Fishel, Inc. v. Charel Co., 134 F. Supp. 551 (S.D.N.Y. 1955) (notice on the clasp of an article of costume jewelry was valid).

[79] 274 F.2d 487 (2d Cir. 1960).

[80] S. Rothenberg, Legal Protection of Literature, Art and Music § 69 (1960).

[81] Basevi v. Edward O'Toole Co., 26 F. Supp. 41, 46 (S.D.N.Y. 1939).

[82] Heim v. Universal Pictures Co., 154 F.2d 480 (2d Cir. 1946).

copyright office.[83] Indeed, no one was certain of the answer.[84]

SAVINGS CLAUSE

The main source of protection against forfeiture for the accidental omission of notice from a few copies of a work was the savings clause.[85] However, in fact, many copyrights were not saved, because the provision was narrowly construed.[86] In one recent case, the provision was applied when, after 25 copies out of the 1000 ordered for a second printing of the work had been printed and distributed without notice, the proprietor discovered the error and destroyed the remaining 975.[87] However, in another case, a preliminary injunction was denied where there had been evidence of copies without notice and the plaintiff did not establish sufficient evidence to show that those without notice constituted an extremely minor percentage of the copies distributed.[88] In fact, the clause would not be applied if the notice was omitted on all the copies,[89] or even if it was omitted on all but the first

[83] *Regulations, supra,* note 5, § 202.2(a)(3) reads: "Works first published abroad, other than works eligible for ad interim registration, must bear an adequate copyright notice at the time of their first publication in order to secure copyright under the law of the United States."

[84] *Hearings, supra,* note 17.

[85] 17 U.S.C. § 21 (1909) provides: "Where the copyright proprietor has sought to comply with the provisions of this title with respect to notice, the omission by accident or mistake of the prescribed notice from a particular copy or copies shall not invalidate the copyright or prevent recovery for infringement against any person who, after actual notice of the copyright, begins an undertaking to infringe it, but shall prevent the recovery of damages against an innocent infringer who has been misled by the omission of the notice; and in a suit for infringement no permanent injunction shall be had unless the copyright proprietor shall reimburse to the innocent infringer his reasonable outlay innocently incurred if the court, in its discretions, shall so direct."

[86] Note, IOWA L. REV., *supra* note 13 at 1127.

[87] Perkins Marine Lamp & Hardware Corp. v. Long Island Marine Supply Corp., 185 F. Supp. 353 (E.D.N.Y. 1960).

[88] Kramer Jewelry Creations v. Capri Jewelry, Inc., 143 F. Supp. 120 (S.D.N.Y. 1956).

[89] Goes Lithographing Co. v. Apt Lithographing Co., 14 F. Supp. 620

published copy.[90] Only one or a very few copies could, in general, have been published without notice or with defective notice in order for the provision to save the notice.[91] The courts felt that anything more liberal would be tantamount to making the notice requirements optional.[92]

Thus, failure to comply with the technical, and often ambiguous, provisions on notice in the 1909 statute caused many works for which authors had desired copyright protection to be thrown into the public domain.[93] Such results prompted the liberalization of the notice requirements in the new Act. It was here that stronger protection against forfeiture than the savings clause was needed.

PART TWO—REVISION

Whereas mostly everyone who participated in the development of the new notice provisions, users and creators alike, agreed that the technical forfeiture resulting from strictly construed and ambiguous provisions of the former statute was unjust,[94] there was little agreement on the best method of eradicating the problem. Those faced with the task of drafting the Revision had to contend with two opposing groups whose arguments revolved around two opposing yet equally valid aims: "to assure all authors the benefit of

(S.D.N.Y. 1936); United Thrift Plan, Inc. v. National Thrift Plan, Inc., 34 F.2d 300 (E.D.N.Y. 1929).

[90] National Comics Publications, Inc., v. Fawcett Publications, Inc., 191 F.2d 594 (2d Cir. 1951).

[91] Krafft v. Cohen, 117 F.2d 579, 581 1(34th Cir. 1941).

[92] United Thrift Plan, Inc., v. National Thrift Plan, Inc., 34 F.2d 300, 302 (E.D.N.Y. 1929).

[93] *Copyright Law Revision, Part Two: Discussion and Comments on the Report on the General Revision of the U.S. Copyright Law*, 88th Cong., 1st Sess. (Comm. Print, 1963) [hereinafter cited as *Part Two*] 373.

[94] *Study No. 7, supra* note 3, at 63; A. HANSON, OMNIBUS COPYRIGHT REVISION, COMPARATIVE ANALYSIS OF THE ISSUES 131 (1973).

copyright protection for all of their works and to facilitate the dissemination of works. . . ." [95]

Although the roles of the two basic groups—authors (meaning authors in the larger sense of creators) and users of copyrighted works—overlapped (authors are, prior to creating, users),[96] the two groups seemed to be in distinctly separate camps. Those who were in favor of the elimination of the notice requirement were, for the most part, creators such as writers,[97] photographers,[98] performing rights organizations.[99] Nimmer, a well-known scholar on copyright, also opposed the notice requirements.[100] The motion picture producers believed the value of the notice to be overrated.[101] Opponents of the notice requirements asserted that:

- It conflicted with the notion that every creator is "entitled to the fruits of his labor"
- Most other countries do not have such formalities and, in keeping the notice, the United States is behind the times
- The notice is useless, since it is necessary to look beyond the notice for information
- The notice caused unjust forfeiture.[102]

In contrast, proponents of the notice requirement argued that:

- Without notice many works in which no one is interested would be kept out of the public domain and thus hamper the free flow of scholarly and cultural ideas

[95] *Study No. 7, supra* note 3, at 47.

[96] A. Kent, *The Viewpoint of an Author*, in COPYRIGHT: CURRENT VIEWPOINTS ON HISTORY, LAWS, LEGISLATION 108 (1972).

[97] *See Copyright Law Revision, Part Five: 1964 Revision Bill with Discussions and Comments*, 88th Cong., 1st Sess. (Comm. Print 1965) [hereinafter cited as *Part Five*] 253; *see Study No. 7, supra* note 3, at 60–61; *see Hearings on 4347, supra* note 17, at 1962–4.

[98] *See Hearings on 4347, supra* note 17, at 1194.

[99] *Id.* at 220.

[100] *Part Two, supra* note 93.

[101] *Part Two, supra* note 93 at 352; *see Hearings on H.R. 4347, supra* note 17, at 1037–38.

[102] *Study No. 7, supra* note 3, at 46.

- Notice is increasingly necessary because of technology and a greater number of secondary users
- The author has a duty to the public to fulfill these requirements in exchange for his limited monopoly
- Notice is effective in providing a starting point for discovering the identity of the owner and the duration of the copyright.[103]

The groups constituting the proponents were the broadcasters,[104] publishers,[105] librarians,[106] and professors.[107]

Arising from these two viewpoints was a compromise: under the new Act, the notice requirement was retained but the requirements of notice were relaxed and, subject to safeguards for innocent infringers, a significant amount of protection against forfeiture was provided.[108] Although writers have characterized the provisions as a codification of recent judicial opinions,[109] that is only partly true. The new provisions go beyond the substantial compliance doctrine developed by many counts.

BASIC REQUIREMENTS

The general notice requirements are set forth in sections

[103] *Id.* at 57.

[104] *See Hearings Before House Committee on Patents* 74th Cong., 2d Sess. at 469 (1936); *Study No. 7, supra* note 3, at 45.

[105] *Hearings, supra* note 104, at 223–224; *Study No. 7, supra* note 3 at 62; *see Hearings on H.R. 4347, supra* note 17 at 1207.

[106] *See* J. Rogers, *Use of the Copyright Notice by Libraries, No. 9, Copyright Law Revision Studies,* prepared for the Subcommittee on Patents, Trademarks and Copyrights of the Committee on the Judiciary, 86th Cong., 1st Sess. (1959) (hereinafter cited as *Study No. 9*); *See Copyright Law Revision, Part Four: Further Discussions and Comments on Preliminary Draft for Revised U.S. Copyright Law,* 88th Cong., 2nd Sess. (Comm. Print 1964) [hereinafter cited as *Part Four*] 364; *See Hearings on H.R. 4347, supra,* note 17 at 121.

[107] *Study No. 7, supra* note 3, at 64.

[108] OMNIBUS COPYRIGHT REVISION, *supra* note 94; A. Goldman, *Copyright as It Affects Libraries: Legal Implications, Current Viewpoints,* printed in COPYRIGHT: CURRENT VIEWPOINTS ON HISTORY, LAWS, LEGISLATION, *supra* note 96 at 35; S. REP. No. 94–473, *supra* note 2 at 121.

[109] For example, OMNIBUS COPYRIGHT REVISION, *supra* note 94.

401 and 402 of the Revision.[110] Although notice is required when a work is published "on all publicly distributed copies from which the work can be visually perceived," [111] problems of publication under the 1909 statute [112] have been greatly diminished. Whether the publication is divestitive is no longer an issue in that, under Revision, copyright "subsists from its creation," enduring "for a term consisting of the life of the author and fifty years after the author's death." [113] Furthermore, the Act does not provide grounds for holding that display of a work of art without notice forfeits the copyright.[114] The statute specifically states that: "A public performance or display of a work does not of itself constitute publication." [115] Moreover, notice need only be placed on "publicly distributed copies," not publicly displayed ones.[116]

The same section answers the formerly unanswered question regarding works first published abroad without United States copyright notice.[117] Notice on publicly distributed copies is required "whenever a work protected under this title is published in the United States or *elsewhere*" (emphasis added).[118] Thus, works published abroad need the proper notice in order to secure United States copyright. Although author groups opposed this provision on the grounds that foreign publishers, whose activities may be hard for an author to control, are often unfamiliar with our require-

[110] Section 401 is entitled "Visually perceptible copies"; Section 402 sets forth the comparable requirements for sound recordings. A detailed analysis of that section as well as a detailed analysis of Section 403, "Publications incorporating United States Government works" is beyond the scope of this essay.

[111] Section 401.

[112] *See* notes 23–32 and accompanying text *supra*.

[113] Section 302(a).

[114] S. Rep. No. 473, *supra* note 2, at 126.

[115] *See* definition of "Publication," Section 101.

[116] Section 401; S. Rep. No. 94–473, *supra* note 2 at 126–27.

[117] *See* notes 80–84 and accompanying text *supra*.

[118] Section 401.

ments,[119] the phrase was put in on the basis that the value which notice has in United States works is the same as that in foreign editions of works copyrighted here.[120] The "increased flow of intellectual materials across national boundaries" as well as the retention of "gains in the use of notice on editions published abroad under the Universal Copyright Convention" were also influential in the decision to insert the phrase.[121]

The three basic elements are retained for the form of the notice.[122] Whereas previously, authors often put the years of both the original work and the compilation in order to protect themselves,[123] the present provision states clearly that, in the case of compilations, "the year date of first publication of the compilation or derivative work is sufficient." [124]

While graphic and other artistic works, those under the former classes (f) through (k), now generally need a year date,[125] a date is not necessary "where a pictorial, graphic, or sculptural work, with accompanying text matter, if any, is reproduced in or on greeting cards, postcards, stationery, jewelry, dolls, toys, or any useful articles." [126] Producers of such useful articles did not want a date requirement, because they were often uncertain of the date of publication of such items and thus would not know what date to insert on the notice.[127]

The greeting card publishers, textile distributors and makers of maps and reproductions of works of art also did not

[119] H.R. REP. No. 83, 90th Cong., 1st Sess. 111 (1967).
[120] S. REP. NO. 473, *supra* note 2, at 127.
[121] *Id.*
[122] Section 401(b); S. REP. No. 473, *supra* note 2, at 127.
[123] *See* notes 46–60 and accompanying text *supra.*
[124] Section 401(b)(2).
[125] Under 17 U.S.C. § 5(1909), classes (f) through (k) did not need a date on the notice: *see* 17 U.S.C. § 19 *supra* note 3.
[126] Section 401(b)(2).
[127] *Part Two, supra* note 93, at 352.

want to have to insert a date, since the date, if anything older than the present, would allegedly undermine the commercial value of the works in this era of love for things which are new.[128] Greeting card publishers also cited the fact that they often reuse sections of previously copyrighted artwork and would not know the date to insert, since the new work could not be considered a compilation or derivation.[129] Librarians opposed an exception to the requirement of a date. They asserted the need for dates on maps when someone searches for boundaries during a certain time period. The absence of dates on maps under the 1909 statute, stated the librarians, caused a great deal of confusion.[130] What the provision under Revision finally does is give the greeting card publishers and the textile distributors their exception, but not the mapmakers.[131]

A problem under the 1909 statute in inserting the correct name of the proprietor[132] is partly solved by the section at hand, which allows less than the full and complete name: what is required is the name "or an abbreviation by which the name can be recognized, or a generally known alternative designation of the owner."[133] Such a relaxation reflects judicial opinion to the extent of the "generally known alternative" but goes beyond it in allowing the "abbreviation."

The final subsection in the general requirements provides that the notice shall be positioned "in such manner and loca-

[128] *Hearings on S. 597 before the Subcomm. on Patents, Trademarks and Copyrights*, 90th Cong., 1st Sess. at 728–9, 778; *Part Two, supra* note 93, at 268.

[129] *Hearings on S. 597, supra* note 128, at 729.

[130] *Hearings on H.R. 4347, supra* note 17, at 449; *Study No. 7, supra* note 3, at 63.

[131] Greeting cards are specifically listed as part of the group whose notice does not need a date. Textiles are "useful articles" under the definition in section 101: "A 'useful article' is an article having an intrinsic utilitarian function that is not merely to portray the appearance of the article or to convey information." However, maps do not come within the category of "useful articles" since their function is merely to convey information. Thus, under Revision, the year date must be in the notice on maps.

[132] *See* notes 33–45 and accompanying text *supra*.

[133] Section 401(b)(3); *see* S. Rep. No. 473, *supra* note 2, at 127.

tion as to give reasonable notice of the claim of copyright."[134] This liberalization diminishes the possibility that the notice will be improper simply because the first element is not "accompanied by" the name and date, because each repetition of a design does not have notice, or because the notice was not on what the court held was the title page or page immediately following.[135] The location need only further the purpose of the notice: to give "reasonable notice." The provision was feared by some, mainly librarians, to be so vague that it would mislead users. That is, the notice could be hidden and yet be characterized as "reasonable."[136] However, others pointed out that this flexible approach has worked quite well for works under the Universal Copyright Convention.[137] Furthermore, as a compromise measure, the section contains a provision directing the Register of Copyrights to prescribe guidelines for the location.[138] Such guidelines, which will mitigate any potential confusion arising from this section,[139] seemed to appease librarians, who, from a practical standpoint, would prefer a requirement specifically designating a place for each type of copyrighted work.[140]

CONTRIBUTIONS TO COLLECTIVE WORKS

Revision of this section was extremely important to magazine writers and photographers, since most of their work appears in collective works[141] and, under the former law, was vulnerable to forfeiture on the basis of lack of notice.[142]

[134] Section 401(c).
[135] *See* notes 61–79 and accompanying text *supra*.
[136] *Hearings on H.R. 4347, supra* note 17, at 1575.
[137] S. Rep. No. 473, *supra* note 2, at 127; Note, Iowa L. Rev., *supra* note 13 at 1124.
[138] Section 401(c); the guidelines are not to be considered exhaustive.
[139] H.R. Rep. No. 83, *supra* note 119.
[140] *Hearings on H.R. 4347, supra* note 17, at 450.
[141] *Hearings on H.R. 4347, supra* note 17, at 255.
[142] *See* notes 33–45 and accompanying text *supra*.

Chance of such forfeiture has been eliminated under the new Act as long as the collective work bears a notice.[143] First, while a separate notice for each contribution is permitted, a single notice on the entire collective work is sufficient to cover the author's copyright in the contribution.[144] Second, if the contribution does not bear its own notice and the general notice of the collective work in which the contribution is published contains the name of someone other than the copyright owner of the contribution, the copyright on the contribution is not forfeited. Instead, the copyright is treated as if the wrong name has been used under Section 406(a).[145] Thus, the provision effects a compromise between creators and users by protecting against loss of the copyright and, at the same time, shielding from liability innocent infringers who have dealt in good faith with the person named in the general notice.[146]

The exception to the single notice rule would be copyrights on "advertisements inserted on behalf of persons other than the owner of copyright in the collective work."[147] Such an exception was opposed by newspaper publishers[148] on the grounds that the newspapers do have an interest in advertisements created by the newspapers' own skill and effort. Since the ads can be photographically "lifted" from the newspapers, newpapers desire protection of the ads. The most practical means of protection would be under a single notice for the periodical.[149] Despite this viewpoint, the drafters of the statute believed that an undue burden would not be imposed on owners of the advertisements to insert a notice. A congressional report accompanying the new statute stated that

[143] Goodis v. United Artists Television Inc. 425 F.2d 397 (2d Cir. 1970); S. Rep. No. 473, *supra* note 2 at 129.

[144] Section 404(a).

[145] *See* notes 176–179 and accompanying text *infra.*

[146] Section 406(a); S. Rep. No. 473, *supra,* note 2 at 179.

[147] Section 404(a).

[148] H.R. Rep. No. 83, *supra* note 119 at 113.

[149] *Hearings on H.R. 4347, supra* note 17, at 1403.

it "is common for the same advertisement to be published in a number of different periodicals." [150] The exception is, according to the report, "justified by the special circumstances." [151]

OMISSION OF NOTICE

Under the revised law, a copyright which omits the notice is saved from forfeiture under certain conditions.[152] Section 405, which balances the needs of the owner against those of the innocent infringer,[153] "not only represents a major change in the theoretical framework of American copyright law, but . . . also seems certain to have immediate practical consequences in a great many individual cases." [154] That is, while the copyright would have been lost because of omission of notice under the former statute,[155] in a number of situations, it will not be lost under the present law. Forfeiture does not take place if any one of the following occurred:

> (1) The notice has been omitted from no more than a relatively small number of copies or phonorecords distributed to the public [156]

Although the Department of Justice wanted the phrase "particular copy or copies" used in the former savings clause,[157] to be in place of "relatively small number of copies," the latter was decided upon so as to be less restrictive than the former language.[158]

> (2) Registration for the work has been made before or is made

[150] S. Rep. No. 473, *supra* note 2 at 129.
[151] *Id.*
[152] Section 405(a).
[153] Omnibus Copyright Revision, *supra* note 94.
[154] S. Rep. No. 473, *supra* note 2, at 129.
[155] *See* note 16 and accompanying text *supra.*
[156] Section 405(a)(1).
[157] 17 U.S.C. § 21 (1909).
[158] S. Rep. No. 473, *supra* note 2, at 130; note that "particular copy or copies" was one of the phrases on which the narrow interpretation of § 21 was based.

within five years after the publication without notice, and a reasonable effort is made to add notice to all copies or phonorecords that are distributed to the public in the United States after the omission has been discovered.

This subsection, the source of a great deal of controversy, is a compromise between the view of the users who desired immediate forfeiture in such a situation and that of the creators who wanted no forfeiture.[159] The five-year period was finally decided upon as a reasonable time period, consistent with the registration provisions.[160] A "reasonable effort" has to be made only in relation to copies distributed in the United States because of the otherwise undue burden it would impose on owners to "police the activities of foreign licensees in this situation." [161]

(3) The notice has been omitted in violation of an express requirement in writing that, as a condition of the copyright owner's authorization of the public distribution of copies or phonorecords, they bear the prescribed notice.[162]

The rationale behind this subsection is that, in such a situation, the work would not be published "by authority of the copyright owner" under Section 401(a). This reflects the equitable principle that the owner should be responsible only for what he can control.

Another example of the legislators' balancing of equities is the provision which disallows forfeiture in the above situations, whether the omission be *unintentional or deliberate.*[163] Although this provision, which goes far beyond the limited protection of accidental omission in the 1909 statute,[164] was strongly criticized,[165] the drafters believed that

[159] H.R. Rep. No. 83, *supra* note 119, at 114.
[160] *See* Section 410(c); S. Rep. No. 473, *supra* note 2, at 130.
[161] S. Rep. No. 473, *supra* note 2, at 130.
[162] Section 405(a)(3).
[163] S. Rep. No. 473, *supra* note 2, at 129.
[164] *See* 17 U.S.C. § 21 (1909).
[165] For example, *Hearings on H.R. 4347*, *supra* note 17, at 1880.

distinguishing between intentional and unintentional omissions and making the validity of a copyright depend on such a distinction "would introduce a subjective criterion that would result in injustice and confusion." [166]

While the possibility of forfeiture for omission of notice has been limited by this subsection, innocent infringers are also protected by the act if they can prove they were misled by the omission.[167] The rationale here is an equitable one, based on the historical concept of United States copyright law: one acting in good faith on the assumption that omission indicates that the work is in the public domain should not be held fully liable.[168] The assumption is apparently worth considering in that it was a valid one under the former law.

Such innocent infringers are liable to a certain extent, but not for actual or statutory damages for acts committed before receipt of actual notice of registration.[169] Authors, publishers, and motion picture producers criticized this burden on the proprietor to give an infringer actual notice in that infringers are often unknown until long after the infringement has occurred.[170] However, with that language, the drafters attempted to protest users such as teachers, librarians, and journalists in situations where the infringements would be minor and thus not really destructive of the copyright.

In exchange for the restriction on actual or statutory damages, the creators may still receive profits, an injunction against continuation of the infringement, or a license fee.[171] In fact, the provision for damages was changed from the 1965

[166] H.R. Rep. No. 83, *supra* note 119, at 114.
[167] Section 405(b).
[168] S. Rep. No. 473, *supra* note 2, at 131.
[169] Section 405(b).
[170] H.R. Rep. No. 83, *supra,* note 119, at 114–16; *Part Two, supra* note 93 at 317.
[171] Omnibus Copyright Revision, *supra* note 94.

bill, which reimbursed the infringer against whom an injunction was issued for "any reasonable expenditure incurred by him,"[172] in favor of the creator. In all, under the new act, the remainder of the balancing with regard to damages is left in the hands of the courts. They have broad discretion to grant or limit damages, depending upon the specific situation.[173]

The final subsection here, which upholds the copyright when notice is removed by someone other than the owner,[174] again places a burden on creators to the extent that the situation is in their control. An adoption of recent judicial decisions such as *Peter Pan,*[175] the subsection goes far to protect copyrights in these situations from invalidation.

ERROR IN NAME OR DATE

Again, this section[176] intends to prevent technical forfeitures and at the same time induce use of the correct name and date and protect innocent infringers who have relied on the wrong information.[177] Unlike the former statute, the new provisions do not treat such error as omission, causing forfeiture; rather, they are addressed to the usual consequences of the communication of the wrong name or date to users of copyrighted material.

An error in name does not affect the copyright's validity. However, reliance on the wrong name by acting "under a purported transfer or license from the person named therein"[178] is a defense to infringement. Yet that defense only applies when the work had not been registered before the

[172] H.R. Rep. No. 83, *supra* note 119, at 117.

[173] S. Rep. No. 473, *supra* note 2, at 131.

[174] Section 405(c).

[175] 274 F.2d 487 (2d Cir. 1960); *see* S. Rep. No. 473, *supra* note 2, at 131; *see* notes 61–79 and accompanying text *supra.*

[176] Section 406.

[177] S. Rep. No. 473, *supra* note 2, at 132.

[178] Section 406(a).

undertaking. Therefore, a reasonable burden is placed on the user to search the copyright office records.[179]

An antedated notice results in a situation approved by many courts: any statutory term is simply computed from the year on the notice.[180] The statutory terms under the new law are in relation to anonymous works, pseudonymous works and works made for hire,[181] as well as to presumptive periods of an author's death.[182]

A notice may be postdated up to one year before it is treated as omission of notice.[183] The reasoning behind this provision follows the common occurrence of postdating of works published near the end of the year.[184]

Omission of name or date [185] is treated as omission of notice. As stated above, the name and date need not "accompany" the rest of the notice.[186] The requirement has been changed so that they must reasonably be considered a part of the notice," [187] a relaxation of the former law.

Thus, the new law does eliminate some ambiguities of the prior statute and does mitigate the former threat of technical forfeiture. The drafters accomplished these goals by compromising between creators and users, two sets of groups with opposite aims. However, rather than please both groups, the new statute may prove to satisfy neither.

PART THREE—EVALUATION

In attempting to protect both creators and users of copyrighted works, the Revision gives each group only partial

[179] *See* S. Rep. No. 473, *supra* note 2, at 132.
[180] Section 406(b); *see* notes 46–60 and accompanying text *supra.*
[181] Section 302(c).
[182] Section 302(e).
[183] Under Section 405. *See* § 406(b).
[184] S. Rep. No. 473, *supra* note 2, at 132.
[185] Section 406(c).
[186] *See* notes 134–140 and accompanying text *supra.*
[187] Section 406(c).

protection. Both groups will encounter not only problems which remain from the former law but also a new set of problems which are likely to arise out of the present compromise. The new notice provisions do not ensure that omission or error in the notice will not deprive the creator of the full benefit of his copyright. At the same time, they diminish the value of the notice to the user. Although such restrictions and unanticipated problems are inherent in any compromise, they do indicate that it might have been desirable for the legislature to have sacrificed the appeasing quality of compromise in exchange for greater effectiveness.

With regard to the notice provisions under the new statute, the notice could have been eliminated or it could have been retained as a condition of copyright, with a relaxation of the requirements. The elimination of notice would not only be a more effective protection for creators but would also follow the dictates of practicality, the scheme of the Revision as a whole, and sound public policy. Thus, in the instant case, it might have been better to adopt the viewpoints of the creators rather than try to satisfy both creators and users.

EFFECT OF REVISION ON CREATORS

Although, as shown above, the new statute substantially reduces the possibility of forfeiture of the copyright, formalities continue to exist. Given the fact that authors of works are usually not lawyers or businessmen and generally lack knowledge of copyright law,[188] the notice requirements can still prove to be a "trap for the unwary."[189]

First, the statute sets forth requisites with which creators are likely to have difficulty in complying. The "or elsewhere" provision,[190] the rule that notice must be placed on copies

[188] *See* Sheehan, *supra* note 18, regarding fine artists.
[189] Goodis v. United Artists Television, Inc., 425 F.2d 397, 402 (1970).
[190] Section 401(e).

or works published abroad, imposes a greater requirement on authors than the former law did.[191] It is thus possible, and some say probable, that book pirates will use such a "loophole" to issue competing copies of a book when they discover one without a notice.[192] This possibility is foreseeable since creators in this country often have very little, if any, control over foreign publishers.[193] If such an infringement should occur, the author would then have the burden of proving that the book was printed without his authority.[194]

The second potential trap for authors of works is the continuation of a form of the publication concept,[195] whereby notice "shall be placed on all publicly distributed copies," when a work is "published. . . ."[196] This rule could, arguably, cause as much controversy as the determination of publication under the former act.[197] Although it clears up the problems surrounding *display* of a work, it still leaves open other questions: Will the distribution of a few copies constitute public distribution? Will the public's interest in certain news items postpone the need for notice, as was the case in *King*?[198] Furthermore, the equity in requiring notice for one publicly distributed copy, if that is in fact the requirement, but not in the display of the same work is questionable. One writer has argued that the burden on the re-

[191] Under the 1909 statute, there was a question as to whether copyright in the United States could be secured after the work had been first published abroad without notice (*see* notes 60–84 and accompanying text *supra*).

[192] Note, IOWA L. REV., *supra* note 13.

[193] *Part Five, supra* note 97, at 252–53.

[194] *Id.; see* section 401(a).

[195] KAPLAN & BROWN, *supra* note 8, at 101.

[196] Section 401(a); "Publication" is defined in section 101 as "the distribution of copies or phonorecords of a work to the public by sale or other transfer of ownership, or by rental, lease, or lending. The offering to distribute copies or phonorecords to a group of persons for purposes of further distribution, public performance, or public display. . . ."

[197] *See* notes 23–32 and accompanying text *supra; Part Two, supra* note 93, at 392.

[198] King v. Mister Maestro, Inc., 224 F. Supp. 101 (S.D.N.Y. 1963).

ceiver of the distributed copy to discover the existence of the copyright (on the assumption that it is distributed without notice) is no greater than that on the person who sees a work displayed. In fact, it is probably a lighter burden on the former, since he is more likely to have direct contact with the creator or an agent.[199] Therefore, such an artificial distinction should not be made. It simply gives the creator another problem with which to contend.

Still another requirement for authors is the necessity of the year date on all works other than useful articles,[200] an addition of categories for which the date is necessary. An author of a work in the former classes of (f) through (k), on which a date did not have to be inserted under the prior law,[201] may not be aware that the date is now needed. He is thus left vulnerable to the consequences of omission of notice.

A fourth problem in compliance arises with regard to the name. Although the validity of the copyright is upheld when a contribution to a collective work has no notice but the collective work does have one, there is still a limitation on an infringer's liability if the name in the notice is different from that of the author of the contribution.[202] Thus, an author is not fully protected when a contribution is published with no notice.

Placement of the notice may also be a difficulty even though the requirement has been liberalized.[203] One participant in the Revision hearings focused on the problems arising from computers. While it might be easy to decide what constitutes "reasonable notice" [204] in an ordinary work, it is more difficult in the case of a computer printout, for example. Where

[199] Kunstadt, *supra* note 29, at 253.
[200] Section 401(b)(2).
[201] 17 U.S.C. § 19 (1909).
[202] *See* Section 404(b); *see* notes 176–179 and accompanying text *supra*.
[203] Section 401(c).
[204] *Id.*

should the notice be placed? Must each repetition of the work of a computer bear the notice? [205] Unless the Register's guidelines answer such questions, and questions regarding many other unusual works, the vagueness of the term "reasonable notice" may prove to be harmful to creators when courts hold that what the author considered to be "reasonable notice" was not.

The exception for advertisements [206] is still another point, criticized by many,[207] that producers of the advertisements will have to note in order to protect their creation.

Thus, there are a number of formalities which remain in the notice provisions. The necessity for notice leaves those creators who do not know of the requirements or who do not want to use the notice vulnerable. That the Copyright Office sees many mistakes in the notices in applications for registration [208] shows that it is common for authors to be unaware of all the requirements. Furthermore, many creators do not want to use the notice or even part of it. For some, the date lessens the commercial value of the work; [209] for others, the notice itself defaces the work of art.[210]

The consequences of omission or error may not be as harsh as they were before, but they still have a strong impact. First, under certain conditions, forfeiture of the copyright can still result from omission.[211] That is, in contrast to the statute's intent, a copyright is *not* necessarily retained until the proprietor *intends* to part with it.[212]

Secondly, the three safeguards against forfeiture are not foolproof. It is not clear whether the phrase "relatively small

[205] *Hearings on H.R. 4347, supra* note 17, at 1426.

[206] Section 404(a).

[207] *Hearings on H.R. 4347, supra* note 17, at 1403.

[208] Regulations, *supra* note 5.

[209] *See* notes 125–131 and accompanying text *supra.*

[210] Kunstadt, *supra* note 29, at 253; Sheehan, *supra* note 18; Peter Pan Fabrics, Inc. v. Martin Weiner Corp., 274 F.2d 487.

[211] Section 405(a); *Hearings on H.R. 4347, supra* note 17, at 1817.

[212] *See* Sheehan, *supra* note 18.

number of copies" [213] means "just a few" or "relative to the number distributed with notice." Furthermore, it has been argued that nothing less than omission on an entire printing, or the like, should even be considered as an omission.[214] Therefore, while this clause appears to allow more copies to be published without notice than the savings clause did,[215] creators do not feel that it goes far enough.

The five-year leeway period is arguably another source of aborted protection; authors think that the period does not give a proprietor enough time to discover that a remote licensee failed to insert a notice.[216] Also, the phrase "reasonable effort" [217] is vague enough to cause the same type of line-drawing difficulties as "sought to comply" did under the prior savings clause.[218]

The final protective device may be ineffective unless a great many authors put a requirement expressly in writing that the work is to be published with notice.[219] This subsection is an added requisite,[220] something which authors may have trouble fulfilling.

Even if the copyright is not lost, the protection of innocent infringers reduces the value of the copyright. It has been said that the provision exempting innocent infringers is "another burdensome formality in a different guise." [221] Authors argue that it is impossible to give a potential infringer "actual notice" [222] of registration since they have no means of knowing when an infringement will occur.[223] Furthermore, there

[213] Section 405(a)(1).
[214] *See Part Two*, *supra* note 93, at 317.
[215] 17 U.S.C. § 21 (1909).
[216] Omnibus Copyright Revision, *supra* note 94.
[217] Section 405(a)(2).
[218] 17 U.S.C. § 21 (1909).
[219] Section 405(a)(3).
[220] Kaplan & Brown, *supra* note 8, at 145–46.
[221] *Study No. 7*, *supra* note 3, at 39.
[222] Section 405(b).
[223] Omnibus Copyright Revision, *supra* note 94; *Hearings on H.R. 4347*, *supra* note 17 at 94–95.

is an equitable argument that an infringer should not have to receive actual notice, because he is not really "innocent" if registration has occurred.[224] Therefore, an owner of the copyright should not have to give actual notice to save his chances for full damages when the infringer should have known of the copyright through registration.

Related to this issue is the possibility that it will be too easy for an infringer to show that he was misled by the omission.[225] It is possible that a court will require an infringer to show only that (1) he discovered a copy of a work without notice and (2) he acted on the valid assumption that the work was in the public domain. Thus, it is not known whether the author will then have to show what the infringer could have done so as not to have been "misled." This would be placing an undue burden on one who has registered and who has been infringed by a deliberate copyist. An infringer should at least be required to show that he has searched the copyright office for registration or that he did not have the facilities to do so.[226] Under the new provision, however, too many infringers with shrewd lawyers may be able to shield themselves from extensive liability.

Finally, giving broad discretion for damages to the courts also shows a lack of full protection for the creator. Such grant of discretion, which has been said to be unwise,[227] will make damages depend on the court's sympathy at the time. It may leave the author without adequate compensation, especially since not even actual damages,[228] what are arguably the minimum required to make one whole, are ensured.

Therefore, although forfeiture is highly unlikely, the proprietor may find himself in a position similar to the one

[224] *Study No. 7, supra* note 3, at 61.
[225] Section 405(b).
[226] *See* Omnibus Copyright Revision, *supra* note 94.
[227] *Hearings on H.R. 4347, supra* note 17, at 1867.
[228] *Id.* at 1817.

he would have been in if the copyright had been lost. A valid copyright is useless if an infringement action does not result in relief to the proprietor.

EFFECT ON USERS

Just as copyright owners will probably be disappointed in the protection given to them by the new law, users will also be unhappy with the effects of the provisions. Users believe that Revision has significantly diminished the value of the notice.[229]

First, upholding the validity of the copyright despite intentional omission of notice[230] may encourage intentional omission[231] and thus make insertion of notice the exception rather than the norm.[232] A spokesman for the American Broadcasting Company (ABC) criticized the reason given for the allowance of intentional omission (that otherwise a "subjective criterion" would be introduced[233]) by asserting that the determination of whether an infringer is "innocent" or whether he has been "misled" is just as subjective.[234] According to ABC, it is in the interest of the "legitimate expectancy of the public"[235] to provide that copyright protection be forfeited unless the omission was by accident. Indeed, any accidental omissions were protected under the former law. The new provisions lessen the incentive to use notice.

The second way in which the value has been weakened is by the five-year period. While authors claim that it is too short, users will not have notice for five years from the date

[229] *Id.* at 1207.
[230] *See* Section 405(a).
[231] Note, IOWA L. REV., *supra* note 13.
[232] *Hearings on H.R. 4347*, *supra* note 17, at 450; H.R. REP. No. 83, *supra* note 119, at 114.
[233] H.R. REP. No. 83, *supra* note 119, at 114.
[234] *Hearings on H.R. 4347*, *supra* note 17, at 1880.
[235] *Id.*

of publication (which will not be readily available if the notice is missing) of whether the work can be copied. While the doctrine of fair use [236] will mitigate this problem, many will not copy something which might be dedicated to the public. Those who do would have to prove their innocence. Thus, some have criticized the provisions for violating the doctrine of "innocent until proven guilty." [237] Users argue that to allow an entire printing of a work to go without notice practically voids any strength in the notice requirements.[238] The rationale here is that notice is not a mere formality but a necessity to users of copyrighted works.

Therefore, neither authors nor users are completely satisfied with the new provisions. While users would not be pleased with an elimination of the notice requirement, in view of the greater burden of the requirement on the creators, elimination of the notice would have been the most desirable solution.

ELIMINATION OF NOTICE

According to a major Senate report on Revision, "the fundamental principle underlying the notice provisions of the [Revision] is that the copyright notice has real values which should be preserved. . . ." [239] The values to be preserved are those which the report and others have cited as the major functions of the copyright notice under the old statute:

(1) It has the effect of placing in the public domain a substantial body of published material that no one is interested in copyrighting;
(2) It informs the public as to whether a particular work is copyrighted;
(3) It identifies the copyright owner;

[236] Section 107.
[237] *Hearings on H.R. 4347, supra* note 17, at 466.
[238] *Id; Id.* at 1129.
[239] S. Rep. No. 473, *supra* note 2, at 126.
[240] *Id.*

(4) It shows the date of publication.[240]

However, the notice does not effectively perform those functions, particularly under the scheme of the new Act.

First, the absence of notice has not conclusively shown that the work is in the public domain.[241] Second, under the new statute, notice does not separate those works that are in the public domain from those that are not, since the copyright subsists from the time of creation.[242] It does not show the expiration date, since the new statute simply provides a term of life of the author plus fifty years for most works.[243] Third, the notice does not show whether the work underlying a derivative work is copyrighted since the copyright covers only the new matter [244] and the date of such derivative work is sufficient.[245] Also, the notice does not inform users of the validity of the claim. Anyone can print a notice on a publication, since the copyright office does not check the validity of claims.[246] Furthermore, the notice does not indicate whether the copyright has been assigned. Thus, those desiring the name of the owner must usually go beyond the notice. This need will be especially strong under the new act which allows for divisibility.[247] Licensees and assignees will not necessarily be named in the notice. Finally, notice shows the timeliness of the content of a work, the reason given by most libraries for the primary value of notice,[248] only to the extent that the publication date is close to creation. It

[241] *Hearings on H.R. 4347, supra* note 17, at 1762, 1769; *Study No. 7, supra* note 3, at 60.

[242] Section 302(a).

[243] *Id. But see* 302(c), in which the statutory terms do not depend on author's life.

[244] Section 103(b).

[245] Section 401(b)(2).

[246] *Regulations, supra* note 5, at § 201.2(a)(1)(i).

[247] Section 201(d)(2).

[248] Subcommittee on Patents, Trademarks & Copyrights of the Committee on at 449–50.
STUDIES, 97, 107 (Comm. Print 1960); *Hearings on H.R. 4347, supra* note 17, the Judiciary, 86th Cong., 2d Sess., *Study No. 9,* COPYRIGHT LAW REVISION

is likely that, under the new act, creators who previously had published with notice just to secure copyright will not necessarily publish immediately after creation, since copyright is secured upon creation. Therefore, the two dates may not be close; in such a case, the timeliness would be misleading.

Despite the need to go beyond notice for the information which is, according to the purpose of the notice, supposed to be in the notice, users claim that the notice is necessary as a starting point: it expedites the time needed to find the information.[249] While notice, thus, may be convenient to users, it is not essential. First, the doctrine of fair use [250] under the new statute allows a large percentage of the users that the notice intends to protect—teachers, scholars, journalists, and so on—to use a work even if it is copyrighted. This would preclude the necessity of a scholar who is taking notes to check the notice to see if the work is in the public domain. Secondly, commercial users of copyrighted works, especially those who use a large number of such works, have developed techniques to gain the full information allegedly given in the notice.[251] In fact, checking the records of the copyright office is not a particularly great burden on users.[252] Anyone who is going to great expense would probably not rely on the notice anyway.

Third, it is possible that publishers would voluntarily insert the date of publication in a book, so as to fulfill the libraries' need for the showing of the timeliness of the content, if the notice is not required. The reason for this behavior would be to emphasize the fact that the book is

[249] *Study No. 7, supra* note 3, at 45; *Part One, supra* note 12, at 62; *Part Two, supra* note 93, at 352.

[250] Section 107.

[251] Subcommittee on Patents, Trademarks & Copyrights of the Senate Committee on the Judiciary, 86th Cong., 2d Sess., COPYRIGHT LAW REVISION STUDIES, *Study No. 8,* 71–87 (Comm. Print 1959).

[252] *Part Five, supra* note 97, at 253.

new, since the public seems to place a great deal of emphasis on this factor in judging books.[253]

Finally, users would learn, once notice has been eliminated as a requirement, to look elsewhere for the information desired. In fact, after the public is educated on the elimination of the requirement, it would be in a better position than it is in now, where it relies on a notice which does not always live up to expectations. This reliance can result in a later lawsuit for infringement to a surprised user, a surprise most people wish to avoid.

CONCLUSION

The United States Constitution states:

> The Congress shall have power . . . to promote the Progress of Science and useful Arts, by securing for limited Times to Authors and Inventors the exclusive right to their respective Writings and Discoveries.[254]

It is generally agreed that this purpose is furthered under the copyright law by balancing the interests of creators and users of works. However, how to balance those interests is a source of controversy. In the opinion of this writer, the scales must be weighed in favor of creators to the extent that is necessary to encourage creators to produce works worth disseminating to users. Thus, the copyright law, based on the assumption that economic security from copyright will promote the progress of science and useful arts,[255] should eliminate burdensome technicalities where users would not be harmed by that elimination. Such is the case with notice, where the burden to creators, even under the liberalized provisions, outweighs the value to users. This policy is reflected in the Revision, as shown, for example, by the simplification of the means of obtaining a copyright and the elimination of

[253] *See Study No. 9, supra* note 248, at 107.
[254] U.S. Const., art. I, § 8, cl. 8.
[255] Kunstadt, *supra* note 29, at 235.

the renewal provisions. Thus, removal of the notice requirement would be consistent with the theory underlying the new law, as well as with that of the constitutional provision quoted above.

Mandatory registration might be considered as a solution for the need to furnish information on the copyright to users. While that, like notice, is a technicality, it is arguably so valuable to users as to outweigh the burden to the creators. However, what is clear is that notice is not in that category.

Thus, although the Revision did eradicate many of the problems arising from the former statute, it created new difficulties as a result of the compromise from which it was formed. In place of such a compromise, which satisfies neither creators nor users, the notice requirement should have been removed.

Appendixes

Panels of Judges

Symposium Number One (1939)

Edward A. Sargoy, Stephen P. Ladas, Edward S. Rogers, Dr. Louis Charles Smith, John H. Wigmore, members of a Committee of the American Bar Association appointed by Thomas E. Robertson, Chairman of the Section of Patent, Trade-Mark and Copyright Law.

Symposium Number Two (1940)

Herman Finkelstein, General Counsel, American Society of Composers, Authors and Publishers

Symposium Number Three (1940)

John H. Wigmore, Dean of Northwestern University School of Law

Symposium Number Four (1952)

Judge Herbert F. Goodrich, United States Court of Appeals for the Third Circuit

Justice Roger J. Traynor, Supreme Court of the State of California

Judge George T. Washington, Court of Appeals for the District of Columbia Circuit

Symposium Number Five (1954)

Judge Stanley H. Fuld, Court of Appeals of the State of New York

Chief Judge Leon R. Yankwich, United States District Court for the Southern District of California

Symposium Number Six (1955)

Chief Judge Sam Driver, United States District Court for the Eastern District of Washington

Dean Wesley A. Sturges, President of the American Association of Law Schools

Symposium Number Seven (1956)

Justice George Rossman, of the Supreme Court of Oregon

Lloyd Wright, President of the American Bar Association

Edward A. Sargoy, Louis E. Swarts, former Chairmen of the Copyright Subsection of the Patent, Trade-Mark and Copyright Section of the American Bar Association

Symposium Number Eight (1957)

Chief Judge Charles E. Clark, United States Court of Appeals for the Second Circuit

Chief Justice A. Cecil Snyder, Supreme Court of Puerto Rico

SYMPOSIUM NUMBER NINE (1958)

Chief Judge John Biggs, Jr., United States Court of Appeals for the Third Circuit

Chief Judge Simon E. Sobeloff, United States Court of Appeals for the Fourth Circuit

Judge William H. Hastie, United States Court of Appeals for the Third Circuit

SYMPOSIUM NUMBER TEN (1959)

Chief Justice Frank R. Kenison, Supreme Court of New Hampshire

Chief Judge Alfred P. Murrah, United States Court of Appeals for the Tenth Circuit

SYMPOSIUM NUMBER ELEVEN (1962)

Panel for 1959 National Competition

Chief Judge Charles S. Desmond, New York Court of Appeals

Judge David T. Lewis, United States Court of Appeals for the Tenth Circuit

Panel for 1960 National Competition

Justice Tom C. Clark, United States Supreme Court

Chief Justice Paul Reardon, Superior Court of Massachusetts

Judge Elbert P. Tuttle, United States Court of Appeals for the Fifth Circuit

SYMPOSIUM NUMBER TWELVE (1963)

Panel for 1961 National Competition

Justice Walter V. Schaefer, Illinois Supreme Court

Judge Sterry R. Waterman, United States Court of Appeals for the Second Circuit

Panel for 1962 National Competition

Judge Frederick G. Hamley, United States Court of Appeals for the Ninth Circuit

Judge John Minor Wisdom, United States Court of Appeals for the Fifth Circuit

SYMPOSIUM NUMBER THIRTEEN (1964)

Justice Leonard v. B. Sutton, Supreme Court of Colorado

Justice Samuel Freedman, Court of Appeal of Manitoba

Justice James L. McLennan, Supreme Court of Ontario

SYMPOSIUM NUMBER FOURTEEN (1966)

Judge Carl McGowan, Court of Appeals for the District of Columbia Circuit

Judge Charles M. Merrill, United States Court of Appeals for the Ninth Circuit
Justice Haydn Proctor, Supreme Court of New Jersey

SYMPOSIUM NUMBER FIFTEEN (1967)
Judge Roger J. Kiley, United States Court of Appeals for the Seventh Circuit
Judge Francis Bergan, New York Court of Appeals

SYMPOSIUM NUMBER SIXTEEN (1968)
Justice Byron R. White, United States Supreme Court
Congressman Theodore R. Kupferman, of New York
Congressman Robert G. Stephens, of Georgia
Congressman Wendell Wyatt, of Oregon

SYMPOSIUM NUMBER SEVENTEEN (1969)
Chief Judge Stanley H. Fuld, Court of Appeals of the State of New York

SYMPOSIUM NUMBER EIGHTEEN (1970)
Judge Shirley M. Hufstedler, United States Court of Appeals for the Ninth Circuit
Judge Luther M. Swygert, United States Court of Appeals for the Seventh Circuit
Justice Samuel J. Roberts, Supreme Court of Pennsylvania

SYMPOSIUM NUMBER NINETEEN (1971)
Chief Judge Alfred P. Murrah, United States Court of Appeals for the Tenth Circuit and Director, Federal Judicial Center
Chief Justice Robert B. Williamson, Supreme Judicial Court of Maine
Justice Harry A. Spencer, Supreme Court of Nebraska

SYMPOSIUM NUMBER TWENTY (1972)
Lord Richard Wilberforce, Lord of Appeal in Ordinary of England
Justice Paul C. Reardon, Massachusetts Supreme Judicial Court

SYMPOSIUM NUMBER TWENTY-ONE (1973)
Chief Justice Samuel Freedman, Court of Appeal of Manitoba
Justice George Rose Smith, Supreme Court of Arkansas
Justice William M. McAllister, Supreme Court of Oregon

SYMPOSIUM NUMBER TWENTY-TWO (1977)
Walter Derenberg, Professor of Law, New York University School of Law
Edward A. Sargoy, Former Chairman of the Copyright Subsection of the Patent, Trade-Mark and Copyright Section of the American Bar Association

SYMPOSIUM NUMBER TWENTY-THREE (1977)

Chief Judge Stanley H. Fuld, Court of Appeals of the State of New York and Chairman, National Commission on New Technological Uses of Copyrighted Works

Chief Justice Robert B. Williamson, Supreme Judicial Court of the State of Maine

SYMPOSIUM NUMBER TWENTY-FOUR (1980)

Jefferson B. Fordham, Dean Emeritus, University of Pennsylvania Law School

Page Keeton, Dean Emeritus, University of Texas School of Law

Robert B. McKay, former Dean of the New York University School of Law and Director, Program on Justice, Society, and the Individual, Aspen Institute for Humanistic Studies

SYMPOSIUM NUMBER TWENTY-FIVE (1980)

Charles Clark, Judge of the U.S. Court of Appeals, Fifth Judicial District

Abraham L. Kaminstein, Register of Copyrights, 1960–1971

Page Keeton, Dean Emeritus, University of Texas Law School

SYMPOSIUM NUMBER TWENTY-SIX (1981)

J. Edward Lumbard, U.S. Court of Appeals, Second Circuit

Thomas C. Brennan, Commissioner, Copyright Royalty Tribunal

George D. Cary, Former Register of Copyrights

SYMPOSIUM NUMBER TWENTY-SEVEN (1981)

Charles D. Ferris, Chairman of the FCC

Robert W. Kastenmeier, Congressman from Wisconsin

Barbara A. Ringer, Former Register of Copyrights

Papers Appearing in Copyright Law Symposia Numbers One Through Twenty-Six

Law Schools Contributing Papers to Previous Copyright Law Symposia

University of Alabama School of Law

Joseph G. Cook, *The Fine Arts: What Constitutes Infringement,* Symposium Number Thirteen 65 (1964).

University of Arizona College of Law

George W. Botsford, *Some Copyright Problems of Radio Broadcasters and Receivers of Musical Compositions,* Symposium Number Two 71 (1940).

Calvin Welker Evans, *The Law of Copyright and the Right of Mechanical Reproduction of Musical Compositions,* Symposium Number Three 112 (1940).

William T. Birmingham, *A Critical Analysis of the Infringement of Ideas,* Symposium Number Five 107 (1954).

Boston College School of Law

Mark H. Puffer, *The Supreme Court and Copyright Liability for Retransmissions of TV and Radio Signals: A Dubious Performance,* Symposium Number Twenty-Six 127 (1981).

University of Arkansas School of Law

E. DeMatt Henderson, *The Law of Copyright, Especially Musical,* Symposium Number One 125 (1939).

Eugene Mooney, *The Jukebox Exemption,* Symposium Number Ten 194 (1959).

Baylor University School of Law

Ted Fair, *Publication of Immoral and Indecent Works, with Regard to the Constitutional and Copyright Effects,* Symposium Number Five 230 (1954).

Boston University School of Law

Alan T. Dworkin, *Originality in the Law of Copyright,* Symposium Number Eleven (1962).

Alan G. Kirios, *Territoriality and International Copyright Infringement Actions,* Symposium Number Twenty-Two 53 (1977).

BROOKLYN LAW SCHOOL

Irving Propper, *American "Popular" Music and the Copyright Law*, SYMPOSIUM NUMBER THREE 164 (1940).

UNIVERSITY OF CALIFORNIA SCHOOL OF LAW AT BERKELEY

Donald L. A. Kerson, *Sequel Rights in the Law of Literary Property*, SYMPOSIUM NUMBER TWELVE 76 (1963).

D. E. Harding, *Copyright in Lectures, Sermons, and Speeches*. SYMPOSIUM NUMBER FOURTEEN 272 (1966).

Kent Sinclair, Jr., *Liability for Copyright Infringement—Handling Innocence in a Strict-Liability Context*, SYMPOSIUM NUMBER TWENTY 36 (1972).

Robin Meadow, *Television Formats: The Search for Protection*. SYMPOSIUM NUMBER TWENTY 73 (1972).

UNIVERSITY OF CALIFORNIA SCHOOL OF LAW AT LOS ANGELES

Robert Yale Libott, *Round the Prickly Pear: The Idea-Expression Fallacy in a Mass Communications World*, SYMPOSIUM NUMBER SIXTEEN 30 (1968).

Alan H. Lazar, *Developing Countries and Authors' Rights in International Copyright*, SYMPOSIUM NUMBER NINETEEN 1 (1971).

Lionel S. Sobel, *Copyright and the First Amendment: A Gathering Storm?*, SYMPOSIUM NUMBER NINETEEN 43 (1971).

Barry W. Tyerman, *The Economic Rationale for Copyright Protection for Published Books: A Reply to Professor Beyer*, SYMPOSIUM NUMBER TWENTY-ONE 1 (1974).

David R. Ginsburg, *Transfer of the Right of Publicity: Dracula's Progeny and Privacy's Stepchild*, SYMPOSIUM NUMBER TWENTY-FIVE 1 (1980).

Robert M. Kunstadt, *Can Copyright Law Effectively Promote Progress in the Visual Arts?* SYMPOSIUM NUMBER TWENTY-FIVE 159 (1980).

Marc R. Stein, *Termination of Transfers and Licenses Under the New Copyright Act: Thorny Problems for the Copyright Bar*, SYMPOSIUM NUMBER TWENTY-SIX 1 (1981).

UNIVERSITY OF CHICAGO LAW SCHOOL

Boardman Lloyd, *"Disk-television": Recurring Problems in the Performance of Motion Pictures*, SYMPOSIUM NUMBER SIXTEEN 143 (1968).

Randolph Jonakait, *Do Art Exhibitions Destroy Common-Law Copyright in Works of Art?*, SYMPOSIUM NUMBER NINETEEN 81 (1971).

CHICAGO-KENT COLLEGE OF LAW

Robert W. Bergstrom, *The Businessman Deals with Copyright*, SYMPOSIUM NUMBER THREE 248 (1940).

CLEVELAND-MARSHALL COLLEGE OF LAW

Robert F. Frijouf, *Simultaneous Copyright and Patent Protection*, SYMPOSIUM NUMBER TWENTY-THREE 99 (1977).

UNIVERSITY OF COLORADO SCHOOL OF LAW

Robert L. Wyckoff, *Defenses Peculiar to Actions Based on Infringement of Musical Copyrights*, SYMPOSIUM NUMBER FIVE 256 (1954).

Elery Wilmarth, *Statutory Remedies for Record Piracy*, SYMPOSIUM NUMBER TWELVE 261 (1963).

COLUMBIA UNIVERSITY SCHOOL OF LAW

Franklin Feldman, *The Manufacturing Clause: Copyright Protection to the Foreign Author*, SYMPOSIUM NUMBER FOUR 76 (1952).

Robert E. Young, *The Copyright Term*, SYMPOSIUM NUMBER SEVEN 139 (1956).

Arthur Rosett, *Burlesque as Copyright Infringement*, SYMPOSIUM NUMBER NINE 1 (1958).

Stuart Jay Young, *Freebooters in Fashions: The Need for a Copyright in Textile and Garment Designs*, SYMPOSIUM NUMBER NINE 76 (1958).

Peter H. Morrison, *Copyright Publications: The Sale and Distribution of Phonograph Records*, SYMPOSIUM NUMBER TEN 387 (1959).

Robert Stephen Savelson, *Electronic Music and the Copyright Law*, SYMPOSIUM NUMBER THIRTEEN 133 (1964).

Marion Lozier Woltmann, *The Author and the State: An Analysis of Soviet Copyright Law*, SYMPOSIUM NUMBER FOURTEEN 1 (1966).

John F. Banzhaf III, *Copyright Protection for Computer Programs*, SYMPOSIUM NUMBER FOURTEEN 118 (1966).

Robert Shaye, *Piracy Within the Law: A Consideration of the Copyright Protection Afforded Foreign Authors in the United States and the Soviet Union*, SYMPOSIUM NUMBER FOURTEEN 226 (1966).

Paul Goldstein, *Copyrighting the New Music*, SYMPOSIUM NUMBER SIXTEEN 1 (1968).

Marian Halley, *The Educator and the Copyright Law*, SYMPOSIUM NUMBER SEVENTEEN 24 (1969).

Paul Sherman, *Incorporation of the* Droit de Suite *into United States Copyright Law*, SYMPOSIUM NUMBER EIGHTEEN 50 (1970).

O. Wayne Coon, *Some Problems with Musical Public-Domain Materials under United States Copyright Law as Illustrated Mainly by the Recent Folk-song Revival*, SYMPOSIUM NUMBER NINETEEN 189 (1971).

Edward Samuels, *Goldstein v. California: Breaking Up Federal Copyright Preemption*, SYMPOSIUM NUMBER TWENTY-FOUR 51 (1980).

Susan Millington Campbell, *Copyright and News Values: An Accommodation*, SYMPOSIUM NUMBER TWENTY-FIVE 121 (1980).

CORNELL UNIVERSITY LAW SCHOOL

L. Lee Phillips, *Related Rights and American Copyright Law: Compatible or Incompatible?* SYMPOSIUM NUMBER TEN 219 (1959).

Michael E. Mecsas, *The Effect of the Copyright Act and the Proposed Revision on Educators as Users of Copyrighted Materials*, SYMPOSIUM NUMBER FIFTEEN 134 (1967).

Robert J. Jinnett, *Adherence of the USSR to the Universal Copyright Convention: Defenses Under U.S. Law to Possible Soviet Attempts at Achieving International Censorship*, SYMPOSIUM NUMBER TWENTY-FOUR 85 (1980).

UNIVERSITY OF DENVER COLLEGE OF LAW

John E. Harrington, *Copyright Duration*, SYMPOSIUM NUMBER ELEVEN 96 (1962).

John Rittenhouse, Jr., *Section 24—Renewal Rights, Survivors, and Confusion: A Case Study*, SYMPOSIUM NUMBER ELEVEN 113 (1962).

DICKINSON SCHOOL OF LAW

John J. DeMarines, *State Regulation of Musical Copyright*, SYMPOSIUM NUMBER SIX 118 (1955).

Robert S. Gawthrop III, *An Inquiry into Criminal Copyright Infringement*, SYMPOSIUM NUMBER TWENTY 154 (1972).

DRAKE UNIVERSITY SCHOOL OF LAW

Gary D. Ordway, *Choreography and Copyright*, SYMPOSIUM NUMBER FIFTEEN 172 (1967).

DUKE UNIVERSITY SCHOOL OF LAW

J. Roger Shull, *Collecting Collectively: ASCAP's Perennial Dilemma*, SYMPOSIUM NUMBER SEVEN 35 (1956).

UNIVERSITY OF FLORIDA LAW SCHOOL

William H. Garland, *Our Copyright Law: Growing Pains in International Society*, SYMPOSIUM NUMBER ELEVEN 82 (1962).

FLORIDA STATE UNIVERSITY COLLEGE OF LAW

Steven L. Sparkman, *Tape Pirates: The New "Buck"-aneer$*, SYMPOSIUM NUMBER TWENTY-ONE 98 (1974).

GEORGETOWN UNIVERSITY LAW CENTER

Peter F. Nolan, *Copyright Protection for Motion Pictures: Limited or Perpetual?* SYMPOSIUM NUMBER EIGHTEEN 174 (1970).

GEORGE WASHINGTON UNIVERSITY LAW SCHOOL

Maurice B. Stiefel, *Piracy in High Places—Government Publications and Copyright Law*, SYMPOSIUM NUMBER EIGHT 3 (1957).

Carl R. Ramey, *A Copyright Labyrinth: Information Storage and Retrieval Systems*, SYMPOSIUM NUMBER SEVENTEEN 1 (1969).

William L. Mentlik, *Federal Preemption in the Field of Intellectual Creations—An End to the Common Law Copyright*, SYMPOSIUM NUMBER TWENTY-THREE 115 (1977).

Michael A. Newcity, *The Universal Copyright Convention as an Instrument of Repression: The Soviet Experiment*, SYMPOSIUM NUMBER TWENTY-FOUR 1 (1980).

UNIVERSITY OF GEORGIA SCHOOL OF LAW

W. Marion Page, *Copyright Laws in Georgia History*, SYMPOSIUM NUMBER TWO 151 (1940).

HARVARD UNIVERSITY LAW SCHOOL

Paul Gitlin, *Radio Infringement of Music Copyright*, SYMPOSIUM NUMBER ONE 61 (1939).

Melville B. Nimmer, *Inroads on Copyright Protection*, SYMPOSIUM NUMBER FOUR 2 (1952).

Arthur L. Stevenson, Jr., *Moral Right and the Common Law: A Proposal*, SYMPOSIUM NUMBER SIX 89 (1955).

Ronald Cracas, *Judge Learned Hand and the Law of Copyright*, SYMPOSIUM NUMBER SEVEN 55 (1956).

Raya S. Dreben, *Publication and the British Copyright Law*, SYMPOSIUM NUMBER SEVEN 3 (1956).

Nathan Newbury III, *Protection of Comic Strips*, SYMPOSIUM NUMBER EIGHT 37 (1957).

G. T. McConnell, *The Effect of the Universal Copyright Convention on Other International Conventions and Arrangements*, SYMPOSIUM NUMBER NINE 32 (1958).

Samuel A. Olevson, *English Experience with Registration and Deposit*, SYMPOSIUM NUMBER TEN 1 (1959).

Arthur R. Miller, *Problems in the Transfer of Interests in a Copyright*, SYPOSIUM NUMBER TEN 131 (1959).

Robert A. Gorman, *Copyright Protection for the Collection and Representation of Ideas*, SYMPOSIUM NUMBER TWELVE 30 (1963).

Thomas B. Morris, Jr., *The Origins of the Statute of Anne*, SYMPOSIUM NUMBER TWELVE 222 (1963).

S. Paul Posner, *State and Federal Power in Patent and Copyright*, SYMPOSIUM NUMBER FOURTEEN 51 (1966).

Matthew Nimetz, *Design Protection*, SYMPOSIUM NUMBER FIFTEEN 70 (1967).

Allen W. Puckett, *The Limits of Copyright and Patent Protection for Computer Programs*, SYMPOSIUM NUMBER SIXTEEN 81 (1968).

David P. Griff, *Royalties Without Copyright: Proposals for a Payments Agreement Between the United States and the Soviet Union*, SYMPOSIUM NUMBER SEVENTEEN 51 (1969).

Julian H. Spirer, *In re Johannesburg Operatic and Dramatic Society v. Music Theatre International: Boycott of the South African Stage*, SYMPOSIUM NUMBER TWENTY 140 (1972).

Michael S. Oberman, *Copyright Protection for Computer-Produced Directories*, SYMPOSIUM NUMBER TWENTY-TWO 1 (1977).

Jeffrey G. Sherman, *Musical Copyright and Infringement: The Requirement of Substantial Similarity*, SYMPOSIUM NUMBER TWENTY-TWO 81 (1977).

Michael V. P. Marks, *The Legal Rights of Fictional Characters*, SYMPOSIUM NUMBER TWENTY-FIVE 35 (1980).

Frank Gibbs, *Copyright Misuse: Thirty Years of Waiting for the Other Shoe*, SYMPOSIUM NUMBER TWENTY-THREE 31 (1977).

HOFSTRA UNIVERSITY SCHOOL OF LAW

Richard W. Schleifer, *On Behalf of Richard M. Nixon: The Copyrightability of the Nixon Presidential Watergate Tapes*, SYMPOSIUM NUMBER TWENTY-SIX 53 (1981).

UNIVERSITY OF IDAHO COLLEGE OF LAW

Reginald Ray Reeves, *Superman v. Captain Marvel: or, Loss of Literary Property in Comic Strips*, SYMPOSIUM NUMBER FIVE 3 (1954).

Val D. Greenwood, *Fair Use and Photocopy*, SYMPOSIUM NUMBER TWENTY-FOUR 113 (1980).

UNIVERSITY OF ILLINOIS COLLEGE OF LAW

William G. Wells, *The Universal Copyright Convention and the United States: A Study of Conflict and Compromise*, SYMPOSIUM NUMBER EIGHT 69 (1957).

INDIANA UNIVERSITY SCHOOL OF LAW

Don Metz, *Rights of Federal Government Personnel under the Copyright Act*, SYMPOSIUM NUMBER TWELVE 96 (1963).

STATE UNIVERSITY OF IOWA COLLEGE OF LAW

Charles W. Joiner, *Analysis, Criticism, Comparison and Suggested Corrections of the Copyright Law of the U.S. Relative to Mechanical Reproduction of Music*, SYMPOSIUM NUMBER TWO 43 (1940).

Frank Miller, *A Re-Examination of Literary Piracy*, SYMPOSIUM NUMBER THREE 2 (1940).

Gilbert K. Bovard, *Copyright Protection in the Area of Scientific and Technical Works*, SYMPOSIUM NUMBER FIVE 68 (1954).

UNIVERSITY OF LOUISVILLE SCHOOL OF LAW

William F. Burbank, *Television—a Public Performance for Profit?* SYMPOSIUM NUMBER FIVE 133 (1954).

UNIVERSITY OF MICHIGAN LAW SCHOOL

Clinton R. Ashford, *The Compulsory Manufacturing Provision: An Anachronism in the Copyright Act*, SYMPOSIUM NUMBER FOUR 48 (1952).

Richard W. Pogue, *Borderland—Where Copyright and Design Patent Meet*, SYMPOSIUM NUMBER SIX 3 (1955).

Roger Needham, *Tape Recording, Photocopying, and Fair Use*, SYMPOSIUM NUMBER TEN 75 (1959).

John L. Wilson, *The Scholar and the Copyright Law*, SYMPOSIUM NUMBER TEN 104 (1959).

Timothy M. Sheehan, *Why Don't Fine Artists Use Statutory Copyright?—An Empirical and Legal Survey*, SYMPOSIUM NUMBER TWENTY-FOUR 157 (1980).

UNIVERSITY OF MISSOURI SCHOOL OF LAW

Stephen E. Strom, *Depreciation and Income Aspects of Copyright Under the Internal Revenue Code of 1954*, SYMPOSIUM NUMBER EIGHT 103 (1957).

UNIVERSITY OF NEBRASKA COLLEGE OF LAW

William F. Swindler, *News: Public Right v. Property Right*, SYMPOSIUM NUMBER TEN 285 (1959).

Marilyn Hutchinson, *Section 2 of the Copyright Act: A Statutory Maverick*, SYMPOSIUM NUMBER NINETEEN 143 (1971).

UNIVERSITY OF NEW MEXICO SCHOOL OF LAW

Juan G. Burciaga, *Divestitive, Publication—A Two-Century Dilemma*, SYMPOSIUM NUMBER TWELVE 201 (1963).

NEW YORK UNIVERSITY SCHOOL OF LAW

Arthur S. Katz, *The Doctrine of Moral Right and American Copyright Law: A Proposal*, SYMPOSIUM NUMBER FOUR 78 (1952).

Dino Joseph Caterini, *Contributions to Periodicals*, SYMPOSIUM NUMBER TEN 321 (1959).

Rita E. Hauser, *The French* Droit de Suite: *The Problem of Protection for the Underprivileged Artist under the Copyright Law*, SYMPOSIUM NUMBER ELEVEN 1 (1962).

Roger M. Milgrim, *Territoriality of Copyright: An Analysis of Assignability under the Universal Copyright Convention*, SYMPOSIUM NUMBER TWELVE 1 (1963).

Ciro A. Gamboni, *Unfair Competition after* Sears *and* Compco, SYMPOSIUM NUMBER FIFTEEN 1(1967).

Andrew O. Shapiro, *The Standard Author Contract: A Survey of Current Draftsmanship*, SYMPOSIUM NUMBER EIGHTEEN 135 (1970).

NORTHWESTERN UNIVERSITY SCHOOL OF LAW

Marshall J. Nelson, *Jazz and Copyright: A Study in Improvised Protection*, SYMPOSIUM NUMBER TWENTY-ONE 35 (1974).

NOTRE DAME LAW SCHOOL

David C. Petre, *Statutory Copyright Protection for Books and Magazines Against Machine Copying*, SYMPOSIUM NUMBER FOURTEEN 180 (1966).

OHIO STATE UNIVERSITY COLLEGE OF LAW

Sheldon M. Young, *Plagiarism, Piracy, and the Common Law Copyright*, SYMPOSIUM NUMBER FIVE 205 (1954).

UNIVERSITY OF OKLAHOMA SCHOOL OF LAW

Howard B. Pickard, *Common-Law Rights Before Publication*, SYMPOSIUM NUMBER THREE 298 (1940).

Milton D. Andrews, *Copyrighting Reproductions of Physical Objects*, SYMPOSIUM NUMBER TWELVE 123 (1963).

UNIVERSITY OF OREGON SCHOOL OF LAW

Nathan Cohen, *State Regulation of Musical Copyright*, SYMPOSIUM NUMBER ONE 91 (1939).

UNIVERSITY OF PENNSYLVANIA LAW SCHOOL

Thomas A. Reed, *The Role of the Register of Copyrights in the Registration Process: A Critical Appraisal of Certain Exclusionary Regulations*, SYMPOSIUM NUMBER EIGHTEEN 1 (1970).

UNIVERSITY OF PITTSBURGH SCHOOL OF LAW

Elizabeth Heazlett Kury, *Protection for Creators in the United States and Abroad,* SYMPOSIUM NUMBER THIRTEEN 1 (1964)

Arnold B. Silverman, *The Scope of Protection of Copyrights and Design Patents in the United States,* SYMPOSIUM NUMBER TWELVE 152 (1963).

ST. JOHN'S UNIVERSITY SCHOOL OF LAW

Stephen A. Gold, *Television Broadcasting and Copyright Law: The Community Antenna Television Controversy,* SYMPOSIUM NUMBER SIXTEEN 170 (1968).

ST. LOUIS UNIVERSITY SCHOOL OF LAW

John M. Moellenberg, *The Question of Choice between Copyrighting or Patenting a Design,* SYMPOSIUM NUMBER THIRTEEN 165 (1964).

Russell H. Schlattman, *The Doctrine of Limited Publication in the Law of Literary Property Compared with the Doctrine of Experimental Use in the Law of Patents,* SYMPOSIUM NUMBER FIVE 37 (1954).

UNIVERSITY OF SAN FRANCISCO SCHOOL OF LAW

Philip Stork, *Legal Protection for Computer Programs: A Practicing Attorney's Approach,* SYMPOSIUM NUMBER TWENTY 112 (1972).

SETON HALL UNIVERSITY SCHOOL OF LAW

Daniel E. Nester, *Is CATV Infringing Proprietary Rights in Television Broadcasts?* SYMPOSIUM NUMBER FIFTEEN 153 (1967).

UNIVERSITY OF SOUTH CAROLINA LAW SCHOOL

Marvin C. Jones, *The Sears-Compco Doctrine: Conception, Birth, and Early Years,* SYMPOSIUM NUMBER TWENTY-TWO 197 (1977).

UNIVERSITY OF SOUTHERN CALIFORNIA LAW CENTER

Sara Jane Boyers, *Protection for the Artist: The Alternatives,* SYMPOSIUM NUMBER TWENTY-ONE 124 (1974).

Jacqueline Fabe, *The Fine Artist's Right to the Reproduction of His Original Work,* SYMPOSIUM NUMBER TWENTY-THREE 81 (1977).

STANFORD UNIVERSITY SCHOOL OF LAW

Saul Cohen, *Fair Use in the Law of Copyright,* SYMPOSIUM NUMBER SIX 43 (1955).

Eric Marcus, *The Moral Right of the Artist in Germany,* SYMPOSIUM NUMBER TWENTY-FIVE 93 (1980).

SUFFOLK UNIVERSITY LAW SCHOOL

Charles C. McGuire, *Common-Law Overtones of Statutory Copyright: An Inquiry into the Status of a Federal Common Law of Unfair Competition*, SYMPOSIUM NUMBER THIRTEEN 33 (1964).

Joseph J. Beard, *Cybera: The Age of Information*, SYMPOSIUM NUMBER NINETEEN 117 (1971).

TEMPLE UNIVERSITY SCHOOL OF LAW

C. Harold Herr, *The Patentee v. the Copyrightee*, SYMPOSIUM NUMBER FIVE 185 (1954).

UNIVERSITY OF TEXAS SCHOOL OF LAW

Thomas O. Shelton, *The Protection of the Interpretative Rights of a Musical Artist Afforded by the Law of Literary Property, or the Doctrine of Unfair Competition*, SYMPOSIUM NUMBER ONE 173 (1939).

John Walton Lang, *Performance and the Right of the Performing Artist*, SYMPOSIUM NUMBER TWENTY-ONE 69 (1974).

TULANE UNIVERSITY SCHOOL OF LAW

Richard C. Seither, *UNESCO: New Hope for International Copyright?* SYMPOSIUM NUMBER SIX 74 (1955).

Martin Leach-Cross Feldman, *The Relationship between Copyright and Unfair Competition Principles*, SYMPOSIUM NUMBER TEN 266 (1959).

Leonard A. Radlauer, *The USSR Joins the Universal Copyright Convention*, SYMPOSIUM NUMBER TWENTY-THREE 1 (1977).

VALPARAISO UNIVERSITY SCHOOL OF LAW

R.T. Nimmer, *Reflections on the Problem of Parody-Infringement* SYMPOSIUM NUMBER SEVENTEEN 133 (1969).

VANDERBUILT UNIVERSITY SCHOOL OF LAW

J. Kane Ditto, *Musical Copyrights as Collateral in Secured Transactions*, SYMPOSIUM NUMBER NINTEEN 219 (1971).

VILLANOVA UNIVERSITY SCHOOL OF LAW

William B. Colsey III, *The Protection of Advertising and the Law of Copyright*, SYMPOSIUM NUMBER ELEVEN 28 (1962).

UNIVERSITY OF VIRGINIA LAW SCHOOL

Richard W. Roberts, *Publication in the Law of Copyright*, SYMPOSIUM NUMBER NINE 111 (1958).

Ann W. MacLean, *Education and Copyright Law: An Analysis of the Amended Copyright Revision Bill and Proposals for Statutory Licensing and a Clearinghouse System*, SYMPOSIUM NUMBER TWENTY 1 (1972).

Teri Noel Towe, *Record Piracy*, SYMPOSIUM NUMBER TWENTY-TWO 243 (1977).

WAKE FOREST COLLEGE SCHOOL OF LAW

Charles O. Whitley, *Copyrights and the Income Tax Problem*, SYMPOSIUM NUMBER FOUR 158 (1952).

James A. Webster, Jr., *Protecting Things Valuable—Ideas*, SYMPOSIUM NUMBER FIVE 158 (1958).

Robert Fuller Fleming, *Substantial Similarity: Where Plots Really Thicken*, SYMPOSIUM NUMBER NINETEEN 252 (1971).

WASHBURN UNIVERSITY SCHOOL OF LAW

Ruth C. Trussell, *A Reappraisal of the Impounding and Destruction Provisions of the Copyright Law*, SYMPOSIUM NUMBER TWENTY-SIX 95 (1981).

WASHINGTON AND LEE UNIVERSITY SCHOOL OF LAW

Library Photocopying: An International Perspective, SYMPOSIUM NUMBER TWENTY-SIX 151 (1981).

WASHINGTON UNIVERSITY OF ST. LOUIS SCHOOL OF LAW

Milton H. Aronson, *The Development of Motion Picture Copyright*, SYMPOSIUM NUMBER THREE 338 (1940).

Donald L. Gunnels, *Copyright Protection for Writers Employed by The Federal Government*, SYMPOSIUM NUMBER ELEVEN 138 (1962).

WESTERN RESERVE UNIVERSITY SCHOOL OF LAW

Frank D. Emerson, *Public Performance for Profit, Past and Present*, SYMPOSIUM NUMBER THREE 52 (1940).

UNIVERSITY OF WISCONSIN LAW SCHOOL

Paul P. Lipton, *The Extent of Copyright Protection for Law Books*, SYMPOSIUM NUMBER TWO 11 (1940).

Frank L. Bixby, *Hurn v. Oursler after Twenty Years*, SYMPOSIUM NUMBER SIX 140 (1955).

Edward Silber, *Use of the Expert in Literary Piracy: A Proposal*, SYMPOSIUM NUMBER NINE 149 (1958).

Nancy C. Dreher, *Community Antenna Television and Copyright Legislation*, SYMPOSIUM NUMBER SEVENTEEN 102 (1969).

YALE UNIVERSITY SCHOOL OF LAW

Walter L. Pforzheimer, *Copyright Protection for the Performing Artist in his Interpretive Rendition*, SYMPOSIUM NUMBER ONE 9 (1939).

Irving E. Bernstein, *The Motion Picture Distributor and the Copyright Law,* SYMPOSIUM NUMBER TWO 119 (1940).

Bruce E. Fritch, *Some Copyright Implications of Videotapes (Suggesting the Need for Statutory Revision),* SYMPOSIUM NUMBER THIRTEEN 87 (1964).

Frank T. Laskin, *All Rights Unreserved: The Author's Lost Property in Publishing and Entertainment,* SYMPOSIUM NUMBER SEVEN 91 (1956).

Daniel M. Singer, *International Copyright Protection and the United States: The Impact of the Universal Copyright Convention on Existing Law,* SYMPOSIUM NUMBER SEVEN 176 (1956).

Monroe E. Price, *The Moral Judge and the Copyright Statute: The Problem of* Stiffel *and* Compco, SYMPOSIUM NUMBER FOURTEEN 90 (1966).

John Iskrant, *The Impact of the Multiple Forms of Computer Programs on Their Adequate Protection by Copyright,* SYMPOSIUM NUMBER EIGHTEEN 92 (1970).

Frank R. Curtis, *Protecting Authors in Copyright Transfers: Revision Bill §203 and the Alternatives,* SYMPOSIUM NUMBER TWENTY-ONE 165 (1974).

Jerry E. Smith, *Government Documents: Their Copyright and Ownership,* SYMPOSIUM NUMBER TWENTY-TWO 147 (1977).

References

Statutes and Case

STATUTES

NEV. LAWS OF 1973, 204
N.H. REV. STATUTES (1973), 203
N.H. LAWS OF 1974, 204
N.Y. GEN. BUS. LAW (1967), 204, 1967), 204
N.C. GEN. BUS. LAW (1968), 117*n*15, 184*n*165; GEN. STAT. (1939), 124*n*35, (1974), 117*n*15; (1974), 117*n*15; (1975), 205
OHIO CRIMINAL CODE (1974), 205
ORE. LAWS OF 1973, 205
PA. CONST. STAT. (1973), 184*n*167; TITLE 18, SECT. 4116 (1971), 205
S.C. CODE 66-101 (1942), 124*n*35
TENN. CODE ANN. (Supp. 1971), 117*n*15: CRIM. OFF. (1971), 206
TEX. REV. CIV. STAT. ANN. (Supp. 1974), 117*n*15; PENAL CODE 1974), 206
UTAH LAWS (1973),206
VA. CODE (1972) 206
WASH. SESS. LAW (1974), 206

GREAT BRITAN ...) ... ...

U.K.: Copyright Act, 1911, 1 & 2 George 5, 131*n*70; Copyright Act, 1956 405 Eliz. 2, 13n170; Performers' Protection Acts, 1958–72 6 & 7 Eliz. 2. 131*n*71

CASES

Advisers, Inc. v. Wiese-Hart, Inc., 238 F.2d 706 (6th Cir. 1956), *cert. denied,* 353 U.S. 949 (1957), 255*nn*54, 55
Aeolian Co. v. Royal Music Roll Co., 196 F.926 (N.D.N.Y. 1912), 192*n*220
Harry Alter Co. v. Graves Registrations, Inc., 101 F. Supp. 703 (N.D. Ga. 1951), 256*n*62
Alva Studios v. Winninger, 177 F. Supp. 265 (S.D.N.Y. 1959), 225*n*89, 227*n*103, 228*n*106, 241*n*177
American Tobacco Co. v. Werckmeister, 207 U.S. 284 (1907), 215*n*30
American Visuals Corp. v. Holland, 239 F.2d 740 (2d Cir. 1956), 247*n*7
Associated Music Publishers, Inc. v. Debs Memorial Radio Fund, Inc., 46 F. Supp. 829 (S.D.N.Y. 1942), *aff'd,* 141 F.2d 852 (2d Cir. 1944), 85*n*69

References

Statutes and Cases

STATUTES

CASES

Works Cited

AMERICAN BAR ASSOCIATION SECTION OF PATENT, TRADEMARK, AND COPYRIGHT LAW, Comm. Reports 153 (1973), 160*n*23

Andrews, *Copyrighting Reproductions of Physical Objects*, 12 ASCAP COPYRIGHT SYMPOSIUM (1963), 227*n*99, 229*n*115

Annotation, *Making, Selling or Distributing Counterfeit or "Bootleg" Tape Records or Phonograph Records as Violation of Federal Law*, 25 ALR FED. 207 (1975), 156*n*7

Baer, *Performer's Right to Enjoin Unlicensed Broadcasts of Recorded Renditions*, 19 NCL REV. 202 (1941), 124*n*35

Bard and Kurlantszick, *A Public Performance Right in Sound Recordings*, 43 GEO. WASH. L. REV. 152 (1974), 117*n*15, 135*n*85

The Blooming Blank Tape Market, 89 BILLBOARD, No. 28, July 16, 1977, 138*nn*97, 98, 139*nn*99, 100

BOWKER, COPYRIGHT (1912), 216*n*43

Brown, *Publication and Preemption in Copright Law: Elegiac Reflections on Goldstein v. California*, UCLA L. REV. 1022 (1975), 12*n*36, 24*n*74, 142*nn*150, 152, 182*nn*150, 153, 183*n*160, 184*n*164

Brylawski, *The Copyright Office: A Constitutional Confirmation*, 44 GEO. WASH. L. REV. 1 (1976), 65

BUSH, TECHNOLOGY & CQPYRIGHT, 269 (1972), 88*n*80

CAHILL, JUDICIAL LEGISLATION (1952), 187*n*184

Callman, UNFAIR COMPETITION, TRADEMARK AND MONOPOLIES (3d ed. 1975), 66, 71*n*1, 172*n*96

Cary, *The Common Law and Statutory Background of the Law of Musical Property*, 15 VAND. L. REV. 397 (1962), 160*n*28, 167*n*68

Cary, *The Quiet Revolution in Copyright: The End of the "Publication" Concept*, 35 GEO. WASH. L. REV. 652 (1967), 249*n*22

Chaffee, *Reflections on the Law of Copyright*, 45 COLUM. L. REV. 503 (1945), 71*n*3, 125*n*43, 162*n*40

Chapman, *The Supreme Court and Federal Law of Unfair Competition*, 54 TRADEMARK REP. 573 (1964), 174*n*105

Comment, *Copyright Fair Use*, 1969 DUKE L. J. 73 (1969), 72*n*8, 74*n*16

Comment, *Copyright Protection for Sound Recordings*, 19 ST. LOUIS U. L.J. 189 (1974), 155*n*2, 157*n*10

Comment, *Copyrights: Concurrence, Revision and Photocopying*, 79 DICK. L. REV. 260 (1975), 94*n*102

Comment, *Copyrights: States Allowed To Protect Works Not Copyrightable Under Federal Law*, 58 MINN. L. REV. 316 (1973), 176*n*117

Comment, *Goldstein v. California and the Protection of Sound Recordings*, WASH. & LEE L. REV. 604 (1974), 163*n*45, 175*n*110, 193*n*221

Comment, *Goldstein v. California: Breaking Up Federal Copyright Preemption*, 74 COLUM. L. REV. 960 (1974), 190*n*200

Comment, *Performers' Rights and Copyright: Protection of Sound Recordings from Modern Pirates*, 59 CALIF. L. REV. 548 (1971), 165*n*61

Comment, *Photocopying and Copyright Law*, 63 KY. L. J. 256 (1975), 86*n*73

Comment, *Record Piracy and Copyright*, 23 MAINE L. REV. 359 (1971), 156*n*8

Comment, *The Sound Recording Act of 1971: End to Piracy on the High C's*, 40 GEO. WASH. L. REV. 944 (1972), 162*n*39, 169*n*83, 171*n*93, 179*nn*131, 132, 180*n*138, 185*n*56

Comment, *Sound Recordings' Copyright: The Disk Dilemma*, 36 U. PITTS. L. REV. 887 (1975), 156*n*7

Comment, *The Twilight Zone: Meanderings in the Area of Performers' Rights*, 9 UCLA L. REV. 819 (1962), 162*n*39, 169*n*85

Comment, *The War Against Record Piracy*, 39 ALBANY L. REV. 87 (1974), 178*nn*128, 129, 179*n*130

4 CONG. REC.—House, H10875 (Sept. 22, 1976), 92*n*94, 93*nn*98, 99, 95*nn*107, 110, 100*nn*125, 126, 102*nn*130, 131, 134, 103*n*35, 112*n*168

63 CONG. REC. (1940), 125*n*42

68 CONG. REC. (1940), 125*n*42

84 CONG. REC. 14799 (1939), 125*n*41

120 CONG. REC. 976 (1974), 181*n*148

122 CONG. REC. H10910 (1976), 5*n*7, 46*n*138

Cook, *The Fine Arts: What Constitutes Infringement*, ASCAP Copyright Symposium 13 (1964), 226*n*94
Copinger, Law of Copyright (7th ed. 1936), 225*n*93
Copyright—Fair Use Doctrine, 23 ALR 3d 139), 76*n*28
Copyright—The Librarian and the Law (Rutgers Univ. 1972), 88*n*80
Copyright for Sound Recordings, Circular 56, Copyright Office (1973), 180*nn*137, 138
Copyright Law Revision, 87th Cong., 1st sess. 39 (1969), 35*n*100
Copyright Law Revision, Part One: Report on the *General Revision of the U.S. Copyright Law*, 87th Cong. 1st Sess. (Comm. Print 1961), 248*n*12, 282*n*249
Copyright Law Revision, Part Two: *Discussion and Comments on the Report on General Revision of the U.S. Copyright Law*, 88th Cong., 1st Sess. (Comm. Print 1963), 35*n*101, 36*n*36, 260*n*93, 261*nn*100, 101, 264*n*127, 270*n*170, 274*n*196, 282*n*249
Copyright Law Revision, Part Four: *Further Discussions and Comments on Preliminary Draft for Revised U.S. Copyright Law*, 88th Cong., 2d Sess. (Comm. Print 1964), 262*n*104
Copyright Law Revision, Part Five: *1964 Revision Bill with Discussions and Comments,* 88th Cong. 1st Sess. (Comm. Print 1965), 36*n*103, 261*n*97, 274*nn*193
Copyright Law Revision, Part Six: *Supplementary Report of the Register of Copyright* (1965), 36*n*103, 37*n*108, 38*n*110, 39*n*113
Copyright Law Revision, Part Seven: *Subcommittee on Patents, Trademarks and Copyrights, Senate Committee on the Judiciary*, 86th Cong., 2d Sess. (Comm. Print 1960), 246*n*3, 262*nn*104, 105, 265*n*97, 278*n*124, 281*n*241, 283*n*249
Copyright Law Revision, Part Eight: *Subcommittee on Patents, Trademarks and Copyrights of the Senate Committee of the Judiciary*, 86th Cong., 2d Sess. (Comm. Print 1959), 282*n*251
Copyright Law Revision, Part Nine: *Use of Copyright Notice by Libraries* (Rogers), 262*n*106, 283*n*253
Copyright Law Revision, Hearings on H.R. 2223, 94th Cong., 1st Sess. (1975), 35*n*99, 40*nn*116, 117
Copyright Society of the U.S.A., Studies on Copyright, the Meaning of "Writings" in the Copyright Clause of the Constitution (Study No. 3, Fisher ed. 1963), 164*n*46
Countryman, *The Organized Musicians*, 16 U. Chi L. Rev. 239 (1949), 150*n*149

Crossland, *The Rise and Fall of Fair Use*, 20 So. CAROLINA L. REV. 153 1968), 74*n*17, 75*n*21, 76*n*30, 77*nn*33, 34, 78*n*39, 81*n*51

Diamond, *Copyright Problems of the Phonograph Record Industry*, 15 VAND. L. REV. (1962), 161*nn*33, 34, 36, 162*n*38

Diamond, *Sound Recordings and Copyright Revision*, 53 IOWA L. REV. 839 A1968), 127*n*49

DOWNBEAT—MUSIC HANDBOOK (1976), 130*n*62

DRONE, THE LAW OF PROPERTY IN INTELLECTUAL PRODUCTIONS (1879), 160*n*24

Dunaj, *Tape Piracy and Applicable Florida Criminal Laws*, 48 FLA. B. J. 338 (1974), 184*n*168

Engdahl, *Preemptive Capability of Federal Power*, 45 U. COLO. L. REV. 51 (1973), 13*n*39

FEATHER, PLEASURES OF JAZZ (1976), 150*n*149

40 FED. REGISTER 4965 (1959), 70

42 FED. REGISTER 223 (1977), 70

42 FED. REGISTER 233 (1977), 70

42 FED. REGISTER 21527–21528 (1977), 129*n*61

43 FED. REGISTER 31 (1978), 70

43 FED. REGISTER 58 (1978), 70

Federalist, No. 32 (1961), 187

Goldman, *Copyright as It Affects Libraries: Legal Implications, Current Viewpoints, in* COPYRIGHT: CURRENT VIEWPOINTS ON HISTORY, LAWS, LEGISLATION, 262*n*108

Goldstein, *Copyrighting the New Music*, ASCAP COPYRIGHT SYMPOSIUM 16 (1968), 148*n*146, 17 BUFFALO L. REV. 355 (1968), 178*n*128

Goldstein, *Federal System Ordering of the Copyright Interest*, 69 COLUM. L. REV. 49 (1969), 165*n*60

Goldstein, *"Inconsistent Premises" and the "Acceptable Middle Ground,"* 21 BULL. COPYRIGHT SOC'Y, 25 (1973), 16*n*50

Gorman, *Copyright Production for the Collection and Representation of Facts*, 12 ASCAP COPYRIGHT SYMPOSIUM (1963), 228*n*110

HATTERY and BUSH, REPROGRAPHY AND COPYRIGHT LAW (1964), 88*n*80

Hearings Before House Committee on Patents, 74th Cong., 2d Sess. (1936), 262*n*104

Hearings on H.R. 4347 Before Subcomm. No. 3 of the House Comm. on the Judiciary, 89th Cong., 1st Sess., Ser. 8 (1965), 249*n*17, 257*n*74, 259*n*84, 261*nn*97–99, 265*n*130, 266*nn*135, 140, 141 269*n*165, 276*nn*205, 211, 277*n*223, 278*nn*227, 228, 279*nn*232, 234, 235, 280*nn*237, 238, 281*nn*241, 248

Hearings on S. 597 Before the Subcomm. on Patents, Trademark, and Copyright on the Senate Comm. on the Judiciary, 90th Cong., 1st Sess. (1967), 149*n*148, 155*n*3

Hearings on S. 646 and H.R. 6927 Before Subcomm. No. 3 of House Comm. on Judiciary, 92d Cong., 1st Sess. (1971), 157*nn*12, 14, 158*n*16

Hearings on H.R. 2223, 94th Cong., 1st Sess. (1975), 245*n*1, 130*nn*63, 65, 131*n*73, 136*n*91, 137*nn*92–95, 138*n*96, 140*n*104

Hearings, on H.R. 6063, 95th Cong., 1st Sess. (1977), 142*nn*113, 116, 117, 143*nn*118–21, 144*nn*123–28, 145*nn*129–34, 146*nn*135–41

Hearings on Pending Bills to Amend and Consolidate Acts Respecting Copyright Before the Senate and House Committees on Patents, 60th Cong., 1st Sess., 265–67 (1908), 164*n*46

HENRY, COPYRIGHT, INFORMATION TECHNOLOGY, PUBLIC POLICY (1976), 88*n*80

Henry, Copyright, Public Policy, and Information Technology, 183 SCIENCE 384 (Feb. 1, 1974), 88*n*80

HENTOFF and SHAPIRO, HEAR ME TALKIN' TO YA (1955), 150*n*149

Hirsch, Toward a New View of Federal Preemption, 1972 U. ILL. L. F. 515, 4*n*9, 13*n*39

H.R. REP. No. 7083, 59th Cong., 2 Sess. (1907), 63*n*44

H.R. REP. No. 222, 60th Cong., 2d Sess. (1909), 162*n*44, 208*n*5

H.R. REP. No. 1270, 80th Cong., 1st Sess. (1947), 125*n*43

H.R. REP. No. 83, 90th Cong., 1st Sess., 152 (1967), 31*n*91, 73*n*12, 264*n*119, 270*nn*166, 170, 279*n*233

H.R. REP. No. 487, 92d Cong., 1st Sess., reprinted in U.S. CODE CONG. and AD. NEWS, 159*n*23, 179*nn*132, 134, 180*nn*136, 139, 181*nn*146, 148, 183*n*157

H.R. REP. No. 93, 93d Cong., 2d Sess. (1974), 181*n*148

H.R. REP. No. 5345, 94th Con., 1st Sess. (1975), 127*n*55

H.R. REP. No. 1476, 94th Cong., 2d Sess. (1976), New Copyright Act, 4*n*12, 5*n*14, 73*n*12, 90*n*88, 91*n*92, 92*n*96, 93*nn*100, 101, 94*n*104, 95*n*106, 96*n*14, 97*nn*115, 116, 98*n*118, 99*nn*120, 121,

124, 102*nn*130, 131, 133, 104*nn*142, 143, 105*n*145, 106*n*149, 235, 238, 196*nn*239, 240, 197*nn*244–46, 198*nn*247, 199*nn*253, 254

H.R. REP. No. 1733, 94th Cong., 2d Sess. (1976), 102*n*132, 108*n*158, 109*nn*160, 162, 110*n*165

H.R. REP. No. 1733, 94th Congress, 2d Sess. (1976), 102*n*123, 104*n*144, 107*nn*152, 155, 108*n*158, 109*nn*160, 164, 110*n*166

HOMELL, COPYRIGHT LAW (4th ed. 1962), 246*n*6, 248*n*47, 255*nn*53, 60

Hudon, *The Copyright Period*, 49 ABAJ 759 (1963), 71*n*2

INFORMATION HOTLINE, July-Aug., 1976; 72*n*5, 92*n*94

7 INFORMATION NEWS AND SOURCES, 35 (Feb. 1975), 77*n*36

Jonakait, *Do Art Exhibitions Destroy Common Law Copyright in Works of Art?*, ASCAP COPYRIGHT SYMPOSIUM (1971), 251*n*29

KAPLAN, AN UNHURRIED VIEW OF COPYRIGHT (1967), 2*n*4, 21*n*61

Kaplan, *Performer's Right and Copyright: The Capitol Records Case*, 69 HARV. L. REV. 409 (1956), 169*n*85

KAPLAN & BROWN, CASES ON COPYRIGHT, UNFAIR COMPETITION AND OTHER TOPICS, BEARING ON THE PROTECTION OF LITERARY, MUSICAL AND ARTISTIC WORKS (1960), 67*n*85, 247*n*8, 250*n*26, 251*n*32, 274*n*195, 277*n*220

Kaul, *And Now State Protection of Intellectual Property?* 60 ABAJ 198 (1974), 28*n*86

Kent, *The Viewpoint of an Author*, in COPYRIGHT: CURRENT VIEWPOINTS ON HISTORY, LAWS, LEGISLATION (1972), 261*n*96

Keziah, *Copyright Registration for Aleatory and Indeterminate Musical Compositions*, 17 BULL. COPYRIGHT SOC'Y 311 (1970), 148*n*146

Korman, *Limitations on the Right of Public Performance and Other Rights Under the 1976 Copyright Act* (1977), 81 CURRENT DEVELOPMENTS IN COPYRIGHT LAW (CCH), 144*n*127

Kunstadt, *Can Copyright Law Effectively Promote Progress in the Visual Arts?*, 23 BULL. COPYRIGHT SOC'Y 233 (1976), 251*n*29, 275*n*199, 276*n*210

Kurlantzick, *The Constitutionality of State Law Protection of Sound Recordings*, 5 CONN. REV. 204 (1972), 156*n*7, 166*n*63

Lang, *Performance and the Right of the Performing Artist*, 21 ASCAP COPYRIGHT LAW SPMPOSIUM (1974), 147*n*145

LATNAM, COPYRIGHT LAW REVISION (1960), 72*n*6, 76*n*27, 80*n*45, 82*n*59, 86*n*72

Leeds, Handler, Berenber, Brown, and Bender, *Product Simulation: A Right or a Wrong?* 64 COLUM. L. REV. 1178 (1964), 12*n*37

Liebig, *Style and Performance*, 17 BULL. COPYRIGHT SOC'Y 40 (1970), 147*n*145

Line and Wood, *The Effect of a Larger-Scale Photocopying Service on Journal Sales*, J. DOCUMENTATION 234 (Dec. 1975), 88*n*80

Maclean, *Education and Copyright Law: An Analysis of the Amended Copyright Revision Bill and Proposals for Statutory Licensing and a Clearing-House System*, 20 ASCAP COPYRIGHT SYMPOSIUM (1972), 93*n*98, 95*n*111

Messina, *The Tape Piracy Cases: Judicial Creation of a Federal Copyright Interest in Sound Recordings*, 17 BOSTON COLL. IND. & COMM. L. REV. 169 (1976), 191*n*212, 193*n*223

Mitgang, *New Copyright Law Held a Boon for the U.S., N.Y. Times*, October 10, 1976, 108*n*157

Nelson, *Jazz and Copyright*, 21 ASCAP COPYRIGHT SYMPOSIUM (1974), 147*n*145, 150*n*149

NICHOLSON, MANUAL OF COPYRIGHT PRACTICE FOR WRITERS, PUBLISHERS AND AGENTS (2d ed. 1956), 247*n*9, 249*n*21

NIMMER, COPYRIGHT (1972, 116*n*10

NIMMER, COPYRIGHT (1976), 72*n*9, 82*n*59, 86*n*72, 87*n*78, 88*n*80, 89*n*83, 161*n*32, 162*n*38, 164*n*48, 166*n*66, 167*n*71, 169*nn*81, 85, 175*nn*111, 112, 177*nn*124, 125, 179*n*132, 191*n*212, 192*n*216, 207*nn*l, 2, 209*n*13, 211*n*22, 213*n*29, 214*n*35, 215*n*37, 219*n*63, 228*n*107, 229*n*113, 236*nn*149, 151, 238*n*163, 239*n*169, 241*n*170, 242*nn*182, 186

Nimmer, *The Right of Publicity*, 19 LAW & CONTEMP. PROB. 203 (1954,) 165*n*55

Note, *Burlesque of Literary Property as Infringement of Copyright*, 31 NDL 46 (1955), 82*n*59

Note, *Copyright—New Light on Sears and Compco; State Copyright Laws Are Not Totally Preempted By the Copyright Act*, 5 TEX. TECH. L. REV. 843 (1974), 176*n*118

Note, *Copyright Law Revision-Copyright Notice, Governmental Ownership of copyright, and the Manufacturing Clause*, 52 IOWA L. REV. 1121 (1967), 248*n*13, 259*n*86, 274*n*192, 279*n*231

Note, *Copyright Protection of Sound Recordings*, 23 DRAKE L. REV. 449 (1974, 156*n*6

Note, *The Future of Record Piracy*, 38 BROOKLYN L. REV., 406 (1971) 165*n*59

Note, *Legal Protection for the Author*, 14 HDL 443 (1937), 77*nn*34, 35

Note, *"Occupation of the Field" in Commerce Clause Cases, 1936–1946*, 60 HARV. L. REV. 262 (1946), 15*n*44

Note, *Parody, Copyrights, and the First Amendments*, 10 U.S.L. REV. 564 (1976), 82*n*59

Note, *Photocopying as Fair Use*, 24 BOSTON COLL. AND COMM. L. REV. 141 (1975), 87*n*70

Note, *Piracy on Records*, 5 STAN. L. REV. 433 (1953), 156*n*8, 157*n*13

Note, *Preemption as a Preferential Ground*, 12 STAN L. REV. 208 (1959) 3*n*9, 15*n*42

Note, *The Preemption Doctrine: Shifting Perspectives on Federalism and the Burger Court*, 75 COLUM. L. REV. 623 (1975), 4*n*10, 13*n*39, 18*n*55

Note, *Protection of Sound Recordings Under the Proposed Copyright Revision Bill*, 51 MINN L. REV. 746 (1967), 164*n*53

Note, *Williams and Wilkins Co. v. U.S.: Library Photocopying of Copyright Materials*, 1974 UTAH L. REV. 127 (1974), 85*n*71

Nuclear, *"Moratorium" Legislation in the State and the Supremacy Clause: A Case of Express Preemption*, 76 COLUM. L. REV. 392 (1976), 4*n*9

OMNIBUS COPYRIGHT REVISION, COMPARATIVE ANALYSIS OF THE ISSUES (Hanson), 1973, 260*n*94, 262*nn*108, 109, 270*n*171, 277*nn*216, 221, 278*n*225

Ordway, *Choreography and Copyright*, 15 ASCAP COPYRIGHT SYMPOSIUM (1967), 121*n*30

Parody, *Copyrights, and the First Amendment*, 10 USFL REV. 546 (1976,) 72*nn*8, 9

Preliminary Draft for Revised U.S. Copyright Law, U.S. Copyright Office, 1963, 34*n*98, 38*n*112, 39*nn*114, 115, 42*n*123, 43*n*124, text, 53–54

Price, *The Moral Judge and the Copyright Statute: The Problem of Stiffel and Compco*, 14 ASCAP COPYRIGHT SYMPOSIUM (1966), 176*n*115

PROSSER, LAW OF TORTS (1971), 170*n*89

Public Hearings on Tape Piracy, 5 PERG. ARTS REV. (1974), 158*nn*15, 17, 18, 159*n*22, 171*n*93

Register of Copyright, *Report on General Revision of U.S. Copyright Law*, 87th Cong., 1st Sess. (1961), 35*n*101, 36*n*103

Richards, *The Value of the Copyright Clause in Construction Copyright Law*, 2 HASTINGS CON. L. Q. 221 (1975), 72*nn*4, 5, 87*n*79

Ringer, *The Demonology af Copyright*, PUBLISHERS WEEKLY, Nov. 18, 1974, 71*n*2

Ringer, *The Unauthorized Duplication of Sound Recordings*, Senate Comm. on Judiciary Subcomm. on Patents, Trademarks, and Copyright, 96th Cong., 2d Sess. (1961), 156*n*8

Rogers, *Use of Copyright Notice by Libraries*, Copyright Revision Study No. 9 (1959), 262*n*106

Rosenfield, *The Constitutional Dimension of "Fair Use" in Copyright Law*, 50 N.D.L. 790 (1975), 72*nn*5, 9, 73*n*10, 76*n*31, 86*n*71, 88*n*81

Rosenfield, *Customary Use as "Fair Use" in Copyright Law*, 25 BUFFALO L. REV. 1196 (1975), 76*n*31, 77*n*36, 78*n*39, 85*n*70

ROTHENBERG, LEGAL PROTECTION OF LITERATURE, ART AND MUSIC (1960), 258*n*80

Savelson, *Electronic Music and Copyright Law*, 13 ASCAP COPYRIGHT SYMPOSIUM (1963), 148*n*146

Schrader, *Sound Recordings: Protection Under State Law and Under the Recent Amendment to the Copyright Code*, 14 ARIZ. L. REV. 689 (1972), 180*n*141, 182*n*149

Schulman, *Fair Use and the Revision of the Copyright Act*, 53 IOWA L. REV. 832 (1968), 78*n*38, 90*n*89

S. 3008, 88th Cong. 1st Sess., 14*n*103

S. 597, 90th Cong., 1st Sess. (1967), 127*n*49, 133*n*79

S. 361, 93d Cong., 1st Sess. (1973), 127*nn*50, 51

S. 22, 94th Cong., 1st Sess. (1975), 5*n*13, 135*n*88, 245*n*1

S. 111, 94th Cong., 1st Sess. (1975), 127*n*54

S. REP. No. 983, 93d Cong., 2d Sess. (1974), 127*n*52, 135*nn*86, 87, 142*n*114

S. REP. No. 1035, 93d Cong., 2d Sess. (1974), 127*n*53

S. REP. No. 1, 94th Cong., 1st Sess. (1975), 128*nn*56–58, 130*n*68, 131*nn*68, 69, 134*n*80, 135*n*84, 85, 136*nn*89–81, 141*n*112, 148*n*147, 151*n*150

S. REP. No. 473, 94th Cong., 1st Sess. (1975), 4*n*12, 5*n*15, 33*n*96, 31*n*120, 44*n*130, 45*n*132, 39*n*149, 54*n*162, 91*nn*90, 91, 92*n*75,

94*n*103, 95*nn*105, 110, 96*n*113, 105*n*145, 106*n*148, 109*n*164, 244*n*195, 245*n*2, 262*n*108, 263*n*114, 264*nn*120–22, 265*n*133, 266*n*137, 268*nn*150, 151, 154, 158, 269*nn*161, 163, 270*n*168, 271*nn*176, 177, 272*nn*179, 184, 280*nn*239, 240

Shaw, *Publication and Distribution of Scientific Literature*, 17 COLLEGE & RESEARCH LIBRARIES 294 (1956), 86*n*72

Sheehan, *Why Don't Fine Artists Use Statutory Copyright?*, 22 BULL. COPYRIGHT SOC'Y 242 (1975), 249*n*18, 273*n*188, 276*nn*210, 212

SHEMEL & KRASILOVSKY, THIS BUSINESS OF MUSIC (1964), 155*n*1

STATE LAWS AGAINST PIRACY OF SOUND RECORDINGS: A HANDBOOK FOR ENFORCEMENT AND PROSECUTION (1974), 183*n*158

Stevenson, *The Doctrine of Fair Use as It Affects Libraries*, 63 L. LIB. J. 254 (1970), 74*n*19, 75*n*20

TAUBMAN, PERFORMING ARTS MANAGEMENT AND LAW (1972, 165*n*54

Ten Years of Federation, 60 HARV. L. REV. 262 (1946), 15*n*44

U.S. CODE CONG. & AD. NEWS 5819–20, 5*n*19, 33*n*96

U.S. COPYRIGHT OFFICE, *The Copyright Notice, Cir.* 3 (1976), 246*n*4, 247*n*8, 254*n*46

U.S. COPYRIGHT OFFICE, COPYRIGHT LAW REVISION, 88th Cong., 1st Sess., *Report of Register of Copyrights* (Comm. Print 1964), 35*n*99, 37*n*106

U.S. COPYRIGHT OFFICE, *Implementation of the Privacy Act of 1974*, 42 FED. REGISTER, (Dec. 5, 1977), 26, 170

U.S. COPYRIGHT OFFICE, Regulations, 37 C.F.R. (1972), 246*n*5, 249*n*21, 259*n*83, 276*n*208, 281*n*246

Wagner, *Copyrights and the Copyright Bill*, PUBLISHERS WEEKLY, Oct. 18, 1976, 72*n*12, 94*n*102

Wagner, *House Passes S22, CONTU Offers Photocopy Guides*, PUBLISHERS WEEKLY, Oct. 4, 1976, 109*n*161

Waxman, *Performance Rights in Sound Recordings*, 52 TEX. L. REV. 42 (1973), 162*n*39, 166*n*62, 168*n*74, 170*nn*88, 89

Yankwich, *What Is Fair Use?*, 22 U. CHI. L. REV., 205 (1954), 73*n*11, 76*n*23, 81*n*54

Yarnell, *Recording Piracy Is Everybody's Burden*, 20 BULL. COPYRIGHT SOC'Y (1973), 158*nn*16, 17

Index